White Screens, Black Dance

White Screens, Black Dance

*Race and Masculinity in
the United States at Midcentury*

PAMELA KRAYENBUHL

Oxford University Press is a department of the University of Oxford.
It furthers the University's objective of excellence in research, scholarship,
and education by publishing worldwide. Oxford is a registered trade mark of
Oxford University Press in the UK and in certain other countries.

Published in the United States of America by Oxford University Press
198 Madison Avenue, New York, NY 10016, United States of America.

© Pamela Krayenbuhl 2025

All rights reserved. No part of this publication may be reproduced, stored in a retrieval system, transmitted, used for text and data mining, or used for training artificial intelligence, in any form or by any means, without the prior permission in writing of Oxford University Press, or as expressly permitted by law, by license or under terms agreed with the appropriate reprographics rights organization. Inquiries concerning reproduction outside the scope of the above should be sent to the Rights Department, Oxford University Press, at the address above.

You must not circulate this work in any other form
and you must impose this same condition on any acquirer.

CIP data is on file at the Library of Congress

ISBN 9780197699072 (hbk.)
ISBN 9780197699089 (pbk.)

DOI: 10.1093/9780197699119.001.0001

The manufacturer's authorized representative in the EU for product safety is
Oxford University Press España S.A., Parque Empresarial San Fernando de Henares,
Avenida de Castilla, 2 – 28830 Madrid (www.oup.es/en or product.safety@oup.com).
OUP España S.A. also acts as importer into Spain of products made by the manufacturer.

for my mama, Pamela A. Morgan, who made all of this possible

Contents

List of Figures	ix
Acknowledgments	xiii
Author's Note	xvii

Introduction: Danced Masculinities on American Screens	1
1. The Nicholas Brothers: Classy and Dignified	30
2. Gene Kelly: Brash and Athletic	70
3. Elvis Presley: Virile and Phallic	111
4. Sammy Davis, Jr.: Modish and Chameleonic	149
Epilogue: Masculinities Danced on Post-1970 Screens	194

Notes	211
Selected Bibliography	235
Index	241

Figures

1.1 Harold Nicholas dances a George M. Cohan-style Irish jig-and-clog with the Goldwyn Girls in the "I Want to Be a Minstrel Man" number from *Kid Millions* (1934).   38

1.2 The Nicholas Brothers dance (and restrain an Eddie Cantor in blackface) during the "Mandy" number from *Kid Millions*.   39

1.3 Harold Nicholas sings in Spanish and both Nicholas brothers dance cinematically in the titular number from *Down Argentine Way* (1940).   42

1.4 Fayard Nicholas swings around a lamppost in *The Great American Broadcast* (1941); Gene Kelly does something similar in *Singin' in the Rain* (1952).   45

1.5 In *Sun Valley Serenade* (1941), "Chattanooga Choo Choo" is first sung by Tex Beneke, and then both sung and danced by the Nicholas Brothers and Dorothy Dandridge.   47

1.6 In the "(I've Got a Gal In) Kalamazoo" number from *Orchestra Wives* (1942), Fayard Nicholas mimes some of the lyrics.   49

1.7 In their famous "Jumpin' Jive" number from *Stormy Weather* (1943), the Nicholas Brothers jump over each other into the splits on a grand staircase, and complete the number by sliding down narrow ramps.   53

1.8 In the "Be a Clown" number from *The Pirate* (1948), the Nicholas Brothers and Gene Kelly grab onto one other for balance and collapse into a pile together.   56

1.9 When the Nicholas Brothers dance on the December 14, 1952 *Colgate Comedy Hour* Christmas Show, Fayard's snaking arms move so fast they blur in the video image.   60

1.10 During the Nicholas Brothers' appearance on the November 14, 1964 episode of *The Hollywood Palace*, Fayard dances quite sensually to "My Kind of Town."   65

1.11 On the February 27, 1965 episode of *The Hollywood Palace*, Harold Nicholas sings "That Old Black Magic" while Fayard Nicholas embodies some of the lyrics.   66

1.12 On the February 23, 1977 episode of *The Jacksons*, the Nicholases dance in bell-bottomed suits with short afros, soon joined by a young Michael Jackson.   68

X FIGURES

2.1 During the *An American in Paris* (1951) dream ballet, Gene Kelly dissolves into an image of Cuban-born dancer Raphaël Padilla in the Henri Toulouse Lautrec poster *Chocolat dansant dans un bar.* 71

2.2 In the "The Babbitt and the Bromide" number from *Ziegfeld Follies* (1945), Gene Kelly sweeps up Fred Astaire for a waltz. 77

2.3 In the "I Begged Her" number from *Anchors Aweigh* (1945), Gene Kelly choreographs a moment of pause for clenched fists and splayed palms. 80

2.4 During the "Worry Song" number, Gene Kelly wears what is today called a "muscle tee" while he dances with Jerry mouse. 80

2.5 Marlon Brando's costuming in *A Streetcar Named Desire* (1951) echoes Kelly's tight costuming in *Words and Music* (1948). 81

2.6 In the "Niña" number from *The Pirate* (1948), Gene Kelly employs the palm/fist dichotomy and jumps over a group of seated women in a manner similar to the Nicholas Brothers. 84

2.7 In *The Pirate*'s dream ballet, Gene Kelly is scantily clad and brandishes a sword as the pirate Macoco. 85

2.8 In "The Hat My Dear Old Father Wore upon St. Patrick's Day" from *Take Me Out to the Ball Game* (1949), Kelly performs both upright, Irish-style tapping and more grounded, swinging Africanist tap. 88

2.9 Gene Kelly "whitens" the *An American in Paris* dream ballet's jazz steps, but he still wiggles his prominently displayed buttocks. 92

2.10 In the "Why Am I So Gone About That Gal?" number from *Les Girls* (1957), Gene Kelly's Black dance vocabulary expands to include Elvis Presley's iconic "knee flaps." 96

2.11 During the "Dancing, A Man's Game" *Omnibus* special (December 21, 1958), Gene Kelly incorporates basketball player Bob Cousy's "pivot" into a stylized dance. 98

2.12 Gene Kelly and Sugar Ray Robinson wear matching outfits and perform "punching" movements later in "Dancing, A Man's Game." 99

2.13 In his televisual performance of "Ballin' the Jack" during his November 21, 1959 *Pontiac Star Parade* special, Gene Kelly performs Africanist hip swings and once again uses the palm/fist dichotomy. 106

2.14 On the October 23, 1963 episode of *The Danny Kaye Show*, Gene Kelly's reprise of "Ballin' the Jack" includes a mobile center of gravity, loose arms, active hips, and a "cool" slide on his knees. 107

2.15 In his final sailor suit number ever, on the November 28, 1965 episode of *The Julie Andrews Show*, Gene Kelly performs bells as he did in *Anchors Aweigh* and a butt wiggle as he did in *An American in Paris.* 108

FIGURES xi

3.1 After singing the first verse of "Hound Dog" on the June 5, 1956 episode of *The Milton Berle Show*, Elvis Presley throws his knees back and forth and completes the phrase on his toes. 112

3.2 During his final *Stage Show* appearance on March 24, 1956, Elvis Presley performs a version of his leg-flapping dance while he strums his guitar. 121

3.3 During Elvis Presley's September 9, 1956 performance on *The Ed Sullivan Show*, the cameras cut him off below the chest when he most obviously launches into a dance sequence. 127

3.4 Highlighting the frenetic energy of his uncensored dance on the October 28, 1956 episode of *The Ed Sullivan Show*, Elvis Presley follows his intense dance moves with a faux-casual pose in opposition. 128

3.5 Elvis Presley's "charm" in the titular number of *Loving You* (1957) consists primarily of a danced demonstration of sexuality. 132

3.6 In *Jailhouse Rock* (1957), Elvis Presley places his hands on his pelvis as he moves it forward and back, drawing the viewer's eye toward it. 133

3.7 As Specialist Tulsa McLean in *G.I. Blues* (1960), Elvis Presley performs a hip-swinging military-style dance to the titular song. 138

3.8 When Elvis Presley performs a pelvic solo dance for the "Slicin' Sand" number in *Blue Hawaii* (1961), the camera offers "crotch shots." 140

3.9 Elvis Presley's extreme artificial tanning, together with his signature black hair dye, allows him to visually blend in with his character's native Hawaiian friends. 141

3.10 In the finale of *Girls! Girls! Girls!* (1962), Elvis Presley leads women representing a variety of cultures in dancing the twist together. 142

3.11 During the "C'mon Everybody" number from *Viva Las Vegas* (1964), the camera frames the hip movements of Elvis Presley and Ann-Margret as a danced conversation. 145

3.12 Elvis Presley's dominant dance move for the titular number of *Viva Las Vegas* is a chest shimmy, accentuated by his open shirt. 146

3.13 The "Comeback Special" (December 3, 1968) dissolves from Elvis Presley to Black dancer Claude Thompson performing a modern dance. 147

4.1 In *Rufus Jones for President* (1933), Sammy Davis, Jr. as President Rufus Jones performs perches and places a sassy hand on his hip. 156

4.2 In *Sweet and Low* (1947), Sammy Davis, Jr. stands out from the rest of the Will Mastin Trio with swinging hips and machine gun tapping. 160

4.3 During his 1949 *Hollywood House* television appearance, Sammy Davis, Jr. creates the illusion that his top half floats separately as his bottom half taps at breakneck speeds. 162

xii FIGURES

4.4 While performing "The Birth of the Blues" on the August 8, 1954 episode of *The Colgate Comedy Hour*, Sammy Davis, Jr. jumps up on the bar set and swings his pelvis in circles, later engaging in Presley-style leg flaps. 163

4.5 During the drunken fever dream sequence in *Anna Lucasta* (1958), Sammy Davis, Jr. pops back and forth between his suit and a sailor uniform as he looks seductively into the camera and dances in a mix of styles. 171

4.6 Sammy Davis, Jr.'s performance as Sportin' Life in *Porgy and Bess* (1959) embodies Davis's own style of dance and dandyism. 174

4.7 During his 1961 appearance on *Playboy's Penthouse*, Sammy Davis, Jr. dances a contrast between deeply rooted downbeats and a buoyant jump off a balcony set piece. 177

4.8 As a gunslinger named Will in *Robin and the 7 Hoods* (1964), Sammy Davis, Jr. performs a graceful, Astaire-style traveling tap sequence. 181

4.9 During the series finale of *The Sammy Davis, Jr. Show* (April 22, 1966), Davis performs a tap number using both Gene Kelly- and Bill Robinson-inspired dance styles. 184

4.10 During his 1968 appearances on *The Hollywood Palace*, Sammy Davis, Jr. begins to wear his natural hair onscreen and lifts Diana Ross, Fred-and-Ginger style, in a tribute sequence. 186

4.11 Outfitted in a hot pink chemise, gold necklace, and black leather boot-pants for *Sweet Charity* (1969), Sammy Davis, Jr. as "Big Daddy" the cult leader does "the swim," shot between the legs of a follower. 188

4.12 Sammy Davis, Jr. performs "Mr. Bojangles" in a brown jumpsuit and bowler hat on *The Flip Wilson Show* in 1972 (left), and "Get It On" in day-glo yellow with pelvic thrusts on his *Sammy!* special in 1973. 193

Acknowledgments

Many people, across several institutions, have made this book possible. First, I am deeply grateful to the Andrew W. Mellon Foundation for funding nearly all my graduate work, including the Mellon Fellowship in Interdisciplinary Studies that generously supported my first five years as a PhD student at Northwestern and the 2015 Mellon Summer Seminar in Dance Studies that connected me to a group of stellar colleagues from several disciplines. Second, Oxford University Press and especially my editor, Norm Hirschy, brought the manuscript to fruition. Norm's enthusiasm for, patience with, and championing of this project (for *years* now) has been crucial for its success. Third, the University of Washington Tacoma School of Interdisciplinary Arts & Sciences Mini-Grant Program and the University of Washington Royalty Research Fund (RRF) provided the funding and teaching release necessary to get this project over the finish line—relatedly, thanks to Danica Miller for encouraging me to apply for the RRF and to Kara Luckey for her excellent feedback on my proposals.

I conducted research for this book at several archives, where I thank the staff for their assistance and patience: the Howard Gotlieb Archival Research Center at Boston University, the Jerome Robbins Dance Division at the New York Public Library, the Schomburg Center for Research in Black Culture, Special Collections at the UCLA Library, the Margaret Herrick Library, and the Paley Center for Media in both Los Angeles and New York City. Many thanks in particular to Martin Gostanian at Paley-LA, who not only let me stay late in the Scholars Room several times, but also managed to dig up interesting articles for me (unprompted!); and Jane Klain at Paley-NYC, who provided extremely hard-to-obtain information about Sammy Davis, Jr.'s hundreds of television appearances. Additionally, special thanks to Alison Hinderliter at the Newberry Library in Chicago for hunting down a lecture recording that had fallen through the cracks of online cloud services.

The lion's share of my work on this project occurred during the COVID-19 pandemic era, so I never could have completed it without the regular protected time of both virtual and in-person writing groups, which pulled me out of isolation and into the company of dear academic friends. On the virtual side, my Northwestern PhD crew: Hannah Spaulding, Annie Sullivan, Ilana Emmett, Simran Bhalla, Reem Hilu, and Catherine Harrington. These women not only co-wrote with me on Zoom and read drafts during the pandemic, but also provided solidarity in the before times, when we spent countless hours in Chicago

xiv ACKNOWLEDGMENTS

cafes and bars together. On the in-person side, my University of Washington Tacoma faculty crew: Randy Nichols, Chris Demaske, Andrea Modarres, Emma Rose, Riki Thompson, and Ed Chamberlain. Writing (and eating, and drinking) with them in living rooms, backyards, forest cabins, and beyond has been a highlight of my time at UWT.

Other close colleagues have also made this book possible outside of a cowriting context. In reverse-chronological order: At UWT, my thanks to Maria-Tania Bandes Becerra Weingarten for being my musicals buddy; to Danica Miller and Ellen Bayer for their friendship, informal mentorship, and enthusiastic support of my work; and especially to David Coon, media studies mentor extraordinaire, who has made my time as a junior faculty member much less miserable than it could have been. At Northwestern University in Qatar, my thanks to Scott Curtis, Amy Sanders, and lea bowman for their broad moral and intellectual support. At Northwestern, many faculty shaped and mentored me as a scholar—Jacqueline Stewart, Mimi White, Hamid Naficy, Lynn Spigel, Ariel Rogers, Neil Verma, and my dissertation chair, Jacob Smith—but especially Susan Manning and Miriam Petty. Susan almost single-handedly ushered me into the field of dance studies, and Miriam not only gives fantastic feedback, but is also the dearest mentor-friend I could ever ask for. Without these two brilliant and generous women role models, neither this book nor my academic career would exist.

Various other folks have had focused, specific impacts on this book. Mario LaMothe graciously shared his astute, concisely phrased characterization of half my argument—blackbodying—with me in summer 2015 and I am forever indebted to him for that! That same summer, Tara Willis confirmed my suspicion that Gene Kelly read as Black to at least some viewers, which renewed my faith in the project's importance. Miranda Baldwin in Chicago, Kate Hallstead in Seattle, and Brynn Shiovitz and Lynn Dally in Los Angeles have all helped me identify tap and vaudeville steps. Daniel Immerwahr provided feedback on my initial proposal for OUP. Anthony Stewart helpfully framed Sammy Davis, Jr. to me as "the original Black best friend," and Ken Eisenstein gifted me a key out-of-print film on a thumb drive.

As for engagements with earlier versions of this work: I thank Anthea Kraut for citing the dissertation version of this and enabling its further development; the anonymous reviewers for their feedback; Harmony Bench and her Dance 7902: Analyzing Movement graduate students at the Ohio State University for their feedback on both Chapter 3 and Chapter 4 in their early stages; Brynn Shiovitz for her feedback on Chapter 4; and Andrea Modarres and Clark Bernier for their feedback on the Introduction. And special thanks to Racquel Gates for her general interest and support as I've navigated this project's interdisciplinarity.

On a personal level, I am deeply grateful for the close friendship of Arielle Grant and Randy Nichols, both of whom have shepherded me through multiple years of this book and its struggles. Their cheerleading and general care for me have been relentless, and they deserve medals. I am also grateful for the unwavering support of my family—my sister Charlotte and both of my parents—who have been there for me not only throughout the writing process but also the various work, school, and life processes that have paralleled and preceded it. They have each sacrificed space, sleep, time, and money to get me here and I am so lucky to have them in my corner. Finally, my sincerest thanks to Clark and Mawdy Bernier, who fed me, sat with me, and surrounded me with love during the final stages of this project—we can go outside now.

Author's Note

On Positionality, Intentionality, and the Scholarly Process

I come to this project as something of an outsider. Though I was born in the United States and have lived here for most of my life, that is where my commonalities with the stars I write about in this book begin and end.

I am a ninth-generation Californian who grew up in a middle-class, mixed-race family: I am of Western European (French, Swiss), Hispanic (Californio), and Indigenous (Achomawi, Atsugewi, and Yana) descent. Though I am white-presenting, the cultural contexts of my own upbringing share little with those of Irish Americans from the Northeast or whites from the South (Gene Kelly and Elvis Presley, respectively); my experiences growing up in this country were of course yet more different from those of African Americans (the Nicholas Brothers and Sammy Davis, Jr., also all from the Northeast). Furthermore, I was born over fifty years after my case studies, who hailed not only from those different backgrounds but also a very different time in U.S. history. Finally, I am a (cis) woman, so I have never experienced the U.S. as a man.

In short, my positionality places me at a remove from the ways my case studies were raised and perceived by American society, as well as the versions of the U.S. that they inhabited. My analysis in this book attempts to make use of this distance, though of course it could never be objective, and I cannot fully remove myself from my own cultural and temporal lens. This is why I wish to make clear to the reader "where I am coming from" when I make sense of these men's masculinities in relation to race, ethnicity, and class. At the same time, there are artifacts of midcentury discourse that remain despite my contemporary lens: I have tried to preserve some of the terminology used around racial and gender formations while minimizing the replication of slurs and other hateful speech.

My academic training is in film and media studies, so that is the first scholarly frame I bring to this subject matter. But I also approach this project from the perspective of a dancer/choreographer. I have trained in classical ballet for over thirty years, co-founded two dance companies and performed with four, and choreographed contemporary ballets of my own for over a decade. This experience helps me to see a range of possible steps and gestures at every turn, so it is natural for me to ask, "Why this movement and not another?" That said, my dance training has been almost exclusively Europeanist in style; while I have

xviii AUTHOR'S NOTE

taken occasional courses in (West) African and Africanist (tap, jazz, hip-hop) dance over the years, I understand myself to be an outsider to Africanist movement vocabularies. This is where my secondary academic training in dance studies comes in. As will become apparent during the introduction, I define Black and Africanist dance versus Europeanist dance in terms established by dance scholars, especially Black dance scholars. I understand Black dance intellectually, but I do not know it deeply in my body as I do the primarily Europeanist form of ballet.

But this is a book of dance-media history and cultural analysis, not phenomenology or embodied knowledge. By uniting the disciplinary methods of film and media studies and dance studies (as well as my personal dance background), I intend to demonstrate the richness of interdisciplinary approaches for reading moving bodies and moving images *together*. I hope to show that both, combined, help us to see meaning in mediated performance more clearly. But I also aim to provide descriptions and analyses that are legible to all readers—scholars, students, dancers, fans, and laypeople alike.

While working on this project, I have often been asked how I arrived at this book in particular. Like many scholarly monographs, it began about a decade ago, as a dissertation. I was originally interested in the relationship between U.S. dance and media cultures writ large during the post-World War II era, as this period saw a great deal of mediated dance not only in Hollywood musicals, but also in experimental film, amateur film, and on early television. I was fascinated then (and remain so now) by the ways that the cultural and technical practices of dancers, choreographers, and film/television makers shaped each other during this period and set precedents that still affect the ways that dancers and camera operators work across media today. But as my dissertation committee member Susan Manning sagely pointed out, I had sketched out an entire career's worth of work in my dissertation prospectus, not a single project. Luckily, at some point in the first half of 2014 I had created a note-to-self on the desktop of my laptop entitled "SECOND BOOK" with the idea "Dance, Race, (class?) Masculinity in the American Film Musical." In October of 2014, I realized this needed to be the subject of my dissertation (and this, my first book) instead. The expansion into television occurred soon thereafter, such that the blueprint for this book was finalized in November 2014. But this sequence of events doesn't fully answer the question.

In trying to excavate exactly how this idea popped into my head, I've reasoned that it was the product of the intellectual milieu my mentors created for me during that period: In autumn of 2013, I took a "Media Performance" seminar with sound studies scholar Jacob Smith, who would later become my dissertation chair. The following term, winter of 2014, I took an independent study on screendance with dance scholar Susan Manning. In spring of 2014, I took an independent study on postwar TV with television scholar Lynn Spigel and a "Black Stardom" seminar with film scholar Miriam Petty, who would become my third committee member. Engaging deeply with the scholarship in each of these areas in quick succession allowed me to envision this project at the crossroads of them all. I hope it will be a testament to both the possibility and necessity of interdisciplinary inquiry.

As I often tell my students, I also hope this book changes the way you see when you watch dance on screen, whether that's TikToks, YouTube videos, movies, television, video games, or some other medium entirely.

Introduction

Danced Masculinities on American Screens

On May 7, 1985, many of his colleagues and admirers gathered to watch Gene Kelly receive his Life Achievement Award from the American Film Institute. Best known for his starring roles in 1940s and 50s Hollywood musicals, Kelly was a white dancer-actor with formal training in both ballet and tap dance. During the CBS television broadcast of the ceremony, Black tap dancer-actor Gregory Hines made a brief speech. He admitted to Kelly, "Over the years, I've borrowed a couple of your steps—more than a couple." The audience laughed at this sheepish admission from one star performer to another. A few minutes later, Fayard Nicholas, of the Black dance duo the Nicholas Brothers, addressed Hines' admission in his own remarks: "Gregory Hines, don't worry about stealing Gene Kelly's steps, because he stole them from us!" Everyone laughed again, and then the ceremony continued. Though these may at first seem like harmless quips among fellow artists, this book takes them seriously. Indeed, they are a rare if playful glimpse into the culture of (masculine) dance in twentieth-century Hollywood. If Hines, as a Black man and among the best American tap dancers of his generation, admits to "borrowing" a white dancer's steps, Fayard Nicholas, among the best tap dancers of *his* generation, completed the circle of borrowing to set the record straight about the originators of jazz tap dance. Nicholas subtly highlights the irony that the white star being celebrated during this broadcast is not, in fact, fully responsible for the dance innovations that made him famous; he informs or perhaps reminds the audience that Kelly performed a great deal of Black dance during his film and television career, including his "borrowings" from the Nicholas Brothers. Fittingly, this reminder was broadcast on national television; all four men involved in this exchange were not only dancers, they were dancers made famous by popular media.

White Screens, Black Dance tracks the use of Black dance by stars like Kelly and the Nicholases on mid-twentieth-century American screens, and reveals how integral it was to constructing a range of masculinities for these stars. The long midcentury, which I am defining as roughly 1940–1970, was a dynamic period in United States history, one characterized by signific cultural and political shifts. It was also a landmark era for both American dance and the American media industries. Hollywood cinema was in its golden age, television was switching

White Screens, Black Dance. Pamela Krayenbuhl, Oxford University Press. © Pamela Krayenbuhl 2025.
DOI: 10.1093/9780197699119.003.0001

2   INTRODUCTION

coasts and growing rapidly, and the fight for civil rights became more acute with each passing year. During and after World War II, women enjoyed greater access to the workplace; when the men returned from the fighting, white men experienced a crisis of masculinity and Black men encountered heightened American hypocrisy regarding the so-called "equality" they had fought for during the war. At the same time, American dance was at its own turning point: vaudeville had died, but Russian expatriate George Balanchine was developing and solidifying his vision of American ballet, and modern dance was in its heyday; musicals were hot both on Broadway and in Hollywood and, as the men returned from war, social dancing was also on the rise again.

This book explores the conjunction of all these phenomena in the moment when they came together to produce a higher volume of men dancing on American screen(s) than ever before or since. In this rare period where dance and American masculinity were not entirely at odds, men's virtuosic movements on film and television actually helped to define a range of available masculinities that were recorded for generations of American audiences to "read" and copy. These stars have thus served as models of gender expression for not only aspiring dancers but also young men (as well as women and nonbinary folks) writ large. *White Screens, Black Dance* unpacks the articulation of these masculinities via the career trajectories of three Black and two white dancer-stars: the Nicholas Brothers and Sammy Davis, Jr., and Gene and Elvis Presley. It argues that these stars' masculinities were fashioned primarily through Black movement vocabularies, which signified differently on their different bodies. Focusing on some of the most famous Black and white dancing men of the era, it pays special attention to the performers' transitions between film studios and television networks, whose different production contexts each brought their own grammars to bear on their presentations of dance on screen. By analyzing the ways that the Nicholas Brothers, Gene Kelly, Elvis Presley, and Sammy Davis, Jr. each negotiated screen spaces and constructed different masculinities using the same Black dance lexicon, *White Screens, Black Dance* articulates how four major models of danced masculinity were developed across media during a period of rapid social and cultural change in U.S. history. Parsing these models requires understanding the contexts in which they developed, so in the sections that follow I will unpack the operant terms in this book's title—that is, what I mean by "Black Dance" and "White Screens"—as well as provide a brief history of men dancing in the United States, and illustrate how the legacies of blackface minstrelsy interact with all of these.

"Black Dance" in the United States

Much of what was understood as "American" dance during the mid-twentieth century (and still today) was profoundly influenced by African American dance.

INTRODUCTION 3

Indeed, not only tap and jazz dance, which were most heavily performed by Black dancers prior to the 1940s, but also white-dominated modern dance and American ballet, are deeply indebted to what cultural historian Brenda Dixon Gottschild terms "Africanist" aesthetics.[1] Moreover, numerous mainstream American social and popular dances have also found their origins in African American communities.[2] I trace these same influences through the film and television dances performed by screen dance stars during the mid-twentieth century. Though the styles I examine in this book range from jazz tap to Broadway ballet to rock 'n' roll—thus spanning both concert dance and popular dance—all are united by the common presence of Black vernacular movement forms.

There has been a great deal of debate about the use of the term "Black dance" among scholars and artists of dance since its widespread journalistic adoption in the late 1960s. Dance scholars Thomas F. DeFrantz and Takiyah Nur Amin have outlined these debates, highlighting in particular their sense that "the term 'black dance' seems to have been invented by white critics as a shorthand for work they felt uncomfortable with or ill-prepared to address."[3] In 1971, Carole Y. Johnson, on the other hand, used the term in a positive, celebratory manner and advocated that it should "include any form of dance and any style that a Black person chooses to work within."[4] After falling out of use due to its "controversial invention and frequent use as a condescending label," the term resurfaced in the 1980s and 90s.[5] Richard Long's 1989 *The Black Tradition in American Dance* defines the term thus: "Black dance, Black stance and Black gesture are non-verbal patterns of body gestures and expressions which are distinctively Black African or originate from their descendants elsewhere."[6] In this book, I use "Black dance" as Long does, with a particular focus on the United States. To track Black dance across multiple bodies and screens, I draw from the specific articulations of movements, stances, gestures, and comportments by DeFrantz and Gottschild.

DeFrantz has described many of the corporeal attributes associated with Black social dances in the United States, and he has traced the ways in which the Black social dance vocabularies that crystalized in the 1920s and 30s recurred in both Black and white social dance "crazes" throughout the twentieth century. In particular, he cites "unexpected contortions of the spine or bending of the knees . . . and strangely mechanical locomotions or freezes" as characteristic of the "eccentric dances" of the 1920s.[7] He further explains:

> Some social dances of this era traveled from rent parties and nightclubs to the theatrical stage and back again. These dances, including the black bottom and the Charleston, featured extravagant body part isolations, especially in sinewy or sudden motions of the pelvis and spine, and rolling gestures of the torso, shoulders, elbows, and knees in unexpected continual waves or accented, rhythmic jerking. The snake hips dance, popularized by the impressive performances of Earl "Snake Hips" Tucker . . . emphasized successional

4   INTRODUCTION

movements that included the hips and pelvis, coupled with twisting motions of the feet.[8]

DeFrantz indicates a lineage from these social dances to similar dances of the 1960s such as the mashed potato, the Freddie, the frug, the good foot, and most importantly, the global phenomenon of the twist.[9] In this study, I will be tracking these same Black social dance movements through a different path to the 1960s: the bodies of screen stars.

More broadly, Gottschild has delineated the key characteristics of what she calls "Africanist" performance, best understood in contrast to "Europeanist" movement idioms.[10] Europeanist dance forms, such as ballet, Irish step dance, and square dance, all operate according to a logic of solidity: straightened torso, tightened core muscles, and a high center of gravity around which the limbs revolve. In contrast, Africanist forms, such as tap dance, jazz dance, and hip-hop, operate according to a logic of flexibility: moveable torso, counterbalanced and shifting contractions of different muscle groups, and a low center of gravity that allows any body part to become the focal point. Whereas Europeanist dances privilege specific rules, choreographed routines, and a sense of beginning and end, Africanist dances privilege improvisation, repetition, and often a refusal of resolution. For the purposes of tracking aesthetics, Gottschild has theorized five Africanist elements that are frequently adopted by Europeanist, especially American versions of Europeanist, dances. These include 1) "embracing the conflict," or a tendency toward paired oppositions such as both awkward and smooth, fast and slow; 2) "polycentrism/polyrhythm," such as the feet moving to one rhythm and the arms moving to another, providing opportunities for the paired oppositions of item 1; 3) "high-affect juxtaposition," in which one's comportment might shift abruptly from passive to challenging or joyous to frightened; 4) "ephebism," generally defined by looseness, speed, vitality, and intensity; and 5) "the aesthetic of the cool," an all-encompassing attitude that ties together the previous items under a mask of effortlessness or calculated carelessness, also potentially expressed in playful changes of affect as in item 3.[11]

Following DeFrantz and Gottschild, this book tracks these African American-originated movement vocabularies and Africanist aesthetics across dancing bodies both Black (Harold and Fayard Nicholas, and Sammy Davis, Jr.) and white (Gene Kelly and Elvis Presley), highlighting them across the long arc of these dancers' careers and analyzing the ways in which they signify within varying contexts. I highlight bent knees and a low center of gravity, mobile torsos and hips, the separate articulation of individual body parts, rhythmic repetition, and iterations of the "cool" aesthetic as demonstrated in general bodily comportment and costuming. It is important to understand that on their own, without the "mainstreaming" effects of Europeanization, Black dances have not generally been well received by white-dominated mainstream culture. Gottschild writes, "By Europeanist standards, the Africanist dancing body is vulgar, comic, uncontrolled, undisciplined, and, most of all, promiscuous. The presumption of promiscuity is allied with and leads directly to the sexually licentious stereotypes that the Europeanist perspective attributes to Africanist dance and, by extension, African peoples."[12] As a result, white culture more generally and Golden Age Hollywood in particular have historically circumscribed Black dance, relegating Black dance acts like the Nicholas Brothers to "novelty" or "specialty" numbers that appeared separately from white narratives.[13] The "cool" movements themselves were then appropriated by white bodies and often inserted into more Europeanist numbers, where they merely appeared exciting and innovative rather than vulgar or promiscuous.[14]

This book traces the ways in which Blackness was sanitized, appropriated, adapted, and performed by differently racialized, differently classed, and thus differently privileged male bodies at midcentury, and identifies the masculinities that were constructed in the process. Of course, both race and class are themselves social constructs, and therefore slippery in their signification. I attend chiefly to a Black/white binary here because it looms large in midcentury media discourses and dances, but the history of racial and ethnic performance in the United States is more complicated. In fact, both Black and white dancers who performed Black dance on film and television often did so in contexts that mixed racial and ethnic signifiers, blurring the lines of "Otherness." Thus, Black movement vocabularies were often used alongside physical or musical markers of "exotic" stereotyped Latin, Irish, Polynesian, South Asian, and/or Arab culture and identity. This racial and ethnic blurring, alongside other costuming, framing, and narrative contextualizing strategies, were all central to American screen media's role in sanitizing Black dance and rendering it a "safe" means of mainstream expression. But however unstable the categories, masculinities were always wrapped up with racial and ethnic performance, and this imbrication had real effects. On the one hand, racial and ethnic blurring strategies provided Black stars rare opportunities to flourish in the white-controlled and dominated star system, finally claiming positive masculinities for Black men after earlier patterns of onscreen emasculation and hypersexualization. On the other hand, these strategies also enabled white dancers to perform some measure of Blackness *as* masculinity; that is, whites used Black dance as a means of confirming, even insisting on their masculinity and virility—thus, race and masculinity are conflated in the dances themselves. More broadly, I argue, whites' performances of Africanist aesthetics in dance on popular screens allayed anxieties about potential failures of white American masculinity during the postwar years; at the same time, Black bodies in proximity to these white ones often remained a major source of anxiety for mainstream audiences.

6   INTRODUCTION

American Men, Dancing

White Screens, Black Dance conceptualizes gender in general and masculinity in particular as a continual, dynamic process of identification that is shaped by both ideology and historical moment.[15] It also sees gender as constituted by the performance of signs whose meanings are not fixed, and mean differently in conjunction with race and class.[16] The codes of masculinity available at any given historical moment are both numerous and contradictory. For Black men in the United States at midcentury, the options were few and fraught, with public discourses trapping them in a paradox between invisibility and hypervisibility.[17] After the Harlem Renaissance's "New Negro" of the 1920s and 30s—itself a proud refusal of Jim Crow oppression and demeaning stereotypes—faded in the wake of the Great Depression, Black men writers like Ralph Ellison and James Baldwin expressed a sense of invisibility and absence.[18] In parallel, despite years of screen and stage stardom as a symbol of Black talent and potential, Paul Robeson was blacklisted across media in the 1940s and 50s for his political activism. After World War II, many Black intellectuals pushed for conformity to white masculinity to further the cause of the Civil Rights Movement (a stance that would soon read as feminizing once the aggressive masculinity of the Black Power Movement took hold in the late 1960s). The (in)famous Moynihan report of 1965 claimed that a dearth of strong Black fathers was causing nationwide issues with the "Negro family."[19] Any public assertion of masculinity was circumscribed by white society as either insufficient or dangerous.

On the other hand, the contradictory nature of normative (and therefore white) American masculine expectations was brought into particular relief by the post-World War II "crisis" in American masculinity.[20] Though it can be said to have several immediate causes, such as men's return to the workplace and women's removal from it; the exodus to the suburbs—and the need for an income to support it; the entrenchment of the corporate economic structure; and the Kinsey reports on both genders, historians have traced the midcentury white male's struggles to "prove" his masculinity back to the turn of the nineteenth century, when white manhood became entangled with the competitive values of modern capitalism. No longer defined exclusively by communal and familial relations, men were also pressured to demonstrate a "self-made manhood" that fused male identity to the workplace.[21] By the early twentieth century, there was a shift in ideology from a "manliness" focused on character traits and morals to a "masculinity" characterized by physical strength and aggression; "femininity" as weakness began to be invoked as a threat to it. At this time, some of the most dominant means of "proving" masculinity were corporeal, as bodybuilding, baseball, and athletics more generally became wildly popular. Physical, bodily fitness was rhetorically linked to mental and spiritual

INTRODUCTION   7

fitness, and together the two defined a desirable, powerful white masculinity.[22] By midcentury, distinctions between middle- and working-class masculinities became acute: conformist suburban father figures vs. nonconformist urban delinquents. But the physical labor involved in working class occupations better fit the image of masculine strength inherited from the turn of the century, so the primary means of embodying masculinity for white-collar men moved to the home, where he could exert power and control as patriarch.[23] As film scholar Steven Cohan and others have pointed out, matters were further complicated by the addition of sexuality into the definition of masculinity. That is, as men were funneled away from the working class's more physically legible character-istics of traditional manhood, object choice became a means of differentiating the manly white-collar worker from the unmanly white-collar worker. This con-flation of gender and sexuality was codified by the U.S. military, for which the opposite of heterosexual masculinity was the "sissy," whose outward effeminacy was presumed to be an indicator of same-sex object preferences.[24] Thus, white, middle-class men who did not conform to the more stringent standards of Cold War era manhood were at risk of being condemned as not only effeminate or weak, but also as sexually deviant and sick.

But even when properly performed, the association of this masculine power with *whiteness* had been highly unstable since its conception. Turn-of-the-century white men felt themselves to be under threat by African Americans, immigrants, and the "New Woman." Historian Gail Bederman has described how the triumph of Black boxer Jack Johnson over white reigning champion James J. Jeffries upset race relations in 1910: because a Black man won the "fight of the century" to become the world champion of masculinity, white men started race riots all over the country.[25] At the same time, social dance crazes began to grip the white middle-class "New Woman" across the country, and their dance partners in the "animal dances" such as the "turkey trot" and the tango were not their middle-class white husbands, but "exotic" Italian and Jewish immigrants. These "lounge lizards" danced sensually and offered an alternative masculinity to the aggressive, athletic norm. Film scholar Gaylyn Studlar has explained how Italian-American silent cinema icon Rudolph Valentino's stardom in the 1910s and 20s was grounded in and exemplified this alternative (danced) mascu-linity, which normative white male critics received as threatening and even dan-gerous.[26] As the first major Hollywood star to dance his masculinity, Valentino also highlighted how contradictory masculinity could be: his star text was soft, sensual, and exotic but he was also depicted as a ruthless, terrifying "Other." In the context of Hollywood stardom, Valentino destabilized standards of mascu-linity "with connotations of sexual ambiguity, social marginality and ethnic/ra-cial otherness."[27] As we will see, later male screen-dance stars followed a similar pattern.

8   INTRODUCTION

This book examines dancing men and masculinity in particular, rather than dance and gender more generally, in part because the mid-twentieth century saw such an explosion of men dancing in the public eye.[28] Never before or since have so many dancing men enjoyed a central presence in popular culture; from the 1940s–1960s men—primarily white men—graced screens big and small, often without the accompaniment of women to 'justify' the dance or share in the spectacle. But just as Valentino was not well received by the male critics of his historical moment, white men who danced without women (and without blackface) during the midcentury period engaged in a subversive act and risked rebuke as "sissies." Concert dancing, cabaret and show dancing, dancing for fun—dancing for any reason other than courtship of a woman—was perceived as a feminine undertaking; to put one's body on display as spectacle and for the sake of visual pleasure was to join the ranks of ballerinas and showgirls, not one's fellow men.[29] However, a few pioneering white male dancers endeavored to "prove" their masculinity by connecting their dances to the reigning physical markers of early twentieth century men: athleticism and sports.

Dance historian Ramsay Burt has described how early twentieth-century Ballets Russes star Vaslav Nijinsky carefully engineered a "spectacle of famed and mythologised strength and agility on stage," performing expansive leaps that could "give Nijinsky the appearance of mastering the space, and, by doing so, dominating the audience."[30] In addition to these actual feats of athleticism, his costuming as a tennis player for the experimental ballet *Jeux* (1913) is said to have been intended to "canonize him as a modern man" via its referentiality to sport.[31] Dance historian Maura Keefe has similarly detailed how white American modern dancer Ted Shawn linked his dances of the following decades explicitly to sports, exemplified in his work *Olympiad* (1936).[32] Originally called *Sports Dances* and choreographed specifically for his touring company of "Men Dancers," *Olympiad* was very well received by audiences at the time. Less metaphorical than *Jeux*, the work included segments inspired directly by various sports, such as basketball and boxing, in order to reassure audiences of the dancers' masculinity.

African American men, on the other hand, danced sans women or pointed reference to sport throughout the first half of the twentieth century, but the only masculinities available to frame these performances were negative stereotypes constructed through blackface minstrelsy (which I will discuss later in this introduction). In particular, the prevalence of Black male dancers on street corners, stages, and film screens during the early 1900s both fed and was fed by the stereotype of the "coon." Film scholar Donald Bogle sets apart the "coon" from other negative stereotypes of African American men in film (toms and bucks) as purely "an amusement object" that depicts the Black male as lazy and shiftless.[33] His dances appear simple and organic, a natural expression of his empty-headedness. A sub-genre of this category is the "pickaninny," a singing and dancing African American child. In their important history of jazz dance, Marshall and Jean Stearns describe "picks" as an entire genre of vaudeville act, usually hired to accompany white performers: "It was child labor, theatrical style. Many dancers started as picks only because it was one of the few ways for a Negro to get into show business."[34] Unlike the tom (derived from *Uncle Tom's Cabin*), a spineless figure who submits congenially to white authority, or the buck, whose dangerousness and brutality are linked to his sexual insatiability, the coon and pick (also derived from *Uncle Tom's Cabin*, via the character Topsy) are defined by their entertainment value—by dancing itself. This aspect of the coon figure highlights one of white Americans' long-held and fundamentally racist assumptions about Black Americans: that they are inherent performers, innately good at singing, dancing, and feats of athleticism.

By the dawn of the twentieth century, African American men were known for their "buck" dancing, a flat-footed stomp-based dance form that serves as one of the basic units of tap dancing, and "wing" dancing, in which legs and arms "flap" like wings; together they formed the "buck and wing."[35] Early Edison films of the 1890s offer records of buck dancing; by the 1930s Bill "Bojangles" Robinson became the most famous Black male dancer on screen by performing a more complex descendent of this dance. At the same time, Black vaudeville duo Bert Williams and George Walker (re)introduced the "cakewalk," derived from a plantation dance and filtered through minstrelsy stages but updated with Walker's "strut" and Williams' "mooch" or "grind" of the hips. As the Stearnses explain, "The Williams Mooche, or Grind, while employing movements similar to the Twist and later dances of today, had a subtle flow that would have made our rock-and-roll devotees look like mechanized monkeys."[36] Williams and Walker's cakewalk was a central element to the quite popular Broadway musical *In Dahomey* (1903), and its format provided the framework for the musical comedy dances that developed into the signature Broadway style of the following decades.

That Black men's dancing was not articulated in mainstream popular culture as "sissy" or as a sign of masculinity "in crisis" like it was in the case of white men directly results from the fact that their dances—for the public, anyway—were always already circumscribed by white theater owners or film directors.[37] Moreover, the aforementioned racist stereotypes that assumed Black men to be either lazy and effeminate or hyper-sexualized spectacle were all but reaffirmed by their dancing. These issues with stereotypes continued to plague Black men's dances throughout the twentieth century; reflecting on his concert dance career of the 1970s and 80s, Bill T. Jones has highlighted his own experiences of intersecting stereotypes about Black men and male dancers:

10   INTRODUCTION

> There is something about the spectators saying, in effect "Perform for us. Show us your body." So it made me extremely aggressive, and maybe that was my desire to impose masculine control—I also assume it was racial . . . It was a cruel and ironic way that I saw myself. You know: you're a black man—take off your shirt. You're allowed to wiggle your hips in public. You know that they're all thinking, "Oh, I bet you have a dick down to your knees."[38]

Jones' articulation of the assumptions about Black masculinity and the sexualization of his body that undergirded his being "allowed to wiggle [his] hips in public" help to paint a picture of the very narrow yet contradictory range of masculinities available to Black men in the twentieth century. They also demonstrate how assumptions about the Black male body and its aggressive sexuality allowed Black dancing men to retain a sense of normative masculinity.[39] Thus, Black men were often able to work as dancers during the first half of the twentieth century precisely because of racist structures that understood Blacks as "natural" dancers available for whites' consumption.

"White Screens" in the United States

In the mid-twentieth century, both the major Hollywood film studios and the burgeoning television studios were owned and operated by white men targeting a white national audience. Both media produced narratives and spectacle that drew from previous forms of American popular entertainment like vaudeville and Broadway theatre and, as such, relied rather heavily on song and dance. In Golden Age Hollywood film (1927–1962), dance and music were the fundamental ingredients of one of the most popular genres: the musical.[40] This genre found its roots largely in Broadway theatre and famously featured romance plots, excessive spectacle, a sense of escapism, and of course the joyous and highly memorable song-and-dance numbers that still circulate online today.[41] Over the past forty years, film scholars have demonstrated that while Golden Age Hollywood musicals relied on an ultimately conservative formula of white hetereosexual romance, they were also an environment in which more marginalized gender, sexual, and racial identities could be explored and expressed under cover of these normative narratives.[42] By the 1950s, the classical musical birthed a subgenre designed to court the large generation of young "baby boomers:" the rock 'n' roll musical—another white-dominated genre.[43] This book sees both types of musical as places where stars danced out the contours of masculinities—shaping both adult and teen viewers' visions of American manhood.

At the same time, the then-new medium of television was on the rise. Though experiments with television began in the 1920s, and the Radio Corporation

INTRODUCTION 11

of America (RCA) introduced television to the American public at the 1939 New York World's Fair, television sets were not widely available and programming was fairly scant until 1947 or so.[44] As the three major American television networks—the American Broadcasting Company (ABC), Columbia Broadcasting System (CBS), and the National Broadcasting Company (NBC)—began to develop distinct genres of programming in the late 1940s and early 1950s, the talent available to them came as often from old vaudeville (often via radio) as it did from Hollywood film. In contrast to Broadway theatre, which by midcentury was respected as "legitimate" theatre where complex narratives and deep characterizations could reveal truths about the human condition, vaudeville was a now-defunct form of lowbrow entertainment. Having reached its peak between the 1880s and 1920s, vaudeville consisted of traveling shows featuring a "variety" format of many different performers and modes of entertainment, from dancing to juggling to magic tricks, which generally lacked a narrative thread. Vaudevillians were often ethnic minorities who hailed from the lower classes, and acts were frequently built from families: parents and children or sets of siblings would perform and travel the vaudeville circuits together. By the time television was taking off in the 1950s, children who grew up performing in vaudeville were adults who could host variety shows broadcast live to living rooms across the U.S. Often called "vaudeo" (vaudeville + video), this genre of mixed performance programming was central to the development of television as a medium.[45] Although scholars tend to separate television from film due to their distinct histories, industries, and aesthetics, *White Screens, Black Dance* demonstrates how danced masculinities were developed just as much in these non-narrative televisual formats as they were in narrative film formats.

Of course, industrial and aesthetic differences between film and television did mean that dances, and the masculinities they helped to construct, looked and signified differently in each medium. Golden Age musicals, as well as some of the higher-budget rock 'n' roll musicals later on, provided dancers with ample rehearsal time, spacious and often dynamic sets, a very mobile camera with a range of editing possibilities available after footage was shot, and opportunities for second and third "takes." The visual sharpness of 35mm film projected on the big screen additionally meant that viewers were able to fully perceive the crisp precision of hands, feet, and facial expressions, as well as larger-than-life views of set and costume details—often in rich Technicolor by the 1950s. Midcentury television, on the other hand, entailed minimal rehearsal time, much smaller and sparer sets, and limited camera movement, and until the 1960s was usually broadcast live. The fuzzy lines of the cathode ray tube television screen offered viewers far less detail and often no color, but its ability to transmit stars into the domestic space of one's living room—with free admission!—provided a different sort of opportunity: a more intimate performance. Indeed, while actors

12 INTRODUCTION

in Hollywood cinema rarely broke the fourth wall, variety television was carefully constructed to be a "marriage of spectacle and intimacy," with frequent direct address to the camera by performers appearing as themselves rather than characters.[46] Performance styles and masculinities both shifted, therefore, between more expansive, theatrical, and "polished" on film to more controlled, casual, and "raw" on live television. The details of these shifts operated differently for each case study in this book and were especially dependent on which medium "made" each star, but these shifting conditions and contexts for danced masculinity on screen are among the central factors that destabilized and multiplied each star's masculinities over time.

Despite their vast differences, both the film and television industries (and, increasingly, the music industry as well) revolved around "star systems." These cadres of performers were recognizable and distinguishable to the general public through their images, personal and professional identities, and signature performance styles. As such, a star persona can be read as a "text," multiply constructed by media institutions, actors' performances, discourses in the press and fan publications, extratextual public appearances, audience reception, and so on.[47] Major star personae constitute some of the primary texts through which cultural historians have examined both trends in and models for expressions of (white) masculinity since Hollywood's star system first developed in the 1910s. Looking at the long midcentury, film scholars have tended to discuss the masculinities expounded by 1940s noir films and westerns, ranging from dark and dangerous to rough and rugged, as well as the later wave of "rebel" films starring Marlon Brando and James Dean.[48] Less attention has been paid to the complex masculinities performed in musicals, but one of the most important insights produced in this area is Steven Cohan's contention that men's musical numbers, brimming with masculine spectacle, serve to "feminize" these dancing men by framing them with a *to-be-looked-at-ness* comparable to that of the more traditional feminine spectacle—which Laura Mulvey has suggested is fundamental to the classical Hollywood visual economy wherein women are passive figures to be looked at and men are active, voyeuristic figures.[49] Cohan further suggests that, against the backdrop of established western or gangster film masculinities, "Hollywood musicals reimagined American masculinity for postwar audiences in the kind of spectacular terms that would later come to dominate a televisual popular culture, but with more mobility and flexibility."[50] But, "like *film noir*, the integrated dance musical represented urban experience in ways highly responsive to postwar anxieties about male authority and masculinity, though to be sure, the musical went to one extreme (visual excess), and *film noir* to the other (visual spareness)."[51] Cohan's observation that a typical star in postwar musicals "constructs his masculinity out of the show-business values of spectatorship and spectacle" provides an important analytical foundation for understanding the

INTRODUCTION   13

specificities of individual midcentury masculinities.[52] Still, the role of dance it-self in shaping spectacular masculinity has been almost entirely overlooked.[53] Television scholars have shown that white men, especially Jewish men, performed visibly "ethnic" masculinities on television in the late 1940s and 1950s, but here again, dance and dancers have rarely been considered.[54] This book uncovers the role of dance in general—and Black dance specifically—in the constructions of multiple stars' masculinities.

Though the star system of Hollywood film and the star system of broadcast television were built differently, many aging film stars did try to transition to tel-evision as the Hollywood studio system was collapsing in the late 1950s.[55] At the same time, stars made on 1950s television also tried to break into the "big money" available in Hollywood, with varying levels of success. In these film and television landscapes, white dancing men secured strong positions as top stars in both Hollywood musicals and variety television/"vaudeo"—these included Fred Astaire, Gene Kelly, Danny Kaye, Donald O'Connor, Mickey Rooney, and Dick van Dyke as well as Elvis Presley. But neither system left much room for Black performers at all, let alone space for them to blossom as stars. White film studio heads, as well as the risk-averse white executives whose corporate sponsorship underwrote television programming, were reluctant to greenlight any onscreen content that might alienate fellow whites in the South.[56] The imperative to tiptoe around "Southern sensibilities," and many whites' opposition to racial integra-tion both onscreen and off, affected both the structure of Hollywood musicals and the range of hosts selected for variety television programs in the 1940s and 1950s. These contexts made it exceedingly difficult for Black performing artists to attain star status. In Hollywood, Black actors could only obtain top billing in Black-cast films, and the studios only made eight Black-cast musicals between 1927 and 1960.[57] On early television, Black-hosted variety series were often pitched and occasionally aired locally in the late 1940s but none were broadcast nationally.[58] When NBC's *The Nat King Cole* Show was finally greenlit for na-tional television in 1956, a national sponsor could not be secured, so Cole him-self canceled it in 1957 with the famous observation "Madison Avenue is afraid of the dark."[59]

Black performers did occasionally achieve stardom in both modalities, but as many scholars have established, Black stardom in white-controlled and largely segregated industries was complicated.[60] Especially because of the limited roles available to Black actors, such as maids and servants to white leads, Black performers in Hollywood did not generally achieve star status in the white main-stream even as they garnered significant attention among Black audiences and in the Black press. In narrative television, the rare Black-led sitcoms on early tel-evision like *Amos 'n' Andy* (1951–1953) and *Beulah* (1950–1953) trafficked in the same stereotypes that Bogle identified in film (though both were adapted

14   INTRODUCTION

from radio programs), so they allowed little room for star-building.[61] But Black performers frequently found ways to challenge the shallow and offensive bounds of the roles they were forced to play in these industries; their stardom was achieved in part through small subversions, resistances, and signifyin(g), a Black vernacular practice of layered meaning-making and critique that has been theorized by scholars of African American history and culture.[62] Such practices allowed Black performers to establish a critical distance—knowingly, and often playfully—from the stereotypes they were assigned by the white media industries. As a result, even roles and performances that were condemned by Black middle-class organizations like the NAACP for their negative representation, and which today read primarily as racist caricature, were often received with more ambivalence in the Black community at large.[63] It is within this model of a more complicated Black stardom that I situate my analysis of the Nicholas Brothers and Sammy Davis, Jr.

Because of the enduring power of the coon stereotype, the most effective means for Black men to access widespread visibility in white film and television—and thereby, a measure of stardom—was through dance (and/or musical) performance. In 1940s film, this meant fleeting appearances in "specialty" numbers, which were generally extraneous to a film's white-centered plot and could be conveniently cut for screenings in the South.[64] Black tap acts like the Berry Brothers, the (Four) Step Brothers, and the Nicholas Brothers all performed such numbers in the musicals put out by Universal, Paramount, and especially Twentieth Century Fox during this period.[65] On 1950s television, it meant guest appearances on the vaudeo variety programs that were hosted by white former radio men like Ed Sullivan and Steve Allen, or white former vaudevillians like Milton Berle. The earlier tap and jazz acts, in addition to newer performers like proto-rock 'n' roll artists Chuck Berry and the Treniers, were broadcast into America's living rooms on all three networks into the 1960s. In all cases, the relative freedom of expression that these brief onscreen appearances offered Black artists, wherein they performed their own work rather than lines scripted by white writers and were generally empowered to carry themselves in the same ways that they had found fruitful in live shows, provided them a means to build some of the strongest Black star texts of the midcentury period. And yet, white performers remained the main conduit through which most white Americans were exposed to Black dance and music, through an appropriative process I call *blackbodying*.[66]

From Blackface to Blackbodying

Though there is a long and varied history of white appropriation of Black culture in the United States, the middle two chapters of this book are interested in articulating a particular type of appropriated performance. I define *blackbodying* as the embodiment of Black or Africanist movements, gestures, and corporeality by a nonblack performer, usually without any explicit acknowledgment of their source in Black culture. Blackbodying is a cousin of blackface minstrelsy, a pejorative and caricatured form of song-and-dance performance by predominantly white men in black makeup that dominated U.S. popular culture between 1830 and 1930. Blackbodying does away with blackface minstrelsy's application of burnt cork to the face and instead channels Blackness through embodied performance alone. Unlike most forms of blackface minstrelsy, this type of performance lacks mocking and caricaturizing undercurrents, and instead seeks to hide its act of appropriation. In this latter regard, blackbodying is a close relation to dance scholar Brynn Shiovitz's concept of covert minstrelsy. Focusing on Golden Age Hollywood in particular, and thus examining the era just prior to but also overlapping with the one I tackle in this book, Shiovitz shows how Hollywood musicals' "less visible forms of blackface minstrelsy transitioned White audiences away from associating an Africanist aesthetic with visible Blackness while at the same time removing Black visibility from the screen" from the dawn of the talkies in 1927 through the early 1950s.[67] As she indicates, this was often achieved by shifting the primary sensory signifiers of minstrel performance from burnt cork blackface to other means, such as props and sets that evoked blackface masks, as well as sonic references such as the use of dialect, dubbed taps, and musical or lyrical quotations. Like blackbodying, covert minstrelsy also often depended on the blurring of "Othered" ethnic and racial categories to integrate its use into white Hollywood. Unlike blackbodying, however, covert minstrelsy often retained the element of racist caricature that it inherited from the "original" form of blackface minstrelsy which predates the birth of cinema. It also tended to operate referentially, with specific performances by key figures such as white *The Jazz Singer* (1927) star Al Jolson (who inaugurated the era of the "talkies" with a blackface number) and Bill Robinson serving as source material for later citational performances.

Blackbodying, on the other hand, retains different inheritances from blackface minstrelsy: it rarely has a specific referent performance or individual and instead generally consists of a condensation of many Black performers' movements and gestures. In this regard, blackbodying operates similarly to dance scholar Susan Manning's notion of metaphorical minstrelsy, a 1930s convention in modern dance wherein white dancers "did not mimic others but presented an abstraction or personification of others—Oriental, Indian, Negro."[68] Unlike the modern dancers of the thirties, however, the white men on midcentury screens who performed a range of jazz and social dances were not aiming to produce abstractions of other identities; they *did* merely mimic the movement vocabularies of others—primarily Black men. Of course, there were

16 INTRODUCTION

also non-dancers engaging in similar practices at the same time. Film and jazz studies scholar Krin Gabbard understands Marlon Brando's 1950s acting style as "jazz acting" and "minstrelsy in whiteface" because of its heavy borrowing from African American comportments sans blackface, "finding new ways to play out fantasies of African American masculinity."[69] Notably, both Brando and James Dean took dance classes with African American modern dancer and choreographer Katherine Dunham during this same period, suggesting that perhaps dance was not too far beneath the surface of their acting.[70] Indeed, Brando and Dean's "jazz acting" might be understood as a subtype of blackbodying, where the cultural borrowing is limited to comportments and everyday gestures. This book seeks to uncover the white masculinities made possible by a broader range of blackbodied movements that were available at midcentury, and juxtaposes them with the masculinities those same sets of movements made possible for the Black bodies to whom they originally belonged.

In order to explicate the stakes and significance of blackbodying as a cultural practice, I must first make clear the legacy of blackface minstrelsy from which it derives. The first form of mass culture that was born in the United States, blackface minstrelsy blended comedy, popular music, dance, and theatre, and was performed primarily by working-class white men. One of its defining features was its makeup: a light-colored exaggeration of the mouth (and sometimes eyes) accompanied by dark burnt cork applied to the rest of the face; this was often accompanied by parodic imitation of African-American dialect and behaviors, which together resulted in racist caricature of Black people. But blackface minstrelsy was a complicated performance modality, dense with contradictory meanings and serving multiple cultural and social functions for various audiences over the course of its over hundred-year reign in American society. Cultural historian W.T. Lhamon, Jr. has demonstrated that this complexity is already present in minstrelsy's early years, when it wrangled with increased racial mixing in the North during the 1820s and 30s: unlike the more unidimensional middle-class propaganda of the period, which was often merely pro- or anti-abolitionist, working-class minstrel performers expressed both alliance with and disdain toward Blacks.[71] Cultural historian Eric Lott emphasizes the complexity of racial feelings underlying the form as it matured. He writes,

> Minstrel performers often attempted to repress through ridicule the real interest in black cultural practices they nonetheless betrayed—minstrelsy's mixed erotic economy of celebration and exploitation . . . The very form of blackface acts—an investiture in black bodies—seems a manifestation of the particular desire to try to take on the accents of "blackness" and demonstrates the permeability of the color line . . . It was cross-racial desire that coupled a nearly insupportable fascination and a self-protective derision with respect to black people

and their cultural practices, and that made blackface minstrelsy less a sign of absolute white power and control than of panic, anxiety, terror, and pleasure.[72]

Tracing the cultural work that minstrelsy did in simultaneous separation of and transgression between Blacks and working-class whites, Lott argues that blackface minstrelsy—like its descendant, blackbodying—constituted an appropriation of Black *masculinity* in particular.[73] And over the course of the nineteenth century, though "based on the social violence of cultural caricature, it paradoxically resulted in the blackening of America," as it brought elements of Black culture, however falsified, into the mainstream.[74] After the Civil War, minstrelsy became an even more complex performance medium as Black performers entered the fray: they sometimes blacked up and sometimes did not, but their engagement with existing minstrel stereotypes was both requisite and transformative, using Africanist cultural practices to establish a critical distance, however subtle, from the stereotypes of white supremacy.[75] But Black participation in minstrelsy did not translate to access as new media industries were born. Hollywood carried on the tradition of blackface performance as a reinscription of white power; political scientist Michael Rogin takes up this thread and examines the blackface musical's relationship to constructions of "Americanness" and nation.[76] In particular, he demonstrates how blackface performance contributed to the whitening of Jewish immigrants—an observation which is also fundamental to Shiovitz's discussion of minstrelsy's increasingly covert forms in 1930s Hollywood.

As a period of transition, when overt blackface performance was still present but covert minstrelsy was on the rise in Hollywood, the 1930s is worth examining in some depth. Al Jolson, having birthed a blackface musical trend in the late twenties, performed in blackface seven times in 1930s Hollywood; fellow film veteran Eddie Cantor joined him with six blackface appearances.[77] But newer and younger musical stars also blacked up in the thirties. And unlike the lion's share of blackface minstrelsy over the prior century, the dance numbers that participated in what Rogin calls "New Deal Blackface" included a surprisingly large number of female performers. It is beyond the scope of this book (and certainly this introduction) to provide a robust theorization of the gendered ramifications of this shift when blackface minstrelsy as a form of mass culture was in its twilight years, but it is instructive to take a brief look at the representational foundations for the later performances I examine throughout *White Screens, Black Dance.*

In the 1936 film *Dimples*, starring white child actor Shirley Temple and choreographed by Bill Robinson (who does not appear, but who is now remembered as Temple's dance partner in several other films), Temple never dons blackface, though this had occurred in *The Littlest Rebel* (1935). However,

18   INTRODUCTION

the entire film is a nod to both mid-nineteenth-century lower-class whites' relative proximity to Black folks (and their facility with minstrel performance) and middle-class whites' growing engagement with racial fantasies in the theatre. As such, the film sees Temple as an urchin with a band of white children street performers, whose singing is accompanied several times by Black boys with harmonicas (played by Thurman Black and Jesse Scott, who formed the act The Two Black Dots); one of her middle-class rescuers first stages *Uncle Tom's Cabin* (with Temple cast as Eva), and later features her in a minstrel show. Temple is surrounded by performers in blackface during both shows-within-the-show, including a brief appearance of Stepin Fetchit (Lincoln Perry) during her "Dixie-Anna" minstrel number, wherein he responds to her "interlocutor" question in his usual caricatured drawl.[78] As in Temple's famed tap-dancing appearances alongside Bill Robinson in films like *The Little Colonel* (1935), *The Littlest Rebel* (1935), and *Rebecca of Sunnybrook Farm* (1938), she serves as the little "angel" who mediates racial boundaries and smooths over racial difference.[79] Shiovitz has demonstrated how Robinson's clandestine strategies to lend sonic complexity to their shared tap sequences (with the camera giving Temple visual credit for Robinson's work) allow her to perform covert minstrelsy, but here Temple's solo innocent whiteness in seas of masculine blackface (with the exception of her scene with Topsy in *Uncle Tom's Cabin*) renders her what film scholar Ara Osterweil calls an "ideological mulatto," performing Black tap dances taught to her by an absented Robinson, but with the "credit" for the source of her virtuosic allure indicated by dozens of blacked-up men surrounding her.[80] While Temple's dances on film do not qualify as blackbodying, since their sources are repeatedly made clear (whether through the presence her Black choreographer and teacher, or through caricatured masks as in *Dimples*), she clearly marks a transition toward the normalization of white bodies delivering Black dance on American screens.

Other young white stars *did* appear in blackface roles for minstrel numbers during the New Deal Era, however. Most prominent are Judy Garland and Mickey Rooney, both of whom were major Hollywood musical icons of the period. In *Everybody Sing* (1938), Garland appears in only her fourth film role as a youngster with a dangerous interest in jazz. When her parents try to ship her off to Europe, she escapes and auditions for a musical show by performing a jazzy update on "Swing Low, Sweet Chariot" in blackface. The spectre of *Uncle Tom's Cabin* remains here, with Garland outfitted as a pickaninny in the image of Topsy, wearing a gingham short dress with uneven knee socks and a wig made of unruly locs. The lyrics she sings try to contend with modernity's changes to the pastoral South, going so far as to suggest "*Uncle Tom's Cabin*'s got a new routine / Liza crossed the ice in a limousine / While Simon Legree shakes his tambourine / Way down south in Dixie." While wearing the caricatured disguise that was first developed by Northern whites as a means to comfortably indulge in antebellum Southern fantasies, Garland refigures (or perhaps disfigures) a Negro spiritual to sing of a new post-bellum, jazz age ideal of the South, where the master–slave relationship has dissolved into racial harmony—and even Black wealth!—brought on by the dissemination of modern Black music. Her accompanying dance is more a mere miming of the words, allowing the camera to frame her primarily in medium shots and medium close-ups that highlight the whites of her eyes and blackface makeup. Though not particularly relevant to the rest of the film's plot, this audition number simultaneously tries to excuse its racism and offers an (albeit absurd) explanation for why such racism might be falling out of fashion: a revisionist history reassuring white spectators that all is now well in the South. Whether this choice works to appease and appeal to imagined white Southern viewers or quietly endorse New Deal supports of the rural South (or both!), it certainly suggests that a blackface minstrel number remains the de facto method of Southern racial address in white Hollywood.

When Garland is joined by Mickey Rooney for a fuller blackface minstrel performance in *Babes in Arms* (1939), the New Deal is a front-and-center issue.[81] Playing children of vaudevillians whose fortunes were ruined by the advent of talking pictures, Garland and Rooney spend the film planning an old-fashioned minstrel show. Before Mother Nature aborts the show with a hurricane, the production observes the traditional minstrel show structure, opening with the troupe parading in, and presenting a brief tap dance by a Topsy-like pickaninny before Garland and Rooney appear as the blacked-up endmen who respond to the interlocutor. Rooney inhabits the minstrel mask a bit more deeply than Garland, with heavier and more consistent use of dialect, and ostentatious rolling eyes. While Garland's implementation of the form is less affected, cross-racial mimicry opens up the possibility of cross-gender performance for her, which she would undertake several more times on screen when performing old vaudeville numbers with male costars.[82] Rooney's subsequent tap dance to the Cantor classic "Ida" indicates its double origins: Black vernacular innovation inherited via Jewish blackface (by a Scottish-American boy). The film's finale insists on a modern update with an indoor show, sans blackface, featuring tuxedos and evening gowns. This is framed as Rooney making good on and setting an example of "the American Dream," so the final song, "God's Country," lays it on thick with explicit celebration of America's melting pot in contrast to European dictatorships. Thus, after one young man sings, "Got no goose step," referring to the signature military marching style of Nazi Germany, Garland follows with a sung and danced American alternative: "But we've got a Suzy Q step." Her brief Suzy Q step, a popular dance craze of the period that likely originated as a Black vernacular jazz dance, is the only lyrical reference to African Americans in their celebration of diversity (which mentioned Greta Garbo, Norma Shearer, the Marx Brothers, etc.). Of course, it is not acknowledged as such and might therefore be understood as a moment of blackbodying. In Rogin's view, *Babes in Arms* "exemplifies the New Deal blackface musical" because its use of "minstrelsy mobilizes the entire history of American entertainment in the service of making Americans."[83] Remaining in a post-blackface mode of blackbodying, the number and film end with Rooney as FDR and Garland as Eleanor Roosevelt, answering questions about the social and financial needs of multiple foreign and domestic groups with a singular solution: "(just) dance." African Americans are notably not represented among these groups (Native Americans, for example, are), but the suggested dancing for everyone else consists once again of Black vernacular jazz, primarily a Lindy-Charleston. By enlisting Black culture, unmarked, in the project of uniting the nation's various other interest groups, the final number participates in what Gottschild terms the "invisibilization" of Africanist aesthetics.[84] Ironically, then, as film scholar Carol Clover once pointed out, "there was a perverse honesty to traditional blackface, as it "does point to where credit might be due" regarding the source of the song and dance being used to construct these young performers' star texts.[85]

Two of the most prominent blackface dance numbers of the 1930s are removed from the structure of the minstrel show proper, and are instead presented within their films as standalone tap dance "tributes" to Bill Robinson. These are Fred Astaire's "Bojangles of Harlem" number in *Swing Time* (1936) and Eleanor Powell's "The King of Harlem" number in *Honolulu* (1939). At a surface level, the framing of these numbers as intended to "honor" the most famous Black tap dancer alive at the time is an attempt to excuse and justify the use of blackface, implying that while it might normally be a *dis*respectful practice, this exceptional use of it is the opposite. There have certainly been critics who defend such numbers with this line of reasoning.[86] And, though I once again note the grim irony, to both name and visually indicate one of the cultural sources of the dance form that was making white stars all over Hollywood is rather more honest than the umpteen numbers which ignore and even hide that source altogether. However, any pretense of tribute or homage fades quickly upon closer inspection, especially in Astaire's number, rendering both examples of covert minstrelsy. As several scholars have pointed out, "Bojangles of Harlem" bears both the visual and rhetorical trappings of minstrelsy, if not its larger structure.[87] The introductory shot uses the black bottoms of huge shoes as a face, where exaggerated lips are placed; Astaire's ostentatious costume includes a polka-dotted bow tie and large white gloves. All (barely) covert references to minstrelsy's cruel caricature, none of these are relevant to Bill Robinson's star text or performance style. Also crucial here is the fact that Astaire's tap dancing style is far more similar to that of John "Bubbles" Sublett, with whom he actually studied, than that of Robinson, with whom he probably did not—Astaire here performs Sublett's "down in the heels" style of rhythm tap, rather than Robinson's "up on the toes" style.[88] Ultimately less interested in who *exactly* Astaire is borrowing his moves from, the number reassures the viewer that Astaire has mastered the "swinging" jazz rhythms that Black artists in Harlem produced and which were now in mainstream vogue.

Powell's tribute is more directly reminiscent of Robinson's costuming and tap style, but it, too, carries more covert elements of minstrelsy than the use of blackface alone. Where Astaire's exaggerated lips were displaced onto his set, Powell wears hers on her face, seemingly mocking the subject she otherwise goes to great lengths to match with her checkered vest, tailored suit jacket, and pleated pants. Choreographically, Powell makes clear reference to the "stair dance" for which Robinson was most famous, tapping up and down a small staircase's two sides as he was known to. And like Garland, Powell also uses this racial masquerade as an opportunity to indulge in explicit gender masquerade as well, laying claim to the artistry of a dance form that had long been dominated by men.[89] As Shiovitz has pointed out, however, Powell's affected gestures push the so-called "imitation" into the realm of clowning and covert minstrelsy as she shifts the focus from the sounds of the feet (and how their sonic qualities change according to angle, force, and materials) to the carriage and movement of the arms. Powell's tap tempo never speeds up, as Robinson's tended to, and the rhythm is roughly half as complex as Robinson's tended to be.[90] Thus, though the visual signifiers of Powell's number—costume and basic choreography—bear a closer resemblance to Robinson's work than Astaire's, the heart of it is still missing (even if we put the blackface aside for a moment). In both cases, the so-called homage to a great performer suggests that the most important thing Robinson brought to tap dance was his Blackness, not his stylistic or rhythmic contributions. Both numbers insist that the best use of this Blackness, for their purposes, is a brief interlude of mockery and the familiar, cheap chuckles of stereotype before its signifying mask is discarded and the "real story" of the film's plot can continue.

All of these 1930s blackface dance numbers, and others like them, participated in covert minstrelsy's project of the "general remapping of Africanist sensibilities onto White bodies."[91] While providing last gasps of the United States' first form of mass culture as it was falling out of fashion in the face of more modern amusements, these twilight uses of the form served precisely to ensure that these modern amusements operated according to the same racial economy as the older ones. That is, the Hollywood musical as a genre, as well as the screen industries as a whole, depended on the same extractive cultural logics as had blackface minstrelsy before them. What Hollywood was beginning to innovate in the New Deal Era were ways of hiding that extraction and papering over the primarily Black sources of the jazz music and dance that were fueling the American cultural industries (film, music, radio) with various types of spectacle. Though blackface numbers continued to appear throughout

22   INTRODUCTION

the 1940s, most were framed within the context of nostalgic, biographical films about earlier white performers who had engaged in blackface minstrelsy.[92] Subjects included George M. Cohan, Al Jolson, Eddie Cantor, and vaudeville twins Rosie and Jenny Dolly—Betty Grable and June Haver perform in blackface during *The Dolly Sisters* (1945). The use of blackface thus became an indulgence reserved for historical accuracy.

This book looks at how song-and-dance performance operated once minstrelsy, both overt and covert, began to disappear in the 1940s and after—that is, once mainstream audiences became accustomed to seeing Black dance performed almost exclusively by white bodies, with little to no reference to Black bodies at all. In the early 1950s, as blackface became a rare occurrence onscreen, and even covert minstrelsy began to give way to blackbodying as the primary means of embodied racial appropriation, there were nevertheless occasional hints that Hollywood films "knew" they were pulling a fast one. An important model for excavating evidence of this knowingness is Clover's article "Dancin' in the Rain," which demonstrates the extent to which the 1952 classic *Singin' in the Rain* depends on Black dance and yet ironically fails to appropriately credit this source; meanwhile, it obsesses over other forms of 'credit where credit is due'.[93] Even the famous titular number is clearly indebted to histories of Black dance:

> If we [today] do not know the racial resonances of the trope of the street-dance-interrupted-by-policeman, Kelly and his colleagues surely did. Perhaps he even got a kick out of responding to Jolson's [*The Jazz Singer*] performance in blackface with a performance of his own in black space. In any event, the setting of what has been called "the single most memorable dance number on film" is yet another racial gesture, one that puts Kelly where a black man used to be . . . What *Singin' in the Rain* doesn't-but-does know is that the real art of the film musical is dance, that a crucial talent source for that art is African-American performance, and that, relative to its contribution, this talent source is undercredited and underpaid.[94]

Writing in the 1990s, Clover discovered what I now term *blackbodying* in what is currently the most beloved Golden Age musical. As this book will demonstrate, it was a widespread phenomenon and played a major role in constructing masculinity through dance in both film and television during this period.

In a sense, *White Screens, Black Dance* ultimately offers a deep dive into what we might understand as the final phase of Gottschild's "invisibilization" process. Over a long history of cross-pollination, the significant Africanist elements of mainstream and therefore unmarked "American" dance and culture have often been papered over and forgotten. Gottschild reminds us that

INTRODUCTION   23

this forgetting is not accidental or neutral, however, and results directly from "the politics of exclusion" on which the United States was built.[95] So, where earlier phases of this cross-pollination still clearly marked Black cultural elements as "Other," their dissolution into unmarked elements has allowed dominant white culture to integrate Africanisms into its own corporeal lexicon from the mid-twentieth century onward. In other words, if blackface minstrelsy made explicit the sources of its exploitative entertainment, and practices like covert minstrelsy and metaphorical minstrelsy provided initial, transitional means of displacing the visibility of that source material, blackbodying is the final step in the process of invisibilizing the Black people who originate and innovate Black dance. The result is Black vernacular movement being spread and popularized by white bodies—a phenomenon that continues in today's media landscape, and which had been occurring prior to the Hollywood system but which was solidified and repeated into a *convention* in midcentury screen media. Black innovators are sidelined by white-controlled media industries as their artistic production not only rakes in profits for those white industries but is also stripped of its cultural specificity. *White Screens, Black Dance* looks under the hood of this now classically American process, telling a story that begins and ends with Black ownership of Black dance, and exposes invisibilized blackbodying by white men (enabled by white media industries) in the middle. But rather than simply demonstrating *that* and *how* Black comportments, movement vocabularies, and styles were transposed from Black to white performers as part of larger processes of racial capitalism, *White Screens, Black Dance* argues that more is going on: as with its use in earlier minstrel performances, Black dance has been mobilized on American film and television in the further project of crafting and performing a range of American masculinities. Forged by the bodies of our biggest screen stars and recorded for posterity, these danced masculinities have crystallized into models that we still live with today.

Considering that the long midcentury in the United States extended from the World War II draft through the postwar crisis in white masculinity and the ramping up of Civil Rights and Black Power discourses, as Black veterans confronted a distinct lack of the values they had fought for abroad, it is no surprise that the resulting societal tensions imbricated masculinity with race and class. This book argues that this imbrication of tensions is borne out in a further tension of moving body and image: within the white-controlled film and television industries, Black dance became the vehicle through which some of the era's biggest starring men embodied masculinities defined by more than the war. But as we will see, both Black and white men's midcentury constructions of danced masculinities for the masses were haunted by the stereotypes inherited from nineteenth-century blackface minstrelsy.

Black Dance on White Screens: Constructing American Masculinities

This is an interdisciplinary book of dance-media history, applying analytical methods from dance studies, film studies, television studies, and star studies. To understand when midcentury stars were using Africanist versus Europeanist movement vocabularies, I use the method of movement analysis. Close attention to the sets of steps; hand gestures; comportments of arms, head, torso; stances of the legs; and facial expressions employed by the performers allows us to read and interpret their movements textually. Even in everyday life, humans have learned to "read" one another for indications of mood, truthfulness, authority, sexual interest, and so on; within the context of a staged and recorded performance, choreographed or intentionally improvised bodily movements take on their own range of meanings which are made yet more legible through re-viewings. In writing about these movements and their qualities, I depend at times on formal terminology from the dance form being used (e.g., ballet or tap dance), but for the sake of legibility to those unfamiliar with dance, I try to describe the movements in plainer language and include screen grabs as figures to elucidate the movements.

The second major approach employed in this project consists of the twin film and media studies methods of cinematic and televisual analysis. I remain attentive to framing, camera angle, and camera movement throughout my analysis of my case studies' onscreen dances. The realities of the cinematic and televisual apparati are often forgotten in analyses of dance on screen, wherein the only "unique" attribute of the two media is assumed to be the mass consumption of their products. But the filming contexts are often very different; whereas midcentury Hollywood films tended to use a single camera, the variety shows on television often used a multi-camera setup. The visual quality of the final products was also vastly different: sharp, fine-grain images projected on the big screen versus the sometimes jagged lines of a cathode ray tube television set. And live television, sometimes with studio audiences, encouraged a different kind of presence from stars than did the many takes of a Hollywood film. Differing set sizes and prop budgets also affect the range of possibilities available to dancing bodies. In all of my case studies, dancing bodies move differently on vast and elaborate film sets than they do on smaller, more compact television sets (these differences remain in location shooting for each medium). Moreover, as will become apparent, major shifts from one medium to the other most often coincided with changes in corporeal and dance style.

Like most scholars who perform visual analysis of midcentury television, my work here has been limited by what is available. My case studies remain popular celebrities with large fan followings who ensure that much is freely available online, and even more is available at repositories such as the Paley Center for Media. Still, kinescopes of live TV were not always made or saved, and at times their quality is extremely poor, though it is worth remembering that midcentury viewers would not have seen much better on their own television sets. It is also important to note the politics of what was saved. The records of Gene Kelly's and Elvis Presley's screen performances are nearly complete, whereas there are several gaps in the availability of the Nicholas Brothers' and Sammy Davis, Jr.'s film and television appearances. Of greatest personal disappointment to me, for example, is that I have been unable to find recordings of the several times that (both) the Nicholas Brothers and Sammy Davis, Jr. appeared together on screen. That white megastars' televisual legacies were more carefully preserved than those of Black stars is indicative of the differences in career opportunities more generally.

Finally, from both star studies and history I inherit the method of primary source analysis. I refer when possible to newspaper reviews, magazine articles, and other historical texts in an attempt to paint a picture of the perspectives of people living through the time period in question. While this is by no means a study of audiences' reception of these stars and their dances, I do note critics' and fans' reactions as indexes of viewer interests and attitudes at their respective historical moments. In all cases, I have also made use of interviews with the stars and commentary by their colleagues and peers where it is relevant in illuminating their own approaches to their dances, what they looked like, and what they meant. The ultimate goal behind these mixed methods is to paint the clearest possible picture of how these men's dances signify changing social identities on screen during the substantial social turmoil of the midcentury period.

The body of this book is divided into four major case studies, each of which makes reference to similar and contemporaneous performers, followed by an epilogue that gestures to the 1970s and beyond, showing how the models of masculinity danced at midcentury remain influential even today. I am sensitive to the fact that my case study structure runs the risk of perpetuating a long tradition in Western scholarship of producing great-man histories, but my intention here is not to praise these performers as the best in the game (that has been done elsewhere); rather, their careers illuminate a period in the U.S. marked by its anxiety over racial difference and miscegenation, in which its most famous screen stars nevertheless performed models of masculinity using Black dance. As indicated earlier in this introduction, I choose to focus on men during this era in part because of its so-called (white) masculinity crisis, and in part because of how frequently men danced on screen during it. This is not to say that analyses of women's dances on screen are not also important, but I want to understand the specific relationship between Black dance and constructions of midcentury

26   INTRODUCTION

masculinity.[96] I have thus chosen case studies who had active careers throughout the era, spanning both film and television.

I begin with the Nicholas Brothers, two of the very few Black dancers who were able to gain mainstream media visibility during the 1940s and 50s—I argue this had much to do with the ways in which their masculinity was contained by film and television structure but that their jazz tap dances forged an elegant Black masculinity despite those constraints. I then understand Gene Kelly and Elvis Presley as white dancers who therefore possessed bodies that could more easily access screen spaces, where their performances of Blackness via blackbodying helped them build sexy, working-class masculinities. Finally, I present Sammy Davis, Jr. as a Black performer "in perpetual motion" who combines styles and strategies from all previous case studies to offer an ever-shifting masculinity of the dandy. I examine each star text roughly chronologically, beginning with biographical and early-career context before homing in on their dance trajectories across different roles, mediums, and decades. In so doing, I trace transformations in the corporeal presentation and performance of masculinity over time, as all five men negotiate changes in American cultural trends as well as social and political climate. While I find it important to both begin and end with Black stars, the chapter order also reflects successively later "beginnings" of each performer's stardom within the midcentury period. Thus, while the Nicholas Brothers' screen stardom was arguably established in 1940, Gene Kelly's came about in roughly 1944, Elvis Presley's in 1956, and Sammy Davis, Jr's sometime between 1956 and 1959.

I have chosen these particular stars because all used Africanist aesthetics in general and Black dance in particular to establish a range of (always unstable) masculinities, which were defining qualities of their star texts. Despite this instability, I have provided general characterizations for each star's "model" of masculinity, reflected in each chapter title. But the patterns and relationships I uncover between Blackness, dance, and masculinity can be found in slightly different formations across many other, often lesser-known midcentury stars, some of which I mention briefly in relation to my primary case studies. Thus, my analysis of the Nicholas Brothers could be applied in similar terms to the Berry Brothers or the Four Step Brothers; Gene Kelly might be likened to Donald O'Connor or Danny Kaye (though Kaye offered a different ethnic presentation). Elvis Presley's borrowings from Black performance cultures were mirrored in more minor movement flourishes by Jerry Lee Lewis and Carl Perkins, and the dance crazes he inspired among white teenagers across America signify similarly across their bodies. Only the final case study, Sammy Davis, Jr., has no immediate contemporaries to my eye. Though his chameleonic approach to both performance and masculinity did serve as a model for later figures (such as Ben Vereen, for example), there was no other performer like him at midcentury.

Chapter 1 tracks the *classy and dignified* danced masculinity of Harold and Fayard Nicholas, a pair of African American jazz tap dancers from Philadelphia, from childhood precociousness in thirties short films to mature, suave masculinity on sixties television. The Nicholas Brothers' Cotton Club fame was already well established by the time they transitioned from Vitaphone short films to Hollywood features in the 1940s. At this point, their star text was characterized by class, grace, and youthfulness. Their signature moves included split-jumps, split-slides, and elaborate hand flourishes, as well as a vivacity that Gottschild might describe as "ephebism." These attributes allowed them access to white spaces and a film contract with Twentieth Century Fox, but the brothers experienced increasing industry marginalization and attempted emasculation as their bodies matured into grown, virtuosic Black men. Attending to this process of maturation through their excisable Fox dance sequences and culminating in *Stormy Weather* (1943), I argue that the Nicholases employed various corporeal strategies to resist both emasculation and relegation to the margins of the musical genre. This series of micro-resistances against this status quo culminated in a brief moment of true integration in *The Pirate* (1948), their final film appearance. Afterward, their television career emerges as a period of important innovation in their style, responding to changes in the social landscape as well as in musical styles. It was not until the end of their career on 1960s TV that their hips swung freely and their style adapted to the post-bebop context, with fresh dances defined by heavier international influences and fluid, polyrhythmic, and groovier movements. The Nicholases' career thus underscores the constraints Black dancers faced when seeking to perform Black dance (and Black male sexuality) in midcentury Hollywood. Still, the brothers ultimately found the space on Civil Rights-era television to innovate their jazz-based style of Black dance and embody a sexy, cosmopolitan masculinity that earlier industry constraints had subdued.

Chapter 2 uncovers shifts in the *brash and athletic* masculinity embodied by Gene Kelly, who was foremost in the post-Fred Astaire generation of screendancers who replaced blackface with blackbodying. While born to a middle-class family, Kelly's explicit claim to manhood at the beginning of his career was staked largely via appeals to working-class masculinity and many historically Black dance steps (such as "ballin' the jack") and bodily comportments (such as wide, deeply rooted stances). His early 1940s fashioning of a "wolf"-style figure in musicals tied together Black tap dance traditions, athleticism, and what I call the "palm/fist dichotomy," in which Kelly's hands exhibit contrastingly splayed palms and tight fists. The rest of his 1940s performances then see increasingly ambiguous performances of both gender and race, as Kelly more frequently plays up his Irish ethnic identity. His most explicit use of blackbodying to bolster his masculinity occurs during his 1950s ballet period, but in his late fifties

28 INTRODUCTION

transition to television with "Dancing, A Man's Game," he erases the centrality of African American innovations in the history of tap dance. When he nostalgically looks back at vaudeville as an aging dancer on 1960s television, Kelly again falls back on emphasizing his Irish ethnic identity. Still, some of his final televisual dances confirm that, for Kelly, masculinity is danced most effectively through athletics and Africanist aesthetics.

Chapter 3 examines the *virile and phallic* but sometimes gender-ambiguous blackbodying dances of Elvis Presley; though best known for his appropriation of Black music, he never could have earned the "pelvis" moniker without performing Black dance as well. With a trajectory moving in the opposite direction from the first two case studies, Presley transitioned from the intimacy of the early television screen in his 1956 "breakout" appearances to the thin narratives of thirty film productions until his 1968 "Comeback Special" on NBC. His standard movements, sometimes copied directly from Black performers such as Jackie Wilson, include legwork similar to the "wings" of the buck and wing, shoulder shimmies, hair choreography, and of course a mobile pelvis. As these movements further developed during the rock 'n' roll musicals of his early film career, they negotiated between masculinities of working-class Southern delinquency and gender ambiguity. An analysis of his first several post-Army films challenges the myth that his military service "tamed" him, for his dances became particularly spectacular as he embraced "the twist" during the early 1960s. After a deeply feminized final dance number in *Viva Las Vegas* (1964), Presley's dancing recedes in the late 1960s, exchanged for karate moves in bejeweled jumpsuits during the seventies. Having replaced Black bodies even more frequently than did Kelly for much of his career, Presley benefitted from the same sexual appeal of Africanist hip movements that prevented the Nicholases from using them until old age.

Chapter 4 unpacks Sammy Davis, Jr.'s *modish and chameleonic* masculinity of the dandy, achieved in part through his early-established and uncanny ability to absorb and replicate the corporeality of others. In the 1950s on variety television and in his first two films, he embodied a mélange of styles—including those of the earlier case studies—and established himself as a multi-talented mimic determined to "dance down the barricades" between Black and white. In the 1960s, when he was best known as the Black member of Frank Sinatra's otherwise white "Rat Pack," Davis performed a playboy masculinity, defined differently in various genres: suave tuxedoed soft-shoe in lounge settings, cowboy-style rapscallion tap on film sets, and youthful, trendy social dances on *Hullabaloo*. These culminated in a playful intermixing of performance styles and peacocking for his counterculture send-up number in *Sweet Charity* (1969). In the early 1970s, Davis's dancing slowed down and demonstrated the nostalgia of a master (though much more fashionably than Gene Kelly), looking back on the entire history of Black popular dance since vaudeville while still appearing hip, if a bit ostentatious—wearing natural hair, skin-tight body suits, and rings on every finger. Like the Nicholas Brothers, Davis the dandy was finally explicitly sexy in the dances of his later television career.

In the epilogue, I address how all four of these men served as role models and/or influences for future performers; their star texts are now seen to represent certain ideals of masculine dance virtuosity, virility, and popular appeal. Thus, understanding the dynamics of their screen-danced masculinities, undergirded as they were by Black dance, provides insight not only into the midcentury social and cultural landscape, but also the ways in which this period set the stage for future generations of male dance stars on popular screens, ranging from John Travolta to Michael Jackson to Gregory Hines to Channing Tatum. I offer analysis of a few key film and television texts in each star's case, before moving to the question of social media. Contemporary social media stars, especially those on the popular app TikTok, use Black dance to perform gender identities in ways that echo their forebears. I offer brief examples of the connections from past to present in hopes of demonstrating potential avenues of screendance and blackbodying analysis in future scholarship. Indeed, TikTok, Instagram, and YouTube are arguably the largest reservoirs of contemporary blackbodying and invite deeper analysis. Ultimately, then, a study of these midcentury dance stars' codetermining codes of race and masculinity helps to illuminate similarly entangled constellations of danced identity today.

1

The Nicholas Brothers

Classy and Dignified

During the November 10, 1951 episode of *All Star Revue*, Ed Wynn strolls across his set and "bumps into'" Fayard and Harold Nicholas, each dressed in suits and bow ties. They want to dance. Wynn tells them, "I cannot take great artists like you and let you dance in this sort of atmosphere. Now I want you to picture a marvelous palace . . . ." At this point, Wynn opens the curtain behind them, only to reveal a disappointing street scene backed by dingy storefronts. Pausing for effect, Wynn continues, "You boys will have to dance in this crummy street, here." "Picture, the Palace, though," confirms Harold. "Yes, please do." So the Nicholas Brothers perform a familiar routine, quite similar to the one they danced in the film *Down Argentine Way* (1940) and on *Texaco Star Theater* (September 18, 1951). But the visual irony is clear: in place of *Down Argentine Way*'s black-tie event on a vast veranda, or the tuxedo tails performance on *Texaco*'s raised stage, the brothers are made to perform on a "crummy street" set. Certainly Wynn is using this irony humorously—it is hard to imagine the always well-dressed Nicholases performing anywhere *but* a Palace Theatre—and yet the humor is uncomfortable. For one thing, neither of the Nicholases could reasonably be described as a "boy," since Harold is thirty years old and Fayard is thirty-seven, so the choice of words recalls the racist tradition of infantilizing Black men inherited from chattel slavery. Moreover, the gag makes light of the structural inequalities that led most African American tap dancers to hone their art in the streets rather than a dance studio; Fayard and Harold were some of the very few Black dancers of the era who were *not* at one time or another associated with street performance.[1]

Fayard and Harold Nicholas constitute this book's first case study because they are two of the most influential male dancers of the twentieth century. However, though the brothers are famous among dancers, classic film buffs, and the African American community, they lack the level of fame attained by white performers of their era such as Fred Astaire and Gene Kelly. They nevertheless enjoyed long careers that spanned the Great Depression, World War II, the Civil Rights Movement, and beyond. As such, their careers also spanned numerous platforms and media: from the live stage of the famous Cotton Club nightclub in New York (where Blacks performed for whites) to broadcast television in both

White Screens, Black Dance. Pamela Krayenbuhl, Oxford University Press. © Pamela Krayenbuhl 2025.
DOI: 10.1093/9780197699119.003.0002

the United States and Europe. The brothers occupied an unusual position among Black jazz tap dancers, for they were granted exceptional levels of public visibility despite continued marginalization as artists of color. They were two of the first Black performers to secure a standard Hollywood contract (with Twentieth Century Fox) but appeared only briefly in every film; they were merely listed as "specialty" in film credits. They never had speaking roles and were instead contained within these "specialty" song-and-dance numbers, which were generally irrelevant to the films' plots. This was done so that their numbers could easily be physically cut from a film strip in the event that white Southern sensibilities were offended by the presence of Black dancers in white cast films. Thus, the Nicholas Brothers experienced a sort of segregated integration through which they were both everywhere and nowhere in Hollywood.[2]

In this chapter, I argue that the Nicholas Brothers' onscreen performances were designed to resist both this relegation to the media industries' margins and the industries' attempts to emasculate them as they aged. They created dances specific to each medium (stage, film, television) with an ever-evolving jazz style that embodied a dynamic and sophisticated Black masculinity legible to both Black and white audiences, while also marshaling costume, styling, and comportment choices that took advantage of racial ambiguity. Though Hollywood never allowed them speaking parts and did what it could to mask their mature masculinity, the Nicholases took advantage of their choreographic control over their numbers to claim their space first on the big screen, and then smaller screens throughout the U.S. Overall, the Nicholases' career maps a trajectory of innovating Black dance on screen that first negotiates between containment and resistance in Hollywood cinema and later blossoms into a freer, funkier, and more soulful Black masculinity on television.

Stylistically, the Nicholases were often classified in popular discourse as "flash" dancers—a label that connotes a gymnastic, acrobatic quality—due to their signature inclusion of spectacular flips and jump splits in their performances. Dance experts, however, have nuanced this description a great deal since the 1980s. Maurice Hines, who—along with his brother Gregory Hines—was once described as being "the next Nicholas Brothers," explains, "I don't like the term 'flash act.' [. . .] To me, the Nicholas Brothers were never flash because they did close floorwork too. They could do *everything* [. . .] Flash . . . trivialized them."[3] Tap dancer Leonard Reed agrees with this assessment, insisting that "Flash dancers didn't do too much, just flips and turns and spins. And there were a lot of great flash dancers, like Jack Wiggins, Johnny Nitt, and Blue McAllister . . . . But Fayard and Harold were not flash dancers."[4] Thus, while flash was an element of the Nicholases' dances, it was reductively used as a stand-in term for much more complex type of performance than most midcentury viewers realized. Especially during their 1940s contract with Twentieth Century Fox, the flash element of the

32 WHITE SCREENS, BLACK DANCE

Nicholases' dance style, thanks to its spectacular memorability for non-dancer audiences, sometimes served to distract from the small resistances they mounted from their marginalized position in Hollywood cinema.

Rather than flash dancers, the Nicholases are best understood as jazz dancers. This term comes from the only biography about them: *Brotherhood in Rhythm: The Jazz Tap Dancing of the Nicholas Brothers*, by dance scholar Constance Valis Hill. For Hill, the brothers' jazz style is characterized by Africanist elements such as a low center of gravity, asymmetrical diagonality, angularity, and momentum-driven "flow."[5] Positioning them as primarily *jazz* tap dancers has important social and political ramifications within the 1940s context. In *Tap Dancing America*, Hill's cultural history of tap dance, she explains the important cultural legacy that the Nicholases inherited, innovated, and brought to mainstream American audiences:

> Jazz was the quintessential modernist expression of the twenties, and jazz tap dance was a form of expressive production that led to a specifically African American modernism. The speedy, swinging, rhythmic propulsion of this modern drum dancing—dissonant in the clatter of its taps, yet exciting in its offbeat, rhythms—defined the new Jazz Age twenties and sounded out a new breed of artists who would finally "shed the costume of the shuffling darky" for the more formal elements of rhythmic expression: its essential abstractness, form (angularity and asymmetry), succession and repetition (visual and aural), and the play of weightedness against weightlessness.[6]

Accordingly, the Nicholases integrated Black vernacular jazz steps, including elements of the Charleston, into their tap dance. They also incorporated elements of the "class act" tradition in Black tap dance, which required controlled precision, a veneer of effortlessness, and an overall sense of dignity achieved through immaculate formal costuming and a sense of composure. Altogether, then, the Nicholas Brothers performed a unique combination of Black dance traditions: the basic buck and wing elements of tap dance, additional flash acrobatics and class act styling, all with jazz modifications to their steps and rhythms. Over the decades, this core style continued to evolve alongside evolutions in jazz music, which is no doubt what allowed the Nicholases to remain popular performers for half a century.

The Nicholas Brothers' particular mix of Black dance traditions, as well as the sheer precision and idiosyncratic upper-body style they developed together, helped to cement them as Black stars in a mostly white Hollywood during the 1930s and 40s. As film scholars such as Krin Gabbard, Arthur Knight, and Miriam Petty have shown, Hollywood has long refused to acknowledge the centrality of Black cultural producers to the musical texts and performances that

THE NICHOLAS BROTHERS   33

it has marketed to mass audiences via images of white bodies, even as these marginalized performers were celebrated as stars in Black communities.[7] A partial corrective to this refusal on the part of Hollywood, this chapter explores the fragile and liminal mainstream visibility of two of the few Black performers who *were* able to gain access to its mass audiences. Hitherto, discussions of the film musical genre have lacked a nuanced look at the Nicholases' actual bodies and how they moved (or were constrained from moving). Thus, the first half of this chapter unpacks the Nicholases' early stage and screen careers from 1925–1948, during which they developed the basics of the signature style they would continue to inhabit and modify for decades to come. In the first half of this period, the Nicholases danced a contradictory young masculinity—presenting themselves as both boys *and* "little men"—that was also always partially constituted by the films' understanding of their Blackness.[8] Over the course of the 1940s, the Nicholases navigated the constraints Hollywood placed on their film appearances by first taking advantage of racial ambiguity and then performing micro-resistances, overall embodying a dignified Black masculinity and virtuosity. The second half of the chapter shows how changing social and political tides during and after the Civil Rights Movement allowed the brothers to draw together an even broader array of dance styles for television audiences. The Nicholases' television career is usually glossed over or forgotten, so this chapter recuperates their mature televisual phase as their most unfettered, when they were finally able to dance a grown and sexy Black masculinity.[9] While the details may have been inscrutable in the lines of the television screen, the Nicholases nevertheless performed semi-improvisational post-bebop dances in living rooms across the 1960s' U.S.

The Nicholas Kids Become the Nicholas Brothers

College-educated New Orleans-style jazz musicians Viola and Ulysses Nicholas had three children: Fayard Nicholas (1914–2006) was born in Mobile, Alabama, followed by Dorothy Nicholas (b. 1920) in Chicago, Illinois, and Harold Nicholas (1921–2000) in Winston-Salem, North Carolina. Their parents traveled a great deal, performing in Black vaudeville theatres all around the North and Midwest, which is what exposed the three Nicholas siblings to jazz music, dance performance, and film at a very young age. Fayard in particular claims to have accompanied his parents in the orchestra pit while still in a bassinet.[10] It was in this environment that young Fayard (at roughly the age of eleven) spearheaded a dancing act called "the Nicholas Kids" in 1925: as the leader of the pack, Fayard convinced his sister Dorothy to join his dance routines, and soon four-year-old Harold as well. As early as 1926, they "stopped the show"

34   WHITE SCREENS, BLACK DANCE

at the Lincoln Theatre in Baltimore, forcing the likes of Leonard Reed (who is credited, alongside partner Willie Bryant, with inventing the Shim Sham Shimmy) to wait for his turn to perform. When the Nicholas family more or less settled in Philadelphia, they lived on the historically well-to-do Lombard Street and the children were enrolled in a private, integrated school called the Stanley School.[11] Ulysses and Viola performed at the highly respected Standard Theater as the "Nicholas Collegians," where they and their band dressed in the attire of Ivy League college students. It was around this time that the Nicholas Kids lost Dorothy but gained almost immediate acclaim.[12] One of their signature moves, a rise up from the splits without using hands, was developed in this early era. Fayard recalls seeing "Ginger" Jack Wiggins do a split in his "Tango Twist" at the Lincoln Theatre and going home to practice it himself, only to realize that he could both go lower and pull himself up without using his hands to push off the ground.[13] He also practiced a range of other steps at home, preferring more diffi-cult steps to simpler ones, such as the time step:[14]

> I could do all the tough steps, but never get that damn time step down. That was
> the hardest thing for me to get. After I learned it, I never used it. They say that
> the time step is the basic building block step for tap dancing. I went and saw a
> show and they would start off with a time step, do another step, go back to the
> time step . . . and I said, "That's monotonous. Don't they know other steps?"
> Right then I said I wouldn't do the time step anymore . . . and never did.[15]

Thus, by 1930, the Nicholas Brothers were both absorbing the dance styles of the many great performers who surrounded them and distinguishing themselves with their own innovations. This marked the dawn of their professional career in Philadelphia, when Harold was still about seven years old. The brothers recall that Ulysses encouraged them to "do their own thing," and when he would see Fayard copying other dancers' steps around the house, he would say "I like what you're doing with your hands—do more of that!"[16] They took his advice; all of the brothers' dances on screen would exhibit emphatic presentational flourishes of the hands, twisting and blooming like flowers. Fayard's stylized handwork was even remarked upon within the industry. Choreographer and film dance director Nick Castle, who often helped the Nicholases stage their film numbers, describes Fayard as having "the most beautiful hands in show business," with Fred Astaire coming in second.[17]

In late 1931, while performing at the Pearl Theatre in Philadelphia, the Nicholas Kids were spotted by the manager of New York's Lafayette Theatre, Jack Schiffman, who invited them to audition for a job at the Lafayette. Apparently knowing the opportunity of a lifetime when they saw it, Ulysses and Viola Nicholas had, by early 1932, given up their own jobs and moved the family to

New York City, where they became managers for the newly rebranded Nicholas Brothers.[18] In New York, the family moved into the Sugar Hill section of Harlem, another well-to-do area—W.E.B. DuBois and Duke Ellington also lived nearby at this time.[19] After opening for a week at the Lafayette Theatre in March of 1932, in "identical three-piece tailored suits . . . which Ulysses had had made especially for the stage," the Nicholases were invited back for a second week in April.[20] It was after this second run that Ulysses Nicholas received a phone call inviting his sons to audition for the top stage in Harlem: the Cotton Club. At the end of the audition, Fayard remembers that Duke Ellington leaned toward Cab Calloway and remarked, "That was wonderful. They are original." Fayard, at this point a precocious young teenager, responded, "Thank you, Mr. Ellington! You are original, too!"[21] The brothers were thus booked for the Cotton Club, where they debuted in October of 1932. It is worth noting that the Nicholases not only arrived in Harlem in the midst of the Great Depression, but also during a period in which the Harlem Renaissance was still flourishing. Thus, the Nicholases were among the privileged few stage performers nationwide who were not only still working but also performing before full houses (of wealthy white audience members). They were paid $750 for their first week at the Cotton Club.

Soon a regular fixture of Harlem, the Nicholas Brothers were exceptional in their relative remove from the local tap milieu. The most prominent hotbed of masculine tap dance innovation in the 1920s and 30s was the Hoofers Club, which was "a small back room to an old pool hall in a basement two doors down from the Lafayette Theater."[22] Famously, the only rule of the club was "Thou shalt not copy each other's steps — Exactly." In this room, veterans challenged each other and younger dancers challenged the reigning talents before an "informal panel of peers, whose judgments could be cruel and mocking and were driven by an insistence on innovation."[23] This environment of challenge, stealing, and productive critique spurred future superstars like John W. "Bubbles" Sublett and Bill "Bojangles" Robinson to hone their craft. The Nicholas Brothers, on the other hand, did not have access to this community—they were too young, and their parents were too set on the brothers' high "professional" aspirations. Thus, even in this key period of growth and mounting fame, their challenges and innovations were entirely based on interacting with each other and watching other acts perform onstage.[24]

The Nicholases were also granted special privileges in the Cotton Club due to their youth and performance of "gentlemanliness." Both brothers looked several years younger than they were; they are sometimes identified as being eight and fourteen when they began at the Cotton Club in 1932, rather than eleven and seventeen. Marshall and Jean Stearns describe their countenance at these performances: "Dressed immaculately in top hats and tails, they played at being sophisticated in a way that delighted everyone . . . . Harold twinkled

36 WHITE SCREENS, BLACK DANCE

cherubically—'he was so cute the ladies didn't notice what he was doing,' says dancer Leon James. 'They just wanted to mother him.'"[25] The brothers recall that their perceived innocence allowed them access to white spaces during a time of extreme segregation at the Cotton Club, which did not admit Black patrons. Harold explains, "We were the only ones that could go out front and sit and talk with the audience, 'cause we were youngsters." Fayard adds, "But I'm glad we *did* go out there 'cause we could show them that Black people had class."[26] It was thus important to the brothers, especially in retrospect, that they were able to serve as a representation of the Black "class act" even offstage, mingling in an otherwise strictly segregated environment of wealthy white patrons—while their parents were forced to wait in the wings or backstage by the kitchen.

The Nicholas Brothers' first screen appearances served to solidify both their "jazz tap" dance style and their "class act" grace and costuming, while also introducing them to screen audiences as part of the larger 1930s Black jazz scene. Their debut in *Pie, Pie Blackbird* (1932) occurred quite early in their career, the same year they made their big break at the Cotton Club. While still at the Lafayette, they were recruited for this Vitaphone/Warner Brothers short subject, one of the few formats that offers a visual record of Black vaudeville, music, and dance performance from the 1920s and 30s. The film premiered in Harlem, several months before their inaugural appearance at the Cotton Club. Constance Valis Hill argues that their performance in the short both "summarized the past and predicted the future of the Nicholas Brothers' tap dancing."[27] Indeed, this rare recording of African American dance performance in the early 1930s marks a key moment in the birth of jazz swing dance, as evidenced in the brothers' combination of traditional tap steps with Charleston variations. In Hill's reading, "their jazz choreography ... suggests that they were moving into a more streamlined style distinguished by lightness, speed, angularity, and swinging rhythms."[28] This dance (versions of which they regularly performed at the Cotton Club as well) introduces any audience who did not see the brothers live on stage to the optics of a Nicholas Brothers performance: one brother dances while the other watches, and then the second responds in a friendlier version of the challenge dances that would have occurred at the Hoofers Club. In this way, the brothers "riff" on one another's steps, building upon and complicating each other's dances more often than simply dancing together in unison. This hallmark of specifically African American style tap dance would remain central to the Nicholases' performances for years to come.

The brothers held similar roles in other Vitaphone/Warner Brothers "Black shorts," including *An All-Colored Vaudeville Show* (1935) and *The Black Network* (1936). These were part of Warner Brothers' series "Vitaphone Varieties" and then "Pepper Pots," both catalogues that were available for individual booking by exhibitors rather than packaged into preconstituted programs for forced block booking.[29] While it is impossible to determine just how many theatres chose to exhibit the Nicholases' shorts, vaudeville was certainly one of the more popular subjects of these reels. But as African American film historian Thomas Cripps points out, the "Black shorts" in particular represented increased public visibility for Black performers, as they "brought the best in African-American vaudeville, vernacular dancing, and the more commercial forms of jazz to film."[30]

The Nicholases are costumed in matching suits and pocket squares for *An All-Colored Vaudeville Show*, and upgrade to three-piece suits for *The Black Network*. The brothers recall wearing very similar dress as youngsters in everyday life: "They [Viola and Ulysses] always made sure we were dressed sharp," remembers Fayard. Nicholas adds, "When we were walking down Lenox Avenue on a Sunday afternoon, everyone was saying how cute we were, dressed up in ties, double-breasted suits, pants with pleats in the back—so immaculate."[31] In *Vaudeville Show*, the brothers perform entirely in unison; in *Black Network*, they incorporate both unison dancing and challenge dancing. But in both cases, their "young gentlemen" aesthetic is clear: in the former, they playfully adjust their ties and smooth their hair as a businessman might; in the latter, they complete their dance with a handshake. In this way, there is a certain parallelism between the Nicholases' star personas and their actual lives—a performance of "class" and professionalism, not only through manner and movement style but also through dress. Already by this point mid-1930s, the brothers not only performed sophistication but also demonstrated a mature understanding of the jazz dance vocabulary as they added their own swing elements and established their "class act." The brothers' upper-class status within the Black community, as well as their immaculate dress and graceful stylings (such as Fayard's hand flourishes) set them apart as much as their youthfulness. Their still-developing masculinity at this juncture is thus primarily defined by their "gentlemanliness," which, alongside their age, is precisely what rendered them so acceptable to whites. This would become particularly evident in their Hollywood debut.

A Class Act Arrives in Hollywood

The Nicholas Brothers' first big feature in Hollywood, Samuel Goldwyn's *Kid Millions* (1934), inaugurated a contradictory budding masculinity for them: they were petite like children but performed like adults. The resultant tensions are immediately obvious during Harold's first appearance in the film. Clearly familiar with the format of the brothers' Cotton Club performances, in which the young brothers danced alongside the Cotton Club Girls, Goldwyn placed young Harold together with his own Goldwyn Girls for the "I Want to Be a Minstrel Man" number, written specifically for the film.[32] As the opener to the film's diegetic

"Minstrel Night," Harold sings of wanting to be a dandy like George M. Cohan. Harold in fact mimics the "jig-and-clog" style of Cohan as he sings about him, demonstrating his fluency in this Irish style of tap (see Figure 1.1).[33] The lyrics create a strange optical/cognitive disconnect, in which little Harold (age 13), whose own tap dancing proficiency had already exceeded that of many so-called minstrel men, expresses a desire to be a white man in blackface.[34] This tension is further highlighted minutes later, when Eddie Cantor's character is blacking up for his own performance: he remarks to his Black valet, "This is tough to put on and take off... you know, you're lucky." The attempt at humor here, in its effort to ease tensions around Cantor's actual privilege in being able to don and remove blackness at will, in stark contrast to his nameless companion's oppression due to his race, brings into focus the strangeness of Harold's sung lyrics. Since blackface minstrelsy was a fraught imitation and even mocking of Black dance to begin with, Harold's sung yearning for that dying-off performance style reads not as being desirous of skills he had already surpassed, but rather as being desirous of white, adult masculinity: the privilege of being able to take off the blackface. Moreover, any follower of the Nicholases' career would know that their entire dance style was far too current, jazzy, and innovative to draw any but a glancing comparison to this earlier form of tap.

There is also a strange sexual tension present: the group of scantily clad white Goldwyn Girls crowds around Harold adoringly (see Figure 1.1), as he represents, in the context of the song, that minstrel man who "thrills [them] like nobody can." Of course, Harold is still clearly a child; were he a grown Black man, he would certainly not have been allowed to occupy this space among a spate of white women. But unlike the white female child star, whose innocence was perceived as "an impenetrable shell that deflected adult sexuality and was, in turn, capable of transforming for the better the adults who came into her orbit,"

Figure 1.1 In the "I Want to Be a Minstrel Man" number from *Kid Millions* (1934), Harold demonstrates his facility with George M. Cohan-style Irish jig-and-clog (left); a horde of Goldwyn Girls surrounds Harold adoringly (right).

Harold's position as a Black boy implies that he is mere years away from being a Black man—and therefore a potential threat to these adult women.[35] That the white women fawning over him sing not about the precious innocence of this child, but rather the "thrill" of this Black body as a would-be minstrel man indicates how racial and sexual difference complicate more common narratives of child stardom.[36] Indeed, this wave of adoration gestures toward a latent sexual desire that threatens miscegenation—a taboo topic in the 1930s.

Then, in the film's finale, both brothers join a freshly corked-up Eddie Cantor and the chorus girls for the number "Mandy." If, as cultural historian Eric Lott has argued, one of the contradictions of blackface minstrelsy was to admire the virtuosity of Black dance while simultaneously portraying Black bodies as buffoons, this number renders the split concrete: the Nicholases demonstrate their genuine talent with smooth pacing and control of the scene, while Cantor plays the masked clown who must awkwardly excuse himself. Cantor, whose dance vocabulary is clearly limited to a basic time step and comedic stunts, is repeatedly physically prevented from dancing while the Nicholases, flanking him on each side, pass the proverbial spotlight back and forth between them, gesturing to each other when they feel it is time to switch over. Little Harold in particular contains and restrains Cantor (see Figure 1.2), once again an action that certainly would have raised more eyebrows were he twice as large or twice as old. After finally being given a turn, Cantor's character seems to back away in embarrassment, leaving the brothers to do one of their more standard twosome routines. This routine is particularly light-footed and speedy, both in pace and duration. Both brothers, together and separately, include literal on-the-toes choreography to enhance their sense of corporeal weightlessness (see Figure 1.2). This final number, then, resolves the tensions begun by Harold's singing "I Want to Be a Minstrel Man." If Cantor is the minstrel man, having demonstrated his

Figure 1.2 In the "Mandy" number from *Kid Millions*, Harold Nicholas restrains Eddie Cantor while Fayard begins a solo (left) and the brothers dance on their toes (right).

40 WHITE SCREENS, BLACK DANCE

effort in applying the burnt cork, he isn't a dancer (or a dandy, for that matter) worth looking up to; he both does not know when it is his turn to dance and cannot keep up when it finally is. After he exits in shame, the Nicholas Brothers, on the other hand, skillfully embody a contradictory masculinity: their youth has gained them access to roles in which they are intimate with white chorus girls and whites more generally, but in order to be taken seriously as dancers they must also demonstrate maturity, refinement, and adroitness.

The Nicholas Brothers' performance of skill, refinement, and indeed *artfulness* in *Kid Millions* was notable enough to be remarked upon by the Black press. In the words of a review in *The Chicago Defender*,

> Though very young in age, the boys give every appearance of being well versed in the art of stagecraft and showmanship, and even now can be listed in a class with those whom one might call perfect showmen.
>
> New York's nocturnal prowlers are well familiar with the work of the Nicholas kids, for it is they who add so much class and punch to the Cotton Club's latest revue. Theatre-goers know of their work for it was they who made Eddie Cantor's picture, "Kid Millions" much greater than it would have been without the artistic tap, tap, tap of their capable feet. Yes, the entire country knows of these sepia sons of rhythm for they have appeared by demand here, there and everywhere.[37]

Whether these claims of national popularity are meant only to describe the African American community or the entire country at large, their status as "classy" and "artistic" here is clear. And, as the *Defender* article intimates, that their professional career started so early allowed them, as classy *young* Black men, their exceptional mobility in and through predominantly white spaces. It is once again important to note the Nicholases' relative privilege amongst Black performers in this regard. Though they were regularly reduced to marginalized roles in musical films, the Nicholases were fortunate never to be associated with slavery or Southern plantation narratives. This is both a function of their socioeconomic position as the children of Northern, college-educated parents and of their age; while Bill Robinson, for example, was born at the tail end of the Reconstruction era in Richmond, Virginia and spent his early years busking, the Nicholases grew up with money and honed their craft during the Harlem Renaissance in the North. The review's description of them as "sepia" also highlights their status as lighter-skinned members of the Black community, another axis of privilege that makes their presence in Hollywood a bit easier.

These historical and contextual differences allowed the Nicholas Brothers to fashion a very different career in show business than most Black dancers of the period, and their plethora of experience in performing for white audiences before even arriving in Hollywood made the Nicholases far more aware of the politics of their racial difference (and the advantages of their age) than they are able to let on. Hill reads the brothers as wearing a "mask" during their childhood and tween years—that of the "Precocious Innocent":

> On the "face" of the mask . . . Harold and Fayard are the "Nicholas Kids," with their sparkling eyes and twinkling feet; behind that mask, they resist being entrapped within the naiveté of the boy-child. "We were kids, but we danced like men," says Fayard, describing what people said about their dancing . . . . In their mastering of the form of tap dancing, they surreptitiously undermined the superficial perception that they were merely naive, and ultimately powerless, little black boys.[38]

She places the Nicholases amongst the pantheon of Black actors in American film history who, in the formulation of Thomas Cripps, *do* something *with* the stereotypes they are assigned to play: the brothers mature *through* the mask of the Precocious Innocent (and sometimes also the minstrel man) rather than remaining confined by it.[39] Thus, even from their earliest appearances in feature-length films, we might read the disconnect between the Nicholases' immature bodies and their performance of adult male dances as an index of resistance. They dance a nascent Black masculinity that refuses the negative imagery of the pickaninny by marshalling skilled precision and debonair attire.

While they were fairly consistently employed in Hollywood throughout the remainder of the 1930s, the Nicholas Brothers' truly "big break" was their song-and-dance cameo for the Twentieth Century Fox Technicolor film *Down Argentine Way* (1940). This performance solidified the format of the standard Nicholases film number, and they would go on to cite and re-perform it several times during their television career. Here, the brothers' relatively light skin allows them to pass as Latin or otherwise exotic, even as they continue to perform Black jazz tap dances. This contextual exoticism also allows them latitude to dance a more sensual masculinity via greater pelvic mobility. As the brothers enter the film's swanky outdoor veranda-style Club Rendezvous (full of white patrons) in Buenos Aires, they hand their hats and canes to valets. When they launch into the titular "Down Argentina Way," it is almost immediately apparent that Harold, now nineteen years old, has grown into a young man, crossing from the threshold of childhood smiles and winks into suave and self-assured maturity. While he sings in Spanish and softly sways his hips, hand on his solar plexus, Fayard's hips swing far more emphatically, complementing the rhythm he shakes out with maracas (see Figure 1.3). Then, with extremely lively arms whose flights upward match the similar kicks of their legs—perhaps to accentuate the "Latin flavor" of their dance—the brothers balance speedy footwork with luxurious slides to produce an emphatically syncopated rhythm. After their initial dance in unison, they also incorporate the challenge dance format, just as they had in their earlier Vitaphone shorts. Once Harold completes a complex series of turning cramp rolls and chugs, for example, Fayard upstages him with elaborate one-footed wings, swinging the free leg out into a balletic *attitude* to counterbalance the working leg. As Fayard does his one-footed wings, Harold "conducts" the movements while watching, as if manipulating a super-human marionette. Harold's response contains a flip-into-split and rise up that garners him a great deal of applause from the diegetic audience. While he continues, Fayard play-conducts his movements just as Harold had done for him. Fayard then tops his brother's accomplishment by jumping into the splits and then hopping in a circle while still in the spits.

At this point, the competition escalates: Harold pirouettes into splits, Fayard jumps over his handkerchief into the splits and shimmies forward while holding them, and they join forces as Harold slides through Fayard's legs in the splits. The Nicholases complete the number with their first bit of truly cinematic choreography: they split-slide side by side toward the camera, looking directly into the lens and giving "ta-da!" presentations of their arms and facial expressions (see Figure 1.3). When they rise up to bow and exit, they once again present themselves directly to the camera. The breaking of the fourth wall marks the performance as distinct from their stage performances at similarly swanky clubs (whether the Cotton Club or elsewhere), which are directed toward the enjoyment of their clientele; in this case, the diegetic audience is clearly secondary to the movie theatre viewer. The unique contributions of the cinematic apparatus to the Nicholases' dance become particularly clear, here: the Argentinian diegetic context frees the brothers to perform sensuality that would not have been

Figure 1.3 In *Down Argentine Way* (1940), Harold places his hand on his solar plexus and gently sways his hips while he sings as Fayard swings his hips more dramatically while playing the maracas (left); the brothers' final "ta da!" split-slide breaks the fourth wall (right).

as welcome to white patrons in their stage act, and the camera's presence allows them greater intimacy with a mass audience as their bodies literally become "larger than life" on the cinema screen. They dance confidently, playfully, and a bit sexily—for all audiences.

If the Nicholas Brothers here finally read as young adults—most notably Harold, who has grown from 75 percent of Fayard's height in *Kid Millions* to just an inch or two shorter—this is largely attributable to their performance of a Latinesque masculinity, one which is always already sexualized, even if only implicitly. That Harold sings in Spanish is by no means the only signifier at work, as the brothers' light, tan skin tone and short, conked (chemically straightened) hair physically facilitate such a reading. The skin tone allows their Blackness a flexibility in signification which, especially on-screen, can read as Latin and therefore appealingly exotic; their conked hair both hides its natural texture and helps them to pass as an *other* Other. The added hip movements of their Latinesque dance, which do not appear in similar Nicholas numbers, mark the brothers' pelvises as present and active at the most basic level, which prepares them for their flirtatious interactions with a young Dorothy Dandridge in *Sun Valley Serenade* the following year. In this way, their dancing prowess is finally being linked to their own nascent sexuality—the very "threat" that made Harold so titillating for the group of white women in *Kid Millions* six years prior—even as it is buried beneath their professional and classy tuxedos' coattails, lapel pins, and matching watch chains.

Thus, if the Nicholases' Vitaphone appearances in "Black shorts" allowed them to both dance as classy young gentlemen and embody a Black jazz vocabulary among other Black jazz artists, their first Hollywood films introduced the problem of racial difference as they interacted with white casts. In these films, they performed contradictory masculinities of childhood innocence versus adult charisma and virtuosity; they also played with racial ambiguity once outside of all-Black performance contexts. But the contradictions of their childhood masculinity when performing amongst whites soon gave way to a clear spatial segregation from white casts (in the U.S.) and increasing hints of an adult sexuality kept under wraps.

Micro-Resistance Buried by Flash

Down Argentine Way put the Nicholas Brothers on the map of mainstream popular culture. Though they appeared only briefly in the film, they were a major selling point for audiences. Fayard once recalled an anecdote in which an audience responded with such fervor that the projectionist had to rewind the film and play their sequence again.[40] Similarly, *The Atlanta Constitution* listed the

Nicholases as the primary descriptor of the film: "'Down Argentine Way,' with the Nicholas Brothers."[41] This mass appeal and major success clearly lodged it in the brothers' memory, as they would return to it several times during their broadcast television appearances over a decade later; it also won them a five-year contract with Twentieth Century Fox. The significance of this contract should not be understated; with it, the Nicholases joined the very small group of African American performers—including Lincoln Perry ("Stepin Fetchit") and later, Lena Horne—who first secured long-term contracts with major studios. Though they continued to be confined to excisable numbers due to racist production practices, their consistent visibility in musicals during the 1940s carved out a space for showcasing Black male bodies performing Black dance where all—including Fred Astaire and Gene Kelly—could enjoy it and be influenced by it.

After the broken fourth wall and presentation directly to viewers in "Down Argentina Way," the Nicholases' performances became more discernibly cinematic. By this, I mean that the brothers' dances began to expand beyond traditional notions of stage space, following a larger trend in musicals toward the "integration" of narrative and number and the accompanying tendency to place dance numbers in less and less stage-like, more "everyday" spaces.[42] Film scholar Arthur Knight has argued that it is not simply an ironic coincidence that the terminology of "integration" was used to describe the increasing attempts at seamlessness between narrative and number, *and* to describe desegregation during the same period, especially given the genre's insistence on creating all-white (or deeply segregated) utopias.[43] It is perhaps doubly ironic, then, that the Nicholases' numbers displayed one of the central characteristics of the integrated Hollywood Musical, a performance space in which, as noted musical scholar Jane Feuer argued, "the proscenium is reborn out of ordinary space and the world is a stage."[44] But the brothers' segregated integration also does not end here; as contracted dancers, they regularly worked throughout the 1940s with Twentieth Century Fox's white dance director, Nick Castle. Castle lent a certain consistent cleverness to the dances he directed; among the most remarked-upon is a Gene Kelly number in *Summer Stock* (1950), in which Kelly appears to spontaneously create a dance with the sounds of a squeaky floorboard and the contrasting "scratch" sound of a discarded newspaper.[45] Though I by no means wish to credit Castle for the Nicholases' incredible virtuosity or their own creativity, his work with the Nicholases helped to incorporate them into the Hollywood musical production apparatus, with the important result that in the 1940s, the Nicholas Brothers brought Black dance directly into the increasingly idiosyncratic grammars of the "integrated" musical genre. And they were the only Black dancers to do so on a regular basis—most other instances of Black dance in Hollywood were performed by white dancers.[46]

Figure 1.4 Fayard swings around a lamppost in *The Great American Broadcast* (1941) (left); Gene Kelly does something similar in *Singin' in the Rain* (1952) eleven years later (right).

The first and clearest example of this segregated integration of the Nicholases into a musical plot occurs in *The Great American Broadcast* (1941). Almost halfway through the film, enterprising businessman-turned-radio broadcaster Rix Martin (John Payne) is preparing for a radio broadcast in a Toledo, Ohio train station. Inside, a group of Pullman Porters (portrayed by The Ink Spots) begins to play and sing the song "Alabama Bound," after which the camera moves out to the tracks, where the Nicholases (also costumed as Pullman Porters) dance to the Ink Spots' tune. In the process, they push over suitcases to dance on top of them, swing through railings, and jump through train windows while fellow station employees, both white and Black, smilingly look on. Notably, Fayard also swings around a lamppost, a move that Gene Kelly would go on to make iconic in *Singin' in the Rain* (1952) (see Figure 1.4). These seemingly spontaneous interactions with the film set's "everyday" elements fall under the category of what musical scholar Jane Feuer has termed *bricolage*, a notion she adapted from anthropologist and father of structuralism Claude Lévi-Strauss to describe the sense of "tinkering" that accompanies the many prop dances that came to define the Hollywood musical genre.[47] Feuer argues that, while these prop dances give the appearance of being spontaneous interactions with everyday materials, they are in fact some of the most heavily "engineered" moments of musical films, citing the extensive process photography necessary for numbers like Fred Astaire's dance with shoes that come to life in *The Barkleys of Broadway* (1949). However, there is a crucial difference between the Astaire-Kelly brand of bricolage and what the Nicholases do here: whereas Astaire and Kelly were white mega-stars with remarkable creative control and access to vast production departments willing to engineer whatever they and their choreographic collaborators could dream up, the Nicholases as Black specialty performers (even on long-term contract) were offered no such privilege. Instead, for them

46 WHITE SCREENS, BLACK DANCE

to claim this presumed-white form for themselves, preempting Kelly even at his most famous act of bricolage, should be understood as an act of resistance.

To better understand the Nicholases' small act of resistance here, it is important to acknowledge the particular context of *The Great American Broadcast* and their costuming as Pullman Porters. During the period in which the film is set (1919), the ethos of slavery arguably lived on in the labor conditions of Black Pullman Porters: these men were assigned 400 hours of work per month, with their three to four hours of sleep per night being deducted from their already minimal pay. Indeed, the Brotherhood of Sleeping Car Porters (BSCP) itself argued these conditions to be dehumanizing—and emasculating—in its efforts to construct a company union, claiming that "The porter has no manhood in the eyes of the company."[48] In fact, parallel with the release of *The Great American Broadcast*, it was BSCP leader A. Philip Randolph who organized the March on Washington Movement to protest segregation in the armed forces and generally promote fair working opportunities for African Americans.[49] Thus, it is particularly meaningful that the Nicholas Brothers' resistant use of the presumed-white technique of bricolage occurs when they are cast as dehumanized Pullman Porters. Wearing the costume of the emasculated, the brothers claim a masculinity defined by innovation and highly skilled dance performance. Of course, their number was nevertheless poorly integrated into the film. After they complete their performance and the camera cuts back to Payne's Rix Martin setting up for the broadcast, where both he and the Ink Spots applaud enthusiastically, his white companion then chuckles and remarks, "Those boys are terrific; they oughtta be on the stage." Martin responds, "Yeah, they're swell. Say, how long before this thing'll be ready for testing?" The brief pause between topics here indicates exactly where the number might easily be cut out in the South; moreover, it is no little irony that the Nicholases had already performed on not just *a* stage or two but *the* top stages in the country before being demeaned as grown Pullman Porter "boys" for this film.

Later that year, with Fayard turning twenty-seven and Harold turning twenty, the brothers' appearance in *Sun Valley Serenade* (1941) finally acknowledges, albeit obliquely, that they are sexual beings whose dance might express more than the joy of pure entertainment; artistically, it also resists the sanitization of jazz into big-band swing. In their "Chattanooga Choo Choo" number, they dance with fellow African American performer Dorothy Dandridge, who would, in her offscreen life, go on to marry Harold Nicholas in 1942. The number begins in a ski lodge, just after Tex Beneke and other band members sang the same song in harmony while "hanging out" at the tables—playing cards, sharing drinks, and so on (see Figure 1.5). While Beneke and the other white performers sang, the all-white Glenn Miller Orchestra was visible in the background, "rehearsing" (according to the scene's inaugural shot of a sign on the lodge door). But after the camera pans away from the singers to showcase the band with several shots of its musical crescendo, it keeps panning toward an elaborate train station set, as Dandridge strolls in theatrically wearing a black dress and discovers the Nicholas Brothers already there in light-colored suits and boater hats.

Importantly, the Nicholases are not costumed here as Pullman Porters, but rather as fellow passengers at the train station. The opportunity certainly presents itself, because the white chorus's lyrics to the Chattanooga Choo Choo song include the line "Boy, you can give me a shine."[50] But here, the Nicholas Brothers are romantic interests rather than menial service workers. They jump up when they spot Dandridge and proceed to perform their own scene-within-a-scene with her, their singing and dancing far outmatching the previous rendition of the chorus by the loitering teens. Whereas the white chorus' performance had been comparatively flat and low-energy, the Nicholases' and Dandridge's performance is bursting with flirtatious possibility (see Figure 1.5). Indeed, Fayard in particular is presented as a vaguely sexual being for the first time, sidling up to Dandridge at every opportunity as Harold watches and attempts to follow suit during their dance together (thus making it ironic that *Harold* is the one who married her the following year). Still, the performance itself never reaches the stage of actual partner dancing, and Dandridge gets on the "train" before long, leaving the Nicholases to their usual brotherly duet. This aborted flirtation not only prevents a full display of Black romance and sexuality, but also reminds the viewer that, unlike a Fred and Ginger would be, Fayard and Dorothy are not the focus of the musical.

In the absence of the brothers' love interest, the choreography becomes considerably faster; it also includes a backflip by Harold launched from Fayard's hands, as well as handsprings and bells by both brothers. These impressive, acrobatic "flash" elements serve as the spectacle to replace the sparks of the

Figure 1.5 In *Sun Valley Serenade* (1941), Tex Beneke sings the first chorus of "Chattanooga Choo Choo" with the Glenn Miller Orchestra playing in the background (left); Fayard Nicholas dances flirtatiously with Dorothy Dandridge during the final chorus while Harold swings under the railing to join them (right).

48 WHITE SCREENS, BLACK DANCE

relationship that might have otherwise bloomed during this dance. They were also highly memorable and popular among audiences; Leonard Reed recalls, for example, seeing an enthusiastic reception of *Sun Valley Serenade* in an all-white theatre in Birmingham, Alabama, where, "For some reason, they did not cut the Nicholas Brothers out, and the people were screaming. You couldn't hear the rest of the picture when they finished their dance."[51]

Given this approbation by white—and even Southern white—audiences, it is crucial to note that, while the songs they danced to in most of their films had already been performed by white bands and singers mere minutes beforehand during the films' plots, the brothers' dance performances recast these jazz tunes with an insistently Black style. A review of *Sun Valley Serenade* in *The Washington Post* that named the Nicholases as one of the film's highlights described them as "a pair of sepias so packed with rhythm that it practically runs out of their ears."[52] The emphasis on rhythm here is both an accurate descriptor and a clear marker of the Nicholases' performance of jazz's Black heritage. What originally made jazz so exciting (and dangerous, just like rock 'n' roll after it, in the eyes of white conservatives) in the 1910s and 20s was the infectiousness of its Africanist rhythms; the emergence of swing's (mostly white) big bands like the Glenn Miller Orchestra tamed jazz and served to erase its "color." Indeed, as neatly summed up by Amiri Baraka, swing "sought to involve the Black culture in a platonic social blandness that would erase it forever, replacing it with the sociocultural compromise of the 'jazzed-up' popular song."[53] Thus, the much-hailed presence of the Nicholases' number literally danced the Glenn Miller Orchestra's version of "Chattanooga Choo Choo" back into a Black song (both sonically via their danced rhythm and visibly via the very presence of their bodies). In this way, the "Chattanooga Choo Choo" scene from *Sun Valley Serenade* enacts and embodies the racial and cultural conflict implicit in jazz performance of the late-swing era. The Nicholases' resistance over the course of the number is therefore a response to both the hollowing out of Black cultural production *and* the erasure of Black sexuality.

Sun Valley Serenade was not alone in rendering visible jazz-swing's racial tension, nor was it the only moment when the Nicholases were allowed to demonstrate at least some interest in the opposite sex. In fact, the Nicholases follow-up performance in *Orchestra Wives* (1942), released less than a year later, embodied similar tensions—both racial and sexual. Once again, the Glenn Miller band plays the first chorus of "(I've Got a Gal In) Kalamazoo" and a group of white singers gathers around a microphone in front of them to sing the second chorus. Then, after moving slightly and slowly throughout the song up to this point, the camera pans right at breakneck speeds to reach a small stage on the other side of the room in time for Fayard and Harold to emerge with the first beat of the next chorus. Their costumes for "Kalamazoo" return to their traditionally formal white ties and tuxedo tails, as if to mark a more streamlined, simpler number than their previous performances for Twentieth Century Fox. Indeed, unlike "Chattanooga Choo Choo," "(I've Got a Gal In) Kalamazoo" brings out the slower end of the Nicholases' repertoire: shuffle-ball-changes, slides that slowly pull the legs together, and ballet-inspired leg movements such as *battements* and *ronds de jamb*. But this isn't to say that there aren't quick, crisp steps or impressively complex choreography—it may be more accurate to say that the brothers' use of the pregnant pauses of staccato rhythms at the slightly slower tempo gives the *appearance* of more streamlined choreography.

The Nicholases do not have a female dance partner this time; instead, the content of the song itself is the vehicle through which they indicate their maturity and interest in women. Whereas the white chorus had simply ignored the words to "Kalamazoo," the female singer punctuating it only with unrelated theatrical facial expressions, Fayard and Harold treat the lyrics as more of a script, which they act out together in the form of a conversation about a girl in Kalamazoo. Thus, when Harold sings, "Years have gone by—my, my how she grew," Fayard interjects, "Man, did she grew [*sic*]!" before Harold continues his narration: "I liked her looks when I carried her books in Kalamazoo." As he does so, he reaches down, as if to playfully smack a bottom, and pulls it up to indicate growth. Then, a few bars later, when Harold exclaims, "Oh, what a gal! A real pipperoo," Fayard once again interjects with "She's a fine chick." This time, he uses both hands to mime her body, in the manner of miming an hourglass figure (see Figure 1.6). In this way, Fayard in particular (but with assistance from Harold's facial expressions) adds a sexual dimension to the song that was perhaps ripe for emphasis but entirely subdued when the white chorus sang it. It is subtle, momentary, and rendered harmless once again by the brothers' seeming youthfulness and impeccable dress, but this element of sexuality is undeniably present.

Figure 1.6 In the "(I've Got a Gal In) Kalamazoo" number from *Orchestra Wives* (1942), Fayard mimes the playful smacking of a bottom (left) and the contours of a female body (right).

50 WHITE SCREENS, BLACK DANCE

And yet, the film's diegetic context once again cannot sustain this sexual element for long, so it is once again sublimated into impressive, "flash"-y spectacle. This spectacle has Fayard and then Harold performing a variation on their customary turn-into-jump split. Recalling the breaking of the fourth wall that ended their number from *Down Argentine Way*, Fayard then gives a glance at the camera—as if to imply, "Watch this!"—before running toward and catapulting off a nearby column; as usual, Harold escalates and "outdoes" his brother's move by performing his own run into a backflip off another column, landing in a split. Harold recalls this backflip off the column to be Nick Castle's idea, one that at first intimidated him: "Are you crazy? Let me see you do that!" Castle, of course, could not, but was certain that Harold could, so he had assistants hold Harold with a belt the first few times he tried it; sure enough, he soon mastered the stunt.[54] In a separate telling of this event by Fayard, he suggests that this idea was sudden: "We were rehearsing and Nick said, 'Stop the music! I've got an idea! . . . I've got an idea where you walk up the wall, do a back flip, and go into a split!'"[55] This seems to complicate Feuer's concept of *bricolage*; in Fayard's telling, the set was not carefully engineered to include columns for the benefit of the Nicholases' spectacle, but rather they really were the materials that so happened to be on the set and available for choreographic exploitation. Thus, though they were denied the budgets and expansive creative freedom of bigger names, the Nicholases participated in pure bricolage, without what Feuer terms its "twin image" of engineering; the dance was made to adapt to the *mise en scène* of the film rather than the other way around. The number then ends with perhaps the brothers' most iconic move, executed for the first time on screen: side splits through the air launched via a jump from the top of a platform and a bounce on mini-trampolines.[56] After the gravity-defying bricolage and stunts, the viewer almost forgets that the Nicholases ever implied sexual desire at all; the sexuality of their mature masculinity is subsumed into their virtuosity.

These last few acrobatic sequences, by now commonplace in the brothers' repertoire, are precisely the accomplishments that earned them a reputation as a flash act. Indeed, their handsprings, flips, and splits demonstrate a truly gymnastic skillset that distinguished them from many other acts and has become one of their hallmarks due to its "wow" factor. This is also what allows their routines to stand out in historical memory—a quick image search for the brothers on any online search engine turns up photo after photo of their jumps and splits. However, this number also demonstrates that the Nicholases did much more than simple tap routines peppered with exciting gymnastics as sensational punctuation. Halfway through the number, the music quiets down and loses percussion as the lights dim and a spotlight appears on the brothers. They perform sensuous slides, quite similar to ballet's *glissés* and *ronds de jamb à terre*, perhaps their smoothest ever drop into and rise up from the splits, and sweeping arms and hands to accompany all of it. This clear choreographic refusal of the flash label and emphasis on their refined, graceful movements aligns them with nebulously "classical" dance, synonymous in mainstream culture with the "high art" of ballet and, especially in the 1940s, Fred Astaire's ballroom-inspired style.

This stylistic similarity to Astaire suggests a potential parallel between their performances of masculinity during this period, but the Nicholases' racialized status in Hollywood complicates this. Musical scholar Steven Cohan used Astaire's masculinity as a case study for the peculiar tension within the cinema's "feminizing" of the song-and-dance man via the camera's gaze toward male dancing bodies—a gaze that classical Hollywood cinema usually reserved for female bodies. For Cohan, Astaire's slight frame (unlike the more muscular physique of white action stars, and Gene Kelly) made him an unlikely candidate for physical spectacle, so the camera's focus on him and others like him "offered an alternative representation of masculinity."[57] More specifically, "[a]s a star text . . . 'Fred Astaire' is a highly theatricalized representation of maleness on screen which oscillates between, on the one hand, a fictional character grounded in the static and reductive binarism of traditional gender roles and, on the other, a musical persona whose energy choreographs a libidinal force that revises conventional masculinity and linear desire."[58] That Astaire's masculinity was an unconventionally spectacular one, and that as a result he could so often be represented by metonymies of his body such as his legs and his signature top hat, places him among the most visually memorable male stars of the era—and our cultural memory of him is inextricably linked to the very grace and "class" he continually embodied.

The Nicholas Brothers' similarly costumed performances of dignity read differently because their dancing was consistently rendered as *only* spectacle, lacking the ambiguity provided by an in-depth performance of conventional gender roles. Where Astaire's dance numbers continually worked through what fellow musical scholar Rick Altman would term their "dual focus," with a female co-star to romance and thereby resolve the problems of heterosexuality and sexual difference, the Nicholases' intimacy with a female dance partner or even description of a "fine chick" in Kalamazoo was continually interrupted by pure spectacle.[59] Thus, their greater feminization via greater spectacle helped to circumscribe their performance of masculinity, and thereby neutralized the "danger" of sexually mature Black men in the eyes of white audiences. In short, the Nicholases were never treated like debonair Astaire on the Hollywood screen because their Blackness got in the way, but whereas Astaire needed female partners to reassure audiences of his masculinity, the Nicholases needed spectacle to sublimate the threat of theirs. But even without Astaire's visibility as leading man in musical plots, the Nicholases brought a comparable sense of "class" to their performances as proud Black men. It is perhaps poetic, then, that their most

52 WHITE SCREENS, BLACK DANCE

famous film appearance (and final film on their Twentieth Century Fox contract) was in a Black-cast musical, *Stormy Weather* (1943).

As one of the most successful Black-cast musicals ever produced in Hollywood, *Stormy Weather* and its titular song have received a great deal of critical attention and noteworthy scholarly analysis.[60] Arthur Knight holds that "*Stormy Weather* [the film] represents an important cultural road not taken by Hollywood and U.S. culture more generally at a crucial historical moment."[61] The biggest hit to feature the Nicholas Brothers, *Stormy Weather* was uniquely poised to launch their career into the next stage; indeed, it is the film for which they are still best remembered today. However, even in this Black-cast musical, the Nicholases are merely guest performers who "close the show" rather than named characters woven into the film's plot, which centered around a romance between characters played by Bill Robinson and Lena Horne. The practical reason for this is that they were not originally slated to be in it at all; they were added at the last minute to prevent Fayard from being drafted.[62] While it might seem strange that the Nicholases weren't originally cast in a musical about African American performers during the interwar period, I argue that this decision in itself indicates the brothers' interstitial place in the Hollywood landscape, defined by their socioeconomically privileged background and independence/isolation from the Hoofers Club set as well as the limitations imposed on their career and potential mainstream visibility by racist production and projection practices. Put reductively, they were "too white" to play major roles in a black cast musical—but "too Black" to ever be assigned substantial roles in mainstream (white cast) musicals.

Their "Jumpin' Jive" number is in many ways the pinnacle of their hybridization of the "class act" and the "flash act" alongside resistive bricolage—but this time, as a part of the Black community rather than the outsiders segregated in an otherwise white film. At the beginning of the number, the Nicholases blend into the arrangement of bodies in a large room, emerging from the crowd on cue to shift attention from bandleader Cab Calloway toward their own spectacular audiovisual performance. They jump up and hop rhythmically onto a nearby table in order to then join Calloway in the club's designated thrust stage space. However, the stage cannot contain them long; after they perform their introductory sequence side-by-side, they jump up onto and across drum-like pedestals that are distributed amongst the members of the orchestra. There is no separation between the flash portion of their dance and the rest of it; the brothers seamlessly weave these impressive feats into their highly rhythmic jazz tap, whose smoothness and constant flow accentuates their tuxedos to mark the number as a class act, too. The performance continues as the brothers jump up to the platform stage, the piano, and back down again to the floor (landing in the splits, of course), echoing each other's steps and arm movements while seeming to float

Figure 1.7 In their famous "Jumpin' Jive" number from *Stormy Weather* (1943), the brothers jump over each other and land in the splits on each step to descend the grand staircase (left); they then complete the number by sliding down the narrow ramps on the sides of the staircase (right).

around the space via quick turns and slides. The brothers then move diagonally toward the camera as if to invite us to follow, and the camera cuts to a grand double staircase that was not visible before, a second stage whose spatial relation to the first is utterly unknown. This gives the impression that the Nicholases' physicality not only pushed the boundaries of the stage space but also, via their proximity to the camera, cinematic space as well. In the famous finale to the number, the Nicholases begin at the top of the staircase and take turns jumping over each other's heads to land in the splits on the step below, making their way down each step before then hopping back up the stairs one final time and unexpectedly sliding down narrow side-ramps in the splits (see Figure 1.7). This final choreographic choice functions as another use of bricolage, in which the Nicholases turn a seemingly unintentional element of set design into an opportunity to demonstrate their dance skill.

It is no wonder, then, that the number "lodges" so well in memory and received such rave reviews from the mainstream press—according to the *Los Angeles Times*, for example, "[c]rowds stormed the box offices of five theaters" to see this "sepia saga."[63] *Stormy Weather* was the culmination of the Nicholases' journey through Hollywood: after a decade of micro-resistances and dancing an ever-maturing Black masculinity, they hit a wall. Indeed, Hill surmises that their expression of a mature, attractive masculinity was at least part of the reason the Brothers' contract was not renewed after World War II:

> Perhaps the most pressing reality to confront Fox executives in any consideration of contract renewal was that in June 1943, Harold was twenty-two and Fayard twenty-eight. Sporting a whip of a mustache over his lip, Harold was a dashing figure on film, and Fayard was unabashedly sexy, especially in the way

54 WHITE SCREENS, BLACK DANCE

> he stroked his fingers and swerved his hips while singing a song. It seemed as
> if the brothers had, all of a sudden, grown from boys to men. No longer were
> they the cute youngsters who had charmed and disarmed audiences with their
> dimpled smiles and jubilant rhythm dancing. Precocious sophistication had
> given way to a mature sexuality.[64]

Of course, the shift Hill describes did not actually occur "all of a sudden;" it had
been brewing since *Down Argentine Way*, but the description of the brothers at
this juncture is apt.

This moment in summer 1943 was also when race riots and "zoot suit" riots
were breaking out in Harlem, Detroit, and Los Angeles, and the film might easily
have been considered part of the problem. The corps of men who performed
in the number just preceding the Nicholases wore the wide-brimmed hats,
long jackets, and draped watch chains of the zoot suit. At a time when lavishly dressed Black men were a dangerous presence in the real world, the presence of lavishly dressed Black men onscreen was a political statement. In fact,
NAACP director Walter White praised Fox for choosing to go through with the
film's June release despite the riots.[65] It is also important to note the hairstyles
at play here. In the context of 1940s urban Black life, the conked hair sported
by the Nicholas Brothers, Cab Calloway, and many of the members of his band
in *Stormy Weather* had a political dimension as well. In cultural studies scholar
and historian Kobena Mercer's reading, the conk—like the zoot suit and jive-
talk—"answered back" against a status quo in which Black men were "[s]hut out
from access to illusions of 'making it'" in white-controlled society.[66] In his autobiography, Malcolm X disparages the conks of his youth as attempts to look
more white,[67] but Mercer suggests that the significance of the practice is more
complicated: "The conk involved a violent technology of straightening, but this
was only the initial stage in a process of creolizing stylization. The various waves,
curls and lengths introduced by practical styling served to differentiate the
conk from the conventional white hairstyles which supposedly constituted the
'originals' from which this Black style was derived as imitation or 'copy.'"[68] On
the heads of the Nicholas Brothers, the conk might be read as an embodiment of
the tensions they also performed with the rest of their bodies: the simultaneous
desires to perform a proud Blackness and retain mainstream access and visibility
in white Hollywood.

Despite Hill's citation of the brothers' mature Black masculinity and sexuality as the most likely reasons for Fox's decision not to renew their contract,
Fayard has insisted it was *they* who refused to renew with Fox after being routinely relegated to specialty numbers; for him, this did not constitute full employment.[69] Regardless of who made the decision, what is clear is that Fayard
and Harold's Hollywood film career was not only *limited* by racist employment

practices, but also *destroyed* by it. At the same time that Fred Astaire, Gene Kelly, Donald O'Connor, and Danny Kaye were enjoying the pinnacles of their careers as Hollywood's beloved song-and-dance men, the Nicholas Brothers found themselves without work in the American film industry. That is, "[n]ow too old to be cast as a pair of carefree teenagers, and too talented and too proud to accept roles as tap-dancing shoeshine boys, Fayard and Harold were still too young (and sexually potent) to play the role of veteran hoofers past their prime, as had Bill Robinson in *Stormy Weather*."[70] Moreover, there was little to be gained by returning to the club circuit, as the federal government's postwar 20 percent "entertainment tax" on all public entertainment venues had severely curtailed nightclub and ballroom performance opportunities.

Post-Fox Mature Masculinity

The Nicholases spent the rest of the 1940s working one-off performances in a variety of venues—a touring show or two, the Vitaphone short *Dixieland Jamboree* (1946), the Broadway musical *St. Louis Woman* (1946), in which Harold secured a starring role, and a few more film cameos. Fayard was drafted in 1943 and served for thirteen months. During that time, Harold made two film appearances of his own: *Reckless Age* (1944) and *Carolina Blues* (1944), "B-movie" musicals. During these interstitial years, both Harold's solo appearances and their later trio performance with Gene Kelly in *The Pirate* (1948) left behind the formal tendencies of their Fox numbers. No longer associated with tuxedo tails, the Nicholases performed in tighter and flashier costumes that highlighted the spectacle of their performances.

The clearest example of this focus on spectacle was both their first "integrated" performance since 1934 and their final appearance in Hollywood film. According to Fayard, "Gene Kelly always wanted to dance with us, but he could never find the right story. He didn't want us to come on like we were servants, and all of a sudden I'm whistling and tapping a little bit."[71] Once they were reunited after the war, the Nicholas Brothers were asked to join Gene Kelly in *The Pirate*, a film set in the Caribbean and featuring Kelly as a circus performer, Serafin, who impersonates the pirate Macoco. The Nicholases were cast as fellow (nameless, lineless) circus performers who appeared in the background at several moments in the film but were mainly brought onboard for the "Be a Clown" number toward the end. Once again, the brothers' tan skin tone, especially in the context of the liminal space of the Caribbean, allows them to read as ambiguously raced and therefore exotic, an *other* Other. For their entrance, they use the split-slide through legs trick that they debuted in *Down Argentine Way*: Gene Kelly stands erect with legs spread apart, Fayard slides in under them and pops up in front, and Harold follows by siding under both of them and popping up in front of Fayard. All three wear tight-fitting bright yellow and turquoise clown outfits and the Nicholases flank Kelly through numerous gymnastic maneuvers—round-offs, kick-ups, toe-touches (split-jumps), climbing atop one another, and a final somersault—as well as barrel rolls, kicks, runs, jumps, and Cossack steps. Kelly's choreography for the trio was physically challenging but rather choreographically simple. None of the three did any tap dancing or intricate footwork, nor were there any tempo changes to vary the steps. This is notably the first time the Nicholases did not control their choreography themselves, and Kelly's version of a Nicholas-appropriate number leaned into the flash aspect, ignoring the complexity of their jazz tap vocabulary.

Though this scene was progressive with regard to its interracial performance, its racial politics in context are more complicated. At this point in the plot of the film, Kelly's Serafin character is about to be hanged for the crimes of Macoco (as whom he has been masquerading), so his noose hangs in wait nearby. During the "Be a Clown" number, Kelly leads the three of them right up to the hanging noose, which all confront with fright as they bug their eyes, reach toward their necks, and turn away. In an era when lynchings of Blacks by whites were still a common occurrence, the optics here are uncomfortable at best, and in a certain sense symbolic of the reasons for the Nicholases' dying Hollywood career. Indeed, this was their last Hollywood musical number ever, and in it, they had to confront a noose while wearing clown costumes. If there is a redeeming factor, it is that for these brief moments, Fayard and Harold were integrated and almost equal—while Kelly was the star, they all did the same steps, all grabbed onto one another for balance, and all collapsed into a pile together twice during the number (see Figure 1.8). This is as much bonding as the Nicholases had experienced on commercial film with a white dancer their entire lives (though a

Figure 1.8 In the "Be a Clown" number from *The Pirate* (1948), the Nicholas Brothers and Gene Kelly grab onto one other for balance (left) and collapse into a pile together (right).

home movie in the RKO lot with Fred Astaire once captured a similar camara-derie). Still, it is hard not to read this opportunity as giving the brothers too little, too late.

With fewer and fewer opportunities to work in American show business in the U.S. after World War II, the Nicholas Brothers found themselves moving to Europe in 1948. They performed in several European films over the course of the following decade, during which time both moved back and forth between the U.S. and Europe. Sometimes one brother would leave the other behind to switch continents, and they often reunited under unusual conditions: in 1953, for example, they appeared in two Mexican films together: *El Misterio del carro express* and *El Mensaje de la muerte*. This period also saw them interacting more with groups of (white) back-up dancers and chorus girls in Europe, as Harold had as a child in *Kid Millions*. But these European performances also functioned as a representation of American entertainment abroad, allowing the Nicholases to take advantage of international recognition for work they had already done in the U.S., offering quotations and callbacks to their most famous dances, espe-cially their finale from *Stormy Weather*.

Meanwhile, the musical as a genre was losing steam within Hollywood, partially due to external factors such as the rise of television and the 1948 Paramount Decree, in which the U.S. Supreme Court ordered the breakup of the major studios. Stylistically, Hollywood musicals were struggling to in-novate by the late fifties, depending on increasingly wacky forms of bricolage and camera tricks to keep audiences interested in their dance numbers, which choreographically offered more of the same. Rare injections of innovation did occur, and once again came from the Black community, but most roles remained reserved for white cast members, so the classical Hollywood musical was stuck in a rut. The future of musical mass entertainment, it seemed, was in television.[72]

Television, Nostalgia, and Innovation

By the late 1940s, experiments with broadcast television had already attracted various kinds of stage performers. Indeed, Bill Robinson himself first danced on *Texaco Star Theater* in June 1948; his final appearance on the show occurred just two months before he died in November 1949. Though American television was by no means quick to integrate, it nevertheless offered more opportunities for Black performers to be seen by mass audiences than did the Hollywood film industry following World War II. But these opportunities did not come easy and required the support of powerful allies, often the Jewish ex-vaudevillians who were first to succeed in the early "vaudeo" (vaudeville + video) years of the

58 WHITE SCREENS, BLACK DANCE

television industry. Milton Berle, for example, recalls a dispute over his desire to bring the Four Step Brothers onto *Texaco Star Theater*:

> I remember clashing with the advertising agency and the sponsor over my signing the Four Step Brothers for an appearance on the show. The only thing I could figure out was that there was an objection to black performers on the show, but I couldn't even find out who was objecting. "We just don't like them," I was told, but who the hell was "we"? Because I was riding high in 1950, I sent out the word: "If they don't go on, I don't go on." At ten minutes of eight—ten minutes before showtime—I got permission for the Step Brothers to appear. If I broke the color-line policy or not, I don't know, but later on I had no trouble booking Bill Robinson or Lena Horne."[73]

Given Robinson's 1948 and 1949 appearances mentioned above, the date of this recollection may be inaccurate, but the sentiment remains: even America's most beloved early television program hosts met resistance when it came to booking Black talent for their live vaudeville-style variety shows.

Importantly, though, Black performers' appearances in America's living rooms, however few at first, would have constituted some white Americans' first experiences of diversity, or in the parlance of the time, "integration." Indeed, as scholar of African American film and television Christine Acham has argued, "[t]elevision was the most significant way of crossing over into the mainstream U.S. milieu. More effective than any other venue, television broadcast African Americans to a mainstream U.S. audience as no medium had done before."[74] For the Nicholas Brothers, this release from the contract-governed Hollywood musical (from which their performance might easily be cut if necessary) meant a series of opportunities to reference, remix, and reformulate their signature steps. Unlike white musical stars who made the move to television, the Nicholases had more or less always played themselves during their film career due to a lack of access to speaking parts and actual characters, so there were no major shifts in character from "roles" to "selves." Also unlike many other song-and-dance men such as Gene Kelly, who spent most of their television years nostalgically yearning for the old days of vaudeville, the Nicholases made old routines fresh and brought new trends to bear on their jazz dance style. In so doing, they innovated beyond their old flash and class act combination toward a more fluid, loose, groovy, and funky style of movement.

To introduce the Nicholas Brothers on the September 18, 1951 episode of NBC's *Texaco Star Theatre*, Milton Berle begins, "Fresh from their European triumph, one of the greatest, if not the greatest young dancing performers that we have on the stage or nightclub floor today: the sensational Nicholas Brothers!" Of course, the Nicholases were no longer "young" at this point: Fayard was a month shy of thirty-seven and almost a decade into his marriage to Geraldine Pate, and their son, Tony Nicholas, was now about seven years old. Harold, an even thirty, had fathered a daughter, Harolyn Suzanne, with Dorothy Dandridge by this point, and the two would divorce about a month after this television appearance. But even as Berle himself is only about six years older than Fayard, he refers to these grown Black men as if they are children, denying their maturity and, by extension, their masculinity. Though Berle is no doubt appealing to older viewers' memory of the petite young men who appeared in a series of shorts and films like *Kid Millions*, this inaccurate emasculation of the Nicholases functions as a television-specific containment strategy—a reminder that the television industry was also a participant in U.S. society's racist discourses despite offering more representational opportunities to Black folks than the film industry. And there is an accompanying visual reference back to their experience of Hollywood segregation as well; the brothers come out wearing tails and perform a variation on their choreography from *Down Argentine Way*. So, just as he had at age twenty-six, Fayard hop-turns in the splits and jumps over his hanky; Harold repeats the original split-slide through Fayard's legs. Unlike their original veranda-style performance space in *Down Argentine Way*, however, the *Texaco Star Theater* set offers a simple platform from which they can jump into the splits, so they incorporate this signature trope as well. This is indicative of the Nicholases' 1950s televisual strategy more generally: they recombine elements from past performances with newer choreography in order to adapt to the televisual space and update their existing star personae.

Two months later, on November 10, 1951, the Nicholases appeared on *All Star Revue: The Ed Wynn Show* and performed yet another variation on "Argentina." Though they wear suits and bow ties instead of tails this time, the song and steps are familiar. The biggest differentiation, in fact, is the introduction, which I quoted as the opening anecdote to this chapter. As I suggested at the outset, for Ed Wynn to quip "You boys will have to dance in this crummy street, here" after asking them to "picture a marvelous palace" both infantilizes them and makes all-too-apparent the brothers' exceptionality as one of the very few Black dance acts that did *not* once dance in the streets and who *had* been invited to several palaces—not only the Palace Theatre in New York City, but also Buckingham Palace after a command performance at the London Palladium before the King of England in 1948. It also runs the risk of mocking these achievements, symbolically relegating their talent to a "crummy street" as punishment for their racial difference. It is particularly ironic, then, that Fayard and Harold perform their *Down Argentine Way* "class act" choreography, originally set for a white tie evening at a swanky club in an imagined Buenos Aires, on a television studio set meant to represent a plain street with basic storefronts. Visually, this segment of *All Star Revue* has the effect of confining two fully grown, thickly mustachioed, emphatically masculine Black men to the urban inner city—in this way, it is an unfortunate reproduction of the status quo in major cities throughout the United States at a time when the white middle class was fleeing to the suburbs.

The Nicholases' appearance on *The Colgate Comedy Hour* Christmas Show, which was hosted by Abbott and Costello and aired December 14, 1952, included their first new choreography since debuting on television, the newness of which is made especially apparent by their extremely elaborate hand and armwork. Perhaps realizing that the full band behind them was too loud for their tapping to be audible, the Nicholases emphasized a more visual aspect of their performance. During their quick and increasingly complicated time steps, Fayard's hands and arms in particular snake and flutter to accentuate his lower body—indeed, their twisting often seems to propel him forwards, backwards, or in a circle. Harold's slightly more compact upper body nevertheless finds its own contrast in his more active, expansive lower body (see Figure 1.9). Both brothers perform in a presentational mode, occasionally crossing their hands only to then open them out into a wide, open gesture. But more often than usual, the brothers perform slightly different but harmonizing choreography—each plays to his own strengths while retaining a unison of rhythm with the other. This new choreographic approach inaugurates the crowning phase of the Nicholas Brothers' career: one in which they perform definitive individuality even as they complement one another. The speed of this fluidic dance and isolation of opposite appendages is a departure from their past combination of joint precision and challenge dance formations, one which marks their final maturity as separate men with separate lives, families, and identities. Unlike the Four Step Brothers, for example, who retain the unison/challenge (or all/one) binary formation during their television career, the Nicholases introduce variation to their

Figure 1.9 On the December 14, 1952 *Colgate Comedy Hour* Christmas Show, Fayard's snaking arms move so fast they blur in the video image and seem to propel him through space (left); Harold complements Fayard's upper body with his wider range of fluidic leg motion (right).

duets that replaces the previous challenge-style habit of taking turns and one-upmanship. However, I am not attempting to claim that the Nicholas Brothers' innovation is in some way superior to or more advanced than the Four Step Brothers' famously high-speed tapping, scatting, and challenge format; I instead want to highlight the extent to which Fayard and Harold continued to distinguish themselves from similar performers throughout this period. Their complementary and harmonizing choreography made an argument for a *different*, complex, and fluidic Black masculinity during an era where stereotyping made this a radical act.

After Fayard and Harold complete their new choreography and bow during this episode of *The Colgate Comedy Hour*, they do not exit but rather continue dancing. At this point, the brothers return to their recent habit of performing variations on "Down Argentina Way" by introducing yet another version. These multiple "Argentina" routines no doubt seem like an uninteresting repetition from the contemporary standpoint—especially as they are presented side-by-side in the context of this written chapter—but it might behoove a contemporary reader to consider that each 1950s television iteration of the 1940 number probably reaches a new audience. If we conceptualize this multiplication of "Argentina" as a "rerun" in the age of live TV, we begin to see the deeper links between early television and the vaudeville/nightclub performance circuit of prior decades; just as performers would repeat numbers and choreography for new audiences as they moved to new stage settings, the Nicholases perform roughly the same choreography for America's growing television audience.[75] Like reruns in later decades, these re-performances would have provided the pleasures of recognition, familiarity, and new observations for viewers who had seen the 1940 film or a previous TV appearance, *and also* introduced the excitement of the number and/or the brothers themselves to first-time viewers. Thus, while the Nicholas Brothers' move to television coincided with dynamic updates to their dancing style, it also in some ways structurally echoed the performance contexts of their youth.

The Nicholases' second appearance on Ed Sullivan's *Toast of the Town* on December 13, 1953, which opened the day's episode, played with this concept of nostalgia but also refused it with more new choreography. Sullivan describes their opening as "very exciting . . . because here are the two great dancing stars of the country and of the world" (and proceeds to take credit for discovering them at the Cotton Club and introducing them to Fred Astaire years before). He then creates a Cotton Club-like context for the performance: "So tonight we're going to take you up to Harlem, make believe, up to the Chez George, where you'll find a—well, you could say a typical—Cotton Club chorus line led by the widow of the late Bill Robinson, preparing the stage for the dynamic entrance of the Nicholas Brothers." The episode then fades to a shot of this "Club Chez George"

62 WHITE SCREENS, BLACK DANCE

set, where the camera tilts down to reveal a revolving door through which six chorus girls sashay in furs, followed by Harold Nicholas. He appears to have entered the club as a patron, and excitedly removes his hat when he apparently spots his brother; Fayard jumps from a platform into the splits as a means of greeting him. The women clear away and the Nicholases begin dancing entirely new choreography together before a grand staircase and platform with ornate railing, apparently meant to represent the club's stage. This indicates an interesting disconnect between what Ed Sullivan suggested (nostalgia) and what the brothers chose to choreograph (new work); their dancing here looks very different from their last few television performances of variations on "Argentina," to say nothing of how it had looked two and a half decades prior when they were a major presence at the now-closed Cotton Club. Indeed, Fayard and Harold danced an even more fluid, seemingly improvisational number than ever before. This was their first television appearance that did not include a nostalgia number or harken back to the heyday of the vaudeville and club circuit, despite what Sullivan seemed to have set up for them.

In many ways, the Nicholases took the theoretical principles that governed swing and lindy to a lived extreme for this number. Once solely the purview of Fayard's extra flourishes, hands and arms are essential to both brothers' choreography here, and perfectly timed to either complement or coincide with each other. Fayard claps enthusiastically as he and Harold step in time with one another. He then partners Harold as he might a female lindy partner, launching him into a quintuple pirouette with ease. Both follow up with more clapping, emphatically swinging hips that exceed their sway in *Down Argentine Way*, and arms moving freely in alternating vertical extensions that would not reach mainstream dance until the 1960s. This loose but energetic new choreographic style does, at the number's halfway point, transition to their more familiar series of flash additions such as splits, jumps, and flips. The brothers take turns jumping over increasing numbers of female corps members, eventually stopping at five. Harold follows with a split slide through the legs of a row of the chorus girls and Fayard concludes the section with one last split jump over the group.

It is important to note the ways in which this sequence resists the perceived "flatness" of the television screen's *mise en scène*, for which it has so often been criticized:[76] while the first series of jumps were performed roughly across the frame, along the x-axis, the dancers were all arranged such that Fayard's concluding jump over the whole group was pointed *toward* the camera, along the y-axis. This use of spatial depth is further emphasized by the exit strategy, according to which the female dancers exit by splitting into two rows and walking toward the camera while the Nicholases run to the back to mount their grand staircase for one last jump into the splits. Thus, even though the television set was certainly smaller and more limiting than the sprawling film sets the

Nicholases were accustomed to, their choreography adapted in relationship to the new format to retain at least some degree of dynamism.

At the same time, the Nicholases treat the television studio as a distinctly different space from a film set; rather than always facing the camera(s), the brothers rotate through the performing space freely. Harold at one point faces Fayard by turning his back on the camera(s) and in this position performs a twisting, rising arm flourish in unison with him that seems to be performed more for his brother's benefit than for the camera's, since his turned back partially obscures our view of the gesture. And, while both brothers were always full-body dancers, they are now moving their hips, arms, and heads far more than ever before. More accurately, they are dancing exuberantly *with each other* rather than depending on the jazz era's challenge format, or even performing merely side-by-side as a dance team; they "partner" one another and playfully bump their bottoms together as chorus girls fill in behind them. It is possible that they do all of this in awareness of the fact that their rhythmic taps are far less loud or pronounced on television; since they are now performing live rather than via recording, louder taps cannot be dubbed in later. Or perhaps being unbound by long-term contracts provides the Nicholases with the freedom to experiment and take risks—certainly their unabashed hip movement here falls squarely into the realms of both the adult and the sexy. As ever, the Nicholas Brothers' onscreen performance demonstrates the innovative use of Africanist dance's loose, swinging hips and arms even as they mix dance styles and influences. But what is new on television is their use of space, interaction with each other, and an overall more fluidic dance style.

At this juncture, during the mid-1950s and the rise of the Civil Rights Movement's struggles for equality, work in the United States became particularly scarce and limiting for the Nicholas Brothers (Harold, who had always been as much a singer as a dancer, found few venues in which to sing in the U.S. during this period, and never on television). Thus, when they were offered opportunities to return to Europe, the Nicholases took them. Harold stayed for nearly a decade, but Fayard became homesick and returned to Los Angeles in 1958.[77] Thus, the brothers did not perform together again until 1964. From a dance-historical perspective, it is unfortunate that circumstances prevented the Nicholases from producing more work together during this period, as their having matured into complementary, fluid, whole-body tap dancers very much echoed the development of the "funky" "hard bop" developments in jazz music.[78]

Jazz Dance in the Soul Era

When Harold returned to the United States in 1964 at his brother's request to perform just two shows together, he found that the strides toward equality made

64 WHITE SCREENS, BLACK DANCE

in the wake of the Civil Rights Movement rendered Los Angeles living and performing a bit more bearable than it had been when he left for Europe, so he moved back.[79] As a result, the brothers appeared on five episodes of the variety show *The Hollywood Palace* in fairly quick succession over the course of 1964 and 1965.[80] Having performed apart for so long, the brothers were no longer sufficiently in tune with each other's movements to pick up where they left off in terms of dancing *together*, but jazz had also changed, split, and mainstreamed since then. So, even as the Nicholases continued to perform bits and pieces of familiar numbers for nostalgia's sake, their new harmonized dance that was innovative in the fifties was able to give way to a groovier version of the fluidity and loose hips more appropriate to the 1960s context. As we will see in the next chapter, they responded to the era's social and cultural changes quite differently than Gene Kelly; rather than televising a backward-looking vaudevillian masculinity through "The Old Soft Shoe," the Nicholas Brothers trafficked in a movement vocabulary that paralleled the new, overtly sexual masculinity of James Brown.[81]

The brothers' November 14, 1964 appearance on *The Hollywood Palace* has them outfitted in slim-fitting suits and skinny ties, singing as much as dancing. Harold leads his brother in a modified rendition of "My Kind of Town," a hit song debuted by Frank Sinatra in *Robin and the 7 Hoods* less than six months before. The song's original refrain, "My kind of town (Chicago is)" was changed for this performance to "My kind of town (Manhattan is)," which seems to allude to their success on Broadway and early mainstream appeal despite being Black entertainers. After this singing section, which has them hopping up and down (but not doing any splits on) New York skyline stairs, the brothers break into their tap dance at the top. A fairly simple unison routine, it includes the old challenge-style formation of taking turns and watching one another. Eventually, they return to the ground and perform a final set of their standard flash elements: splits, slides through legs, and jumps over each other. Fayard also includes his hopping split from *Down Argentine Way*, but at fifty, his body looks a little less willing to perform it. And instead of including their famous sliding splits toward the audience, they dial down to sliding crouches. But they include a signature final jump off the platform into a split on the ground, proving that "they've still got it," a feat that is perhaps even more impressive to audiences given the Nicholases' age.

Fortunately, even as Fayard's arthritis prevents him from performing the brothers' stunts as easily as he once could, television by this point has finally entered an era in which he is allowed to be "sexy." This episode aired just months after the Civil Rights Act of 1964, and just two years before Sammy Davis, Jr. began hosting his own variety show. So, as Harold sings, Fayard is finally free to thrust his pelvis and place a sensual hand on his chest (see Figure 1.10). Of course, by this time Fayard is (thankfully) no longer one of the only African

Figure 1.10 On the November 14, 1964 episode of *The Hollywood Palace*, Fayard thrusts his pelvis as Harold descends the stairs (left) and clutches his chest, bringing attention to his physicality (right).

American male dancers in the spotlight to lay claim to a more nuanced masculinity than the binary stereotypes of emasculated, grinning clown vs. overpowering and threatening buck inherited from minstrelsy. Indeed, Harriet Jackson's 1966 article "American Dancer, Negro" in *Dance Magazine* cites Arthur Mitchell, Donald McKayle, and Alvin Ailey as the young artists who were by that time "emerging from the minstrel-vaudeville cocoon" and allowing for a "Negro dancer and choreographer who no longer feels he must be confined to dancing 'Negro roles' and to expressing 'Negro themes.'"[82] I would argue that this held equally true for the Nicholases during this period, whose choreography now mixed dance styles more than ever.

A prime example of this stylistic mixing is the brothers' February 27, 1965 appearance on *The Hollywood Palace*. Costumed this time in two-toned slim-fitted suits, the brothers open with a fast-paced rendition of "That Old Black Magic," by that time an American standard that had been famously sung by Judy Garland, Frank Sinatra, and Sammy Davis, Jr. Harold begins the song with melodic and rhythmic scatting, following the long tradition of its use in Africanist expressive cultures. Fayard accompanies him with an exuberant mélange of dance styles: a little salsa, conga, and of course jazz, sometimes miming Harold's words. For the lyrics "down and down I go," Fayard wriggles himself down (see Figure 1.11); for "round and round I go," he spins. Harold then sings, for the first time on screen, about an explicitly sexual experience: being "aflame with such a burning desire," asking a fictive lover to "kiss [him] and put out the fire." Thus, by the 1960s, both brothers are finally able to perform a Black masculinity that is explicitly sexual but not *only* sexual—it also remains cosmopolitan and virtuosic.

This segment is followed by what the now-applauding audience was waiting for: the tapping. With their taps more crystal-clear than ever, the brothers keep both the speed and their exuberant arms going. The number seamlessly

Figure 1.11 On the February 27, 1965 episode of *The Hollywood Palace*, Harold sings "down I go" and Fayard wriggles downward (left) as part of his larger dance mélange (right).

ties together new choreography, old quotations (such as Fayard's jump over the handkerchief into the splits), and a sense of physical freedom (indicated in no small part by freely swinging hips) even in their frequent sonic unison. And as ever, they complete the performance with the spectacular flash elements of the splits: Fayard jumps over his handkerchief into a split, and Harold slides into one through his brother's legs. This virtuosic performance, with its high-speed tapping, traveling across the floor, and selective use of splits for spectacular emphasis, bears a marked resemblance to the electrifying moves performed just a few months before by another virtuoso: James Brown.

Many commentators and fellow entertainers consider Brown's eighteen-minute show-stopping song-and-dance performance on the *Teenage Awards Music International Show* to be the moment that established him as *the* Soul/R&B performer of the era, as well as the moment he was officially introduced to white audiences. The *T.A.M.I. Show* was a two-hour long showcase of 1964 chart-toppers filmed at the Santa Monica Civic Auditorium, bringing together most of American youth's favorite acts of the moment, including Chuck Berry, the Beach Boys, The Supremes, Marvin Gaye, and the Rolling Stones, whose show-closing headliner status famously upset James Brown. In Brown's memoir, he recalled, "I don't think I ever danced so hard in my life, and I don't think they'd ever seen a man move that fast."[83] Brown's moves during the *T.A.M.I. Show* are nevertheless representative of his 1960s screen appearances on broadcast programs such as *The Ed Sullivan Show*, *Shindig*, *The Hollywood Palace*, and even his brief cameo on the 1965 teen flick *Ski Party*. Just as the Nicholases fill out their *Hollywood Palace* appearances with smooth, intricate, and speedy footwork, so too does James Brown. And as Brown sings at the *T.A.M.I. Show*, The Famous Flames (who are incidentally outfitted similarly to the Nicholases) keep time with two-steps, a little grapevine, and some accented quick turns, just as Fayard does when Harold sings. Brown's celebrated exit some seventeen minutes later includes sliding down into several versions of the splits, once again echoing the Nicholas Brothers. Though Brown's seemingly electrified feet do not tap (apart from a brief segment during "Night Train"), they do swivel and almost vibrate at high speeds, in a striking resemblance to the Nicholases' 1965 dance. Of course, unlike the brothers' roots in the jazz rhythms of the Harlem Renaissance, Brown draws from the physicality of the Black Pentecostal tradition of being possessed by the Holy Spirit.[84] This is particularly true of his "open step slide" or "one-foot shimmy," which makes him seem to glide across the floor as if on ice. The Nicholases' dances took a different path through Black vernacular culture, and yet the discernible "steps" in each performance are the same—the result is two generations of Black men using the same movement vocabulary to flesh out proud masculinities of nimble "cool."

Despite the similarity of the movements, the Nicholases and James Brown occupied very different political positions in the 1960s cultural landscape. Young Brown's performances of Soul were invested in a sense of political urgency and radicalism; as ethnomusicologist Portia K. Maultsby has demonstrated, Soul in the 1960s was defined by "a group attitude which mirrored the philosophy of the Black Power Movement."[85] The Nicholas Brothers, on the other hand, were veterans from an earlier era of civil rights struggle, and habitually kept a lower political profile in order to stay employable during shifting tides.[86] Nevertheless, while the James Brown-style reassertion of the Black phallus alongside political radicalism was the most visible brand of Black masculinity during the 1960s, the Nicholas Brothers offer an alternative, smoother model using many of the same steps. Both corporeally and sartorially, their performance of masculinity performs a definitive break from the implied racist restrictions of earlier decades. They innovate a new jazz style to fit with the contemporary musical, political, and socio-cultural landscape.

Passing the Torch

Over a decade later, on February 23, 1977, Harold and Fayard appeared on an episode of *The Jacksons*, a family variety show which featured a nineteen-year-old Michael Jackson and an eleven-year-old Janet Jackson. The Nicholases' segment begins with an announcement by Michael's voice: "Ladies and gentlemen, the world-famous Nicholas Brothers!" Fayard, now sixty-three, and Harold, fifty-six, walk into view wearing brightly colored bell-bottomed suits, their hair grown out for the first time ever (onscreen, anyway). This is the Nicholas Brothers as they have never been seen: in leisure suits rather than bow ties, hair grown out rather than cropped short or conked. They have finally escaped—visually, at least—the necessity of performing "class" for white audiences that governed their entire professional careers. They tap a familiar syncopated introduction before being joined by Michael; the three then tap a trio dance and Michael notably keeps up quite well (see Figure 1.12). Eventually, the rest of the Jacksons (and some friends) join, forming a semi-circle in which all take turns demonstrating their moves. This arrangement recalls traditional African-American vernacular circle dances and with its dual emphases on the collective and the individual.[87] A danced version of call and response, this segment includes a skilled solo by Michael that presages some of the signature stances and spins of his early eighties music videos. It also includes brief solos by Fayard and Harold (who still spryly includes a signature jump into the splits). Of course, the brothers' dancing at this point is certainly not as complex or sharp as it had been in previous decades, but it is nevertheless enthusiastic and energetic. Regardless, the quality of the dancing here is far less important than the optics: the Nicholases once again join a Black cast as they had in *Stormy Weather* over three decades before, but this time on television, and this time with a few white friends in the background. This performance, however, unlike their number in *Stormy Weather*, is not packaged for primarily white audiences because it finally does not have to be in the 1970s. The program, which broke new ground by being the first variety program hosted by a Black family, served as a space where Black hosts could showcase other Black talent.[88] In this sense, the Nicholases were not simply there to perform a specialty number, but were welcomed as the episode's featured guests. And as their dance with him seems to imply, the Nicholases are symbolically passing the torch to young Michael Jackson (and little Janet, too). Indeed, the segment ends with these four (Janet, Harold, Michael, and Fayard) leading the rest in a large group dance. Afterwards, the camera moves in to show Harold and Fayard

Figure 1.12 On the February 23, 1977 episode of *The Jacksons*, the Nicholases dance in bell-bottomed suits with short afros, soon joined by a skilled young Michael Jackson (left); at the end, we see the three embracing (right).

embracing Michael (see Figure 1.12); this would be the new face (and body) of Black masculine dancing for the next several decades.

It could certainly be argued that the Nicholas Brothers only became mainstream stars in retrospect, thanks to the help of television channels playing old movies and the several documentary films that have been made about them since the 1990s. While the consensus in the dance community has always held them as some of the greatest dancers of the twentieth century, they lacked the visibility and star power that were made available to white actors in midcentury Hollywood. But even with their reduced visibility, it is important to remember that the Nicholas Brothers secured a Twentieth Century Fox contract by virtue of a single dance number ("Down Argentina Way"), and from that moment in 1940, the brothers' peerless jazz tap and acrobatic flash abilities, coupled with confidence, charisma, and, importantly, "class," allowed them to begin staking a claim for a Black masculinity on screen that existed beyond stereotypes. With their intricate rhythms, graceful flourishes, and many memorable variations on the splits, the brothers innovated their way from contradictory "little men" to actual, grown men through many small resistances to Hollywood's system of racist constraints, after which they continued to innovate, with increased freedom of movement and sexy self-expression on television. Indeed, a trans-media approach across the long arc of their entire career trajectory illuminates this final development. And as Black male dancers and entertainers of the following generations have made clear in interviews, the youth were paying attention to their dances, looking up to the Nicholases as role models.[89] Despite persistent segregation, containment, and infantilization on the part of the film and television industries, the Nicholases danced dignified, mature, and unapologetically *Black* masculinities across half a century of popular media.

2
Gene Kelly
Brash and Athletic

During the seventeen-minute dream ballet that concludes *An American in Paris* (1951), Gene Kelly and Leslie Caron dance their way through a version of Paris inspired by French impressionist and post-impressionist painters. When the pair arrives in a Van Gogh-ian *Place de l'Opéra*, they encounter a walking poster advertising an Henri Toulouse Lautrec *exposition*. On the back is a fac-simile of Lautrec's drawing *Chocolat dansant dans un bar* (1896), which depicts Cuban-born dancer and clown Raphaël Padilla in a regal pose. Standing be-side the poster, Kelly imitates *Chocolat*'s pose just in time to be superimposed on top of, and dissolved into, the drawing of the Black dancer (see Figure 2.1). Having entered the world of the painting as Padilla, Kelly then performs not an approximation of what Padilla might have danced as an Afro-Cuban ex-slave in the late nineteenth century, but instead American mainstream (and therefore "whitened") 1920s jazz steps like the Charleston, adding light-footed gallops with a solid upper body and carefully placed arms. And as he moves through to another Lautrec painting, he steels himself with tense, flat palms that locomote him through the space. These tense palms are a signature Kelly dance move which, alongside his embodiment of jazz steps descended from African American vernacular dances, work to demonstrate the masculinity of his dance. Thus, through the dissolve in this scene, Kelly literally embodies a Black Cuban dancer and performs Black American dance to shore up his athletic masculinity despite his potentially feminizing tight costume and the spectacularization of his body. The lineage of Black innovation behind the canonical (by the 1950s) jazz steps he chooses to perform is simultaneously "invisibilized" by Kelly's white body and emphasized by the Blackness of the dancer he chose to impersonate.[1]

That Gene Kelly engages in such a direct engagement with histories of Black dance and Black dancers in a mainstream 1950s Hollywood musical is signif-icant in part because, as a star, he is nearly synonymous with the entire genre of the midcentury musical. He starred in nineteen Hollywood musicals, many produced by the technicolor dream factory that was the Freed Unit at Metro-Goldwyn-Mayer, between 1940 and 1960. He is well-remembered, alongside colleague Fred Astaire, for his trick solos and uses of *bricolage* in musical num-bers, seeming to spontaneously incorporate props and set pieces into his dances.

White Screens, Black Dance. Pamela Krayenbuhl, Oxford University Press. © Pamela Krayenbuhl 2025.
DOI: 10.1093/9780197699119.003.0003

GENE KELLY   71

Figure 2.1 During the *An American in Paris* (1951) dream ballet, Gene Kelly poses beside the Henri Toulouse Lautrec poster of Cuban-born dancer Raphaël Padilla in *Chocolat dansant dans un bar* (left), and in the next frame is literally superimposed over Padilla's body (right).

His particular interest in developing the most compelling methods for filming dance (and dancing for the camera) is also well-documented across many interviews and biographies. As such, Kelly figures prominently in canonical academic studies of the Hollywood musical such as Rick Altman's *The American Film Musical* and Jane Feuer's *The Hollywood Musical*.[2] Other scholars have examined the negotiations of gender, power, and Americanness in Kelly's musical performances.[3] But the inspiration for this chapter comes from film scholar Carol Clover's pathbreaking 1995 article "Dancin' in the Rain," which highlights the ironically uncredited—and frequently Black—sources of *Singin' in the Rain*'s phenomenal success.[4] To explore the question of the film's dance authorship, she suggests, is to confront head on some of the racial politics buried just beneath the surface of the Hollywood musical's bright white veneer—politics that, I argue, often show themselves in the context of gender concerns. While Clover briefly mentions Kelly's attentiveness to and participation in the midcentury masculinity debate, it is more fully addressed by Steven Cohan in *Incongruous Entertainment*, where an entire chapter is devoted to Kelly's musical performances of masculinity (and their relationship to sexuality and camp). Indeed, Cohan holds that Kelly's roles in musicals directly contributed to a certain "gender-sexual indeterminacy" about his star persona.[5] This chapter uses the conjunction of Clover's and Cohan's readings of Kelly's film performance as its launching point; from such a perspective, the dissolve into *Chocolat* becomes one of the most overdetermined moments of Kelly's onscreen dance. He not only occupies the space of a Black body within an artwork, but he occupies the body of the first Black celebrity performer in Paris, who famously dressed in the form-fitting clothes of a dandy—itself a theatrical, feminine identity of Victorian men.[6] So, even as he chooses a movement vocabulary that emphasizes his athleticism

72 WHITE SCREENS, BLACK DANCE

and the "coolness" of jazz, Kelly performs an ambiguous masculinity.[7] Blackness serves as both a structured absence and an explicit reference in this and his other dance performances, such that his dancing mobilizes Blackness *as* masculinity.

This chapter argues that Gene Kelly employs Black dance to stabilize this ambiguous, athletic but often spectacularized masculinity. He engages in what I call blackbodying: as a white dancer, Kelly embodies Africanist movements, gestures, and corporeality, usually without any explicit acknowledgment of their source in Black culture, and without the burnt cork face makeup or caricatured elements of blackbodying's ancestor, blackface minstrelsy. Kelly achieves this un-marked form of cultural appropriation not only via his wide stances, low center of gravity, and his choices in tap and jazz dance steps, but also by occupying Black spaces in his film diegeses. There are further important linkages to Black culture in his costuming, especially the tight and form-fitting "muscle tee" he frequently adopted during the first half of his career. The accumulation of these and other codes of Blackness are precisely the means through which Kelly is able to modulate and maintain a certain reassurance of masculinity even as he dances ballet or with other men. His blackbodying operates alongside two other strategies: what I call the "palm/fist dichotomy," and the use of athletic elements in Kelly's dances. The former describes his tendency to tensely splay and tighten his hands and arms; the latter refers to his practice of incorporating non-dance athletic stunts and gestures into dance numbers.[8] Kelly draws these elements together to construct a brash, working-class, white masculinity. Complicating matters, however, said masculinity is often marked as being of explicitly Irish American ethnicity—through character names, costuming, dialogue, and even dance steps—which rather muddies the Black-white racial distinction we might assume today.

Kelly's dance style has been almost universally described as athletic, in part because he was so insistent about this quality himself, but it might be most ac-curate to describe Kelly as possessing a *Broadway* dance style. What initially sets him apart from other male dancers of his era—including the other case studies in this book—is his explicit insistence throughout his career that dancing could be a masculine activity. He seems to define masculinity in the terms bequeathed to his generation by the early twentieth century, when public discourses about the inner quality of *manliness* shifted toward the term *masculinity*, "which re-ferred to a set of behavioral traits and attitudes that were contrasted now with a new opposite, *femininity*. Masculinity was something that had to be constantly demonstrated, the attainment of which was forever in question—lest the man be undone by a perception of being too feminine."[9] A primary means of repeatedly demonstrating this new masculinity was by building plenty of muscle and ath-letic skill. But to say that Kelly's dance style was merely athletic oversimplifies his stylistic complexities; the basic dance styles and vocabularies into which

Kelly frequently integrates gymnastic and sports elements are already multiple and mixed. Kelly biographer Clive Hirschhorn has documented instances of Kelly explicitly "pilfering" tap steps from Clarence "Dancing" Dotson and Frank Harrington, Black dancers who came through Pittsburgh in the late 1920s and early 1930s.[10] His theatrical combination of tap with the ballet he studied later no doubt grew out of his early observations of, dancing on, and choreographing for Broadway productions in the late 1930s and early 1940s, notably at the same time that George Balanchine was choreographing ballet alongside tap in his own Broadway shows.[11] Both men inherited an even earlier precedent on Broadway of white casts and choreographers borrowing Black movement styles and rhythms; as Constance Valis Hill has demonstrated, this can be traced back to *Darktown Follies* in 1914.[12]

Kelly's Broadway dance style, and his manner of blackbodying, thus relies on a complex mix of Africanist and Europeanist influences—these can be disentangled a bit through close analysis. One of the primary differences between these two lineages in tap dance, for example, is in the carriage of the torso and hips: the Africanist style "angled and relaxed the torso" and "centered movement in the hips," whereas the Irish style had an "upright torso" and "minimized hip motion."[13] With the development of jazz in the early twentieth century among African American communities, Black innovators added syncopated rhythms and more movement in the limbs (as in the "wing" leg flaps and wiggling hands of the Charleston).[14] Kelly often uses the Africanist angled torso in his dance solos, as well as some of the more complex and syncopated tap rhythms developed by Black dancers. He also makes frequent use of the low center of gravity, wide stances, and bent knees of Africanist movement aesthetics more generally; his performances largely abide by the Kongo proverb "Dance with bended knees, lest you be taken for a corpse."[15] As we will see, Kelly's tendency toward Black dance styles is made all the more apparent by his occasional reversion to Irish/Europeanist style dances, where he keeps his body as straight as possible—he has cited minstrel man George M. Cohan as influential in this area.[16] But of course, Kelly's personal style also includes a ballet base; ballet steps were especially prominent in his 1950s musicals, which represented a sort of personal "ballet boom" for him. Kelly thus balances the grace and flow of ballet with reassuringly masculine Black dance and athletic feats.

The reassurance of masculinity was especially necessary because of Kelly's ballet base. Since concert dancers in particular were assumed to be neither fiercely competitive (like a shrewd businessman) nor powerful and aggressive (like a ballplayer), they were often relegated to the ranks of the effeminate—and probably homosexual.[17] Unlike male performers of popular or social dance, who were presumed to enjoy dance not as an art form but as a means for seducing women, men who danced on a proscenium stage were seen as simply flitting about like ballerinas. Throughout his career, Kelly was defensive about his dual and seemingly contradictory position as a virile average Joe and a beautiful stage dancer. His frequent collaborator Stanley Donen remembered Kelly as "the only song and dance man to come out of that period who had balls" and, in his opinion, "that's why he was such an explosion on the scene. It was the athlete in him that gave him his uniqueness."[18] But in the actual visual records of his dances, Kelly performs more ambiguity, murkiness, and even anxiety regarding his position as the "manliest" of the song-and-dance men. These contradictions—and the recourse to athleticism in their defenses—were, of course, not new to the masculinity crisis of the postwar era; ballet danseur Vaslav Nijinsky's performance of sport in *Jeux* (1913) and choreographer Ted Shawn's 1930s company of Men Dancers had both called upon athleticism to do similar masculinizing work.[19] But what is new in Kelly's case is the fact that his career functioned as a long-term platform for negotiations of dance and masculinity on screen, where his finessing of multiple dance forms via Blackness was no doubt viewed by millions of Americans each year.

This chapter is structured according to the roughly chronological stylistic and media phases of Gene Kelly's dance-on-screen career. I begin with biographical context about Kelly's ethnic background and childhood experiences to set the stage for his later danced dealings with both his Irish ethnic identity and the question of masculinity in dance. I then unpack the early phase of his screen career, when he played a number of "likeable heels," began to incorporate athletic feats into his dances, and first developed the palm/fist dichotomy. Kelly's dependence on Black dance, style, and bodily comportment—that is, his blackbodying—as a signifier of masculinity became increasingly obvious in the late 1940s. During his ballet phase in the fifties, *An American in Paris* in particular drew together and crystalized all existing threads of his dance style: athleticism, the palm/fist dichotomy, *and* blackbodying as a means to perform masculinity. When he transitioned to television as an aging dancer, his performances constituted a "re-version" to vaudeville as he danced an imagined past. Still, even late Kelly nostalgically reenacts a consolidation of his masculine dance persona that included tropes drawn from his entire film career in a final sailor suit performance.

Muscular Likeable Heels

Though he was born to a middle-class Irish American family in Pittsburgh, Pennsylvania, Eugene Curran Kelly (1912–1996) repeatedly indicated that he was subjected to working class values as a child. That is, he often told a story about being beaten up by neighborhood boys for going to dance classes as a child.[20] It is still unclear, of course, whether their problem was with the form-fitting clothes and Buster Brown collars he and his brother wore on their way to class, or whether it was with the practice of dancing itself. Either way, this tale points to a primary foundation for Kelly's lifelong project of representing dance as a masculine activity: a heavily classed notion of manhood defined by the physical markers of working class male activities such as manual labor and factory work.[21] As a man in a female-dominated field, Kelly was clearly imminently aware of the optics usually associated with dancers on a stage, and this story of bullying implies that the graceful steps of ballet were understood by the neighborhood boys, too, as clashing with normative ways of moving the male body. Recognizing this rift in physical representations of masculine movement, Kelly devoted much of his life to bringing these seemingly oppositional images of male physicality together. He explained in at least one interview that he saw himself as a dancing representative of the working class: "What I wanted to do, was dance . . . for the common man. The way a truck driver would dance when he would dance, or a bricklayer, or a clerk, or a postman . . . I grew up with all these kind of peoples, you know."[22] And this goal was apparently met with some success; Kyle Chrichton wrote for Colliers in 1945, "If you have imagination, you think of Kelly in terms of the corner drugstore, the pool room, the basketball shot from the middle of the floor that wins the game."[23] The question, then, is how he came to construct this image for himself in the years leading up to the above reading by Chrichton.

Gene Kelly was seventeen years old when the Great Depression hit in 1929, which seems to have spurred his creative monetization of his unique skillsets— not just dancing, but also teaching and choreographing. To supplement the income he and his brother earned from dance contests and club appearances, the family took over a failing a dancing school, which in 1932 was renamed the Gene Kelly Studio of the Dance. Kelly taught at both of the school's locations and had a strong impact on its rhetoric as an educational institution. On the back of a 1939 program for one of its recitals, the Studio describes its approach to boys' dancing as innovative: "Our teaching methods are modern and thorough, and stress the benefits of dancing from an artistic as well as a physical standpoint. Here children are taught to love dancing and to dance because it is enjoyable and healthy and right to do so. Our boys' classes in particular have made a decided departure in pedagogy from old 'dancing-school' methods and the results you may judge for yourself as you witness their work tonight."[24] Likely a reflection of the aforementioned sports and athleticism craze that hit when Kelly was young, this mission statement of sorts promotes an understanding of dance as *physical exercise*, particularly for young boys. It also indicates that prioritizing the health and fitness aspects of dance—which resurfaced during the middle of Kelly's career—is already a core value of the Kelly dancing school franchise the year before Gene performed the starring role of *Pal Joey* on Broadway.

76 WHITE SCREENS, BLACK DANCE

Kelly's characterization of Joey falls in line with the kind of man who might be responsible for "the basketball shot from the middle of the floor that wins the game." That is, he projected the character's cockiness and womanizing through the lens of working-class values while preserving just enough naiveté and charisma to win over his audience. Kelly's friends had apparently tried to warn him away from the character, fearing that the distinctly *unlikeable* version of Joey written in the John O'Hara novel (upon which the musical was based) might destroy Kelly's career by forever condemning him to playing "the heel."[25] However, Kelly's success in nuancing the role led him to become synonymous with a "likeable heel" instead.

Kelly's first several roles in Hollywood films held to this pattern of likeable heels; talk of him in magazines and the popular press during this period used these performances as shorthand for his "place" in Hollywood. A 1942 profile in *Liberty*, for example, claimed that, "Unlike Fred Astaire, whose specialty is insouciance on the hoof, Kelly has tapped his way to fame by playing lovable 'heels'— lately on Broadway in John O'Hara's Pal Joey, and currently in Hollywood in For Me and My Gal."[26] Contrasting Kelly directly with Fred Astaire was an increasingly frequent occurrence, which only served to further entrench Kelly as the younger, brasher "average Joe" to Fred Astaire's older, smoother "class act."[27] Comparison between the two would continue for the duration of their careers; Kelly explains this relationship in a 1952 interview:

> Fred's style is easy, intimate, light. My dancing is strong, wide-open, bravura. I envy Astaire his ability to walk across a room with that coltish grace, and give pleasure just by that, or watch him in top-hat, white tie, and tails. They are the specialties of his era: they symbolize the style of the man. He handles them with such assurance. But if I tried I'd rip and roar. Top-hat and tails do not belong to my school at all.[28]

As the face of a second-generation Hollywood song-and-dance man, it was essential for Kelly to both demonstrate a level of dancing skill equal to reigning champion Astaire *and* mark himself as a fresh take on the song-and-dance man persona, thereby symbolizing the innovation of the new generation and selling tickets for musicals with ever-escalating budgets. The likeable heel aided this project, signifying both a class difference and a demeanor difference from Astaire.

Kelly's "The Babbitt and the Bromide" dance duet with Astaire in *Ziegfeld Follies* (1945)—their only onscreen collaboration of the midcentury period— invited further comparison between the two that clearly distinguished both their dancing styles and masculinities.[29] The number begins with a meet-cute on a park bench, where the two gentlemen find themselves similarly dressed and tapping in their seats. Their dialogue sets up an old master/new blood relationship in which the men half-jokingly play themselves: Kelly almost immediately recognizes Mr. Fred Astaire, but Astaire cannot seem to place the young face in front of him. When Kelly mentions his first major hit, *Cover Girl* (1944), Astaire makes an immediate gender jab: "You're not Rita Hayworth!" The tension is now doubled; not only is Kelly marked as the young nobody, but he is challenged to demonstrate how he differs from his femme costar Rita Hayworth, to prove his masculinity. Mirroring the gender challenge by invoking Astaire's frequent onscreen dance partner, actress Ginger Rogers, Kelly shoots right back, "Haha—no I'm not, Ginger." The two men laugh uncomfortably together before launching into their dance duet. Playing the roles of boring, conforming middle-class husbands, the two dancers both offer a commentary on such a bland life *and* assert that they are "regular" people, too. This besuited number is sartorially closer to Astaire's style than Kelly's, but Kelly's stronger influence is evident in the choreography—their dance includes a number of ballet steps, and doesn't fall into Astaire's ballroom-style purview until its third and final segment.[30] The two remain playfully competitive throughout, but in another gender joke, Kelly scoops up Astaire as his waltzing partner in that final segment. Who gets to dance the "male" partner's role? Why, Gene Kelly, of course (see Figure 2.2). Still, even Kelly's ostentatious efforts at being seen as the more masculine of the two do not necessarily feminize Astaire in the eyes of viewers. A comparison article and review of the film in the Christian Science Monitor, for example, still considers Astaire to be "masculine" alongside Kelly:

> The gracious, charming Astaire, lyrical in style, master of intricate rhythms flavored with ballet and ballroom elegance, has long upheld the highest standards of screen dancing. . . . [H]e has been a model of masculine grace and

Figure 2.2 In the final segment of their "The Babbitt and the Bromide" number from *Ziegfeld Follies* (1945), Kelly sweeps up Astaire for a waltz, placing him in the "female" position (left); earlier, he evidences his "openness of thigh" (right).

distinction, elevating the once lowly tap not only by his artistry but by his general good manners, including courtesy to his partners. Gene Kelly, the (comparative) newcomer, is stockier, sturdier, more open of thigh, more resilient of torso, and, though he knows his ballet, less elegant in style. One sees in him great possibilities for modern expressionism.[31]

According to this review, Kelly's brash, youthful masculinity—ironically associated with his balletic habit of being "more open of thigh"—seems to come at the expense of the (differently masculine) gracefulness of Astaire, that bastion of an earlier era. Whereas Astaire is credited with making tap graceful, the author expects Kelly to make it more "expressive," a quality it usually had in its Black vernacular usage.[32] The responsibility falls to Kelly, therefore, to "modernize" the white tap tradition with more Africanisms while Astaire continues to tap with a Europeanist style.

With *Anchors Aweigh* (1945), released just one month before *Ziegfeld Follies*, the likeable heel established a more regular buddy coupling with Frank Sinatra that further bolstered his brash masculinity. Though Sinatra only joined Kelly in two more musicals (*Take Me Out to the Ball Game* and *On the Town*, both released in 1949), the pairing established and reinforced specific "types" for both actors. Kelly leans into the wolfish rascal image, with Sinatra as a meek, awkward, and inexperienced sidekick who becomes his counterpoint. Cohan sees this relationship as part of a larger trend in Kelly's screen roles, which are often made to seem more "manly" (and more clearly classed) by "effete" sidekicks: "These asymmetrical male friendships give Kelly's masculine persona its distinct social inflection as a working-class man: ethnically identified as Irish, psychologized by his dependences on postadolescent male friendships, and manifested in an overexaggerated display of sexual bravado that stands out in comparison with the sidekick's more effeminate behavior."[33] As part of this larger construction, Kelly's dances—both with his "buddy" and without—(re)establish this working-class masculinity through Black-originated tap idioms and various feats of muscular athleticism.

The film follows the shore leave experiences of two Naval officers, Joseph Brady (Kelly) and Clarence Doolittle (Sinatra). From the start, Kelly's character is presented as a ladies' man. When calling ahead to a "Lola" in Hollywood, Joe caresses the phone and croons smooth sweet nothings, which results in cheering on the part of his shipmates. Clarence, in contrast, *feigns* a conversation with a girl while an operator announces the official time on the other end. As such, he seeks out Joe's advice when they reach land—according to Clarence, Joe is "the best wolf in the whole Navy." But as luck would have it, neither young man spent his first night with a young lady; in fact, they both found themselves waylaid by a little boy named Donald (Dean Stockwell) who ran away from home, intending to join the Navy. So, when the two arrive quite late at some temporary sleeping quarters for servicemen, Clarence starts to explain: "[W]e got in a little trouble: we picked up a little kid . . . ." But Joe has a reputation to protect, so he cuts in and continues the story using "kid" as a substitute for "dame," describing the blonde and redhead they supposedly met. And when Clarence can only describe his imaginary girl as "rather interesting" (clearly a descriptor of personality rather than physicality), Joe the heel cuts in again with "Ohh, 'interesting'—you shoulda seen the kid work!" This objectifying remark initiates a tall tale-turned-musical number about the kisses they claim to have received from these women. While Kelly's Joe weaves his story, Sinatra's Clarence admires his chutzpah. As the "wolf" mentor, Kelly encourages his friend while maintaining a confident, open stance that shows off his buttocks. Notably, he manages this because the men's Naval uniform costumes are rather tight. Kelly is said to have preferred the sailor suit for offering a desirable balance between the familiar costuming of a "regular guy" and the form-fitting tights or unitard preferred for showing a male dancer's lines—and he would go on to use such suits again in *On the Town* (1949), *Invitation to the Dance* (1956), and a later television appearance on *The Julie Andrews Show* (1965).[34]

Having finished their yarn, the pals then break into a tap segment led by Joe. Clarence follows along and, in case the viewer has at this point still failed to recognize Joe as the smooth operator and Clarence as the awkward side-kick, Sinatra's tapping looks stiff and bashful beside Kelly's fluid movements, energetic syncopation, and expressive face. This scene also establishes a signature Kelly stylistic trope that will become a defining characteristic of his entire onscreen career: what I call the "palm/fist dichotomy." At key points during the number, Kelly's careful choreographic placement of widely spread open palms in contrast with tightly clenched fists attributes a sense of strength, energy, and vigor to the dance. While they appear less frequently here than they do later, in the ballet boom phase of his career, they enter his movement vocabulary rather early. Separately, the fists signify a retraction, a contraction, a compression of the body, whereas the palms signify an opening up, an extension, a burst of energy. Together, they create a dynamic dichotomy of movement that render Kelly's body particularly active, athletic, and eye-catching. In this case, the fists come first, followed shortly after by the splayed palms (see Figure 2.3). They read as the polar opposite of Fayard Nicholas's graceful hand flourishes; whereas Fayard aimed to embody a "class act" masculinity with this delicate panache, Kelly's tense hands are intended to align him with the working class, evoking manual labor.

His alpha masculinity thus corporeally established, Kelly's character goes on to reinforce it in the context of Sailor Joe teaching a cartoon mouse king—played by an animated Jerry Mouse (of *Tom and Jerry* fame)—how to dance. "The

Figure 2.3 In the "I Begged Her" number from *Anchors Aweigh* (1945), Kelly specifically choreographs a moment of pause for clenched fists (left), followed by splayed palms as the men's bodies open out (right).

Worry Song" number visually inaugurates the second costume element he most frequently chooses to accompany his "manly" dances: what is recognized in contemporary parlance as a "muscle tee" (see Figure 2.4). Kelly's striped sailor-esque tee shirt here is not only quite form fitting, it also has very short sleeves that emphasize his biceps, achieving a look that would soon be associated with the hardened working-class masculinity of Marlon Brando's Stanley Kowalski in the stage and film versions of *A Streetcar Named Desire* (1947, 1951) (see Figure 2.5). To return for a moment to the Kelly-Astaire comparison, Kelly famously once said, "If Fred Astaire is the Cary Grant of dance, I'm the Marlon Brando."[35] This evaluation is in fact quite apt, and worth a slight detour here. Film and music scholar Krin Gabbard has claimed that tight jeans and tight tops came into vogue among American men largely thanks to Brando's Broadway *Streetcar* costume: "Brando was more than willing to display much more of a well-muscled

Figure 2.4 During the "Worry Song" number, Kelly wears what is today called a "muscle tee" while he bounces Jerry mouse on his biceps as if weightlifting (left) and performs a freeze that shows off his buttocks (right).

Figure 2.5 Marlon Brando's costuming in *A Streetcar Named Desire* (1951) (left) echoes Kelly's tight costuming in *Anchors Aweigh* and even more so his costuming in *Words and Music* (1948) (right). Right image courtesy of MGM/Photofest.

physique than audiences were accustomed to seeing. At least some portion of this display surely grew out of Brando's observations of Black dancers and athletes."[36] Gabbard's larger argument is that Brando "may have been the first American actor to practice minstrelsy in whiteface." He places Brando in a genealogy with musical performers Al Jolson, Bing Crosby, and Fred Astaire, noting the popularity of their blackface routines.[37] Given this context, Gene Kelly is the next logical addition to the ranks of "whiteface" performers in postwar Hollywood, having closely observed Black dancers even more than Brando did. Indeed, during the time Kelly spent in Chicago between 1933 and 1935, learning classical dance by day, he spent many of his evenings in jazz clubs, likely absorbing the Black vernacular dance styles swirling around him.[38] Unlike Astaire—recall his blackface "Bojangles of Harlem" number in *Swing Time* (1936)—Kelly never blacked up. Instead, he quoted Black cultures in less obvious, solely embodied ways. It is thus unsurprising that Kelly's costuming in *Anchors Aweigh*—and even more so for his "Slaughter on Tenth Avenue" number in *Words and Music* (1948)—bears strong similarities to Brando as both channel Black-influenced working class white masculinities (see Figure 2.5).[39] But I want to be clear, here, that neither Kelly nor Brando retained the mocking or caricatured elements of minstrel performance; instead, both men engaged in the more subtle practice of black*bodying* to construct their masculinities.

In so doing, however, Kelly (and Brando) instead heavily contributed to the invisibilization of Africanist contributions to American dance and cultural style; without any visible markers of Blackness, Kelly is able to pass off Black postures and movement vocabularies as his own style. His comportments during "The Worry Song," for example, exhibit the pointed elbows and knees of wing dances. Furthermore, the majority of his dance steps are drawn from Africanist tap and vaudeville traditions, echoing the strut of comedic dandies like Black vaudevillian George Walker and the up-on-the-toes tapping of Bill Robinson. Kelly and Stanley Donen also choreographed many emphatically athletic bits of vaudevillian flash, eccentric, and comedic dancing into the number: there are jolly bells/heel clicks, a bit of modified Cossack dancing known in old vaudeville as "Russian kick-outs," and what is today known as a "plank" immediately followed by a high jump over Jerry. Afterwards, Kelly bounces Jerry between his two arms by pumping his biceps in the air as if weightlifting (see Figure 2.4). The remainder of the dance involves a mélange of tapping, more modified Cossack steps, and a little ballet (*pirouettes* and turns *à la seconde*). Even as he mixes a number of movement vocabularies here, what remains constant is the energy with which he attacks and confidently grounds himself in each step, emphasized by the return of the palm/fist dichotomy. Thus, while theoretically teaching a mouse some simple dance steps, Kelly is in fact working to demonstrate his vigor and vitality through a mix of Africanist and Europeanist idioms.

The resultant masculinity of these athletic movements is, however, complicated by the fact that Kelly simultaneously shows off his firm buttocks and thighs in those tight white pants (see Figure 2.4). It is here that Cohan locates the contradiction, incongruity, and ambiguity in Kelly's masculinity: such "very tight" pants "condensed the effeminate/manly dualism that made his virility legible, but in functioning as a theatrical costume as well, it gave him an erotic significance when he danced on screen that exceeded those binary terms."[40] At the same time, however, Kelly performs some of the taut, hard-bodied positions that Dyer cites as the male pin-up's inoculation against the feminizing spectacularity of his body.[41] It is arguably Kelly's blackbodying that seems to tip the scales here: even with the theatricality and feminizing spectacle that threaten to overwhelm the athleticism of his performance, the associations of his muscle tee and tap dance virtuosity with Black masculinity work to reassure us that he is no "sissy."

Stunt-heavy choreography, like that used by Kelly and Donen in "The Worry Song," had been common among Black tap and flash dancers on the Chitlin' Circuit since at least the 1920s, but the high production values of Kelly's films (and the access to such values afforded by his whiteness) allowed him to perform larger-scale stunts than would be possible on a standard vaudeville stage. This is particularly clear in the final dance number in *Anchors Aweigh*, set to the tango "La Cumparsita," where Kelly imagines himself as an exotic bandit, wearing a Zorro-esque mask, red-lined cape, and tight yellow satin bib-front tuxedo shirt. While Kelly has again concocted a blend of dance forms to serve his flamenco adaptation—including wiggling "jazz hands" and almost unmodified *pirouettes* and *sissones* from classical ballet—the number's primary vehicle is Kelly's extremely crisp percussive tapping. In this case, therefore, the tap dance foundation is put to use as an exoticizing tool, a making-Other. Whereas the Nicholas Brothers had used embodied references to Latin dance in *Down Argentina Way* to soften their masculinity and appear sexually "safe" or nonthreatening, Kelly uses them here to channel the smoldering mystery of José Greco, the Italian-Spanish dancer who was then popularizing the Romani-Andalusian dance form of flamenco in the U.S.[42] The brand of masculinity here is thus different from that of the sailor-dances; it is more flamboyant and, in Cohan's words, "an alternative male masquerade" modeled on the sensual and ethnically ambiguous (or explicitly Latin) "matinee idols" of the 1910s and 20s, including Rudolph Valentino and Douglas Fairbanks.[43] But even in the context of this masquerade, Kelly's dance is emphatically athletic. He once again employs the palm/fist dichotomy to demonstrate the virility of the steps, especially the splayed palms. Moreover, the number's most often noted element is Kelly's scaling of the large set pieces, sprinting up a tree trunk, and swinging high above the ground on a large curtain before sliding down a pole to his beloved.[44] Such athletic, masculinity-confirming stunts would be rehashed in both of Kelly's postwar "comeback" musicals, *Living in a Big Way* (1947) and *The Pirate* (1948), after his stint serving in the Navy.

By the end of World War II, then, the basic elements of Kelly's star text and dance vocabulary have been established: he tends to play likeable heels whose roughness and womanizing is balanced by charisma and athleticism. This athleticism, accentuated by his increasing implementation of the palm/fist dichotomy, pervades Kelly's dances, which blend his ballet training with Afro-Irish fusion tap and other exotic forms. Through the use of these elements and his pairings with thinner, slighter, and, in the case of Astaire, "classier" singing and dancing men, Kelly stands out as the muscular, working-class average Joe of the film musical universe. At the same time, his claims to muscle-bound masculinity are complicated by the feminizing spectacle of his tight costuming and occasionally flamboyant performance, as well as a re-masculinizing via these same costumes' gestures toward Black culture alongside his frequent performance of Black dance.

Ambiguously Masculine Ethnic Spectacle

Upon his return from the Navy, Kelly gave several lectures at local Los Angeles universities between 1946 and 1948 that explicitly stated his masculinity thesis. He purportedly argued at UCLA that "dancing is primarily a man's art": "Any dance step you girls can do," he told the predominantly female audience, "I can do stronger. Because I am stronger. Therefore the male can excel in the dance art."[45] An attendee at the lecture described how "[t]he professor deplored the fact that most men associate serious dancing with esthetic groups, and said he tries to offset this opinion by making his cinema routines as virile as possible."[46]

Meanwhile, magazine articles about the Kelly household and the domestic habits of Gene, his wife Betsy, and his daughter Kerry circulated throughout the decade. This combination of Kelly's outspokenness regarding the masculinity of dancing and fanzine writers' interest in "Who Rules These Hollywood Roosts?," for example, underlines the gender tension that built up during wartime and came to a head when men returned home.[47] After several years in which women gained power and responsibility in both the workplace and the home, men faced uncertainty regarding their roles as they reentered peacetime society. Kelly's response seemed to be further exaggerating masculinity in *The Pirate*.

Building on his previous "likeable heels," Kelly's traveling player character in *The Pirate* is a womanizing rapscallion who combats the campiness of his spectacularized, feminized performances by infusing them with athletic feats and increasingly explicit Black dance. The "Niña" number, toward the beginning of the film, introduces all of these elements. In the process of chasing after numerous women (all of whom he addresses as "Niña" to save himself the effort of learning their names) on the streets of a "Port Sebastian," Serafin the thespian (Kelly) scales walls, swings across balconies, and slides down a multi-story pole. He then launches into what can only be described as a "pole dance," swinging around the striped polls of a gazebo in the town square. In the process, Kelly caresses poles, thrusts out his pelvis, and incorporates jazz hands. Once again employing the palm/fist dichotomy, he also includes a wide stance in ballet's second position, up on his toes and in *plié*—a stance that is perhaps familiar to viewers from his dance with Jerry Mouse in *Anchors Aweigh* (see Figures 2.4 and 2.6). Toward the end, he even jumps over a seated group of women in a manner reminiscent of the Nicholas Brothers' similar stunt (though he omits the splits) (see Figure 2.6). Throughout the number, Kelly's many displays of bravado mix

Figure 2.6 In the "Niña" number from *The Pirate* (1948), Kelly employs the palm/fist dichotomy alongside a wide stance in plié and on his toes (left); he then jumps over a group of seated women in a manner similar to the Nicholas Brothers' split jumps (right).

with erotic spectacle and athletic achievement. It is perhaps not surprising, then, that Cohan reads the film as "let[ting] loose the gender-sexual indeterminacy of his dancing" and that he argues, as a result, "*The Pirate* most completely and most provocatively realizes the camp informing Kelly's performing style as well as Garland's."[48] Again, however, I believe there is more to the story. Even in the absence of tap, here, Kelly can be read as blackbodying not only in his wide stances and use of jazz hands but also in his "borrowing" of a signature Nicholas Brothers move. Though he dances with them later in the film, here he steals their step, just as Fayard Nicholas asserted in the 1985 anecdote that opened this book.

When Judy Garland's character Manuela imagines Serafin the thespian (Kelly) as Macoco the pirate in "The Pirate Ballet," Kelly amps up his "flaming trail of masculinity."[49] This is one of the most commented-upon dances of Kelly's forties musicals, and the consensus among film scholars seems to be that Kelly, in perhaps his most scantily clad scene ever, performs a thrilling and erotic dance whose signification is overdetermined. In tiny black shorts and a deep v-neck black tank top, with a thick metal band around his right bicep, Kelly brandishes a sword and flexes his quadriceps as obviously as he flexes his biceps (see Figure 2.7). As Manuela dreams him, he is both sinister and sexy; abusive but virile and appealingly violent. The choreography itself looks much like the danseur's solo variation from a grand pas de deux; it consists mainly of serial and spectacular leaping turns—in short, the most athletic portion of male ballet repertoire. But it also includes yet more of the wide stances and bent knees and elbows of Africanist dance vocabularies. Even when he flies through the air, he appears deeply grounded and strongly rooted due to these positions of his limbs; herein lies part of the attraction.

As a fantastical departure from the film's plot, this low-lit dance sequence seems to serve for most readers as an actualization of the "flaming trail of masculinity" Garland's character sang about longingly in an earlier song called "Mack

Figure 2.7 In *The Pirate*'s dream ballet, Kelly as Macoco sports tight black shorts, a deep-V tank top, and a metal band around his bicep as he brandishes a sword.

86   WHITE SCREENS, BLACK DANCE

the Black." Cohan summarizes his (camp) reading of other commentators' responses thus:

> Whether impersonating Macoco, performing as an actor, or wooing Manuela, Serafin exaggerates feminine as well as masculine characteristics, just as Kelly's dancing is choreographed to achieve homo- and heteroerotic affect. [Jane] Feuer thus can see in Kelly's Serafin an eroticized, effeminate male, even a gay icon, just as [Richard] Dyer can view Kelly's dancing as half turn-on, half send-up, because, in both characterization and performance, the figure's references to gender and sexuality do not fall into alignment, resulting in the ambiguity that the two critics describe. Male yet not entirely manly, heterosexual yet not fully heterosexualized, eroticized yet parodic, Serafin's own "flaming trail of masculinity" cannot be fixed to a determinate meaning one way or the other.[50]

These scholars all seem to agree that Kelly's gender performance here is at its most ambiguous; by performing hyper-masculinity to the point of parody, Kelly refuses any simple reading. But, although the complex state of Kelly's masculinity in this number has been thoroughly discussed, the racial element of Kelly's performance has not been addressed. While his skin is fairly tanned throughout the film (perhaps an accident, but more likely a purposeful means of marking Kelly's character as "Latin," since he claims to come from Madrid), Kelly appears much darker throughout the dream ballet number (see Figure 2.7). This skin tone is not so extreme as to garner comparison with more famous (and much earlier) blackface musical performances such as Al Jolson's "Mammy" (*The Jazz Singer*, 1927) or Fred Astaire's "Bojangles in Harlem" (*Swing Time*, 1936), so one might argue for an interpretation of Kelly as a so-called hot-blooded Latino here, but he nevertheless connotes Blackness when performing the wide, grounded stances and jazz hands of the excitingly dangerous Macoco. Participating in the problematic but now-familiar tendency of commercial media to associate darker skin tones with sinister behaviors, this scene must be understood not only as ambiguously eroticized but also ambiguously racialized.

Concerns about the representation of race in *The Pirate* are not simply confined to the dream ballet; there is also the issue of the Nicholas Brothers' guest performance with Kelly toward the end of the film, which I discussed in Chapter 1. The brothers, not in their signature tuxedo tails for this performance, flank Kelly throughout the "Be a Clown" number in tight bright yellow and turquoise clown outfits. While Kelly choreographed the number to be less complex than standard Nicholas Brothers fare (no doubt so that he could keep up with them), he clearly emulated the brothers' acrobatic, constantly moving style. Taking advantage of their skillset, Kelly created a vaudevillian number with barrel rolls, jump splits, and various tricks such as "coffee grinders" and over-the-tops. As Hill reports, the brothers were unfortunately not given the chance to collaborate on the choreography, even as their signature moves were being used.[51] In this way, Kelly capitalizes on the value of the Nicholas Brothers' appeal as an act without collaborating or allowing their expertise to factor into the creative process. Still, the sequence is an extremely rare example of racially integrated dance on screen in the postwar era, and indicates Kelly's personal comfort in literally intertwining his white male body with two Black male bodies. And yet, as I mentioned in Chapter 1, the sequence includes racially problematic imagery when Kelly leads the three of them right up to a hanging noose. Thus, Kelly benefits from the Nicholases' "incredible vigor" to assure audiences of his own acrobatic prowess while simultaneously dominating the scene as the starring white body who will certainly evade the noose that still signifies as a major threat to the Black bodies flanking him onstage.[52]

Returning to the buddy formula with Frank Sinatra in *Take Me Out to the Ball Game* (1949), Kelly plays a professional athlete (who is also a dancer) for the first and only time in his film career, and explicitly ties this athletic masculinity to his Irish ethnic background. The film is set in 1908, when baseball became extremely popular in America and was increasingly associated with working-class men, so the choice to cast Kelly as essentially professionally masculine here is significant.[53] Also unique to the film is the extent to which Kelly calls upon his own Irish heritage to play an emphatically Irish-American character—while many of his characters had Irish last names and would occasionally be explicitly referred to as such, *Take Me Out to the Ball Game* was the first film in which Kelly performed a long Irish dance number.[54] First, however, Eddie O'Brien (Kelly) and Dennis Ryan (Sinatra) are established as buddies: they return to the Sarasota Baseball Park after a duo vaudeville tour of the country and perform a musical number ("Yes, Indeedy") before their teammates in which they describe the many girls they kissed and left. Much like their similar number in *Anchors Aweigh*, however, it begins with a spoken introduction by Sinatra about other things, such as art shows, bird walks, and museums. It is thus Kelly's character who once again begins the yarn about the women and leads the accompanying comedic song-and-dance full of mime and exaggeration.

Thus, by the time Kelly's big solo performance arrives, at a clambake two-thirds of the way through the film, his character is well established as a bit of a ham. This hamming morphs into an ethnic joke in "The Hat My Dear Old Father Wore upon St. Patrick's Day," as Kelly dons a bright green hat and grabs a cane, cheered on by older fellow Irishmen. Over the course of the long tap sequence, Kelly performs not only obviously traditional Irish-based steps, with a tall and straight upper body that produces evenly timed taps, but also more Africanist movements with bent knees, swinging arms, and more complex rhythms (see Figure 2.8). Ham that he is, it is difficult to tell when the dance is meant to be

Figure 2.8 In "The Hat My Dear Old Father Wore upon St. Patrick's Day" from *Take Me Out to the Ball Game* (1949), Kelly performs both upright, Irish-style tapping (left) and more grounded, swinging Africanist tap (right).

parodic or genuine. Kelly embodies the complex relationship between whiteness and Blackness that tap inherited from both blackface minstrelsy and the larger common history of Irish and African Americans during the eighteenth and nineteenth centuries in the U.S., a history often forgotten due to the "whitening" of the Irish between the Civil War and the early 1900s.

Earlier waves of Irish indentured servants imported to the British colonies, as well as large waves of starving Irish Catholic immigrants during the Great Famine, meant that the white Protestant majority in the young United States often mistreated and discriminated against Irish Americans. In some areas, Irish and African Americans lived in close quarters and experienced cultural exchange. And during the early years of minstrelsy, the Irish had been objects of ridicule alongside Blacks.[55] But as Irish Americans themselves began to participate in blackface minstrel performance, their relationship to African Americans and Black culture became increasingly complicated, and their ability to put on and take off the burnt cork—alongside anti-Black violence perpetrated by Irish Americans and political shifts such as a Jacksonian democracy that more explicitly welcomed the Irish-American working class—served to "whiten" Irish-Americans.[56] Both Irish and African Americans were frequently portrayed as lazy workers but talented (often vaudeville) dancers throughout this period. Given that *Take Me Out to the Ball Game* was set in 1908, Kelly's exaggeratedly jolly jig may or may not have intentionally recalled old stereotypes of the drunken dancing Irishman, but it did make reference, via a slower soldier-like section, to the loss of Irish American soldiers in the Civil War. Certainly, middle-aged adult viewers in the late 1940s who had grown up with this Irish-as-Black phenomenon may very well have read Kelly's performance of Irishness as a performance of Blackness, or at least a racially ambiguous one, even though Irish Americans had thoroughly achieved whiteness by midcentury. Moreover, his expert "hoofing" of both African American and Irish American forms of tap is met with approval by the men around him, demonstrated by cuts to their responses or expressions in the background. The dance, however silly, is meant to reinforce his working-class masculinity as much as the stories about kissing girls at the beginning of the narrative. Kelly's reiterated manhood in this film thus triangulates itself between several confirmations of masculinity at once: heterosexual prowess, ethnic characteristics, and athletic aptitude.

If the early years of Kelly's dance-on-screen career were defined by feats of gymnastic athleticism and oblique references to Black dance and Black culture, his postwar dances were far more explicit in their performances of Blackness. Both the use of body makeup and Kelly's proximity to actual Black dancers (the Nicholas Brothers), in addition to Africanist wide stances and low center of gravity, render Kelly's own racialization just as ambiguous as his eroticized gender performance. Of course, the athletic elements also remain to reinforce Kelly's masculinity, which he began to speak about in interviews and lectures. It is within this context, in which Kelly has so thoroughly established dancing as "a man's game," that he turns to ballet (the most feminized of dance genres) in the 1950s.

Blackbodying as Masculinity During a Ballet Boom

After fits and starts of ballet in more tap-heavy numbers across *The Pirate, Words and Music,* and then *On The Town* (1949), Gene Kelly entered a period of his career (arguably its peak) characterized by extended ballet numbers; because of the increased risk of being perceived as a "sissy dancer," Kelly relied heavily on blackbodying to shore up his masculinity throughout this period. Of his fifties films, his largest ballet undertaking was *An American in Paris* (1951). Though the winner of six Academy Awards, including Best Picture, *An American in Paris* is often forgotten in the shadow of *Singin' in the Rain* (1952). Indeed, in the words of Roger Ebert, "by the 1960s, 'Singin'' was routinely considered the greatest of all Hollywood musicals, and 'An American in Paris' was remembered with more respect than enthusiasm."[57] But at the time, *An American in Paris* staged something of an upset at the *Academy Awards*; musicals were rarely awarded an Oscar for Best Picture, and for 1951 it beat out both *A Place in the Sun* and *A Streetcar Named Desire.* Its success was particularly surprising given that the crew was unable to shoot on location in Paris, and that Kelly choreographed a seventeen-minute ballet to round out the film. In fact, Kelly recalled many years later a comment about its riskiness by the composer and lyricist Irving Berlin: "All dancing? No words? I hope you know what you're doing, kid."[58] Envisioned as a truly "American" capstone performance to a film that worked through the very

90   WHITE SCREENS, BLACK DANCE

concept of Americanness abroad in the aftermath of World War II collaboration and cultural exchange, the number incorporates several dance styles and speaks volumes about Kelly's idea of American masculine dance during the period: Black forms are the manly ones.

Kelly plays Jerry Mulligan (once again a decidedly Irish name), an American ex-G.I. and painter who has chosen to stay in Paris after the end of World War II. Before even reaching the final ballet, Kelly establishes his character's masculinity via several tap-heavy numbers. "I Got Rhythm," for example, is framed as an educational experience wherein Mulligan teaches a group of French children what "la danse Americaine" looks like. As such, he taps his way through the American vernacular dance vocabulary, performing the steps one at a time: "C'est le time step . . . c'est le shim-sham . . . Charleston!" Importantly, all of the named dances he demonstrates originated as Black popular dances that eventually made their way into the white-dominated mainstream. For example, Black dancers Leonard Reed and Willie Bryant famously danced (and may have originated) both the Shim Sham Shimmy and the tap Charleston on the T.O.B.A (Theater Owners Booking Association) vaudeville circuit for Black performers in the 1920s, though the original Charleston likely finds its roots in the African American Juba and later Jay-Bird dances. The act of Gene Kelly's white American body visually spreading (*African*) American dance to this fictional European setting is in fact synecdochic of the larger, real-life process of invisibilization and dispersion: a marketing of uniquely "American" dance that celebrates Africanist movement while simultaneously erasing the Black bodies from which they originated—in other words, adjusting the optics by replacing Black bodies with white ones. Visually speaking, Kelly accomplishes this in a casual sweatshirt and slacks, reading as a working man despite the upper-class, elite associations with his character's profession; together with the Black dance steps, he establishes a masculinity of physical skill ahead of his later graceful romancing.

The film's *pièce de résistance* is the final, seventeen-minute dream ballet, which neatly ties together ballet and tap as well as all three of Kelly's major stylistic signatures: athleticism, the palm/fist dichotomy, and his most explicit case of blackbodying to date. The scene begins with Mulligan finding himself—and a rose—transported into the middle of his own drawing of Paris. As Gershwin's "An American in Paris" composition enters into a lively full swing, the drawing bursts with color and Mulligan is confronted by elaborately costumed and made-up ballerinas in white and then red. Clearly shocked and perhaps a bit threatened, Mulligan disentangles himself from the chiffon and dodges away from these imposing female figures. The camera then tracks him as he stumbles into an imagined Place de la Concorde based on paintings by Raoul Dufy, where multiple layers of dancers-as-passers-by swirl around the square and alternately absorb or deflect Mulligan's body as he dance-walks through the giant set.

Throughout this introductory segment, Kelly's dance movement demonstrates the challenge of making ballet appropriately "masculine:" he promenades about, using a "ballet walk" modified to look more like a track star's warm up. Specifically, he distinguishes himself from classical ballet via his *port de bras* (carriage of the arms): the comportment of Kelly's torso and upper body is always one of a slightly puffed out chest, and especially when performing a dance segment, the initiators of his upper body movement are his elbows and shoulders rather than his core. The particular valence of expression produced by these movements is determined by Kelly's hands, which are always tense unless he is engaged in a romantic partner dance. In this sequence, they once again engage in the palm/fist dichotomy as Kelly's body expands and contracts through the scene. As he includes more and more ballet—a triple *pirouette en dedans* here and a few *pas de basques* there—his hands and arms more emphatically resist ballet's formal vocabulary and remain tense with pointed elbows rather than exhibiting the smooth, round, light, and graceful arms normally associated with this classical form. In other words, the corporeal traditions of ballet cause Kelly to depend even more heavily on his "masculine" alternative appendage usage.

After the scene transitions from the crowded public square to a quiet flower market (based on Renoir flower paintings) and Leslie Caron appears in a baby blue dress and matching satin pointe shoes, Kelly at first relaxes his hands somewhat, but as soon as he separates from her for a moment they become tense again. In this case, Kelly chooses to express emotion by flexing his arm muscles rather than elongating his line and reaching for his mate, as tends to happen in classical story ballets. The next scene then reassures us that men can dance just fine *without women*: amongst sets based on Maurice Utrillo's visions of Montmartre and *le quartier Latin*, a moping Kelly is swept up by a group of uniformed servicemen; together they all don candy stripe jackets and boater hats, also grabbing bamboo canes. When they join a group of women in Rousseau-inspired costumes and a fairground setting, taps have been dubbed in, as if the gender divide must be marked by ballet vs. tap. In fact, Kelly courts Caron in this public setting *by tapping*—their romantic ballet and ballroom scenes were private, the movement equivalent of whispered sweet nothings. Now that his romancing is a public performance, it is danced as entertainment and spectacle rather than graceful tenderness and emotion. To reinforce the separation between the two modes, the next scene is precisely the sensual, private ballet number that the public scene avoided. Back at the *fontaine de la Concorde*, Caron has traded in her bright pointe shoes for barely-there soft sandals. Kelly becomes the traditional danseur insofar as the majority of his performance consists of lifting and carrying Caron, with only brief opportunities to showcase his leaps and turns.

It is at this point that the pair transitions to the scene that served as the opening to this chapter: a Van Gogh-ian *Place de l'Opéra* featuring a walking poster of Lautrec's *Chocolat dansant dans un bar*. As I stated at the outset, Kelly imitates Chocolat/Raphaël Padilla's pose just in time to be superimposed on top of, and dissolved into, the drawing. This is one of the stranger moments of Kelly's entire oeuvre: he cinematically *becomes* a Black body within an artwork, this time lacking whatever tanning, body paint, or lighting effects made his skin appear so dark in *The Pirate*, but ironically posed in one of his most classical *ports de bras* (no sharp elbows or tense fists, here!). The film here literalizes the invisibilization process and allows Kelly to attribute whatever steps he wishes to the frozen form of *Chocolat*. The movements he imagines for Padilla's figure are predominantly mainstream African *American* jazz steps like the Charleston, which also erases the specificity of Padilla's Afro-Cuban background. Existing records of Chocolat give few clues as to what his dance style would have actually been, as his greatest commercial success resulted from his career as a buffoonish clown in his duo act with white fellow clown "Footit."[59] It is safe to say, however, that Kelly takes license with history here and imagines Cuban-European dance through the lens of his own white American experience of Black dance. Indeed, the jazz steps are rendered through what Gottschild would term a "Europeanist" balletic lens as he performs them here: rather than buoyant, hip-directed steps connected to the floor and accompanied by loose, counterbalancing arms, Kelly keeps a solid upper body and his signature tense, carefully placed arms (see Figure 2.9). And as he moves through to the next Lautrec painting, he once again steels himself with tense, flat palms that locomote him through the space. As a whole, the jazz steps' lineage of African American innovation is simultaneously invisibilized by Kelly's whiteness (both physically and interpretively) *and emphasized* by the drawn dancer he chose to embody. Moreover, given his exceptionally tight pants,

Figure 2.9 Kelly "whitens" the *An American in Paris* dream ballet's jazz steps with his erect upper body and signature tense arms (left) but the Blackness of the body he replaces is used to justify wiggling his prominently displayed buttocks (right).

GENE KELLY   93

this quite explicit case of blackbodying justifies both the costuming and Kelly's prominently displayed and actively moving buttocks (see Figure 2.9), since they are used more liberally in Black dance than in white dance. Indeed, the male virility and sexuality associated with the Black dance(r) he embodies do the work of "proving" his masculinity as a contradictory counterbalance to the presumed feminization of said erotic display.[60] All of this is to say that, here, the contradictory stereotypes about Black male dancing bodies (infantilized, feminine pickaninnies and coons vs. dangerous, oversexed, hypermasculine bucks) work to Kelly's advantage as he embodies *Chocolat*.[61]

Singin' in the Rain (1952), for its part, conceals the invisibilization process that *An American in Paris* made clear, with Kelly more implicitly taking the place of Black men from three decades after turn-of-the-century *Chocolat*. It was not always as well received by critics as its predecessor and did not take home any Academy Awards, but most reviewers immediately sensed its popular appeal. In the words of Dick Williams from the *LA Mirror*, "'Singin' in the Rain' may not be the best musical that has ever come out of Hollywood but it is good, solid entertainment and will be popular."[62] Now a regular entry in both American and British "greatest films of all time" lists, the drama of secret vocal dubbing in *Singin'* provides a record of midcentury Hollywood's nostalgia for the era of its early talkies. This canonized film also canonized Kelly's blackbodying and, as I indicated in the opening to both the book and this chapter, hinted at its anxieties around the removal of the Black talent that was foundational to the dances of the entire musical genre. In the article that inspired this book, film scholar Carol Clover suggests that "*Singin' in the Rain* is itself worried . . . more generally about the possibility that too many of the unseen artists whose moves have been put to such brilliant and lucrative use in the 'white dancer's field' of the film musical are black," going so far as to claim that "its real subject is not white women's singing voices, but black men's dancing bodies."[63] She articulates this as the film's "consciously unconscious relation to African-American dance," pinpointing the moment of accidental acknowledgement in the scene where Don Lockwood (Kelly) and Cosmo Brown (Donald O'Connor) propose transforming *The Dueling Cavalier*, their silent film-turned-talkie, into a musical. As Cosmo struggles to come up with a new title that would appropriately reflect the genre change, he blurts out "*The Dueling Mammy*" before quickly correcting himself and, after a short series of half-mumbled "no's," settling on "*The Dancing Cavalier*." Clover's astute analysis of this gaffe and its significance is crucial to understanding the politics of the film:

> Duelling cavalier—duelling mammy—dancing cavalier. "Dancing" is the word the sequence aims toward, the word that will solve the problem of the musical ("We need a musical title"), but it can only be suggested by and arrived

94 WHITE SCREENS, BLACK DANCE

at through a reference to "mammy"—a reference that in a split second puts African-Americans into the picture and acknowledges that the artistic bridge between a brittle eighteenth-century melodrama and a vibrant twentieth-century musical is a racial one. But blackness is no sooner admitted than it is denied, for the next full sentence . . . surely adumbrates a dancing black man, invisible in the given story, but a logical step in the sequence.[64]

In closing with a Charleston, which originated as a Black vernacular dance, Cosmo in fact replaces this adumbrated Black body with his own. Like Kelly would go on to do in his own histories of dance (to be discussed below), O'Connor here erases not only the Black dancing body but the history of Black dance. And after O'Connor's Cosmo enacts this invisibilization in the planning stages for their film-within-the-film, Kelly reenacts it in both the film *and* the film-within-a-film's dream ballet.

Kelly's clearest replacement of a Black dancer occurs in the film's titular dance, which occurs in the streets at night. Per Clover: "the setting of what has been called 'the single most memorable dance number on film' is yet another racial gesture, one that puts Kelly where a black man used to be."[65] As I indicated in Chapter 1, many Black dancers of the early twentieth century honed their craft in the streets, lacking access to appropriate indoor venues to gain both practice and payment for their performance;[66] Clover suggests that surely Kelly and co-choreographer Donen would have been familiar with both this and the very real threat of policemen in Black public-dancing experience. Clover is less interested in the thefts from Black dance and replacements of Black dancers themselves than she is in exposing the film's own anxiety about such theft, especially since it is explicitly a film about giving credit where due, but I would argue that the clear presence of such thefts begs the question: what are these thefts achieving? I further argue that the result of Kelly's position "where a black man used to be" is its function *as* Kelly's masculinity, imbued via embodiment. That Kelly's Don Lockwood is later able to dance out a tale of a young nobody who becomes love interest to a leggy Cyd Charisse and therefore a sexual threat to dangerous gangsters in the "Broadway Melody" film-within-a-film suggests that Black dance makes him manly and attractive to women. The very adumbrated Black male that turned a "white loser to a white winner" in the shift from *The Dueling Cavalier* to *The Dancing Cavalier* (via *The Dueling Mammy*) turns Kelly from a white "sissy dancer" to a virile white star (via blackbodying).

Kelly's last big musical for MGM, *Les Girls* (1957), sees him further contending with not only Marlon Brando-style rugged masculinity but also another blackbodier new to the media scene: Elvis Prelsey. In the film, Kelley plays a vaudeville showrunner, Barry Nichols. His negotiations of late fifties masculinity are perhaps clearest in the film's final number, from a show-within-the-film wherein he seduces a girl enjoying the juke box at a diner, and the girl is played by Nichols' real-life love interest, Joy Henderson (Mitzi Gaynor). Easily and often read as a parody of Marlon Brando's Johnny Strabler from *The Wild One* (1953), Kelly's performance in "Why Am I So Gone About That Gal?" is also his last appearance in one of his signature tight t-shirts—revealed from under a black leather jacket. As Cohan argues, the number

> is a fitting coda to his tenure as a leading man at the [MGM] studio. Jack Cole is credited with the choreography of *Les Girls*, but the ideas behind "Why Am I So Gone About That Gal?"—the playful impersonation of Brando, the recuperation of a confident heterosexual masculinity through dance, the homosocial bonds reinforcing that masculinity—are in keeping with Kelly's athletic, sexually aggressive dancing style and the virile star image it reinforced.[67]

A forty-five-year-old playing a twenty-nine-year-old and courting a twenty-six-year-old, Kelly performs Barry Nichols' stage dance indignantly, ultimately choosing his "pals" over the "gal," as Cohan notes. The colors—Kelly's tight all-black costume and the diner's bright red walls and floor—recall his "flaming" number from *The Pirate*, and his wielding of a chair in its first moments recall his previous wielding of a sword. After jumping seemingly without effort onto the bar and lifting Joy with one arm, Kelly breaks into a passionate ballet that balances tense muscles with extensions and release, building to a speedier jazz segment. Throughout, but especially during the slower ballet-heavy portion, Kelly lifts, pulls, holds, and teases Gaynor. The allure of his aggressiveness here springs from both the strength presumably required for the effortless lifts and the Black movement vocabulary of the second half, especially the swinging hips and syncopated steps. In a clear attempt to resonate as "youthful" here, Kelly's blackbodying choreography even incorporates a few isolated knee flaps and shoulder shimmies, both of which I will discuss in Chapter 3 as being central to Elvis Presley's use of Black dance (see Figure 2.10). The palm/fist dichotomy is also in full masculinizing effect, softening only when he grabs his partner and when he leaves to join the rest of his leather-clad biker gang. This continuation of older strategies but slight shift in both costuming and dance style to correspond to the edgy new rock 'n' roll aesthetic serves to further highlight how Kelly's masculinity had always relied not only on demonstrations of his strength but also the "coolness" afforded by the latest Black dance.

Though *Singin' in the Rain* is today the only one of Kelly's ballet boom films to be considered among the defining works of his career, several of his fifties ballet-heavy films clearly illustrate the ways in which his performance relied on Black corporeal styles to lay claim to his more mature but still-brash masculinity. This is especially true as his use of acrobatics and athletic feats is less

Figure 2.10 In *Les Girls* (1957), Kelly's Black dance vocabulary expands to include the isolated "knee flaps" that Elvis Presley made iconic the previous year.

prominent than it had been in the earlier years (when Kelly was younger and more capable of gymnastic feats). As we will see in the final section, this athleticism makes a major return at the dawning of his television career, alongside continued references to Black dance history, before giving way to what I call "late Kelly," whose performances consistently depend on Irish identity and vaudeville to legitimize his presence as an older dancing man.

Vaudeville Nostalgia on the Small Screen

It is frequently said that the veritable explosion of television during the 1950s period is one of the main contributors to the film musical's demise.[68] This necessitated a major career change for the dancing stars of Hollywood musicals, who often found themselves adapting to the small screen. According to one 1957 article, "Gene Kelly has come back to unpack his trunks and discover to his bewilderment that in the four years he has been headquartering in Europe that the old town has been through an upheaval. 'It's television's great progress and the tremendous influence on the entertainment field of rock 'n roll and a fellow named Presley that amazed me most of all.'"[69] Kelly was thus part of a sea change among his fellow song-and-dance men: as the Golden Age of the Hollywood musical was giving way to new musical film structures and less musical film production overall, these men found themselves experimenting with the small screen throughout the 1950s, both hosting their own series and specials and appearing as guests on variety shows.[70] The new medium provided new challenges and opportunities for these film musical stars, who went from playing fictional characters to playing "themselves." Television appearances thus became occasions to define and reinforce their star texts. And so, the year after his final musical for MGM (*Les Girls*, 1957), Gene Kelly began his shift toward playing "Gene Kelly." But he did so with an awareness that the new version of youthful and virile masculinity—which had been *his* domain during his *Pal Joey* period of likeable heels less than two decades prior—was now embodied by Presley, leaving him to (re)forge the masculinity of his aging star text differently.

This transitional moment in Kelly's career is marked by the 1958 television special he wrote, choreographed, co-directed, and danced for the *Omnibus* series (1952–1961), entitled "Dancing, A Man's Game." The Ford Foundation funded the series with the aim of cultural uplift; it was hosted by British expat Alistair Cooke and its material ranged from lectures and interviews to theatre and dance performances. In the words of television scholar Anna McCarthy, *Omnibus* "invited viewers to imagine not only how television might be better but also how they themselves might be better if only they seized the chance at self-improvement through culture that it offered."[71] When Kelly's high school friend Robert Saudek, the ABC executive who created *Omnibus*, encouraged him to write a special for the program, Kelly probably recognized his opportunity to participate in cultural discourse using more than just his body. Indeed, since "Dancing, A Man's Game" aired just after many of the networks' original "forum" shows reached their conclusion—to say nothing of the highly persuasive direct address of Richard Nixon's "Checkers" speech six years earlier—Kelly and his viewers alike would have been accustomed to direct televisual discourse about "important issues," whether political, cultural, or both. Thus, both television in general and *Omnibus* in particular were an ideal venue for Gene Kelly to spread his gospel and try to change America's mind about the presumed femininity of concert dance. It is against this backdrop that Kelly explicitly defended the (white) song-and-dance man, providing a platform for debating the mainstream definition of masculinity so trenchant in the fifties—and by doing it on national television, he brings this debate into America's living rooms. Likely framed quite differently than his university lectures ten years earlier, Kelly's defense of danced masculinity here depends simultaneously on the middlebrow audience's reverence to "high culture" and its presumed enthusiasm for sports.

As such, Kelly solicits appearances by major sports stars of the day in order to tie the masculinity of sportsmen to that of dancing men. The special opens with a long tracking shot of a gym set, in which male dancers mingle with famous sports stars, all warming up for their various activities. The camera pulls back to reveal Alistair Cooke and Gene Kelly looking out on the gym from a platform above; when their introductory chat is complete, Kelly pops over the railing and down the ladder, landing spryly on the floor. As he strolls through the gym set and the men continue their exercises behind him, Kelly immediately begins laying out the tenets of his argument: that dance and sports are based on the same principles of rhythmic movement. To provide visual proof of these

Figure 2.11 During the opening to the "Dancing, A Man's Game" *Omnibus* special (December 21, 1958), Bob Cousy demonstrates a standard basketball "pivot" (left) and Kelly incorporates it into a stylized dance (right).

claims, Kelly invites demonstrations of key movements from each of his featured sports stars and combines them all into a stylized dance (see Figure 2.11). He further holds that, in fact, many classical ballet movements share their origins with fencing, harkening back to some mythical past when men were "fighting for their lives," thereby linking an art form with the ever-manly act of fighting to the death. Kelly then insists not only that dance is a sport, but also that sports are a dance, whose movements he describes as "beautiful."

In so equating these physical activities, Kelly invites an extension of athletic masculinity from the sports stars to the dancers, as well as an extension of bodily objectification and spectacularization from the dancers to the sports stars—in other words, leveling the playing field between public perceptions of each activity type. He goes on to justify male dancers' skin-tight "uniforms" by pointing out that any men's sport judged by body form (Olympic gymnastics, diving, etc.) requires equally tight—and at times, more skimpy—attire. But for all his attempts to blur the boundaries between America's most beloved and its most stigmatized forms of masculine physical performance, reviewers of "Dancing, A Man's Game" did not always buy what Kelly was selling. Elizabeth L. Sullivan opined in the *Boston Daily Globe* that "[t]his was no sissy show,"[72] but Harry Harris wrote in the *Philadelphia Inquirer* that it "didn't disprove the widespread notion that male ballet dancers are apt to be sissy, but it did establish, most interestingly, a relation between dancing and rugged sports."[73] Thus, Kelly more easily linked the two realms of activity themselves than dispensed with the notion of the "sissy dancer" figure that had haunted his career.

Later in the program, Kelly also provides a history of tap dance—one that invisibilizes Black people's participation in its development. He begins by introducing the buck and wing as the closest thing America has to a folk dance, and entreats Black boxing champ Sugar Ray Robinson to demonstrate with him. Oddly, he offers no actual details about the Black origins of the buck and wing despite inviting the only Black guest on his program to dance it with him. Robinson is also the program's only actual athlete-dancer, a boxing champ who also happens to be a talented tap dancer. As a result, his performance is perhaps the most powerful gesture of the entire special. When Kelly asks Robinson about the most important thing a boxer must have, and Robinson answers, "Rhythm, man, rhythm!," the boxer joins Kelly for a clean, coordinated, and well-rehearsed number. The two parallel one another in "punching" movements and wear matching outfits, suggesting a masculine camaraderie (see Figure 2.12), and Robinson adds his own flair toward the end with expressive hand and arm movements that Kelly lacks. Functionally, the dance proves not only that an exceptional athlete can also be a skilled and compelling dancer, but also that Kelly is every bit as "manly" as his dance partner, a Black star in the manliest of sports. By hosting an integrated dance on television in 1958—that is, smack in the middle of the Civil Rights Movement—with, some argue, the greatest boxer of all time (who also happened to be Black) Kelly therefore harnesses not only the masculine power of sports but also the masculine power of Blackness.

And so, when Kelly and Robinson complete their duet with a smile (see Figure 2.12), one might expect to hear about how the history of tap dance is largely one of Black innovation. Instead, Kelly leaves the buck and wing behind to focus on the Irish, performing several times with an in-house Irish band but glazing over Black contributions and oversimplifying tap's history even as he describes it as "indigenous" to the United States. He proclaims that tap "exists here and only here" and goes on to explain its international appeal: "Tap dancing is admired and appreciated by people all over the world, mainly through the medium of the motion picture." As a means of explaining its uniqueness, Kelly then likens tap dance to "America itself": "a real melting pot of the folk dances of

Figure 2.12 Kelly and Sugar Ray Robinson wear matching outfits and perform "punching" movements together (left); they complete the dance with big smiles (right).

100 WHITE SCREENS, BLACK DANCE

several countries, fused into its present form by a most widely accepted artistic contribution to the world: jazz music." But, without explaining that we specifically have African Americans to thank for jazz music (and therefore also jazz-related dances ranging from tap to the Charleston), Kelly immediately switches gears and attempts to describe the manly origins of tap movements, locating the desire to make sounds by stamping one's feet as a universal trait of men and boys across the globe—"it's a basic masculine movement." He does return to jazz and finally brings up its Black origins only when he gets down to specifics:

> There were two groups who formed the basis of, and synthesized, the tap dance: the American Negro and the Irish immigrant. The beginnings of jazz and its physical interpretation by the Negro, added to the clog dancing of the Irish, developed into an American dance form with amazing swiftness . . . he had in him the beat and the rhythm that went with it.[74]

While finally giving credit where it is due, Kelly here (re)produces a very problematic assumption about Black cultural production: that rhythm, music, and dance are somehow innate to Black bodies and therefore do not require the labor, creativity, or virtuosity assigned to white performing bodies. As the demonstration continues, he emphasizes the centrality of blues and then jazz in the dance's development, but suggests that all of the "Negro" contributions to tap were slow, slouched movements akin to the infamously exaggerated lazy shuffling of Lincoln Perry as Stepin Fetchit. The Irish American clog dancers, in Kelly's telling, were the ones who added tapping, speed, and complexity to the loose, undisciplined movements of their African American counterparts. Formal competitions in precision and clarity of tapping that he attributes to Irish American cloggers were actually integrated; in 1900, a not-yet famous Bill Robinson beat the reigning (also Black) buck and wing champion, Harry Swinton, in a dance contest.[75] The inaccurate racial typing and one-sided innovation suggested here thereby obscure actual African-American craft, experimentation, and creative labor. Selectively highlighting the contributions of his own ethnic forefathers, as if to elevate public perceptions of Irishness as well as masculinity, Kelly offers up not only an inaccurate, but also a casually racist history in this segment. Still, the Black heritage of tap dancing is at least made partially visible for an American public who, if fed solely on a diet of Golden Age musicals, might otherwise believe Fred Astaire to be the father of tap.

Kelly's ensuing appearances on television were far less explicit with regard to either masculinity or the racial and ethnic groups that developed jazz and tap dance. Instead of the lecture-demonstration format of *Omnibus*, most of his later television appearances where in "vaudeo" (vaudeville + video) programs. As Kelly approaches the age of fifty—too old for his youthful muscle tees—the format of these shows allows him to perform a nostalgia for an early childhood that could have been. Kelly not only uses the variety structure as an opportunity to choreograph series of narratively unrelated and stylistically heterogeneous dances, but also takes seriously the historical precedent for it; he performs songs, dances, and skits *about* "old" vaudeville performance. In so doing, Kelly interrupts and reorganizes his previous economy of "masculine" dance components. His blackbodying returns to its less explicit forms of his earlier career (when he played tap-dancing vaudevillians with angled and/or loose torsos), and his demonstrations of athletics are all but replaced with vaudevillian comedy and self-effacement. An established but aging star, Kelly takes himself less and less seriously; the only element of his previous styles that remains is the palm/fist dichotomy, but even this begins to give way to the borrowed styles of the past—and parodies of the future. The first one-hour instantiation of *The Gene Kelly Show* (a special originally broadcast in color, but now only extant in black & white kinescope copies) serves as a clear example of this "vaudeo" trend.

Just days before the April 1959 special aired, an interview was published that indicated Kelly's ambivalent feelings about television: "Television isn't really a dancer's medium. The limitation in the size of the screen is obvious. The viewer doesn't want to see a close-up of the ballerina's face: he wants to see the movement of her whole body, and her relationship to the other dancers."[76] This signaled a change in Kelly's choreographic and performative approach: smaller dancing for a smaller screen. Elsewhere, Kelly also explained that he had to consider television's multiple cameras when choreographing numbers; bodily movement looks different when viewed from a single, highly mobile perspective (on film) than from several largely stationary perspectives (on television).[77] And to Kelly, but not just Kelly, the smaller screen recalled smaller stages: vaudeville and variety. As such, in his introduction to the April installment of *The Gene Kelly Show*, Kelly positions himself as a modernized vaudeville dancer: he explains that while the "old" circuit consisted of major U.S. cities such as Chicago or (his hometown of) Pittsburgh, the "new" performance circuit is international.

Kelly thus harkens back to an imagined vaudeville past for himself, one he had only barely participated in as a child—but one which very much defined the career of fellow hoofer Sammy Davis, Jr., as we will see in Chapter 4.[78] Having played vaudevillians in *For Me and My Gal* (1942), *Take Me Out to the Ball Game* (1949), and *Singin' in the Rain* (1952), Kelly called upon vaudeville's modular and (re)combinatory performance structure for the program. This includes the insertion of old film numbers as one form of variety among many. When he transports the titular "Les Girls" number from the previous year's film to television, he rechoreographs it to resemble the lighthearted fairground scene from the titular "An American in Paris" dream ballet he danced with Leslie Caron and other ballerinas in 1951. Importantly, he marks himself as far more separate from

102   WHITE SCREENS, BLACK DANCE

ballet than he had in *An American in Paris*, even though it was his major mode of performance for much of the previous decade. Now, evidence of Gene Kelly the danseur is entirely missing: he instead offers up a manly hoofer's performance to contrast with *les* (three) *girls*. But this stylistic distancing is not his only means of marking masculinity. Later, in an elaborate new production for the show, "Coffee House," Kelly spoofs the popular private eye series *Peter Gunn* (1958–1961). His character, unshaven Peter Gatt in a striped sweater and slacks, hears gunshots and watches a victim topple acrobatically (and unbelievably—laughs are audible in the kinescope recording) into the "Cha Cha Coffee House." He then finds himself in the midst of a dancing "Cha Cha Gang," whom he joins in a jagged, angular number heavily reminiscent of then-rising star Bob Fosse's choreographic style.[79] Generically recalling not just the popular TV series and Fred Astaire's "Girl Hunt Ballet" in *The Band Wagon* (1953) but also the films noir of the precious decade, Kelly draws (albeit ironically) upon the "grittier, tougher, colder" masculinity of 1940s noir films.[80] After he chases down the femme fatale culprit, the classic Kelly tense-palm makes an appearance during his very sensuous *pas de deux* with a leggy blonde, whose choreography is similar to his bits with Cyd Charisse in *Singin' in the Rain*'s "Broadway Melody" segment.[81]

As soon as the "Coffee House" number ends, Kelly is suddenly back in his suit and clean-shaven with a guitar, parodying Elvis Presley's virile rock 'n' roll masculinity. Importantly, he performs a little dance as he sings the silly "rock" song characterized by excessively bent knees, a wide stance, and overemphatic jumps. Since Presley was a well-established sensation by 1959, Kelly clearly uses him and his imitators as fodder for a joke that his adult audience might appreciate, indirectly reestablishing his own masculinity as superior. He follows the send-up with an explanation confirming the importance of his own dance style: "I guess if you were starting out as a song-and-dance man today, rock 'n' roll would be one of your mainstays . . . but, no matter what new musical styles are developed, there will always be one that will remain unchanged, and that's the standby of the song-and-dance man." From there, Kelly transitions into just that, song-and-dance man mode, singing and dancing about the enduring vaudeville forms that he argues are far less temporary than rock 'n' roll. Before breaking into a surprisingly balletic soft shoe dance whose supposed historical context seems to preclude him from using the palm/fist dichotomy, Kelly sings about the history of popular music and dance forms in "The Old Soft Shoe," a song originally written for the 1946 Broadway musical revue *Three to Make Ready*.[82] He sings, jovially, "When me and my Alice was playing The Palace in '25, there wasn't a word of, we never had heard of that thing called Jive . . . There wasn't a number concerning the Rumba on all that bill, and as for the Conga with Madame La Zonga, there just was nil."[83] Of course, Kelly was just thirteen years old in 1925, so he is singing of an imagined past in which he seems to argue there was a "purity" of show dance, lacking fads entirely. Importantly, the later so-called fads that the song (and therefore Kelly) dismiss are all explicitly dances adopted by the white mainstream from marginalized Others, especially Black and Latin communities across the Americas. Here, he not only seems to denigrate the exoticism of contemporary dances, he also risks claiming some sort of originary homogeneity of "American" popular and show dancing of the vaudeville period, as if the soft shoe and its cousins were not already amalgams and modifications of Africanist and Irish dance forms that were imported by immigrants.[84]

As the song continues, Kelly sings lyrics with oblique references to both the Africanist and the blackface minstrelsy origins of soft shoe dancing:

> Dances come, dances go, like the changes of the moon
> for a fad is always short and sweet
> But you can still stop a show with the lazy daisy tune
> and the easy breezy patter of your feet
> It never could happen that musical tappin' is gone, amen
> Plus science has found that the music goes 'round and comes back again
> And old Swanee River will flow on forever because they played it when
> we gave 'em the old soft shoe

As an aging star staking a claim here for the timelessness of vaudeville as part of his own origin story, Kelly exhibits nostalgia about "Swanee River," also known as "Old Folks at Home," an 1851 minstrel song that itself romanticizes an earlier period—namely the conditions of chattel slavery in the antebellum South. In citing this song, Kelly not only hints at the parallels between minstrel performance-as-masculinity and his own blackbodying-as-masculinity, and seems to wish that cultural institution of minstrelsy as a fount of problematic performance traditions would "flow on forever," but also gestures at the mere two degrees of separation between his own soft shoe and the Black dancers who inspired the minstrels in the first place. The result is similar to that of the absenting of Black bodies in *Singin' in the Rain*; despite refusing to explicitly center Black innovation in his history of tap dance in "Dancing, A Man's Game," Kelly here reveals his "consciously unconscious relation to African-American dance."[85] While he performs most of his simple soft shoe in a rigid, elevated and lengthened—indeed, rather balletic—style, he also inserts a few more grounded stances for contrast. The dance he performs thus embodies the combination of Irish/Europeanist and Africanist forms he inherited from minstrelsy via vaudeville and Broadway, and it is this combination he uses to shore up his masculinity with his television audience. Moreover, it is vaudeville's variety format that allows Kelly to suture together *both* a dance that makes fun of the rock 'n' roll future *and* one that insists on the timelessness of the blackface minstrel past. With

104 WHITE SCREENS, BLACK DANCE

the addition of the grit and sensuality of the *Peter Gunn* spoof number, the first *Gene Kelly Show* positions aging Kelly as a playful master of several dance styles and an authority on dance history and innovation. At this juncture, references to the absented Black bodies in both Kelly's earlier career and the history of "American" dance more generally will become increasingly oblique and implicit, mirroring his 1940s films. Instead, Kelly enters the 1960s by emphasizing his Irish ethnic heritage and decreasing physical stamina.

Kelly's second special, which aired on November 21, 1959, was even more traditionally vaudevillian than the previous—one of the segments is a long comedy sketch specifically about vaudeville—and engages in heavy ethnic humor and stereotyping. The program opens with a tap battalion marching down a long backstage hallway while singing, "Has Anybody Here Seen Kelly?," the lyrics of which remind viewers of Kelly's Irish heritage: "Though his hair's not red; his eyes aren't blue, but he's Irish through and through. Has anybody here seen Kelly? Kelly from the Emerald Isle." As they pass by the dressing rooms of costars Carol Lawrence and Donald O'Connor, they ask after their leader in unison, eventually finding him snoozing under the brim of his hat in a chair. Startled awake, Kelly takes up the leading position and ushers the men onstage, where they perform a regimented tap number together. His Irish identity thus firmly established, he goes on to perform in a series of numbers exoticizing other cultural dances.

For example, Kelly first dances in an indeterminately Hispanic scene (perhaps the setting is meant to be historic Spain?) as a wanted criminal. Taken by a lovely young aristocrat who drops her hanky, Kelly performs a solo dance in front of a crowd. He appears in a flamenco suit and "plays" Hispanic, dancing a flamenco solo—very similar to those popularized in Hollywood by José Greco—to encouraging shouts from the crowd. As he did years prior in *Anchors Aweigh*, Kelly uses the exciting appeal of a cultural dance form not his own (but rhythmically close enough to tap that he can still draw from the Africanist tap vocabulary) to perform an enticing masculinity. This fades to more racist nonspecificity and caricature with the "Bim Bam" number from within the vaudeville skit, which Kelly performs with Lawrence and O'Connor. In the context of a fortune teller request, the three perform a dance with much less care toward the source dance form(s) than the flamenco number, wrapping only a single stereotypical Ancient Egyptian arm movement into a thoroughly American show dance. Lawrence wears harem pants, a bejeweled bikini top, and a fez, or *tarboosh* hat, meant to visually signify the "exotic." At least one reviewer understood the number as merely "Oriental,"[86] which suggests that the lack of cultural specificity translated from performance to reception. Considered in the context of Kelly's long career of variously implicit blackbodying, despite which he almost always refused to "give credit where credit is due," these dances do the reverse; make clear the exotic "flavor" of Othered cultures without engaging them beyond the surface stereotype. Indeed, as Meenasarani Linde Murugan has demonstrated, this was an intentional choice often used to make dance more appealing on small screens.[87] A 1947 article in *Dance Magazine* argues for the visual attractiveness of the dance and costumes of the "Other":

> The most suitable dances for television are those that require both a minimum of floor space and vertical movement, such as to spring a partner into the air. For these reasons, Oriental, tap and rumba routines are ideally suited to the medium. The dances of the far East have been successfully televised since most of the rhythm is expressed by the hands and arms permitting close up camera shots . . . . The picturesque costumes worn for all types of specialty dances have tremendous video appeal. The colorful Oriental and Spanish costumes, the Hawaiian grass skirt, native dress and brief shorts and blouses lend grace and beauty to the dance and emphasize the flavor of the musical accompaniment.[88]

A decade after the publication of this article, which appears to encourage the presence of "Other" bodies as much as their dances, Kelly and friends simply appropriate the signifiers without performing the steps to which they belong.

O'Connor and Kelly later offer a far less exoticizing ethnic slippage joke about themselves, followed by Kelly's first potential gender ambiguity in years—but viewers are reassured both verbally and via blackbodying. O'Connor asks Kelly how he feels; the answer is "tired." Kelly sighs, "It's times like these when I wish our names were Como and Sinatra." O'Connor: "You mean you wish we were Italians?" The joke's double significance lies in the mirrored distinctions between singing/dancing skill and the Italian/Irish ethnic identity of the four performers. In following immediately on the heels of the variously "exotic" dances in the vaudeville skit, this joke extends the program's problematic use of cultural "Others" as its "spice" but centers its ethnic highlighting this time on the star texts immediately at hand. In their implied interchangeability despite their difference, the Italians and Irish are marked as "normal" (read: acceptably white) Others rather than foreign, elaborately costumed Others. The exchange thus sums up the uneven ethnic fluidity of the special.

To accommodate Kelly's tiredness, the two retire to chairs and play a tap guessing game where they tap old numbers from their musicals and guess which one the other is tapping. During the game, Kelly is so excited by O'Connor's tapping "You're Just In Love" from *Call Me Madam* (1953) that he asks to be Ethel Merman—as he taps along, he leaves out the overt drag burlesquing that the two had performed in the vaudeville skit (dancing the can-can in full dresses and wigs), only slightly changing his comportment with a raised chin and eyebrows. Still, the shift risks gender confusion so O'Connor reassures viewers of Kelly's masculinity and thus inappropriateness for Merman's role: "Ethel, how you've changed." Kelly then reassures viewers that he is not too old to keep dancing full-out: he and O'Connor soon get up and dance a fairly rigorous tap number, involving both jumps up and down off their chairs and more than a few barrel rolls. The underlying concern over Kelly's age remains, however; at one point, O'Connor breaks out into an even more rigorous solo dance, and Kelly only looks on disapprovingly. Was the problem that he "went off-script" (though it was clearly planned and rehearsed to unfold that way) or that he "showed up the old master" and threatened his athletic masculinity?

The special's crowning number, a Kelly solo (which actually occurs just before the O'Connor duet), returns to pure vaudeville nostalgia and thinly veiled blackbodying as masculine "cool." Shirtsleeves rolled up (he means business), Kelly performs "Ballin' the Jack." This performance of the number is quite different from Kelly's earlier version with Judy Garland in *For Me and My Gal* (1942). Whereas the earlier version was quick, light, and more influenced by Irish styles, this solo is slow, syncopated, and spectacular—in the sense that Kelly's body expands to take up as much space as possible. Rick Altman once said of Kelly's musical dancing that "The Gene Kelly who stands out, performing numbers which only he could bring off, is not a Gene Kelly *making love*, but a Gene Kelly *showing off*"[89] and I argue that this holds even more true of his television appearances, where Kelly, anxious about the smallness of the screen, would only really "let loose" when he had the limited space all to himself. The number is thus classic Kelly, with just enough wiggle of the hips and buttocks to bring the viewer's eyes to them. It reveals not only a continued use of blackbodying, through his mobile hips, grounded stance, and loose arms, but also through the song and dance choice itself: the "ballin' the jack" and "eagle rock" are both late nineteenth-/early twentieth-century Black social dances.[90] To drive home the dance's masculinity, Kelly also includes an emphatic use of the palm/fist dichotomy (see Figure 2.13). He pulls his hat brim low, flashes his cocky smile, and ends it all with a slide and shuffle on his knees, which at the time would

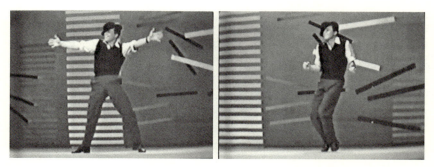

Figure 2.13 In his televisual performance of "Ballin' the Jack" during his November 21, 1959 *Pontiac Star Parade* special, Kelly performs Africanist hip swings and once again uses the palm (left)/fist (right) dichotomy.

have brought to mind both rock 'n' roll performances (like Elvis's) and jazz finales (like Fosse's)—in short, the stuff of youth. Thus, Kelly reinterprets an old vaudeville number as modern, heavily indebted to Black dance in exuding what Gottschild would call its "ephebism."

After several years away from dancing for the comedy-drama series *Going My Way* (1962–1963), Kelly returns to variety programs with segments that continue to reinforce his nostalgia for both vaudeville and his earlier career, as well as emphasize his Irish masculinity. Tap dance remains his primary idiom, further distancing him from his ballet period with Black dance. During the mid-sixties, he appears as a guest on several variety shows. On the October 23, 1963 episode of *The Danny Kaye Show*, Kelly and Kaye, both wearing suits, revisit the entirety of Kelly's musical career according to the organizing principle of "girls," a rhetorical strategy on Kaye's part that reminds viewers of his guest's earlier wolfish brand of masculinity: "The sets were built (the girls were, too). They put you in a sailor suit and you knew just what to do . . . . He was a tiger. Oh, he was incredible."[91] However, all of this was in the past, and in the present, age seems to be an underlying concern. At the beginning, Kaye comments on having known Kelly for some twenty years; after their first joint tap dance, Kaye jokes that they have someone ready with an oxygen tank near the set. And yet, a few minutes later, Kelly appears in familiar rolled-up shirtsleeves for another performance of "Ballin' the Jack." This time, however, the Africanist influences in Kelly's style are made more apparent due to Kaye's accompaniment. Kaye's dance, replicated directly from his own performance of "Ballin' the Jack" in *On the Riviera* (1951), is delicate and understated; he stands tall, erect, and statuesque. Kelly, on the other hand, moves throughout the space. Despite performing ballet steps such as *pirouettes*, he does so in a jazz-inflected style with a mobile center of gravity, loose arms, and active hips. Once again, he slides on his knees for another emphatically "cool" finale (see Figure 2.14). Having perhaps attempted to lower

Figure 2.14 On the October 23, 1963 episode of *The Danny Kaye Show*, Kelly's reprise of "Ballin' the Jack" exhibits a mobile center of gravity, loose arms, and active hips (left); he completes it with another "cool" slide on his knees (right).

audience expectations with jokes about his age and exhaustion, Kelly ultimately calls upon his old tactic (which had been disrupted by O'Connor in 1959) of outshining and outmuscling his more understated, slimmer buddy pairing.

When Kelly appears on the November 28, 1965 episode of *The Julie Andrews Show* at fifty-three years old and performs with Andrews, who is thirty, images of the brash Irish sailor return. Unlike in previous appearances with male colleagues—and instead in the company of a pretty young woman—there are no references to Kelly's age. Instead, he offers demonstrations of ethnic and class identity, in keeping with his early desire to dance as might a "truck driver, bricklayer, clerk, or postman" and his increasing references over the course of the 1950s and 60s to his Irish heritage. He and Andrews sing about and act out fantasies of their "family trees," with most of Andrews' imagined English ancestors generally occupying higher social positions (physicians, obstetricians, opera singers) than Kelly's Irish ones (jesters, magicians, and pirates). Whereas Andrews claims a knight at King Arthur's court, Kelly claims a drunkard who invented the Irish jig by hopping over broken whiskey bottles. Kelly later appears in his classic outfit, a sailor suit, and performs a fairly intense dance, as if to argue for his continued youth and virility (see Figure 2.15). This is the last time Kelly ever appeared in his signature sailor suit, performing steps drawn from the full arc of his film career. Indeed, there are bells from *Anchors Aweigh*'s "The Worry Song" with Jerry Mouse, a barrel roll and hops in "plank" position from *The Pirate*'s "Be A Clown" number with the Nicholas Brothers, and even a butt wiggle from the "Chocolat" dance in *An American in Paris*'s dream ballet (see Figures 2.4 and 2.9). This is a markedly different nostalgia than Kelly has otherwise peddled on television; the dance is not explicitly linked to old vaudeville, nor is it a simple re-performance of a popular number from one of his films. Rather, with a new song and new choreography, Kelly visually signifies

Figure 2.15 In his final sailor suit number ever, on the November 28, 1965 episode of *The Julie Andrews Show*, Kelly performs bells as he did in *Anchors Aweigh* (left) and a butt wiggle as he did in *An American in Paris* (right).

nostalgia for his past formulation of masculinity (e.g., tight costume, athleticism, blackbodying) through a deconstructed approach that signals the past more elementally than just another rendition of "Singin' in the Rain" or "For Me and My Gal." To conclude the number, Kelly salutes—this serves as his final farewell to the athletic masculinity of his youth.

In the late 1960s, when "vaudeo" and the variety format were quickly disappearing from television, Kelly represented one of the last bastions of variety, with hour-long Kelly-hosted specials occurring every now and then. These included *Gene Kelly in New York, New York* (February 14, 1966), *Gene Kelly's Wonderful World of Girls* (January 14, 1970), and *Changing Scene* I and II (September 10 and December 10, 1970). By this time pushing sixty years of age, Kelly was dancing less, but made it clear that he still needed to dance sometimes. A 1972 *Radio Times* article explains this: "At 60 he has the stamina and energy of a much younger man, and he looks it. If he goes too long without doing something, he gets 'edgy.' 'To combat that I usually do something on television—a little song and dance—I call it mini-dancing—on one of the variety shows—to get into shape.' "[92] Here it seems that he still insists on a masculinity tied to being "in shape," a clear holdover from decades past. His tune changed, however, when he reached sixty-seven: "I'm still doing a few television appearances just to pay the rent. I'm not breaking any new ground, just singing and doing a little dance— all that's left of old dad. I never really dance any more you know. It's too much trouble keeping in shape. I'd rather have a drink and a hearty meal . . . I go on television, but I just horse around. Everybody thinks I'm dancing, but I'm not: I do a few steps. No, I don't dance any more, really."[93] These wistful comments suggest that for Kelly, youth and (Black) dance and masculinity were all co-constitutive. When there is not much "left of old dad," it is because he can no longer keep well enough in shape to dance the masculinity that had always defined his star text, so instead he sees himself as a silly old man who "just horse[s] around."

Overall, Kelly's television career underscored several simultaneous tensions underlying the transition away from his preferred format of commercial film. These included nostalgia for the big budgets and resulting "big" production numbers of the old days (as demonstrated by the frequent references to and rehashings of these old numbers), as well as an even deeper nostalgia about vaudeville, whose revue structure reappeared on television in large part because the talent available in television's early New York years was precisely the pool of aging, largely out of (screen) work vaudeville stars of yesteryear. Finally, there was the problem of the increasing obsolescence of the musical era's song-and-dance man, who could argue all he wanted for the primacy and importance of "the old soft shoe" but was, in reality, fast being overshadowed by a young rock 'n' roll star whose hips swayed farther and faster than Kelly's. Of course, television as a medium also posed certain challenges for the aging dancer. Early

110 WHITE SCREENS, BLACK DANCE

TV resembled the stage in that its "liveness" allowed for no breaks or second takes. Dancing almost nonstop for the better part of an hour would have been daunting even for younger dancers. While the variety format did provide some respite, live television still required a perfect "first take," as it were. Even once programs moved over to pre-recording, broadcast schedules simply did not allow for much rehearsal time. In the context of all these factors, as Gene Kelly approached and then passed the fifty-year mark, he used his age (alongside his explicit performances of Irishness) as an explanation and resource for nostalgia. But this was a selective nostalgia: he left behind the gymnastics, limited the athletics, and depended more on the "coolness" of blackbodying alone to claim his masculinity undiminished by age.

Gene Kelly's brand of "masculine" dance is ultimately more complex than it has often appeared, and not only in the camp-inflected ways Steven Cohan has highlighted. Though what I have described as his "palm/fist dichotomy" became a standard element of his dances early on and remained throughout his career, other elements of his dancing as a "man's game" were more variable. He frequently incorporated gymnastic and athletic movements into his early career dances, but his later dances more emphatically bore the mark of his Irish ethnicity. Kelly was very vocal about proving dance's relationship to sports, especially in the 1950s, but as I have argued in this chapter, the masculinity in his dances resulted just as often from costuming, bodily comportments, and dances borrowed from African American culture. In this way, he "tapped into" the virile masculinity associated with Black male bodies even when performing more Europeanist ballet steps in the middle of his career. It is perhaps a bit ironic that his more direct and explicit connections to Black dancers (from the Nicholas Brothers to Raphaël Padilla to Sugar Ray Robinson) disappeared during his later career, especially as the Civil Rights Movement ramped up in the 1960s and Black performers were appearing more regularly on television. In his reversion to an earlier period of dance, his performances of masculinity largely reverted to earlier, invisibilizing, blackbodying as well.

3
Elvis Presley
Virile and Phallic

Milton Berle announces him, and the screen fades to a separate camera, where Elvis Presley debuts "Hound Dog" on American television. Within fifteen seconds, the camera has pulled back from its initial medium shot and Presley's already wide stance erupts into a wave of gyrations, originating from his knees but extending through his entire body, throwing his legs left and right as he extends his left arm to steady himself. He completes the phrase balanced on the tips of his toes, in what would become a signature Presley pose (see Figure 3.1). The dancing increases and continues throughout the rest of the song, becoming particularly pronounced during the breaks without lyrics, which free Presley to leave the microphone and expend his breath on leg-shaking rather than singing.

It is widely believed that this June 5, 1956 performance of "Hound Dog" on *The Milton Berle Show* cemented Presley's status as "the king" of rock 'n' roll music. What is peculiar about this view, however, is that this "Hound Dog" performance was not the first time he had thoroughly demonstrated his facility with the rock 'n' roll *sound*; he had twice performed Little Richard's iconic "Tutti Frutti," among similarly rocking renditions of other songs, on *Stage Show* earlier that year to high acclaim. What stood out about this performance, therefore, was not the sound at all. Indeed, reviews by critics suggested that it was something else entirely: his unfettered hip gyrations. *New York Times* TV critic Jack Gould put it in no uncertain terms:

> Mr. Presley has no discernible singing ability . . . For the ear he is an unutterable bore, not nearly so talented as Frankie Sinatra back in the latter's rather hysterical days at the Paramount Theatre. Nor does he convey the emotional fury of a Johnnie Ray.
>
> From watching Mr. Presley it is wholly evident that his skill lies in another direction. He is a rock-and-roll variation on one of the most standard acts in show business: the virtuoso of the hootchy-kootchy. His one specialty is an accented movement of the body that heretofore has been primarily identified with the repertoire of the blonde bombshells of the burlesque runway. The gyration never had anything to do with the world of popular music and still doesn't.[1]

White Screens, Black Dance. Pamela Krayenbuhl, Oxford University Press. © Pamela Krayenbuhl 2025.
DOI: 10.1093/9780197699119.003.0004

Figure 3.1 After singing the first verse of "Hound Dog" on the June 5, 1956 episode of *The Milton Berle Show*, Elvis Presley throws his knees back and forth (left) and completes the phrase on his toes (right).

Gould was backed by a host of other negative evaluations of Presley's bodily movements; Ben Gross at the *New York Daily News* claimed that popular music "has reached its lowest depths in the 'grunt and groin' antics of one Elvis Presley ... Elvis, who rotates his pelvis was appalling musically. Also, he gave an exhibition that was suggestive and vulgar, tinged with the kind of animalism that should be confined to dives and bordellos ... as he sings, indulges in bumps and grinds and other motions that would bring a blush to the cheeks of a hardened burlesque theatre usher."[2] Even Harry A. Feldman, chairman of a high school music department, purportedly wrote in to Milton Berle himself, complaining that the performance "was in execrable taste, bordering on obscenity. The gyrations of this young man were such an assault to the senses as to repel even the most tolerant observer."[3] This general outcry about the vulgarity of Presley's performance is clearly focused not on his *singing*, which is tossed aside as uninteresting and irrelevant, but his *dancing*. Thus, while Elvis Presley might be a somewhat unexpected figure to feature in a book about dance on screen, Presley's dancing was as crucial as his singing, not only to defining his star persona, but also to defining the 1950s and 60s popular dance-scape.

Numerous scholars, critics, and historians have made clear the ways in which Presley's music and "sound" are at best inspired by, and at worst appropriative of, Black music.[4] It was Presley's whiteness (and thereby, his access to record deals, Hollywood contracts, and extended television exposure) that was able to bring midcentury Black music into the mainstream; he helped to embody the racist division in the music industry between the ghetto of "rhythm and blues" and the gold mine of "rock 'n' roll." Of course, Southern (white) country music had long been influenced by African American blues music, so the cross-pollination itself was not new. But what was new with white-coded rock 'n' roll in general and Elvis Presley in particular was the direct embrace of Black culture, only slightly repackaging it for mainstream white audiences.[5] By being named the king of the genre, Presley became the face—and body—of the tensions, anxieties, and conflicts that rock 'n' roll brought with it as it swept the United States in the mid-1950s.

In an expansion of that thorough excavation conducted by music scholars, this chapter argues that Elvis Presley uses Black dance to perform a virile white masculinity and an often-ambiguous, spectacular sexuality. It unpacks Presley's "wiggling," "shaking," and pelvic mobility, as well as other aspects of his corporeality, such as his hair choreography—all of which comprise dances by a seeming non-dancer. Against a backdrop of older, professional dancers like Kelly and the Nicholas Brothers, Presley stands out as a younger amateur who offers an alternative possibility for dancing masculinity during the midcentury period. Like Gene Kelly, he engages in practices of blackbodying as a response to the era's anxieties around white masculinity, but in a far more transgressive and provocative manner than Kelly, and for a younger generation of viewers; this is not concert dance for "the Greatest Generation" but popular and social dance for budding Baby Boomers. Where Gene Kelly's use of blackbodying served, in conjunction with his palm/fist dichotomy and sports movements, to connote a muscular, athletic masculinity, Presley's blackbodying signified a masculinity of the phallus. Presley's career took off just as Kelly's began to fizzle out; Presley rocketed to fame in 1956, the same year that Kelly's *Invitation to the Dance* was a box office failure. And unlike both Kelly and the Nicholas Brothers, Presley built his career on television *first*, receiving his inaugural Hollywood contract with Paramount only *after* his first six television appearances. In this way, Presley first reached the youth of the United States at home, transmitting his model of reckless "bad boy" Black dance-as-white masculinity to their living rooms, long before he drew them out to the cinema to see him dancing larger than life on the silver screen.[6]

Presley's pelvic thrusts and other aspects of blackbodying were received as vulgar by the white majority—and caused so much handwringing—because they were an embodiment of white fears around racial miscegenation. At the first International Conference on Elvis Presley in Oxford, Mississippi in 1995, Yahya Jongintaba (as Jon Michael Spencer) argued that "the syncopated leg and body movements," which Elvis displays most famously in the "Hound Dog" performance above, are attributable to "the rhythms that undergird African-American culture and give it its distinctiveness." These movements constituted a public expression of Black sexualities, performed by a white body.[7] This begs the question: when a white body engages in Black sexualities, what comes next? In "Elvis from the Waist Up and Other Myths: 1950s Music Television and the Gendering of Rock Discourse," popular music scholar Norma Coates frames this white body/Black sexualities combination in terms of miscegenation fears:

114   WHITE SCREENS, BLACK DANCE

Perhaps the biggest threat of rock and roll was its overt recognition of the plausibility of racial miscegenation. Musical miscegenation could to some extent be contained, as it had in jazz, but rock and roll had a much wider appeal. It was a short step from the fear of musical miscegenation, the primary effects of which were between the ears, to the fear of racial miscegenation, concerned with feelings lower down in the body. Rock and roll thus challenged and put into crisis the prevailing racial and sexual mores of the day.[8]

Framed in this way, the consequences of Presley's overtly sexual blackbodying become clear: interracial sex and therefore a mixed-race future. But that is not the whole story: as with the generation of dancing men before him, the camera's relentless focus on Presley's bodily spectacle also threatens to feminize him by rendering him the passive object to be looked at rather than the active subject doing the looking. Therefore, Presley's danced "feelings" both embody and complicate white culture's simultaneous fear of and sexual desire for the Black "Other" because they are also rooted in gendered anxieties about masculine (versus feminine) bodily performance.

But it is important to remember that Presley's whiteness is what allows him to get away with his provocative movements in the first place. On Black bodies such as those of the Nicholas Brothers, such hip gyrations would have been seen as so hyper-masculine and sexually dangerous that they were simply not an option—but on Presley's white body, they read as a vulgar, feminizing appropriation of sex appeal (with interracial undertones).[9] At least, this is the anxiety that critics' non-dancing white male bodies revealed in their critique of Presley; on the other hand, the hordes of young female fans, operating within the same context of presumed heterosexuality as the reviewers and who screamed and trembled uncontrollably at the sight of Presley's mobile hips, seem to affirm his movements as "masculine" insofar as they signaled heterosexual desire. Thus, the masculinity that Presley danced via Black vernacular movement remained more ambiguous than the insistently athletic but sometimes eroticized and campy masculinity performed by Gene Kelly; the very root of Presley's appeal was its constant transgressions across the categories of both race and gender.

The first half of this chapter shows how the traceable Africanisms in Presley's performances, like the dances themselves, start small and elemental—a single leg flap, for example—but give way, over the course of his 1956 performances, to a clearly discernible wing dance descended from nineteenth-century Black social dances that entered the white social dance sphere in the 1920s.[10] I also demonstrate how his controversial performance of "Hound Dog" goes a step further, exhibiting all five of the Africanist aesthetics Gottschild has outlined as being present in American dance, in order to perform irreverence and virility.[11] With Presley's shift to film, his dances are framed differently, both figuratively and literally, within narrative contexts that emphasize his "bad boy" masculinity via fistfights. The second half of the chapter demonstrates how his post-Army films, contrary to popular opinion, largely follow in the same vein, exhibiting not reform of Presley's dance (as cultural critics claimed at the time), but an evolution toward a newer Black social dance: the twist. The last two instances of Presley's midcentury dancing on screen in *Viva Las Vegas* (1964) present Presley's masculinity as both a danced representation of heterosexual intercourse and a feminized spectacle of gender indeterminacy. After his nostalgic '68 "Comeback Special," which finally features a Black man dancing, Presley switches gears again, dropping any remaining elements of subversiveness and sexuality from his performance in favor of pure, bejeweled spectacle.

A Truck Driver from Tupelo

Much romance has been made of Presley's humble beginnings. Born in Tupelo, Mississippi on January 8, 1935, half an hour after his stillborn twin, Jesse Garon, Elvis Aron Presley was always very close to his mother, Gladys. His father, Vernon Presley, moved the family around a lot as he searched for stable employment and worked odd jobs—Gladys often went to work as well to help the family stay afloat. The Presleys moved to Memphis in 1948, and Elvis spent most of high school living in a Memphis public housing facility called Lauderdale Courts. During high school, Presley was shy. Old friends recall that he never quite fit in, and few of his peers even knew he could sing until he performed in a 1953 talent show—he had failed music class.[12] Later that year, a few months after graduating from high school, he walked into the Sun Records office. For $3.98 plus tax, Presley recorded "My Happiness" and "That's Where Your Heartaches Begin," ostensibly for his mother, but also hoping that Mr. Sam Phillips would be sufficiently impressed to jumpstart his career. He then stopped by the office regularly for the following months to inquire if any bands needed a singer but received no encouragement until June of 1954, when Phillips called him in to try out a new song, "Without You." The session did not go well.

He got a second chance, however, in July, when guitarist Scotty Moore and bassist Bill Black were looking for a singer. These famous sessions together in Phillips' studio produced "That's All Right, Mama" with Presley bringing his own rendition to Arthur "Big Boy" Crudup's blues song. Sam Phillips played the track for Dewey Phillips, the popular disc jockey at WHBQ Memphis (the two shared a name but were not related). Sam later recalled, "What I was thinking was, where you going to go with this, it's not black, it's not white, it's not pop, it's not country, and I think Dewey was the same way."[13] Presley thus embodied precisely what Sam had been searching for, a phenomenon he knew would be wildly

116 WHITE SCREENS, BLACK DANCE

lucrative, particularly in the South: "negro" sounds emanating from a white boy. This is often considered the revolutionary moment of rock 'n' roll; in musicologist Albin Zak's telling of the first Sun Session with Presley, Moore, and Black together, "the story of that night became one of rock 'n' roll's most cherished founding myths."[14]

Of course, Dewey did play the record on his show *Red, Hot, and Blue*, together with its B-side, "Blue Moon of Kentucky," a bluegrass song by Bill Monroe that had been a hit in 1946. At this point, Elvis was still just a nineteen-year-old truck driver who could not dance (at least, he had refused to try at his senior prom), but his record—a unique blend of hillbilly, country and western, rhythm and blues, and even a little pop—was an instant hit throughout Memphis.[15] This is why Sam, Dewey, and the rest of his team were unsure how his unusual (sonically miscegenated) performance might be received at his first few live performances, which occurred at what might be described as "redneck" and "hillbilly" venues. As it turned out, white youth in the still-segregated South not only found it easier to identify with Black sounds when someone who looked like them was *singing* them, but they also found it attractive when a white body *danced* Black dance. Indeed, these early public performances are also where his friends discovered Presley could dance at all, and this was certainly part of the reason the crowds at his second-ever stage performance, at Overton Park, Memphis, on July 30, 1954, loved him. Monroe recalls, "Elvis, instead of just standing flat-footed and tapping his foot, well, he was kind of jiggling . . . I think with those old loose britches that he wore—they weren't pegged, they had lots of material and pleated fronts—you shook your leg, and it made it look like all hell was going on under there." Of the audience response, Presley later recalled, "everybody was hollering and I didn't know what they were hollering at . . . my manager told me that they was hollering because I was wiggling my legs. I went back out for an encore, and I did a little more, and the more I did, the wilder they went."[16]

As Presley performed at increasingly important venues in the South—including the Grand Ole Opry, where he was not a sensation, and Louisiana Hayride, where he was—his developing dance style proved to be both persistent and adaptable. The leg movements quickly morphed into an intentional, carefully timed facet of Presley's performance and were soon accompanied by matching hip movements. Country singer Bob Luman recalled of a 1955 show in Kilgore, Texas, "This cat came out in red pants and a green coat and a pink shirt and socks, and he had this sneer on his face and he stood behind the mike for five minutes, I'll bet, before he made a move. Then he hit his guitar a lick and he broke two strings . . . and then he started to move his hips real slow like he had a thing for his guitar."[17] While some have argued that Presley's early "leg-shaking" and "twitching" resulted from the Holy Roller church experiences of his youth, by the time they made their way to the wider public, there was little about them that resembled religious reverie.[18] Moreover, as a poor white child in Memphis, Presley lived in close social and physical proximity to Black communities. Bo Diddley, a Black R&B artist and fellow Southerner, accused Elvis of stealing his own "wiggle" dance steps.[19] Further, as Gottschild has demonstrated, Presley's "twitching" also resembles the full-body "tremble" for which Black performer Earl "Snakehips" Tucker was famous in the 1920s and 30s.[20] Regardless of precisely where Presley picked up this Africanist aesthetic choice, beginning with a few 1955 shows in Jacksonville, he was inciting near-riots of teenage girls, eager to rip off his clothing.

Presley's clothing, hair, and other styling choices in 1955 serve as an early indicator of how he performed Blackness in a gender-ambiguous way. Though Luman's recollection above places him as costuming himself brightly in general, Presley's preferred costume color scheme was black and pink. Multiple observers noted that he wore eye makeup (at minimum mascara, but often eyeliner as well).[21] In *Vested Interests: Cross-Dressing and Cultural Anxiety*, popular culture scholar Marjorie Garber highlights the multiple transgressions of Presley's hair and costuming:

> Elvis's hair created even more of a furor [than did his purported eyeshadow at Grand Ole Opry]. It was like a black man's (Little Richard's, James Brown's); it was like a hood's; it was like a woman's. Race, class, and gender: Elvis's appearance violated or disrupted them all. His created "identity" as the boy who crossed over, who could take a song like "Hound Dog" from Big Mama Thornton or the onstage raving—and the pompadour, mascara, and pink and black clothing—from Little Richard, made of Elvis, in the popular imagination, a cultural mulatto, the oxymoronic "Hillbilly Cat," a living category crisis.[22]

Thus, Presley's similarities to "Little Richard" Penniman—eyeliner, bright and color-contrasting costuming, pompadour hairstyle—as early as 1955 make for an ambiguous masculinity at the same time as they draw from Black culture. Penniman, for his part, was very much aware of how his makeup, hair, and general flamboyance functioned in relation to his race; he has reflected that his "drag" style and audiences' resultant assumption that he was homosexual is the only reason he was able to perform amongst young white women as a Black man.[23] For Presley, on the other hand, the adoption of Blackness alongside the flamboyant stylings helped them to signify as presumed heterosexuality—this was not the lily-white gender ambiguity of Liberace, after all, it was far cooler.[24] Of course, this is not to claim that Presley was styling himself directly from Little Richard; he had been experimenting with his dress and hairstyle since high school and his oft-cited role model James Dean also wore product-styled haircuts similar to the "pomp." The visual similarity between Presley and Penniman is nevertheless important to understanding the signification of Presley's early ambiguous masculinity.

It was at this juncture that Sam Phillips sold Presley's Sun Records contract to RCA-Victor, as facilitated by Presley's new general manager, "Colonel" Tom Parker. The most immediate result of this move from a small, minor Southern label to a major national label—beyond rereleases of his Sun singles and a few new songs, including "Heartbreak Hotel"—was a meeting with RCA's new publicity director, Anne Fulchino. They immediately agreed that Hollywood was in the long-term plan.[25] Meanwhile, Parker also envisioned mass exposure, and booked Elvis for four episodes on the television variety program *Stage Show*, hosted by former big band leaders Jimmy and Tommy Dorsey. These performances, occurring just after Presley turned twenty-one, catapulted his music, dancing, and style to fame, controversy, and mainstream visibility.

Black Dance Builds a TV Star

Unlike the Nicholas Brothers and Gene Kelly, Elvis Presley did not grow up dancing. As will become apparent, however, even from Presley's first few television performances, there were hints that dancing *was* a part of his performance style; before long, it became the focal point and earned him his nickname, "the Pelvis." Thus, while I do not mean to suggest that Elvis's relationship to dance was as deep or intentional as were those of the Nicholases and Kelly, it is important to understand how Presley, too, *used* dance during his screen performances to the extent that it became integral to his star persona. Like his singing style, his bodily movements repackaged Black vernacular culture for white consumers in a manner reminiscent of the jazz dance crazes of the 1900s–1920s. Specifically, Presley brings to television what dance scholar Thomas DeFrantz describes as the "extravagant body part isolations, especially in sinewy or sudden motions of the pelvis and spine, and rolling gestures of the torso, shoulders, elbows, and knees in unexpected continual waves or accented, rhythmic jerking" of 1920s Black social dances.[26] This controlled (and later uncontrollable) jerkiness helped to establish the virility of the budding star.

It is also important to remember the televisual context in which Presley first appeared. The existing stable of white male singer-performers who appeared regularly on television in the mid-1950s were middle-class men in suits and ties with short, neatly combed hair. Crooners like Frank Sinatra moved little; slightly more uptempo performers like Perry Como occasionally swung their arms for effect but also stood still. In fact, remarking upon the "casual atmosphere of the 1955 Como," television critic Jack Mabley quipped that "Perry almost relaxed himself right out of the business."[27] In debuting rock 'n' roll on television, Presley disrupted not only the preexisting musical landscape but also the visual landscape: with his up-combed pompadour that often became mussed as he whaled vigorously on his guitar and flapped his leg, he stood out immediately. Though he caused no scandals during his first seven television appearances, his performances already contained the seeds of the blackbodying that would get him into so much trouble (and fame) in June. Thus, though he was not noted for his dancing until the *Milton Berle* performance that opened this chapter, it is important to consider the incipient presence of Black dance elements as he began constructing a screen masculinity even in his first few television performances leading up to the controversy.

On January 28, 1956, Cleveland disc jockey Bill Randle was invited onto *Stage Show* to introduce Elvis Presley to American television audiences: "We think, tonight, that he's going to make television history for you." Randle was not wrong, though he might have expected a grander performance based on his knowledge of Presley's live appearances. Presley performed "Shake, Rattle and Roll" and "I Got a Woman," both originally recorded by African American performers (blues singer "Big" Joe Turner in the former case, and R&B/soul singer Ray Charles in the latter). These songs had been included in Presley's touring sets for at least the past year, when he had performed with considerably more physicality than he displays here in the television studio. What little movement remains in this first televised performance is displayed prominently on one of the three studio cameras, which is positioned for long shots of Presley together with Scotty, Bill, and their new drummer, DJ. During the first song, Presley includes only a single, two-beat dance step. The step itself is just that, a step back toward his band playing behind him, but with a syncopated knee-flapping flourish. His ensuing guitar solo is accompanied by a bit of additional knee shaking—the "jiggling" and "wiggling" described by viewers of his early live performances—but he otherwise gives few hints that his hips are about to become a danger to anyone's sensibilities.

Over the course of the next three February shows, a pattern solidifies: Presley performs two songs, pumping his left leg and/or his left shoulder every now and then. Like the leg flap, the shoulder isolation is an element common to Black social dances from the previous decades. At this juncture, these isolated elements do not necessarily amount to a full-fledged "dance." But by his fifth appearance, on March 17, 1956, Presley becomes emboldened. Instead of the standard shaky leg that had become his television signature at this point, Presley dances more— and rocks harder. During "Blue Suede Shoes," he allows the heavy action of whaling on his guitar to rattle his entire body, such that he physically travels while he plays during the instrumental break. This full-body tremble is precisely what Gottschild refers to as a "watered-down" version of Earl "Snake Hips" Tucker's similar movement. Such movement is quite different from how fellow Sun Records performer Carl Perkins would later perform this song on television—in place of the powerful shake, Perkins employs a bit of mime, enumerating his fingers and pointing to his shoes to act out the lyrics "one for the money/two for the show" and "don't you step on my blue suede shoes," respectively. Like Presley, he also occasionally includes dance elements, but unlike Presley's, they resemble the stiff torso and vertical nature of Europeanist folk dance.

Presley continues to tremble in "Heartbreak Hotel" and adds the additional element of hair choreography.[28] By this point, Presley has clearly discovered that if he pops or heaves his chest forward slightly, his meticulously coiffed hair bounces rhythmically. He uses this to his advantage during the pauses between the opening lyrics of the song. Though this is not necessarily a characteristic of Black dance in itself, it recalls similar hair choreography performed by Cab Calloway, which was especially visible in the 1950 and 1951 Snader Telescriptions that Presley could have seen on television in the early 1950s.[29] In making his hair mobile and ostentatious, Presley again approximates the stylings of Little Richard and performs a physical excessiveness, a vigorousness. He would soon be joined in this tactic by fellow Sun Records recording artist and rock 'n' roller Jerry Lee Lewis. Both men used hair choreography to demonstrate the speed and intensity of their "rocking" and "rolling," and these *are* abiding characteristics of Black dance. Finally, during the "Hound Dog" bridge, Presley inserts what I argue is the first actual dance moment of his television career. After the full-body trembling he repeated from the previous song, Presley isolates his left leg and flaps it four times, along with the final chords of Scotty's electric guitar solo. He keeps his left arm straight and hand in a tense open palm, not unlike Gene Kelly's palm from the palm-fist dichotomy. He responds to the music with deeply bent knees and downward gravity; his arm also enacts a "freeze," such that a stark contrast is created between the rhythmically flapping leg and the still arm. Both are characteristics of Black dance. For his final *Stage Show* appearance on March 24, 1956, Presley experiments with variations on the knee-flapping dance, including a version where *both* legs flap in and out to produce a clear wing dance while he continues playing the guitar (see Figure 3.2). Even in the high-angle shot provided, his body—and crotch in particular—appear as electric as Scotty's guitar. His first "full" wing dance, this is Presley's most legibly Black dance to date, and it televisually establishes a visual brand that would follow him for the rest of his career.

After his string of *Stage Show* appearances, Presley's next onscreen performance occurs in a somewhat different context: an episode of *The Milton Berle Show* set on the U.S.S. Hancock aircraft carrier, docked in San Diego, CA. This April 4, 1956, episode was thus filmed outside rather than in a studio, and was staged as a comedy hour rather than a variety show. The most interesting—and

Figure 3.2 During his final *Stage Show* appearance on March 24, 1956, Presley performs a version of his leg-flapping dance in which both legs wing while he strums his guitar.

telling—element of this performance occurs in the comedy routine that directly follows Presley's songs. Milton Berle enters as Elvis's "twin brother" Melvin and, as part of their banter, Elvis thanks Milton's bumbling fool for teaching him everything he knows. In response, "Melvin" explains, "I did, I taught him his singing style. I used to drop grasshoppers down his pants; that's how he keep jumpin' around." Clearly, Berle's comedic commentary focuses not on Presley's vocal manipulations or genre mixing, but on his "atomic powered" dance moves.[30] The joke both belittles Elvis's strange (i.e., non-white, non-mainstream) dance style and seeks an explanation, falling back on silly fantasy as a reassurance. Then, when Elvis suggests that they sing a song together, Berle's performance to "Blue Suede Shoes" includes immediately breaking his cardboard guitar and dancing around like a clown, as well as thrusting his pelvis at Presley. Bearing in mind the historical connection between "clowning" and blackface minstrelsy, it follows that Berle's exaggeration of Presley's Black dance functions much the same way as minstrelsy did: the exaggeration is a response to his discomfort with Black dance, of which he is both dismissive and envious. The comedy of Berle's hyperbole renders the dance more comfortable. He also seems to be egging Presley on, pushing him to unleash the (sexuality of) Black dance entirely.

Thus, by the spring of 1956, televisual Presley has in just four months progressed from a single knee-flap to a full dance that Milton Berle can mock. He performs elements of Black social dances that can be traced to both the decades prior and the century prior: shoulder isolations, arm freezes, and the "wing" of his legs, as well as more general Africanist aesthetics. Though the gender ambiguities for which he is already well known in his live shows (flashy colored costumes and makeup) are not yet visible, the studio audience's screams when he breaks into his wings and "wiggles" are already audible. The stage is thus set for Presley's intensification of all these elements in the second half of 1956.

122 WHITE SCREENS, BLACK DANCE

Elvis the Pelvis

On the June 5, 1956, broadcast of *The Milton Berle Show* from the studio in Burbank, CA, Presley performs two songs and a brief comedic skit. To open, he debuts his new single "Hound Dog," which he sings without a guitar, instead dancing throughout the entire song. During it, he dances *with* the microphone much as Fred Astaire once danced with a hat rack and Gene Kelly once danced with a broom. This therefore recalls the prop dances of Hollywood musicals; like the Nicholas Brothers' and Gene Kelly's swinging around conveniently placed lamp posts, it can be understood as an act of *bricolage*, that playful tinkering with everyday objects that appears spontaneous but is very much engineered in advance of filming.[31] However, unlike those song-and-dance men from Hollywood musicals, whose props were carefully placed in the space ahead of time with the specific intention of their being used for the dance, Presley's microphone stand is a practical tool for his musical performance. Thus, unlike the materials of traditional Hollywood bricolage, the microphone stand *is* as incidental to the dance as it appears to be. Still, Presley's use of his microphone here and his guitar elsewhere as stand-ins for human bodies—recall Luman's description of Presley's dancing "like he had a thing for his guitar" in a Texas show—do similar gender performance work as those similar props in musicals. That he dances an implied heterosexual pairing, most often without a partner (the notable exception is *Viva Las Vegas*, to be discussed below), helps Presley to perform the concept of sexuality itself.

It is important to note that Presley's dancing repertoire here has clearly advanced beyond his previous onscreen experiments: this time, he dances *throughout* the song, maintaining a low center of gravity and a wide stance. He constantly shifts his weight and breaks into sudden bursts of high-energy steps and leg flaps, accentuated by several freezes. This includes the first onscreen instance of what would become a signature Presley move—a freeze up on his toes. Different body parts seem to be moving to the sounds of different instruments at different times (e.g., arms follow the guitar, legs follow the drums), and he adds a "jazz hand" descended from Black social dance and made famous by the Charleston. He also falls into a deep lunge not unlike the splits Chuck Berry often used in his performances. Finally, he concludes by nonchalantly flipping his hair out of his face. This sustained recombination of Black social dances and the grammars of Black expressive movement more generally, unexpectedly erupting from Presley's white body, begin to overshadow the music itself.

These elements are emphasized once again in Berle's imitation, which is frenzied and chaotic, unlike Presley's controlled balance of contrasts. Indeed, in his attempt to move his knees like Presley, Berle's shoes dislodge from his feet and he falls over. Once he stands upright again and a curtain closes to separate Berle and

Presley from the rest of the band, Berle—still in awe—comments on Presley's moves: "I wanna tell you, that beat with your foot is absolutely sensational." But this is reductive; it is not merely Presley's beat with his foot that marks him as doing something quite different from, say, Carl Perkins—who himself often tapped his foot while performing—indeed, Berle's frenzied imitation itself demonstrated that Presley was marking the beat(s) with his whole body. Berle then addresses the second most important element of Presley's performance: his hair. He wants to know what products—pomades, creams, tonics, oils—Presley uses to achieve such an unusual (for most mainstream white audiences) effect. "What do you do with your hair? What, Toni? Do you use—" Presley answers, "Prom!" Both products were marketed to women (not men) in the 1950s, so the joke is well received amongst the primarily female audience. To further emphasize his interest in and attraction to Presley's unusual hair style, Berle literally plays with Presley's hair as they chat. This particular kind of intimacy brings into sharp relief the gender indeterminacy that is crucial to Elvis' star persona; particularly from a white perspective, Presley's careful attention to his highly artificial, pompadour-like hair style and flamboyant dress—both on clear display in this episode—mark him as non-normative or even effeminate. But it is the fact that this flamboyant body performs Black dance—with its vigorousness, mobile hips, and general air of coolness—that allows Presley's performance to nevertheless be read within the confines of heterosexual expectation by female fans.

Within the arc of this episode, this reassurance appears immediately after the discussion of his hair; when Debra Paget (who played Presley's wife in his recently released film *Love Me Tender*) is invited on stage, she screams, tears at, and kisses Presley. Berle asks Presley how he feels about this, and he rolls his pelvis suggestively as he steadies himself on Berle's shoulder and replies, "Cool, man, cool." In case the heterosexuality of Presley's dance was still in question, his pelvis reassures us that he is desirous of Paget, and his verbal response insists that he is nevertheless keeping his "cool." But this pelvic gesture, arguably more vulgar than the dance it references since it is directed at a woman, also reveals the mechanism according to which Presley's blackbodying dance signifies here: by gyrating his legs and freezing up on his toes, Presley centers the viewer's gaze and perception of him on his penis. In styling himself after Black men, he also takes advantage of white cultural fantasies about Black men as hypersexual. As cultural studies scholar and historian Kobena Mercer reminds us, "black men are confined and defined in their very *being* as sexual and nothing but sexual, hence hypersexual."[32] The result is a particular kind of white paranoia first articulated by the deeply influential cultural theorist Frantz Fanon: "[O]ne is no longer aware of the Negro but only of a penis; the Negro is eclipsed. He is turned into a penis. He *is* a penis."[33] By exaggerating his pelvic thrusts, Presley makes himself into a penis, sex on legs, consummate virility. This is his brand of rebellion

124 WHITE SCREENS, BLACK DANCE

against the middle class, and therefore the seed of their outrage: his genitals are symbolically on parade. After Presley leaves to prepare for his next song, Berle feigns confusion about the frenzy caused by Presley's penis: "I don't know what they see in him . . . I can sing as well as he can! If I were only bow-legged! Debra, I can't understand why all the girls—he's number one across the country—why do they go for him?" Debra explains precisely why, herself centering his pelvis and his aesthetic of "cool": "Why Milton, he's young and handsome and sexy and virile . . . and well, he's the hippest!" Paget thus makes it clear that Presley's penis-centric dance reads as "sexy" and "virile" in the eyes of young white females.

We now return to some of the quotations from 1950s white male critics I used to open this chapter: for Jack Gould, this performance was tantamount to a burlesque performer's "hootchy kootchy;" for Ben Singer it was "suggestive and vulgar . . . animalism." Of course, the generational and gendered divide between Paget's "sexy and virile" and Singer's "suggestive and vulgar" is all but obvious. But Gould's contention that Presley reads as a (presumably female) burlesque dancer nevertheless gets at the gender ambiguity of his corporeal presentation. Indeed, in these critics' cultural imaginary, men do not put such effort into dying and styling their hair, nor do they draw attention to their sexual availability via dance; women do. But Presley's combined blackbodying and pelvic focus are also vulgar because they call up associations with "the big black prick."[34] Part of the fear, then, points to what Jongintaba labeled the "black sexualities" aspect of the dance: the danced miscegenation Presley performs with his hips is much closer (physiologically speaking) to *actual* miscegenation than the performance by his vocal cords—and this is why they are so dangerous in the eyes of white reviewers in 1956. For context, Presley danced "Hound Dog" smack in the middle of the Montgomery Bus Boycott sparked by Rosa Parks—on the very same day that he appeared on *Milton Berle*, a federal court ruled bus segregation unconstitutional. Thus, national headlines about the Boycott and entertainment section headlines about Presley exposed the same white American fears of racial mixing, just in different terms.

Despite critics' protests, Presley appeared on *The Steve Allen Show* a month later, on July 1, 1956. His continued presence was largely due to what *Variety* called the "rat race for ratings;" Presley's appearances, especially the more controversial ones, outrated any programming they were up against in a shared time slot.[35] Indeed, Allen gives a nod to Presley's controversial reception the month before when he introduces his guest:

A couple of weeks ago, on *The Milton Berle Show*, our next guest, Elvis Presley, received a great deal of attention, which some people seemed to interpret one way and some viewers interpreted another. Naturally, it's our intention to do nothing but a good show . . . We want to do a show the whole family can watch and enjoy and we always do. And tonight we are presenting Elvis Presley in his—haha, what you might call his first comeback, and at this time it gives me extreme pleasure to introduce the *new* Elvis Presley, and here he is!

Of particular note here is Allen's insistence that his is and has always been a *family-friendly* show and that he intends to both retain that descriptor *and* bring Elvis Presley on as a guest. The solution he offers to this seeming paradox is the suggestion that, in this first "comeback"—a word that would be associated with Presley much more heavily in 1968—Presley will appear somehow "new," re-formed, and tame. In other words, no more "animalistic" Black dance. Writing for the *Daily Boston Globe* the day after Presley's appearance on Allen's show, critic Mary Cremmen notes that the reference to a comeback "proved to be a strange choice of words. His appearance looked more in the nature of a go-away-from."[36] Indeed, the producers of the show ensured that the young man also *dress* the part of the reformed, as Presley appears in a tuxedo and white gloves. He is accompanied by a swell of orchestral music and bows upon arrival. He also carries a top hat, which he does not wear but holds just long enough to pointedly wipe his nose on it and hand it to Allen; this was no doubt staged to emphasize that this working-class boy from Tupelo does not belong in a Nicholas Brothers ensemble. A demure Presley thanks both the fans and Mr. Allen, after which he sings "I Want You, I Need You, I Love You" while wearing his guitar, but he neither plays it nor really moves at all—it is as if the guitar is intended to shield his pelvis from view even as it refrains from gyrating.

This performance is followed by a rendition of "Hound Dog" that reads as both irony and punishment: Allen brings out a basset hound, to whom Presley directs the entire song. Throwing knowing looks toward the in-studio audience and grabbing the dog's face to look it in the eyes, Presley seems to be sharing a joke with his teenage fans. Meanwhile, the filming of the performance takes no risks, either; at several points, it appears that Presley is in fact still including some of his leg-shaking antics, but most of the song is filmed in a medium shot so nothing below Presley's waist is generally visible. What he develops because of all this punishment is a different kind of rapport with his audience, a winkingness that was absent before. The remainder of his television appearances after this point all arguably contain a certain self-censorship that refers back to this moment, when at least some portion of the dance is replaced with a grin over the shared joke: he seems to be saying, "I can't do it here, but you all know I'll keep doing it elsewhere."

The perhaps unexpected outcome of this rather castrated performance was that Allen's show that evening received excellent ratings. So excellent, in fact, that it recorded *more* viewers than its time slot competitor *The Ed Sullivan Show*, an unprecedented achievement for Allen.[37] As a result, Sullivan reversed

126 WHITE SCREENS, BLACK DANCE

his position on Presley—he had previously vowed never to have the vulgar young man on his show, but after this ratings loss, he reversed his position and contracted Presley for three-appearances. In reporting this development, the media attempted to describe Presley's trajectory with clinically descriptive language. In the *Chicago Daily Tribune*, Presley's controversial *Berle* dance was termed "interpretative action" that was then "subdued" on *Allen*.[38] And, according to *The New York Times*,

> Mr. Presley became the center of controversy after his appearance last month on Milton Berle's show, also on N.B.C.-TV last month. The use of bodily contortions in projecting his tunes was considered to be in bad taste by some critics and a number of viewers. However, his appearance on the Allen show was relatively placid, to the satisfaction of critics and the discontent of his admirers.[39]

The descriptors of his reform—"placid" and "subdued"—bring to mind a rabid rodent more than a popular performer, though this does seem to be in line with Gross's original claim of "animalism." Teenage fans' disappointment at the *Steve Allen* performance uses language similarly appropriate to an animal: "Gee, it was awful, they had him tied down in a tuxedo and wouldn't let him move. One time when it looked like he was going to dance, it appeared that someone off camera made him stop. They've ruined Elvis."[40] What is particularly interesting in the reporters' chosen copy is their avoidance of the more practical and economical term "dance," used naturally by the teenage fan. Instead, Presley's originally offending practice is termed "interpretative action" and "bodily contortions" as if his dance is more foreign than Martha Graham's, more impossible than a circus performer's. All of this is to say that a blackbodying Presley, though foreign and threatening to white power structures, was closely watched and therefore commercially desirable. After less than a year of television performances, his solid and citable star persona is monetizing the transgression that would end any Black performer's career in a heartbeat.

Presley's three performances for *The Ed Sullivan Show* were famously partially censored by the camera operators. He seems to anticipate this and begins to experiment with forms of facial emphasis such as raising his eyebrows and crossing his eyes during his September 9 rendition of "Don't Be Cruel," replacing provocative dances with reactionary faces that seem to stand in for his would-be pelvic transgressions. He is afforded occasional full-body shots, for which he indulges in some light leg-jiggling, but when he begins to dance in earnest during the second half of that first episode, there is clearly an intentional reliance on an unwavering medium close-up shot. For most viewers, it is probably clear here that he is doing a great deal with his lower body during these shots, since

Figure 3.3 Though the cameras grant Presley long shots at other points during his September 9, 1956 performance on *The Ed Sullivan Show*, they do cut him off below the chest when he most obviously launches into a dance sequence; only the efforts of his upper body are visible as a result.

his upper body betrays a combination of intense concentration and the facial choreographies of the previous songs, and he temporarily tosses aside his guitar as he usually does when he dances while wearing it (see Figure 3.3). In her review of Presley's performance for *The Daily Boston Globe* the following day, Mary Cremmen reports that "the cameras gyrated more than he did" for "Don't Be Cruel" and that "the cameramen had obviously given up trying to find discreet angles" by the time Presley began "Hound Dog," so "[t]hey showed him from the shoulders up and let it go at that."[41]

It is crucial to keep in mind that Presley continued touring the country for live performances in between his appearances on *The Ed Sullivan Show*—so young people in most major cities were either seeing or hearing about the uncensored version of Presley's dance moves live on stage. Perhaps this has something to do with the fact that his second *Ed Sullivan* show performance, on October 28, 1956, appears to be fairly uncensored. Indeed, when he performs "Hound Dog" and once again brings out his "gyrations," the camerawork this time does not obscure them. But at this point, after so much press about his pelvis, Presley is quite self-aware, so he begins to contrast his frenzied dance moves with a faux-casual binary opposite: calmly crossed legs (Figure 3.4).

Afterwards, when Ed Sullivan arrives and shakes Presley's hand, Presley decides to highlight his freedom from censorship: he first looks over at Sullivan, breaks into his frenzied dance again for a moment, and then returns to normal, calm and grinning. Of course, this is accompanied by screams from the in-studio audience. Here again, Presley is at peak cool: he just got away with his "vulgar" Black dance, having bounced back from censorship, on an extremely well-paid and widely viewed episode of *The Ed Sullivan Show*. And then, a newly "respectable" young white man shakes the hand of the very powerful "Master of Variety," shifts his weight with a certain rebellious swagger that betrays his working-class

Figure 3.4 Highlighting the frenetic energy of his uncensored dance on the October 28, 1956 episode of *The Ed Sullivan Show*, Presley follows his intense dance moves (left) with a faux-casual pose in opposition (right).

background, and immediately moves into a snippet of African American vernacular movement before switching back into "respectable" mode again. It is also worth noting that, while this is among Presley's more masculine and subdued performance outfits, he is nevertheless sporting noticeable eyeliner throughout the episode. Thus, Presley's symbolism as a transgressive "violation" of race/class/gender norms and boundaries is already thoroughly woven into his televisual performance by the tenth month of his screen career.

Presley's final *Ed Sullivan* guest spot on January 6, 1957—his last television appearance until his return from the Army in 1960—was his most flamboyantly costumed. In addition to continued eyeliner, Presley wears a blue velvet blouse with a glittery gold lamé vest. But it was also his most sterilized; the audience did not even see a glimpse of Presley's pants until he prepared to exit the stage after his show was over. As before, there is a great deal of upper body evidence that his lower body is moving, but the cameras never stray from their three positions: medium close-up, close-up, and a cutaway to a shot of the electric guitar for the solos during which Presley would have been dancing most. Indeed, at the end of "Don't Be Cruel," Presley even explicitly marks the breakout dance section by verbally announcing, "here we go!" before dancing vigorously—at-home viewers only saw vigorous arm movements and hair choreography but could have easily deduced that there was more off-camera.

In his biography of Presley, music historian and critic Peter Guralnick suggests that this entire performance of the song, especially its "pumped up ending," can be attributed to Presley's experience seeing a young Jackie Wilson—then merely the lead singer of Billy Ward and his Dominoes—perform his song in Las Vegas.[42] Based on Presley's recollection of the Vegas performance as recorded in his December 4, 1956 jam session with Jerry Lee Lewis and others, in which Presley explicitly demonstrated how Wilson played the song, this is entirely plausible.

In the recording, Presley held that, while Wilson did not render "Hound Dog" very well, Wilson's version of "Don't Be Cruel" was in fact *better* than his own, and when he described Wilson's own elaborate dance for it, he admitted that he did not think himself capable of executing the footwork himself.[43] He explains, "[a]nd he had his feet turned in like this, and all the time he was singin,' them feet was goin' in and out, both ways, slidin' . . . I can't do that one." Yet, Presley does seem to be channeling Wilson with his vigorous final moments in that last *Ed Sullivan* appearance; the arm movements that are visible look nothing like previous Presleyan efforts. Though there are some direct resemblances here, Presley's overall dances originated not directly from a single individual, but from a long history of experiencing Black music and dance. Indeed, Presley's visual similarities to Jackie Wilson and Bo Diddley, like his visual similarities to Little Richard and Chuck Berry, come together as evidence not of Presley copying just one individual, but of "how much a composite of African American culture Presley was."[44] Thus, Presley's entire look, beginning but not ending with his movement vocabulary, was an act of blackbodying. Within the context of his larger career trajectory, this "Pelvis" period of Presley's breakout year on television also set expectations for his corporeality in cinema. For, over the course of the year, Presley developed a combination of Black social dance gestures (the leg flap/wing, the isolated shoulders and chest, the jazz hands) and aesthetics (the low center of gravity, the ephebism, the "cool") that set the stage for constructing a "bad boy" masculinity in his first few films.

A Bad Boy in Rock 'n' Roll Musicals

When Elvis Presley entered the Hollywood filmscape, classical Hollywood musicals were still doing fairly well in theaters, but with their aging song-and-dance men (Gene Kelly was forty-five) they were not necessarily appealing to the emergent teenage market. Though many of Presley's films lacked the high production values of classical musicals, he nevertheless performed dance numbers in many of them. These numbers, especially those in his pre-Army films, do not work through the heterosexual coupling as did many classical Hollywood musical duets (à la Fred and Ginger), but rather find more similarity to Gene Kelly's solo numbers; film scholar Rick Altman aptly described these numbers as containing "not a Gene Kelly *making love*, but a Gene Kelly *showing off*."[45] In similar fashion, though Presley's characters often succeed in wooing female partners with minimal effort, their dances are often more interested in showing off than securing their mates. Presley generally plays some version of himself— a lower class Southerner, a hip-swaying performance prodigy—but especially in the pre-Army films, these characters are more overtly *bad* (and "baaaad," as

130 WHITE SCREENS, BLACK DANCE

Gottschild describes the few whites who would dare to imitate Blacks) than mild-mannered Presley himself.[46] Thus, his otherwise transgressive, gender ambiguous performances (with their hair choreography, eyeliner, tight clothes, etc.) are carefully realigned with normative masculinity by fistfights. But, unlike on television, he is nearly always framed at least partially in long shot when he performs, so his full body is on display—uncensored. And thanks to the narrative universes provided by the cinema, Presley is free to dance in contexts quite different from the television studio. It is in these more fantastical contexts that, like Gene Kelly before him, Presley finds more fodder with which to play with masculinity and experiment with the Black vernacular dances that he was helping to spread via teen dance crazes across the nation.

In *Loving You* (1957), Presley plays a small-town orphan who begins performing throughout the South and accidentally becomes an overnight sensation, even scoring regional television coverage by the end of the film. Presley's diegetic stage performances in *Loving You* often include full-body shots of his onstage dancing interspersed with reverse shots of giddy female teenage audience members, a formulation that mirrors his previous television appearances. However, the film also transports his character's stage act into the everyday scene of a restaurant and includes an extended final performance (being filmed for television within the diegesis) in which Presley dances among his audience. By 1957, the extremity of Presley's fame and fans would have made both scenes an impossibility in real life, but they nevertheless functioned as a fictionalization of the Elvis Presley story and helped to build a narrative context for his particular brand of masculinity.

A little less than halfway through the film, Presley's Deke Rivers prepares to play his first big city show in Amarillo, Texas. As he and a bandmate eat in a local restaurant, a teenage girl recognizes him and announces her desire to hear him sing. Her greaser boyfriend pressures him to do so, nearly starting a fight in the process; to prevent a disturbance and to appease the elderly manager, Presley's Rivers begrudgingly agrees to sing. He pops a nickel into the jukebox—somehow able to choose the instrumental version of a rock 'n' roll tune—but he does far more than simply sing along to it. Surrounded by gleeful fellow white patrons, Presley dances between tables as he sings and claps to "Mean Woman Blues." With more freedom than television studio cameras, the film cuts between multiple distances and vantage points to render his movements maximally visible and dynamic. Indeed, as Presley moves down the aisle of sorts, zig-zagging toward the camera, it dollies back as well and offers close-ups of his hair choreography and supplementary side views. On a surface level, with the camera taking up the vantage point of a bystander, the enthralling magic of Presley's dancing is made intimately available to the film audience. But the scene carries more significance when considered in its narrative context: Presley imports Black music and dance into a thoroughly white Southern establishment. And as usual, his combined sonic—and especially bodily—transgressions here are what excite the white teenage audience, especially the women, surrounding him. In fact, his physicality here is played up before the dance even begins; his excited blonde fan describes him as "the one with the jumpin' beans in his jeans."

But, in case the diegetic and/or non-diegetic audience should mistake this song and dance as a mark of feminine spectacle, it immediately transitions into a confrontation-turned-fistfight. Having been convinced to labor "for free," Rivers asks the greaser boyfriend for free labor in his own field (automobile maintenance). After he responds that Rivers' preferred upholstery color must be "yellow" (the color of cowards), Rivers pulls him up by the collar and the two begin a fistfight—which our hero wins, of course. The blonde girlfriend seems to enjoy the spectacle, but the restaurant manager calls the police. At the risk of stating the obvious, I understand this (obviously choreographed) fight as a pointed extension of the dance that preceded it. The greaser boyfriend no doubt noticed that Rivers' mobile hips, legs, and shoulders were winning over every young woman in the room, including his own girlfriend, so his jealous response is to challenge the performer. This then offers Rivers the opportunity to prove his masculinity the old-fashioned way: a duel of strength. Especially considering both Presley's actual and Rivers' fictional working-class background, winning a fistfight against an auto mechanic reassured all viewers that Presley is no bur-lesque dancer (as the critics would have it), but rather the virile, sexy young man that young Debra Paget described to Milton Berle. What makes the virility and sexiness legible here is a combination of class markers (accent, behavior, occu-pational background) and racial/cultural markers (vocal style, rhythm, dance moves). In this way, the scene is reminiscent of some of Gene Kelly's roles and performances. The emphasis on Presley's white working class positioning and willingness to enter into fistfights is a common reassurance of masculinity across his next two films as well.

The final "number" in *Loving You* refers even more directly to Presley's own life. Having just run away from a scheduled television performance after feeling overwhelmed by his sudden fame and fortune—and betrayed by his manager—Deke Rivers reappears just in the nick of time to sing for all of America. The broadcast was devised as a remedy for Rivers' canceled sold-out show in Freegate, Texas, where local parents claimed he was a bad influence who led teenagers to-ward bad behavior. So when he eventually appears in all denim, rather than the colorful, fancy western garb he had been convinced to wear for many of his pre-vious performances, and opens with the titular ballad, "Loving You," it seems as though he has bowed to the mothers and demonstrated his "true self" to be a harmless young country boy who sings heartfelt slow songs. But Rivers follows up with a provocative full-body performance of "Got a Lot o' Livin' to Do," which is interspersed with reverse shots of the local mothers whose initial disapproval melts into enjoyment of his dancing. The conversion of one particular mother over the course of "Got a Lot o' Livin' to Do" serves as both prescription and description for actual 1950s mothers. That Deke Rivers' harshest critic melts into admiration as she watches The Pelvis in action implies that he really is just a simple, charismatic country boy that any woman—especially a mother—cannot help but love. The irony, of course, is that this "charisma" clearly exudes precisely from that pelvis, this time tightly clothed in slim-fitting blue jeans and mesmerizingly mobile (see Figure 3.5). Thus, it is the danced expression of a sexuality that appeals to women of all ages which marks Presley's masculinity—a sexuality once again borrowed from Black dance movements and aesthetics. He performs Africanist leg-flapping, pelvic thrusts, and shoulder shimmies with bedroom eyes aimed at white women of every age. When he jumps down into an aisle, he nearly sashays from fan to fan. He even completes the number with tempo-slowing steps that once again highlight the conflict between fast and slow, and repeatedly emphasize his pelvis. With perhaps his most dramatic blackbodying since "Hound Dog" on *Milton Berle*, Presley as Rivers cements himself as a male sexpot who eventually receives a "pass" for voluminous pelvic thrusts thanks to his Southern *white* background, which allows white mothers to forgive the lewd gestures since his attention flatters and titillates them as much as their daughters.

The most acclaimed film of Presley's career, *Jailhouse Rock*, was released just months after *Loving You*, in November of 1957. Critics at the time were generally unimpressed; a representative review by Mae Tinee in the *Chicago Daily Tribune* was entitled "Elvis Rocks but Movie Stands Still" and Paul Jones declared in the *Atlanta Constitution* that "[t]he film won't win any awards."[47] Nevertheless, the film did quite well in the box office, breaking records across the South.[48] This time, Presley's masculinity is at its most insistently macho of

Figure 3.5 Presley's "charm" during "Got a Lot o' Livin' to Do" in *Loving You* (1957) consists primarily of a danced demonstration of sexuality; to complete the number, Presley performs tempo-changing dance moves that particularly focus on his pelvis.

his career: the film opens with Presley killing a man in a bar fight. After serving his time in jail alongside an experienced country singer (Mickey Shaughnessy), Presley's Vince Everett strikes out on his own, seeking fame in the music business. Unlike Presley, Everett remains violent, rude, and uncouth, but like Presley, he wins the hearts of teenagers—especially young girls—across the country, eventually landing a Hollywood movie contract. Similar to *Loving You*, *Jailhouse Rock*'s standout scenes occur toward the end, when NBC invites Everett for a "nationwide television extravaganza" and when he performs at a pool party he throws to celebrate his Hollywood success. The television extravaganza number is "Jailhouse Rock," Presley's most elaborate dance performance of his film career, and one that brings the tensions and transgressions between masculinity and femininity, Black and white, into sharp relief.

The scene has Everett performing the film's titular song on a sparse television set mimicking a jail, accompanied by about a dozen white fellow "inmates." As the camera moves in, passing the diegetic television cameras pointed at the set, Everett breaks into song and his fellow jailbirds become his backup dancers. Choreographer Alex Romero, who already had a bit of experience choreographing rock 'n' roll numbers despite the newness of the genre, said that he tried to develop a unique spectacle that would be consistent with the personal style that Presley had already exhibited on television.[49] The result of this awareness and intentionality on Romero's part is that Presley continues to earn his "pelvis" nickname, as he draws explicit focus to the mobility of his hips even more than he had before receiving choreographic direction. One means of achieving this emphasis is the placement of his hands on his pelvis, which draws the viewer's eyes to it as it pops forward and backward again (see Figure 3.6). He continues to use this strategy throughout the number and then

Figure 3.6 In *Jailhouse Rock* (1957), Presley places his hands on his pelvis as he moves it forward and back, drawing the viewer's eye toward it.

in other scenes elsewhere in the film, such as one of the recording studio sessions. No longer primarily knee-driven, the pelvic dance steps involved here also move Presley/Everett around a larger space than previous numbers or television appearances. As opposed to the smaller, accentuating movements that had previously accompanied guitar solos and microphone stands, this more complete and formally choreographed dance number has Presley traveling dynamically throughout the diegetic television studio, surrounded by and interacting with a variety of backup dancers. Thus, in *Jailhouse Rock* he not only gets away with the Africanist pelvic isolation and mobility that got him in trouble on television, but also receives professional choreographic assistance in further exaggerating it.

But within the film's narrative context, Presley's dances are passed off as exclusively white cultural products. Film scholar David James points out that "[i]n both [*Loving You* and *Jailhouse Rock*], Presley emerges from entirely white social and musical milieus . . . the African-American components of his music and his persona appear as his sheerly idiosyncratic genius, the quality of pure Elvisness." By erasing any trace of the Black influences on Elvis's stylization, both films distance themselves from the earlier fears about racial miscegenation and instead "reassure audiences that he and his music are racially immaculate."[50] The same distancing and reassurance are applied to Presley's bodily movements in the film: its diegesis presents his dancing as Everett's/Presley's individual genius (despite technically being the concoction of choreographer Alex Romero). Of course, in reality, Presley's movements are an inheritance from the dances that originally accompanied the very African American rhythms that inspired his music.

The most immediate effect of these particularly mobile hips and the long duration of their movement, especially given the presence of backup dancers, is the resultant sense of spectacle normally associated with more traditional Hollywood musical films. Presley's character also fulfills some of the accusations levied at him by scandalized television critics: during the number, he dances on a pole and a table, both of which are more properly the domain of the "burlesque" dancers to whom his critics compared him. Indeed, film scholar Brett Farmer has pointed to these "orgasmic gyrations" as an instance of "spectacular eroticization, if not homoeroticization, of the male image that is quite unusual in mainstream cinema."[51] He also likens the performance to many of the Gene Kelly dances that I discussed in Chapter 2, ones that Steven Cohan highlighted for their feminization (via spectacle) of the male dancing body. Especially given the jailhouse's homosocial context, this is a valid reading. But importantly, like Kelly's, Presley's body is reinscribed into the confines of normative (presumed heterosexual) masculinity in other physical ways. Where it was athleticism in Kelly's case, here it is the bar fight and murder, which sent Everett to jail in the first place, that reassure us of Presley's conventional working-class masculinity.

Overall, Presley's multiple transgressions, in which the sturdy borders of masculinity become porous to feminine spectacle and assured whiteness actually embodies Blackness, crystalize clearly in the dances of *Jailhouse Rock*.

Elvis's performances in *King Creole* (1958), while less effeminate and spectacular than his main dance number in *Jailhouse Rock*, are more clearly racially transgressive than perhaps any other of his film performances. As James has noted, *King Creole* not only has Presley singing Black music and dancing Black dance as usual, but also quietly "acknowledges Elvis's debt to African American culture":

> His act in the King Creole is introduced by a nightclub dancer whose banana props resemble Josephine Baker's . . . black musicians back him on "Trouble;" and for his introductory number immediately following the credits, Elvis sings "Crawfish." One of his most supple performances, it is a call and response blues duet performed with the marvelous (but uncredited) black jazz singer Kitty White . . . [T]he duet with White is the sole hint of personal association with an African American—let alone a romantic relationship—with a black woman in any of his feature films, and the only dramatization of Elvis's musical indebtedness to the black working class.[52]

Fittingly, perhaps, Presley's only number with sustained dancing is, in fact, "Trouble." In context, Presley is called upon by a nightclub manager (where his character, Danny Fisher, is employed as a bus boy) to jump up on the stage and prove he can sing. His embodied rendition of the song reads rather clearly as Black dance, in no small part because he is, as James mentions, backed by an all-Black brass band and singing rhythm and blues. Moreover, the central physical trope he uses in this context is the jerky isolation, common to earlier Black social dances. These isolations can be seen most clearly in a sequence during which he holds out a limp wrist and pops his pelvis forward and back, and then when he isolates a shoulder, elbow, and wrist successively to match the rhythm of a cowbell being tapped.[53] Even as the circumstantial emphasis is on the racial markers of the number, his aforementioned limp wrist during the isolations is notable, as it was fast becoming synonymous in popular culture of the time with effeminate, queer, even transvestite or transsexual identity formations. In other words, the hand placement is transgressive in terms of gender/sexuality at the same time as the hips and other body isolations, together with the singing style, are racially transgressive. And yet, Presley is singing about how he is "trouble" and his character will be throwing punches—rather than wrists—in mere minutes.

This association between Presley and fighting during this brief pre-Army cinematic period is similar to Gene Kelly's masculinizing strategy at the same time (on his 1958 special "Dancing, A Man's Game") of incorporating a fight into his

136 WHITE SCREENS, BLACK DANCE

final piece of choreography. Indeed, if dancing and fighting are associated at midcentury with femininity and masculinity respectively, it is no wonder both men combined the two on screen. In Presley's case, his clear reverence for James Dean-style rebellion even before he arrived in Hollywood allowed for a fairly seamless transition from censored *Ed Sullivan* performer to fistfighting rags-to-riches characters in cinema. But as Presley matured and "Colonel" Parker accelerated the pace of his film contracts after his Army service, this particular mark of masculinity would be left behind. The Black social dance steps that Presley had been able to enhance under the choreographic tutelage of Alex Romero would, with help from makeup and new, skimpy outfits, continue to signify ambiguously on Presley's spectacular body, even as he adapted them to fit a new cultural moment.

Army Aftermath: The Twists

Elvis Presley was drafted on December 20, 1957, about a month before shooting for *King Creole* was set to begin. After he was granted a deferment to complete the film, Presley was inducted on March 24, 1958—several months before the film was to be released. After training at Fort Hood in Texas, he was assigned to the 3rd Armored Division in Friedberg, West Germany. Presley remained in Germany from 1958–1960. His manager, "Colonel" Parker, declined to have him inducted into the special services unit, where the U.S. government would have dispatched Presley as entertainment for the troops and therefore profited from Presley's performance capital. Instead, Presley became a regular soldier, under strict instructions not to publicly perform or record while enlisted.[54] During this period, the U.S. Army used Elvis as an ideological symbol for West Germans who were uneasy about the American military presence there. German youth (of both East *and* West Germany) had experienced an Elvis craze not unlike the one that had transpired in the United States, so he carried a great deal of meaning by simply being present.[55] As military historian Brian McAllister Linn writes in *Elvis's Army: Cold War GIs and the Atomic Battlefield*, "across much of the world, GIs became public agents of Cold War Americanism, teaching young people their slang, fashions, music, and attitudes, to the great distress of both parents and the communists."[56] Importantly, however, his positioning as just another regular, hardworking soldier did just as much ideological work for *Americans* as it did for Germans. Presley not only took photos with West German female fans and posed at West German memorials, but also shaved off his sideburns and was photographed working hard at maneuvers along with the rest of the soldiers.

The story the U.S. military was able to tell about Presley was one of transformation—with a little discipline, the Army could turn even the biggest

ELVIS PRESLEY   137

troublemakers into good, brave men. As a "regular" person for the first time in five years, Presley was subjected to the same rules as everyone else, receiving no special treatment. Of course, he did live differently when not on duty; rather than living on-post with the rest of the men, he resided in a series of hotels with his family and small entourage. Guralnick has described in detail how Presley entertained young German girls, jammed with buddies, and embraced amphetamines to stay awake, energetic, and alert. Still, despite all this, when Presley's performance blackout ended with the completion of his Army service, the media portrayed him as a changed, tamer man. As *New York Times* critic Bosley Crowther put it, "Whatever else the Army has done for Elvis Presley, it has taken that indecent swivel out of his hips and turned him into a good, clean, trustworthy, upstanding American man."[57] This 1960 article's subtitle was "Elvis—A Reformed Wriggler." But these judgments (including Crowther's, which was made within the context of a film review) seemed to be largely based upon a single film, Presley's first post-Army appearance as the star of *G.I. Blues* (1960). In Linn's reading, "*G.I. Blues* jettisoned the rebellious rock-and-roller of Presley's early movies, and left most of the gyrating to his co-star, Juliet Prowse. Guided by copious comments from the U.S. Army editors, the film portrayed soldiering in idyllic terms."[58] Key here is the role of Army editors, who were themselves shaping Presley into pro-Army propaganda. Indeed, for Linn, "Presley's metamorphosis illustrates the Army's belief, shared by much of the American public, that military service was a path to individual reformation."[59] The only flaw in these readings of a "reformed" Presley is that the "indecent swivel" Crowther mentions is not entirely absent after all.

While it is true that many of Presley's songs in *G.I. Blues* are sung while sitting, or to a baby, or with a puppet, he did find a few opportunities to swing his hips, draw the viewer's eye to his infamous pelvis, and bring back his old winking antics from previous experiences of censorship. Indeed, when he performs the film's titular number as Specialist Tulsa McLean, Presley takes the opportunity presented by the military theme to march in such a way as to swing his hips while doing so (see Figure 3.7). This style of marching is quite distinct from the more traditional military style of marching he employs in the film's final, much tamer number. It is clear that Presley is meant to represent a good, wholesome (reformed) American boy in this final number, as evidenced by its opening shot in which he stands proudly before the American flag. This is definitely the "reformed wriggler" Crowther fondly remembers, but it is mere happenstance that he overshadows the hip-swinger from earlier in the film. To say that Presley is a completely changed, no longer dangerous performer is to see only selectively; Presley's sonic and corporeal indebtedness to African American rhythms remains intact.

138 WHITE SCREENS, BLACK DANCE

Figure 3.7 As Specialist Tulsa McLean in *G.I. Blues* (1960), Presley performs a military-style dance to the titular song in which he swings his hips while marching in place.

Elsewhere in the film, Presley's mini-choreographies recall the tropes of his televisual censorship days. He uses a hand to playfully "stop" a wiggling leg while he plays a song on a train to Frankfurt, standing open-legged as young Fräuleins try to look on. He pops and shimmies his shoulders and he pulls up his pants in the middle of a later performance, drawing the viewer's eye toward his crotch in a perhaps less obvious way than he had in *Jailhouse Rock*, but drawing the eye nevertheless. He also utilizes a number of facial choreographies—bugged and/or crossed eyes, playful pouts, and so on. This is to say, for much of the film Presley *plays at* "singing straight," which results in a certain queering of these performances as not quite up to Army regulation but *passing* as such. Any seasoned viewer of Presley's on-screen performances would have remembered these antics from television and potentially been cued into the charade of reform—one made perhaps more obvious by his far more risqué performances in *Blue Hawaii* the following year. Thus, beginning with his dances in *G.I. Blues* and extending through the rest of the sixties, Presley sometimes toned down but did not eradicate those swinging hips. At times, he would start the movement to allude to it and then, to tease his audience, fail to complete it. Others, he would pause dramatically at points where audiences might expect a breakout dance move. In general, though, the films were pumped out so quickly that there simply was not time to stage complex performances for any of the numbers; beginning in 1960, Presley starred in two to three films per year every year until 1969. But once a year or so, a Presley film was released that *did* include one or more dance numbers and they were not particularly reformed. It is perhaps most accurate to say that after returning from the Army, Presley's dances simply became less frequent than they had been before he enlisted. Entire films were produced that had Presley singing in many situations—while driving, dining, gathering with family, entertaining children—but never dancing. And yet, this intensive shooting and soundtrack-recording schedule did not entirely prevent the Pelvis from expressing itself.

Blue Hawaii (1961) is the first of three Hawaii-set Presley films, and has him starring as Chad Gates, son of a successful Southern CEO who has just returned from Army service and has no interest in following in his father's footsteps. Instead, he has embraced the ways of Hawaii, with native friends and a "native" girlfriend with whom he loves to enjoy the sand, surf, food, music, and dance opportunities of the islands.[60] Gates' local friends demonstrate equal interest in traditional music, rooted in Polynesian culture, and contemporary American fare; as the house band, they excitedly launch into the song "Rock-a-Hula" at the party Gates' parents throw him. When they beckon Gates to join their performance, Presley sings and dances much like he had before entering the Army. For Hawaiian flavor, he holds flower bouquet coconut maracas as he sings and employs knee-driven hip swings in time with his maraca rhythms.

But after the introductory verse, the dance moves into less familiar territory. His dance's new development in this early 1960s context is the clear influence of the popular dance "the twist," whose origins trace to early African American social dances such as the "mess around" and the "ballin' the jack." The dance's popular spread was the direct result of the rhythm and blues song "The Twist" by Hank Ballard, which was famously covered by Chubby Checker in 1960. The twist's main hallmarks include a fairly wide stance, stationary balls-of-the-feet (or one stationary foot and the other foot raised to its tip-toe), and a constant swiveling or *twist*ing of the rest of the body, with arms often in an armchair formation.[61] Presley had always used a fairly wide stance, particularly when wielding an instrument, as he does here. But this time, his movements are no longer simply knee-driven—as they most often had been during his career—nor even hip-driven—as they sometimes had been in numbers such as "Jailhouse Rock"—but *swivel-driven* like the twist. Moreover, he occasionally lifts a leg off the ground to emphasize his weight change and the grounded swivel of the other, and this is another key characteristic of the twist that had been missing from Presley's previous dance numbers. He does not fully commit to the twist, however; his shoulders remain fairly stationary and anchor his upper body while he places his weight in his heels and swivels his toes and hips, stepping sideways to travel a bit while he does so. In these ways, Presley's dance evolves with the rock 'n' roll zeitgeist (still driven by African American culture) even as it retains continuity with his previous signature moves' stronger focus on body part isolation. Notably, despite the Hawaiian location and content of the song (about a woman's hips as she dances the hula), Presley's hips do *not* mimic the pendulum-like hip movements of this native dance but instead cleave to movements more similar to the popular dance of the time, one which teenagers were avidly embodying on *American Bandstand* and at local dances across the country in the early 1960s. Presley's Gates concludes the dance with a full-body shake and deep bend of the knees in order to transition into a slow kick that leads into his long strides out of the room. His Southern mother (Angela Lansbury) is completely scandalized by the dance, announcing halfway through the number that she is coming down with a "dreadful headache." Thus, any lingering claims that the Army somehow cured Presley of his improper Black dance moves are essentially stifled by her pearl-clutching dialogue.

Later in *Blue Hawaii*, Presley dances with his friends and customers (for whom he serves as a tour guide) by a bonfire on the beach. The setup is reminiscent of *Jailhouse Rock* in that it is a fully staged dance number, wherein Presley leads a group of backup dancers in a clearly choreographed sequence and formation. After singing playfully about his friend Ito's ingestion habits with a pair of drums and a casual hip-swinging circle dance ("Ito Eats"), Presley entreats, "Let's slice some sand!" and leads the group in a speedy jig-like dance as he sings "Slicin' Sand."[62] Because everyone is in beach attire, the eye is drawn to the dancers' legs. Within the group, however, Presley stands out in his white outfit; he is clearly meant to be the center of the spectacle. The group then performs a series of variations on a single theme: swinging hips. Choreographically, the basic structure is similar to a number for showgirls; patterns include step-step-step-kick and syncopated walks in a circle. As the star, Presley also breaks away from the rest for an Africanist solo dance full of pelvic pop-walks and then a dramatic drop to the knees for shoulder shimmies and what appears to be a brief air guitar performance. In both cases, Presley's legs remain spread open and his center of gravity is low. When he rises again, the camera stays low, thus keeping his upper body out of the frame and focusing the viewer's eyes once again on his pelvis and exposed thighs (see Figure 3.8); the shot only ends when Presley kicks sand at the camera and it cuts away. All of this is to say: Presley's dance is undeniably erotic, in part because his tight white bathing suit draws the eye to his

Figure 3.8 As the main focus of the "Slicin' Sand" number in *Blue Hawaii* (1961), Presley performs a pelvic solo dance which includes "crotch shots" that draw the eye to his crotch and upper thighs.

crotch, buttocks, and upper thighs, and in part because his hips move more in isolation than they have since *Jailhouse Rock*.

The "Slicin' Sand" number thus has a great deal in common with Gene Kelly's "Pirate Ballet" from *The Pirate*. Not only are both low-lit, fiery scenes in which our male star breaks away from his backup dancers to strike a wide, dramatic stance, but both also include skimpy colorless costumes that draw the eye to the star's musculature (especially his thighs and buttocks) as he dances. Where normally the camera's desiring gaze would be pointed toward a scantily clad woman dancing—and indeed, there are several dancing behind Presley—it is instead pointed at the (also scantily clad) male dancing body. This is additionally complicated by the fact that, diegetically, the main audience for this performance is Gates' male friend Ito; the low-to-the-ground framing in Figure 3.8 is very nearly his exact point of view. In this way, the same complexities about the gendered and sexual nature of spectacle that Cohan highlighted in the context of the "Pirate Ballet" and that Brett Farmer cited when discussing "Jailhouse Rock" apply here: creating his own "flaming trail of masculinity," Presley's "Slicin' Sand" dance, too, achieves both homo- and hetero-erotic affect.[63]

Moreover, there exists the additional layer here (as with Kelly's "Pirate Ballet" dance) of racial and ethnic indeterminacy. Legend has it that Presley's white skin was so pale before the filming of *Blue Hawaii* that producer Hal Wallis personally recommended a particular tanning lamp to properly darken his skin for the role; whether true or not, this rumor does highlight Presley's extreme tanning for the role, which does important signifying work.[64] The result is a skin tone that nearly matches that of his native Hawaiian friends, a visual continuity that not only implicitly signals Gates' spiritual and philosophical ties to Hawaii, but also blurs his ethnic identity—especially alongside his signature black hair dye (see Figure 3.9). At the same time, his dances' continually bent knees, buoyant

Figure 3.9 Presley's extreme artificial tanning, together with his signature black hair dye, allows him to visually blend in with his character's native Hawaiian friends.

steps, and swinging hips are more visually aligned with Black culture than Polynesian dances. The result is a decidedly ambiguous racial/ethnic performance on Presley's part: Southern white man who looks like a Hawaiian native and dances like a Black man. This is reminiscent of the "other Other" position the Nicholas Brothers sometimes held, though unlike them Presley approaches this status from a place of racial privilege.

With his next handful of films, Presley (mostly) moves on from the Army as a narrative device in his films and star persona.[65] His characters hold a range of skilled, often physical professions: boxer, sailor, crop-duster. Inevitably, of course, these characters are also skilled singers and sometimes skilled dancers as well, and there is little distinction between Presley's performances across films. Although the plot structures do not noticeably change or develop over the course of the decade, Presley's dancing does. James argues, correctly, that the "rock 'n' roll elements" of Presley's music and persona largely disappear across this swath of post-Army films: he is no longer a delinquent who starts fights, repels adults, and sings songs governed by African American rhythms.[66] The Africanist elements of his *dancing*—low center of gravity, mobile hips, modified wing dances like the twist—do not disappear, however. They are certainly joined by a range of other elements, but these basic building blocks remain in his dances even as the music they accompany tends toward the pop ballad. What is notable about his dances in 1962 and 1963 is how they transform with the historical moment and with Presley's interests while still retaining their Blackness.

Much as his "Rock-a-Hula" performance reflects the influence of the twist, the major dance numbers in *Kid Galahad* (1962), *Girls! Girls! Girls!* (1962), and *Fun in Acapulco* (1963) evidence the extreme popularity of the twist among teenagers. In *Kid Galahad*, Presley's boxer character dances the twist with his love interest at a picnic with other young white people; in *Girls! Girls! Girls!*, the final number rather impossibly includes a large cast of young women, purportedly from around the world, who first perform their native dances and then all join Presley in dancing the twist (see Figure 3.10). Here, Presley becomes the American emissary of dance—much as Gene Kelly had in *An American in Paris*.

Figure 3.10 In the finale of *Girls! Girls! Girls!* (1962), Presley leads women representing a variety of cultures in dancing the twist together.

What has changed in the decade between the two films, of course, is the sense of global multiculturalism in which all the world's women join together in the grand melting pot of American culture. What remains the same is the symbol of peace and togetherness: a popular dance, spread by a white American man, whose origin lies in Black culture.

Finally, Presley's most elaborate onstage dance performance in *Fun in Acapulco* includes a very fast variation on the twist, woven together with more classic Presley dance moves. Notably, the "Bossa Nova, Baby" twist is no longer a social dance but a concert dance performed as stage spectacle, and it is the only rock 'n' roll (if bossa nova-inspired) number in the film. In this concert dance context, Presley also performs the modified twist in a manner more akin to a buck dance, using his feet to tap out the rhythm of the music, emphasizing certain beats with a heavier/louder step. The result is a rich mélange of older and newer Black dance steps. It is an odd context for the song, however; Presley is performing Brazilian-influenced American music at a club in Mexico, backed by a Mexican band with Mexican instruments in Mexican-styled outfits. Regardless, this is Presley's dancing at its most virtuosic and impressive. Especially during the chorus, he moves fluidly with the exceedingly fast tempo. In addition, all four limbs shift to balance each other out while his twisting trunk causes him to both travel sideways and careen forward and backward; his shifting center of gravity and mobile spine are once again characteristic of Africanist movement.[67] This Black movement vocabulary cements his international playboy masculinity in spectacular fashion.

Despite the sheer production crunch that must have accompanied Presley's nine post-Army films made between 1960 and 1963, this period contained a number of excellent, complex dances by the rock 'n' roll star. In fact, Presley's dances of the early sixties not only failed to demonstrate "reformed" hips, they also absorbed—and likely helped to spread—the twist. Arguably the most famous and widespread Black social dance since the Charleston, Presley's twist began as a mere influence in *Blue Hawaii* and then became one of several Black dance idioms and aesthetics that Presley mixed together in *Fun in Acapulco*. During this period, with the near absence of fights, dirty denim, and other markers of his characters' rugged masculinity, Presley's body became increasingly spectacular and (ambiguously) eroticized. Though this signification of masculinity as pure, phallic sexuality—for example, the crotch shots of his tight white bathing suit in *Blue Hawaii*—arguably peaked during this period, Presley's spectacularism continued in his most feminized dance on film in *Viva Las Vegas* (1964).

Dance as Climax, Dance in Decline

Beginning in 1964, Presley's own dances on screen took a backseat to entire companies of backup dancers, who often lacked speaking parts and were

144   WHITE SCREENS, BLACK DANCE

irrelevant to their scenes and the films' overall plot. In several of these films, such as *Kissin' Cousins* (1964) and *Girl Happy* (1965), Presley merely provides the singing; a corps of other men, women, or both provide the dancing to accompany it. This pattern, together with the move toward often operatic pop ballads as the governing sounds of Presley's films, signaled a generic shift from the rock 'n' roll musicals and teen films of the late 1950s and early 60s to low-budget B-musicals for the mid to late 1960s. As a result, Presley's last major dance appearance on screen occurred in *Viva Las Vegas*. The film's fairly high production values, integrated structure, dual character focus, and inclusion of recent *Bye Bye, Birdie* success story Ann-Margret as Presley's co-star set it apart from the rest of his 1960s films. Indeed, the amount of dancing it allows for Presley gives the discerning viewer a peek into what Presley's dancing career might have looked like if "Colonel" Parker's strict production schedules and low budgets had been disregarded more often.

The plot of *Viva Las Vegas* follows racecar driver Lucky Jackson (Presley) as he tries to both woo Rusty Martin (Ann-Margret) and enter into the city's Grand Prix race. In an early number, after Martin initially rejects Jackson but softens enough for a morning date at the local university dance studio, Presley and Ann-Margret perform an unlikely duet. Martin at first appears to intimidate Jackson with a wild modern dance number, accompanied by her students; when she invites him to join them, he admits "I'm gonna chicken out." But she insists that he perform *something* for the students: "If you don't wanna dance, sing! I know you can do that." He agrees, but after only a few bars of "C'mon Everybody," Presley's Jackson does far more than sing. His movements at first resemble the stylized military march from *G.I. Blues*, but with added stomping to match the lyrics' "stomp your feet real loud;" his legs then open up into a twist-and-tap pattern similar to the one he used in "Bossa Nova, Baby." Importantly, the scene and camera both frame this dance as more than simply a performance; it is an interactive demonstration-workshop in which the Jackson character is also simultaneously courting Martin using her own language: dance. Thus, the steps are not, in the context of the diegesis, intended as only entertainment or even a simple manifestation of feeling; they are part of a mating ritual. In this way, Presley's old steps read anew as not only expressions of African American sexuality performed by a white body; they are also now *overtures* danced in a Black vernacular—even as they are matched with pop music.

This activation of the steps becomes particularly clear when Presley inserts an isolated pelvic thrust with straightened legs, of the sort that would become more exaggerated in the social dances of later decades but which was still uncommon on screen. As he performs it, Presley looks directly at Ann-Margret, instigating a sort of conversation of the hips between them (see Figure 3.11). Especially given the choice to film Presley's next movements from behind Ann-Margret,

Figure 3.11 During the "C'mon Everybody" number from *Viva Las Vegas* (1964), the camera frames the hip movements of Presley and Ann-Margret as a danced conversation.

whose hips also move, the gendered and sexual dynamics of the scene are more explicitly heterosexual than similar scenes featuring similar Presley dancing "at" no one in particular or at male buddies like Ito in *Blue Hawaii*. No longer a Presley "showing off" or vaguely homoerotic, this is a masculinity of direct sexual conquest. The dance continues with suggestive phallic imagery, as Presley hops up onto a gymnast's pommel horse and straddles it while students push him back and forth, mimicking the movements of intercourse. Finally, to conclude the number, the two come together in symbolic coital bliss, begun with a pelvic thrust toward one another. This is followed by a series of squeals and grunts by Ann-Margret during their final steps, performed side-by-side. As they travel downstage, the two take turns stepping over each other's extended legs, representing the rise toward climax. When they reach the front, Presley attempts to dramatically dip Ann-Margret, but loses his balance and the two topple over together. The number then ends with both characters prone on the stage, exhausted from their danced intercourse and having seemingly forgotten the students watching them on the floor. As the most carefully staged Presley dance number since *Jailhouse Rock*, the sequence reaffirms his masculine virility via a mixed usage of Black dance and theatrical symbolism. The film then immediately cuts to the rest of their day on a series of perfectly innocent date activities, making no reference to the erotics performed beforehand.

Later on in the film, after a heated disagreement about Jackson's gambling habits and racing ambitions, both Jackson and Martin enter a talent contest in hopes of winning prize money. In their respective performances, each is accompanied by backup dancers of the opposite sex. But the tenor of the two performances is quite different. Ann-Margret's is performed in bright stage lighting and she is coded as hyperfeminine, luxuriating in fur and jewels before stripping down to a skimpy leotard. Presley's performance of "Viva Las Vegas," on the other hand, is not hypermasculine, but also rather feminizing. Unlike the men who back up Ann-Margret, Presley dances not in a collared shirt and sweater vest but a hot pink shirt and short jacket, both buttoned low to reveal his chest. And his primary dance move in the number is intense shimmying of said chest (see Figure 3.12), a movement his 1950s critics surely would have been quick to associate with female burlesque. Otherwise, he joins fellow decadently costumed showgirls in their movements, one by one. Whereas Ann-Margret accepts jewels from her male backup dancers, demonstrating their conventional heterorelationality, Presley copies the movements of his backup dancers, demonstrating a sort of corporeal solidarity and sisterhood. When Ann-Margret and her dancers perform the same steps, the dancers look at her admiringly to signal implied heterosexual desire, but there are no such markings of desire in Presley's dance; instead, he links arms with his female compatriots and dances beside them jovially, as an equal. Moreover, this practice not only decentralizes Presley from being the main figure in the performance, but also demonstrates the ease with which he embodies the decidedly feminine gestures of his fellow performers. The result is a truly spectacular, feminine masculinity, no longer particularly ambiguous or visibly hetero-erotic. The rise of these pants is far longer and baggier than most Presley has danced in, so his pelvis is not a focal point; the pink blouse peeking out of his jacket does not emphasize male musculature so much as mimic female cleavage. After joining each female dancer in her unique choreography, Presley then leads the entire group in a modified conga line, circling flamboyantly through the space as his hair and shirt billow like the feathers of the women's costumes. Thus, in Presley's last major dance number on film, he dances little masculinity at all. Not only does the song itself have little connection to the rhythm and blues of his original music, but the dance

Figure 3.12 Presley's dominant dance move for the titular number is a chest shimmy, accentuated by his open shirt.

is largely evacuated of Africanisms (except for the shimmy/tremble) in favor of show dance. Absent as well is any attempt to perform a version of normative, heterosexual masculinity.[68] Missing the earlier aesthetic of "cool" and penis-focused eroticism, Presley's big dance finale has dissolved into abstracted flamboyance.

The remainder of Presley's onscreen career featured less dancing in general, but especially less of his own dancing. Occasional shoulder shimmies or swinging hips popped up here and there, but never a full Presley dance number. Of course, it is well known that Presley was unhappy with the many formulaic musicals he was forced to pump out in the 1960s; he had hoped for more serious acting opportunities but "Colonel" Parker prioritized profit margins over Presley's creative fulfillment.[69] It is perhaps not surprising, then, that Presley avoided the additional effort of rehearsing or even improvising dance scenes. Even with his brief return to television in the 1968 NBC "Comeback Special," Presley dances very little. While his fifties rock 'n' roll image is back—sideburns, black leather—only references to the movements are included in the performance. Thus, while wide stances, straddling crouches, and a bit of bumping and grinding do accent "Hound Dog," "All Shook Up," "Jailhouse Rock," and so on, Presley once again leaves the substantial dancing to others. In fact, as soon as he explains that rock 'n' roll actually "sprang from" gospel and rhythm and blues, there is a dissolve from his body to Black dancer and choreographer Claude Thompson, performing modern dance choreography to the gospel vocals of Jean King (see Figure 3.13). In the words of James, "for an instant it appears that a black self is emerging from within him."[70] Thus, Presley somewhat ironically ends his career of dancing on screen by finally allowing his own blackbodying practices to be replaced by an actual Black male dancing body. Insofar as the Comeback Special was also a final farewell to the old bad boy Presley persona—the last time he wore that rebellious black leather—he left his old Black dance moves behind as well.

Figure 3.13 The "Comeback Special" (December 3, 1968) dissolves from Presley's acknowledgement of the Black rhythm and blues' influence on rock 'n' roll to Black dancer Claude Thompson (left) who then performs a modern dance (right).

148 WHITE SCREENS, BLACK DANCE

Instead of further developing the signature moves and stylings of his early career, he became associated in his later years with increasingly bedazzled outfits, such as his famous jumpsuits and capes, and the incorporation of karate moves on stage. When he did move his hips, he did so in a seemingly parodic manner, as if spinning a lasso while riding a rodeo horse. Even the horsing around and the karate moves, however, became scant after 1972. No longer a *dancing* spectacle of both racial and gender ambiguity, Presley became pure, immobile, sideburned spectacle. In this way, he finally transitioned from Little Richard to Liberace.[71]

Presley's style and dance changed a great deal over the course of his career, far more so than the Nicholas Brothers' or Gene Kelly's did. At least in part, this is probably due to the fact that he was not a concert dancer, as they were, but a vernacular dancer. Indeed, because he was always a singer first, Presley's dance styles essentially followed the musical phases of his career. During his first three years in the spotlight, Presley the rock 'n' roll rebel infused his performances of Black music with Black dance, cementing his status as "young, sexy, and virile" by focusing viewers' eyes on his pelvis. With the aid of film narratives as he made the transition to Hollywood in rock 'n' roll musicals, this irreverence became "baaadness." But as the music turned toward pop ballads in his post-Army films, the dances turned toward pop trends like the twist. After culminating—indeed, climaxing—in the heterosexual dance coupling with Ann-Margret in *Viva Las Vegas*, Presley's dance receded as his music ultimately entered the realm of white gospel and country, where both masculinity and sexuality were subsumed into bejeweled spectacle. This trajectory from Black dance as virile sexuality through increasing gender ambiguity to the complete absence of both underlines the reality that male dance stars rarely simply perform *a* masculinity—though defining performances certainly emerge—they perform many masculin*ities*.

4
Sammy Davis, Jr.
Modish and Chameleonic

Sammy Davis stands in total darkness on the set of *The Steve Allen Show* on May 5, 1957. He lights a cigarette and then stamps it out. There is a cut to a close-up on Davis's feet as they tap without music. This is followed by a dissolve to a long shot showing Davis's full body in front of modernist cubes-as-steps in the background. Smartly dressed now in a sport jacket with his shirt collar upturned and rounded out by a neatly tied ascot, Davis taps faster and faster. But Steve Allen suddenly interrupts, "startling" Davis and causing him to fall down alongside a perfectly timed cymbal crash. Allen suggests that Davis might make use of the thirty-four-piece house band available to him. Davis responds, "No, I don't need a musician . . . the only thing I need is these Cye Martin tight pants . . . look, the only thing I need is a little rhythm. Now, have you got any rhythm in you?" Though Allen was a pianist, not a percussionist, he obliges Davis by beginning to play some nearby bongo drums. What ensues is a rhythmic conversation between Davis's taps and Allen's drumming; in an impressive intervention for live television, this is captured in horizontal split screen, with one camera in close-up on Davis's feet after he jumps up onto the on-set cubes, and another on Allen's hands as they slap the bongos. During this initial call-and-response sequence, the sway in Davis's hips looks rather like that of Fayard Nicholas—implying sexuality but not actively demonstrating it. Moments later, however, Davis jumps down from the cube and begins a deeply hybrid segment: Presley-style knee flapping with arms up to emphasize the work of the lower body; Kelly-style wide stances and flat palms before floating across the stage with intricate footwork; Nicholases-style jumping up and down the cubes while tapping, including jumping over Allen's head (though not into the splits). When back up on the tallest cube, Davis even weaves in a wide-legged Kelly freeze, before wriggling his pelvis out of it as Presley might. In stitching together Black dance's many modifications through the lenses of ballet, Broadway, and white working-class aesthetics, Davis embodies an amalgamation of cross-cultural stealing, mimicry, and alteration that had been unfolding since before he was born.

Sammy Davis, Jr. was a singular and somewhat contradictory star; he has been described as paradoxically both "daring and deferential," and as an "establishment rebel."[1] He held many nicknames over the course of his fifty-plus-year

White Screens, Black Dance. Pamela Krayenbuhl, Oxford University Press. © Pamela Krayenbuhl 2025.
DOI: 10.1093/9780197699119.003.0005

150 WHITE SCREENS, BLACK DANCE

performance career, most notably Mr. Entertainment and Mr. Show Business. He was one of the most multitalented performing artists of the twentieth century: dancer, singer, actor, impersonator, gunslinger, musician, and even photographer. Though he always considered himself a stage performer first and foremost, he appeared not only on vaudeville, nightclub, and Broadway stages, but also on radio, television, and film. Davis was keenly aware that these mass media were crucial to building a highly visible star persona, and as such he could be seen on television more often than almost any other performer during the 1950s and 1960s. Throughout his life, Davis often used comedy to insistently make room for Blackness in white-dominated spaces. He also frequently highlighted his exceptionality, calling himself "the only Black, Puerto Rican, one-eyed, Jewish entertainer in the world."[2] Reaching his career peak nearly twenty years later than the Nicholas Brothers, despite being close to them in age, Davis was a major supporter of Dr. Martin Luther King, Jr. and the Civil Rights Movement. Equally important to his reputation as a star are the public scandals over his relationships with white women, including his marriage to white Swedish actress May Britt at a time when miscegenation laws were still on the books in many U.S. states. Sometimes accused of disavowing his Blackness in his attempts to transcend racist societal boundaries, Davis nevertheless rooted most of his performances in Black dance and cultural history.

In this chapter, I argue that Davis actively constructed his masculinity and star persona to be chameleonic—ever-changing and able to match a variety of social contexts—but consistently suave and modish. That is, Davis's use of Black dance contributed to the larger project of styling him as a fashionable smooth operator, with his own star persona ultimately comprising a condensation of many other Black and white stars' personae. Indeed, as African American Studies scholar and cultural critic Gerald Early notes in his introduction to *The Sammy Davis, Jr. Reader*, "For a time Davis, even as much as Frank Sinatra and Dean Martin, personified hipness; as much as trumpeter Miles Davis or boxer Sugar Ray Robinson, he personified a kind of black cool. Davis had the clothes and the moves and the mannerisms."[3] And while his comedic impersonations, music, acting, and even his controversies often overshadowed his original mode of performance, fellow dancers have always acknowledged Davis as a landmark dancer. In their expansive 1968 history of jazz dance, in the middle of an entry about legendary tap dancer John W. "Bubbles" Sublett, Marshall and Jean Stearns paint this picture quietly:

> When old-timers gather o[n] an afternoon in front of Tin Pan Alley's Brill Building . . . they sometimes discuss great entertainers. A hundred names may be mentioned and violently debated, but agreement is never reached except on three or four. Bill Robinson is considered tops because, among other things,

he broke through so many social barriers with his dancing. Sammy Davis, Jr. is mentioned with great respect. Peg Leg Bates, who can execute just about any tap step with one leg, is considered a marvel. On the subject of Bubbles, however, enthusiasm mounts and sparks fly.[4]

Buried in a list of great dancers from the generation before him, whose entire purpose is to highlight the greatness of a different star, Davis nevertheless maintains this broad respect among dancers. But his controversies remain: very often the only Black man in white spaces, both onscreen and off, Davis tried to both metaphorically and literally "dance down" racial barriers throughout the midcentury. Few found his approach effective.

A helpful lens through which to understand Davis's stylish, protean, dancerly masculinity is through the figure of the Black dandy. On the one hand, this figure is a stereotype that finds its origins in blackface minstrelsy, the northern foil to the southern plantation figure of Jim Crow. This sharply-dressed, sophisticated dandy is known as Long Tail Blue, often incarnated in the character of Zip Coon, who serves as a site for ridicule of "uppity" free Blacks with upper-class aspirations.[5] In the original minstrel song "Long Tail Blue" (1827), it is made clear that this urban dandy experiences romantic and sexual success with white women, which gets him into trouble with the law—a narrative that equally applies to the life of Sammy Davis, Jr.[6] The later Zip Coon incarnation, which originated in 1834, contained the threat of the refined Black dandy by refashioning him into a "gangling servant dressed in the master's clothes," "convert[ing] the respectability of Long Tail Blue into an outrageous and blasphemous black buffoon."[7] These figures both persisted throughout and beyond nineteenth-century minstrel stages; thus, any invocation of dandyism by a Black man is necessarily haunted by this history.

On the other hand, the Black dandy is also a reclaimed figure common amongst both earlier vaudeville performers like George Walker and Harlem Renaissance intellectuals like W.E.B. Du Bois.[8] In her book *Slaves to Fashion: Black Dandyism and the Styling of Black Diasporic Identity*, Monica L. Miller sees this reclaimed Black dandy's marshalling of sartorial style as "an index of changing notions of racial identity and the other identities in which race is constructed, performed, and lived—namely, gender, sexuality, class, and nation."[9] Like European dandyism, Black dandyism is a mode of social critique achieved through "a pointed redeployment of clothing, gesture, and wit;" in other words, dressing up as acting up.[10] But unlike the European dandy's highly personal act of self-fashioning, the *Black* dandy's style is simultaneously personal and "representative of 'the race,'" and for Miller, "a racialized dandy is at once ... (hyper) masculine *and* feminine, aggressively heterosexual yet not quite a real man, a vision of an upstanding citizen and an outsider broadcasting his alien status by clothing his dark body

152   WHITE SCREENS, BLACK DANCE

in a good suit."[11] Similar to Miller's example of James Weldon Johnson, best known (aside from authoring the lyrics to "Lift Ev'ry Voice and Sing") for his novel *The Autobiography of an Ex-Colored Man* (1912), Davis's careful focus on cutting-edge fashion might be understood as part of his effort to "signify on" the color line. Davis also grew up in a Harlem shaped, in part, by Johnson, and was taught the value of sharp dressing, especially for Black vaudevillians, as a child performer. As it was for Johnson, Davis's dandyism may well have served as a means for externalizing his sense of his own cosmopolitanism, especially once he achieved international acclaim in the 1960s.[12] And equally relevant for Davis is Miller's estimation that "Black dandyism serves as both liberation and a mode of conformity."[13] Especially as support for Black radicalism grew in the late sixties, Davis's conformity became particularly noticeable. His public image during this decade, the peak of his career, is what prompted the aforementioned descriptions of him as a "daring and deferential" "establishment rebel."[14] For all of these reasons—the pointedly fashionable dress, the sexual conquest of white women, the masculinity with a slight feminine undertone, the implicit critique of the color line, and the simultaneity of liberation and conformity—the figure of the dandy will return throughout this chapter as a means of reading Davis's star text.

Though Davis co-authored two autobiographies with (white) friends Burt and Jane Boyar, and several additional biographies of him have been released since his death, there has been relatively little academic study of Davis's career or body of work. Early suggested in 2003 that "[p]erhaps his story is a complex parable about crossover success, racial self-hatred, and the early days of racial integration,"[15] but not until twenty years later has anyone taken up these questions in-depth; historian Matthew Frye Jacobson's recent book *Dancing Down the Barricades: Sammy Davis Jr. and the Long Civil Rights Era* indeed uses Davis's career to examine the history of Black racial politics in the U.S. over the course of his lifetime. But because Davis as a figure was so defined by his physicality, it is important to attend to the ways in which dance made him who he was. Unfortunately, the Davis media archive is more scattered and incomplete than those of this book's previous case studies; as Early notes, "Davis made very little art that that was of . . . permanent availability: he . . . appeared as a guest on a number of television shows over the years, probably more times than any black person in the history of television, but none of these shows acquired lasting stature."[16] Beyond the incomplete televisual record, one of his most important films, *Porgy and Bess* (1959), is not commercially available in the United States. Nevertheless, Davis was "a fixture" of the midcentury media landscape in the U.S., "a kind of palimpsest of American culture writ large," so this chapter will unpack how this particular palimpsest danced, as a dandy, into and through masculinities onscreen.[17]

The first half of the chapter tracks Davis's stylistic foundations and development from his childhood in vaudeville, through his experience serving in the U.S. Army, and then as a young adult member of the Will Mastin Trio with his father, Sammy Davis, Sr., and "uncle" Will Mastin. The group's inheritance from minstrelsy is quite clear, and only when Davis consciously chooses to leave it behind during the 1940s does he begin to model his developing masculinity on white stars, especially Frank Sinatra. Thus, Davis spends the 1950s transitioning into a suave young standout whose dance style both draws from the many sources—on stage and screen—he has been observing since childhood, and has an implicitly sexual edge to it, demonstrated through his mobile pelvis. During this transition, Davis continues to show facility with Mastin and Sammy Sr.'s old vaudeville style while also taking opportunities to expand beyond it in solo numbers. The second half of the chapter then examines Davis's fully solo career after the older members of the Trio retire. Combining tight pants with a playful dance style that draws together Broadway theatricality, old-school tap, and social dance, Davis embodies a dandified masculinity that crystallizes most clearly in his performance as Sportin' Life in the film adaptation of *Porgy and Bess* (1959) but remains his signature for the rest of his career. In the 1960s, Davis is everywhere: a playboy partying with Frank Sinatra's Rat Pack, an advocate for the Civil Rights Movement headlining many benefit shows, a hip social dancer blending in with the youth on the television show *Hullabaloo*, a host of his own television variety show, and chameleonically adapting to all of these and other contexts. Topping off his peak decade as a decadently dressed and slithering cult leader Big Daddy in *Sweet Charity* (1969), Davis enters the seventies worried about becoming a washed up and penniless old hoofer as in his famous "Bojangles" performance, so he balances his bit of nostalgia for the vaudeville steps of his childhood with an insistently *au courant* danced masculinity.

A Child of Vaudeville

Sammy Davis, Jr. was born in 1925, just four years after Harold Nicholas but a decade before Elvis Presley. Both of his parents, Sammy Davis, Sr. and Elvera Sanchez, were vaudeville dancers, so they returned to the performing life soon after his birth in Harlem. They separated when he was a toddler, at which time Sam Sr. took Davis on the road with himself and performing partner Will Mastin. By the age of three, Davis was performing with Mastin and his father as they toured the Theater Owners Booking Association (T.O.B.A.) circuit with their hoofing act. This network of theatres showcased Black talent throughout the East Coast, the South, and the Midwest, but the pay was often meager. Davis has indeed characterized his childhood with the Will Mastin Trio as a lean time, when meals and lodging were not always within reach. But they did continue to book contracts, even during the Great Depression. In his first autobiography, Davis recalls that they were "booked on [their] reputation as a clean act that could be depended on for fast and furious flash dancing."[18]

Though their "hoofing" speed and tricks classified the Trio as a flash act, they also incorporated the style of the class act (not unlike the Nicholas Brothers). Davis recalls Mastin's careful attention to the group's immaculate suits and explanation to young Sammy: "Never sit around in what you wear on the stage. We've always had the name of the best-dressed colored act in the business and we're gonna keep that name."[19] The dignity of this immaculate dress, however, was often in tension with the physicality and content of the Trio's performances. In his autobiographies, Davis recalls early memories of Will Mastin applying blackface makeup onto him and remarking, "Now you look like Al Jolson"— Mastin refers, here, to the white Lithuanian-American vaudevillian and film actor perhaps best known for his blackface performance in the first "talkie," *The Jazz Singer* (1927).[20] Moreover, looking back on their 1920s, 30s, and even early 40s performances, Davis realized the group's performance style depended on racialized caricatures, an inheritance from minstrelsy that was quite common amongst Black vaudeville hoofers but which he did not recognize as limiting and ultimately demeaning until the mid-1940s. Davis first noticed the issue in other acts' use of dialect, as in the introduction "Gen'men, we's gwine git our laigs movin', heah." In Davis's characterization, "[t]hey were talking 'colored' as Negro acts always did . . . . I watched them doing all the colored clichés, realizing that we were doing exactly the same thing. We'd always done them. They were an automatic part of our personalities onstage. It was the way people expected Negro acts to be so that's the way we were."[21] While Davis does not explicitly connect these linguistic traditions to the blackface he was made up with as a child, both are clearly inherited from blackface minstrelsy and profoundly shaped the entire performance career of the Will Mastin Trio, whose older members never departed from this tradition.

The use of dialect is in fact scripted into the film that features Davis's first onscreen song-and-dance performances. In the Warner Brothers/Vitaphone short *Rufus Jones for President* (1933), Davis co-stars alongside established Black actress and singer Ethel Waters, playing the titular child who dreams that he is elected president of the United States. Enacting the inverse of Davis's offscreen Jolson-esque blackface performance, the film's framing narrative introduces him as having been hit in the face with cake by a neighboring child, so he first walks onscreen with a frosted visage that literature and film scholar Ryan Jay Friedman has read as "virtual whiteface."[22] In consoling him, Ethel Waters speaks in dialect (as do all characters in the film) before breaking into a song sung in "standard English" that lulls them both to sleep. As reviewers in the Black press at the time and contemporary scholars have each pointed out, the script's narrative paints a picture of Black social and political life rife with negative stereotypes—the main concerns of the dreamworld's campaign and new government include porkchops, watermelon, chicken coops, and dice.[23] Nevertheless, the film does allow both stars' talents to shine, thus providing an early record of young Sammy's already-impressive performing abilities as a mere seven-year-old. Upon first being elected, Davis's Jones is brought to a microphone and invited to give a speech, but instead he breaks into song while holding a half-eaten chicken wing. In a double-breasted suit and a newsboy cap, he skillfully mimics Louis Armstrong's gravelly voice (though young Davis's is of course much higher pitched) and expressive mouth as he sings "You Rascal You (I'll Be Glad When You're Dead)," punctuating it with a couple pointed stomps and then following it with a brief tap dance. The dance itself is fairly simple, comprised of a time step with kicks, stomps, and a walkaround, but Davis impressively accomplishes it while still holding the chicken and trying to keep his lowered hat from falling off his head. In the following scene, as he is being sworn in while wearing a tuxedo and top hat, the *wunderkind* seems unable to contain his enthusiasm for performing—he steps and sways his way through his vows and completes the sequence with a stylish spin into a handshake. Finally, when one of his senators claims he "don't do nothin'," Jones rises from his chair and proclaims, "I'll do sump'n'!" before launching into his centerpiece tap solo on the senate floor. Notably, whereas the Nicholas Brothers' upper middle-class upbringing trained them (and allowed them) to largely avoid or refuse the racist linguistic and physical tropes of old minstrel shows, young Davis's more economically desperate position made him (and his guardians) far less discerning.

Still wearing his presidential tuxedo, Davis's Jones performs an ebullient number that demonstrates several classic Black vaudeville steps he has absorbed from his father, Will Mastin, and the other dancers he has seen travelling the T.O.B.A. circuit. Like young Harold Nicholas does as an eleven-year-old, Sammy Davis, Jr. at seven performs several perches on the tips of his toes to break up his time steps, trenches, and buck-and-wings (see Figure 4.1). He also offers some relaxed ball taps, bringing attention to his mesmerizing tiny feet, and walkarounds for some showboating. Already a bit of a ham, Davis does more than just tap: he claps, sticks out his tongue, places a sassy hand on his hip, and makes eye contact with viewers offscreen (see Figure 4.1). Though his achievement is soon eclipsed by adult dancers, particularly a couple doing an impressive lindy hop number, Davis makes his mark as a charismatic young soloist and demonstrates his absorption of the styles that surrounded him during his young life on the road. Thus, even as a child, one of his defining characteristics was the ability to synthesize the performance styles of others, magnify them, and deliver them to audiences with a seemingly effortless comedic panache.[24]

Figure 4.1 In *Rufus Jones for President* (1933), Sammy Davis, Jr. as President Rufus Jones performs perches (left) and places a sassy hand on his hip (right).

Indeed, during this same period, Davis had an encounter with elder tap dance legend Bill "Bojangles" Robinson in which he absorbed some new steps: "Bill Robinson showed me a little step when I was between six and eight years old ... and I remember it like it was yesterday." Recalling this meeting in a 1987 interview, Davis expresses the belief that Robinson "purposely" demonstrated difficult steps that day, and when Davis successfully reproduced them, Robinson merely said, "that's good." Feeling that his eager-to-please young self came across as a show-off, Davis nevertheless conveys a humble pride in being able to pick up steps so quickly as a child.[25] This brief experience of mentorship from Robinson further pulls Davis into a sort of equivalence with the many other young Black performers that Robinson famously took under his wing, including the Nicholas Brothers.[26] Of course, this milieu was not without its representational risks; even more so than the upper middle-class Nicholas Brothers, young Davis as a child performer risked reading as a pickaninny precisely because he and the Trio often lived on the edge of poverty. While there are no surviving images of him *dancing* in rags, there is certainly footage of him *dressed* raggedly, as in *Seasoned Greetings* (1933), starring Lita Grey Chaplin. In the film, young Davis plays a grinning child costumed in a crumpled hat, a partially untucked collared shirt, and uneven, shredded pants held up by suspenders. Together with his lack of formal schooling and his father and Mastin's choice to disguise him as "Silent Sam the Dancing Midget" to fool agents from the New York Society for the Prevention of Cruelty to Children, this image places the grinning child rather in the territory of stereotype.[27]

Even so, Sammy Davis's nascent masculinity developed as did the other aspects of his star persona: through engagement with the gender presentations of the role models he watched closely. One of these men, and perhaps the most influential on Davis's persona for the next twenty years, was Frank Sinatra. The two met in 1941 when Davis was fifteen and Sinatra twenty-six; the Will Mastin Trio was booked for a show in Detroit, Michigan as a replacement for the more successful tap act

Tip, Tap, and Toe. The Trio would be the opening act for Tommy Dorsey—the same Tommy Dorsey who, in fifteen years, would first introduce Elvis Presley to television audiences. Dorsey had recently booked Sinatra to sing with his jazz band, so when Davis met him backstage, he was already familiar with Sinatra's work from Dorsey's latest records. As was his habit with most performers he admired, Davis stood in the wings and watched Sinatra, absorbing the details of Sinatra's relaxed, slouchy physicality as much as his crooning vocalizations.[28] It was this attentiveness to a range of performance styles that arguably kept the Trio working even as the vaudeville circuit had all but collapsed in the early 1940s; Davis had by now expanded his performance repertoire to include not only dances but also singing, impressions, and playing various musical instruments. In this context, it is not entirely clear exactly what so drew Davis to Sinatra. Perhaps Davis noticed that he and Sinatra shared a similarly slight body type, both with narrow shoulders and long faces, so Sinatra's corporeality felt more easily transferrable than the array of other performers he routinely impersonated with exaggeration on stage. Or perhaps he was keenly attuned to the extreme swooning of teenage bobbysoxers in response to Sinatra's calm, syrupy crooning and seemingly shy boyish smile. Indeed, Sinatra's apparent sweetness and vulnerability were played up in movie fan magazines as he first entered Hollywood between 1941 and 1943, despite mainstream media's disdain for him as effeminate.[29] His star text was thus quickly and clearly solidified, further aided by the fact that his first major role was to play himself, an unusual position for a white performer and much more common amongst "specialty" performers of color. Always an avid follower of movies and movie culture, Davis may have noticed all this, too. Regardless, Sinatra's nonthreatening, sensitive, sensual, and thus implicitly sexual masculinity served as the bedrock model for Davis in his late teens and early twenties. The challenge for Davis, of course, was how to embody Sinatra as a *dancer*, and as a *Black* man, both of which were culturally constructed as far riskier to white female innocence than Sinatra's crooning.

Having built up a wide repertoire of talents and having closely observed Sinatra's youthful masculinity, Davis found a way to further hone his performing skills while ostensibly serving his country. After being drafted in 1943, Davis experienced racial violence for the first time. He later spoke and wrote often of the abuses he endured from fellow draftees; as a petite Black man in a newly integrated unit, he was a frequent target of bullies and bigots.[30] His autobiographies suggest he at first tried to fight his way out of the situation, not only punching back but often punching first; this never ended well. However, he also happened to meet George M. Cohan, Jr., son of the famous minstrel man about whom young Harold Nicholas had sung in 1934's *Kid Millions*. The two began to put on shows together, and Davis introduced his first impressions of Sinatra in these shows, but the backdrop of minstrelsy remained: not only was Davis working

158 WHITE SCREENS, BLACK DANCE

with the son of a famous minstrel performer, but Army shows of the period were rooted in and, by regulation, generally expected to follow the conventions of blackface minstrelsy.[31] Davis never elaborated on this context, but it almost certainly informed his relationship to his audiences. In Davis's characterization of the experience, the audience's response planted the seed of his worldview and performance philosophy: that the dance is mightier than the fist. In his audience, he saw his biggest bully transfixed by and appreciative of his art: "My talent was the weapon, the power, the way for me to fight. It was the one way I might hope to affect a man's thinking . . . when I was on that stage it was as though the spotlight erased all color and I was just another guy . . . . It was as though my talent was giving me a pass which excluded me from their prejudice."[32] He pushed himself during these shows to "reach" every audience member, and this push for recognition and approbation from even the most racist white audience members established the model for Davis's entire adult performance career:

> I combed every audience for haters . . . and when I spotted them I was able to give my performance something even more than I usually had, an extra burst of strength and energy, an ability that came to me because I had to get those guys, I had to neutralize them and make them acknowledge me, and I was ready to stay onstage for two hours until I saw one of them turn to his buddies and say, "Hey, this guy's not bad," or until I caught an expression that confirmed the power I knew I had, I dug down deeper every day, looking for new material, inventing it, stealing it, switching it—any way that I could find new things to make my shows better, and I lived twenty-four hours a day for that hour or two at night when I could give it away for free, when I could stand on that stage, facing the audience, knowing I was dancing down the barriers between us.[33]

It is thus at this moment, at the age of nineteen in the Army, that the chameleon's politics began to crystallize: he would become anything, any combination of styles and performative signifiers, in order to "dance down the barriers" between Black and white Americans. Davis believed, in an era long before public discourses of "colorblindness," that his talent could somehow transcend race and make him, briefly, raceless. He also believed that a raceless Black man could somehow be the key to dissolving the color line, even in the most deeply segregated corners of the United States—so he added more white celebrities to the list of those he imitated onstage.

The Charismatic Youth in the Will Mastin Trio

Davis started getting noticed in 1946, having solidified his purpose and honed his personal repertoire while in the Army. At this moment, about a year after his release from the military, the prominent music magazine *Metronome* named him "The Most Outstanding New Personality of the Year." The Trio often still struggled to make ends meet, even as they received rave reviews as the opening act for Mickey Rooney's own post-Army tour. Davis recalls Rooney excitedly calling to share the good reviews with him: "The best dance act to hit Boston in years." "Berry Brothers, Nicholas Brothers better forget it!"[34] Rooney was another early role model for Davis, especially as a fellow child performer and petite man. "I stood in the wings watching every show Mickey did, soaking up his tremendous knowledge of the business, totally awestruck by his talent. He was the multi-talented guy who had to do everything: sing, dance, comedy, impressions, drums, trumpet, everything! And he did them all well . . . . Mickey was the performer I admired more than any in the world."[35] It was in this context, admiring the versatility of Rooney, that Davis began to realize the minstrel tradition was holding him back—professionally as much as racially. In *Yes I Can*, he reflected:

> By a lifetime of habit, by *tradition*, I . . . had been cementing myself inside a wall of anonymity. It didn't matter how many instruments I learned to play, how many impressions I learned to do, or how much I perfected them—we were still doing *Holiday in Dixieland*—still a flash act. That was how we set ourselves up so that was how the audience would see us.[36]

Davis thus spent the late forties trying to break out of the Black vaudeville mold and its stereotyped gestures, incorporating more and more of the styles and strategies employed by white performers even as his father and "uncle" Mastin stuck with those old familiar traditions. For Davis, this was also a choice between minstrelsy's emasculating stereotypes (such as the buffoonish coon) and Sinatra's sensual sexiness. Perhaps his imitations of Sinatra in particular are part of why Sinatra personally requested the Will Mastin Trio as his opener at New York's Capitol Theater in 1947. As Davis tells it, the head of booking had actually suggested the Berry Brothers and balked at the high fee Sinatra wanted for the Trio, arguing "We can get the Nicholas Brothers for that kind of money and they've even got a movie going for them. They're hot."[37] Whether apocryphal or not, this memory highlights the extent to which the Trio remained in the shadow of bigger Black tap acts after barely scraping by for twenty years straight. That the Nicholas Brothers are cited in this story as the superlative act, apparently due to their film fame, demonstrates not only their exceptionality (as discussed in Chapter 1), but also the immense influence of film in building dancers' appeal and stardom—of which Davis no doubt took note.

It is unclear whether Davis personally pushed for his first film role as an adult at this juncture, or whether the group landed the spot by luck, but they appeared soon thereafter in the 1947 short film *Sweet and Low*, part of the Paramount Musical Parade series. In it, the Will Mastin Trio provides a featured performance for white guests; despite being a short film, the structure here is similar to those of the feature-length Fox musicals in which the Nicholas Brothers had appeared in the early forties. All three men are outfitted in black trousers, white mess jackets, and black cummerbunds to perform a speedy version of Glenn Miller's "The Booglie Wooglie Piggie." After a medium close-up shows Sammy Jr. with exaggerated facial expressions, singing the lyrics so fast they're nearly scatted, the camera cuts to a long shot of the trio breaking into a tap dance. At first, they dance largely in unison, but Sammy Jr. is notably drawing the eye not only by being in the center and adding extra, embellishing steps to the shared rhythm, but also by swinging his hips with panache during the walk-steps while the older generation does not (see Figure 4.2). Before long, Sammy Jr. breaks into a solo whose taps quickly gather speed. Traveling little and producing a high volume of flaps and cramp rolls, with the occasional stamp, his feet seem to move faster than the film's frame rate can actually capture. Davis's machine gun tapping here is notably quite different from the style he used in *Rufus Jones for President* over fifteen years prior. Whereas the former was anchored by stomps and digs, deeper into the ground, this performance is light and upright, in the general school of Bill Robinson. He also inserts steps straight out of Robinson's famous "Doin' the New Lowdown" routine, such as shuffles with a pickup and crossover step.[38] But the obsession with speed, here, departs from Robinson's style and has much more in common with that of John Bubbles, often called the "Father of Rhythm Tap." When Mastin and Sammy Sr. take their turns, however, they change the tenor back to their older flash dance style, which Sammy Jr. seamlessly returns to—all three do vaudeville-style tricks on the floor (such as "Russian kick-outs" and "the clock") before a final set of trenches and a swift exit.[39] Davis thus makes clear, at the age of twenty-two, that he is comfortable with and is adept at multiple tap dance styles *and* that he is unafraid of a little implied sexuality, however fleeting.

Figure 4.2 In *Sweet and Low* (1947), Sammy Jr. at first stands out from the rest of the Will Mastin Trio by swinging his hips (left) and then with machine gun tapping that seems to move faster than the film's frame rate (right).

This was reaffirmed on Sammy Davis, Jr.'s first known television appearance, which occurred on the short-lived ABC Los Angeles variety series *Hollywood House* in late 1949 or early 1950. In the partial-episode kinescope that survives, Davis appears without Mastin and his father. Instead, he and series regular Dick Wesson play hotel bellboys (using their own names) who are trying to impress girls. Davis, in a light colored suit with almost comically broad shoulder pads— a clear descendent of the zoot suit of a few years prior—and a floppy bow tie, opens his portion of the skit by asking for tickets to the Hollywood Bowl (a large concert venue) that night; when he's informed that there is "nothing doing in the Hollywood Bowl tonight," Davis responds (with a cut to a medium close-up to emphasize it) that "there will be when we get there." Davis follows this surprisingly suggestive implication with a guttural note and some quick eyebrow raises in the style of a cartoon wolf, perhaps to smooth the brazen sexuality with a bit of comedy. Now established as the ladies' man of the group, he goes on to give Dick some advice for pleasing girls: he explains that his strategy is to sing like a girl's favorite singer, so he demonstrates his singing impersonations for different imaginary girls. He later adds that, when the first strategy doesn't work, he dances; this is followed by another rapid-fire tap dance sequence featuring a fluid sequence of crisp, clear taps. He first establishes the rhythm by slapping the bell desk and cueing in a very spare piano accompaniment before launching into a speedy routine structured as a call-and-response with the piano; he makes heavy use of stop time and adds in a handful of classic moves that make his years immersed in old vaudeville clear to anyone who might recognize them.

Like his tapping with the Will Mastin Trio in *Sweet and Low* a few years prior, Davis's dancing here is in the "rhythm tap" style made famous by John Bubbles. Also dancing in this tradition at the time was Teddy Hale, whose appearance on *Texaco Star Theatre* in 1949 could have inspired Davis's *Hollywood House* performance. But unlike both Hale's and his own style in *Sweet and Low*, Davis in this episode brings down his upper body and bends his knees more. Visually, this has the effect of separating his upper body from his legs, at times creating the illusion that the top half floats separately as the bottom half works at breakneck speeds—the live editing accentuates this by cutting to a shot of his lower body alone for several moments (see Figure 4.3). Common amongst many tap dancers and key to the Africanist tap tradition, the "low-down" look is yet another facet of form Davis absorbed through observation. In this context, it appears to contribute to his characterization in the skit as the young charmer; together with winking smiles, syncopated clapping, and a comportment that might be described as "peacocking," the lowered torso establishes his aura—and model of masculinity—as a grown-up soloist: suave.

Davis appeared on television approximately ten more times during the early 1950s, almost always as part of the Will Mastin Trio. Most often, the Trio appeared

162   WHITE SCREENS, BLACK DANCE

Figure 4.3 During his *Hollywood House* television appearance, Davis brings down his torso and bends his knees more, creating the illusion that his top half floats separately as his bottom half taps at breakneck speeds (left), which is enhanced by cutting to a shot of his lower body alone (right).

on Ed Sullivan's *Toast of the Town* (which became *The Ed Sullivan Show* in 1955) and the *Colgate Comedy Hour*, hosted by Eddie Cantor (who had danced in blackface with the Nicholas Brothers in 1934's *Kid Millions*). Stylistically, Davis spent the early 1950s seeking a balance between the older vaudeville dance act of his father and Mastin, and his own, more modern and varied style. This is evident across their television appearances, all of which appear to include chunks of their stage act with few changes from program to program. However, small evolutions in Davis's style are apparent even in these. By his August 8, 1954 appearance on *Colgate Comedy Hour*, for example, Davis marks himself apart from the older generation via both movement and fashion choices. At first, all three appear in loosely cut suits and bowties, with the older gentlemen in lighter suits and young Davis standing out in a darker one. So attired, they announce their return to the program after several years with a custom song, "This is the Place that We Started From," during which Sammy Sr. and Mastin merely sway, shift their weight, or tap their feet with the music. Sammy Jr., however, throws his hips into it toward the end, and the cameraman responds. While the number is primarily shot with a static camera in a medium-long shot with the three men standing against a curtain, as soon as Sammy Jr. begins to swing his hips, the camera pulls back to a loose long shot. With young Davis's full body now in the frame, he transitions to a few counts of more Broadway-style jazz: throwing his legs side to side with syncopation and adding an exaggerated Charleston-esque wing dance, Davis looks more like a hamming Gene Kelly than like his father or Mastin. Of course, these are still fundamentally Africanist movements and they are contextually safer than when Elvis Presley would reproduce them two years later; as this is a "family" performance of father, "uncle," and son, the sexuality that might otherwise be implied by twenty-eight-year-old Davis's mobile pelvis is circumscribed by the old vaudeville style of music and dance that literally boxes him in.

But later in the program, when he sings "Birth of the Blues," likely for the first time on television, Davis pushes these changes farther with a long solo that presages his late fifties solo style and recalls all three of this book's previous case studies. Here, he has given up the traditional performance uniform of the bowtie and traded it in for a polo-style knit shirt under a very light suit. Highlighting his youth via costume despite the set being a New Orleans bar from yesteryear, Davis sings more than he dances.[40] But when he does dance, it is reminiscent of Kelly's contemporaneous stylization of vaudeville. Davis hops up on the bar in the set, leans back, flattens his palms, and swings his pelvis in circles (see Figure 4.4). A corps of fellow Black dancers kneels below the bar, swaying and clapping along as they gaze up at Davis. To end the phrase, he jumps over them all—this time more like the Nicholas Brothers, though he does not land in the splits. He then breaks the slower rhythm of the song with a "Look out!," and launches into a speedy Kelly-style solo. Similar to the "Gotta Dance" segment of the "Broadway Ballet" in *Singin' in the Rain* (1952), Davis is buoyant with deeply bent knees and marries fancy footwork to the occasional wide stance with flattened palms. Unlike Kelly's fists or the Nicholases' hand flourishes, Davis adds a supported but fluid *port de bras*, such that the arms complement the busy movements of the lower body almost as a runner's arms would—a sort of relaxed windmill. He concludes this segment with two intensive Presley-style leg flaps (but two years prior to Presley's television debut!) before a dramatic drop-slide on his knees (see Figure 4.4). The grand finale has him leading the corps in a travelling train of syncopated waltz steps with limp wrists and a single shaking jazz hand, ultimately finding himself jumping from the raised stage behind the piano onto

Figure 4.4 While performing "The Birth of the Blues" on the August 8, 1954 episode of *The Colgate Comedy Hour*, Davis jumps up on the bar set and swings his pelvis in circles with flattened palms (left) and later engages in Presley-style leg flaps (right).

the café table where his father and Mastin have been watching the whole time. Here, too, he lands on his knees with a final "ta da!" presentation of his arms and a gaze into the camera as his father and Mastin look on. Throughout these many stylistic shifts, Davis begins to demonstrate more of what he has seen and absorbed from not only his stage contemporaries but his screen contemporaries of the late 1940s and early 1950s—while there is no way to know for sure how closely he had been watching Gene Kelly's films, Davis was well known for being a voracious film viewer. Remaining rooted in Africanist aesthetics, he nevertheless performs with many of the Broadway-esque affectations that Kelly added to this same movement vocabulary. And though he is a truly charismatic and magnetic center to this scene, he is careful to end it by acknowledging the rest of the Trio; this level of careful negotiation remained as long as the previous generation shared the screen with him.

It is important to note that the promotion of Davis and the Trio on these major programs, especially by enthusiastic white hosts, was not a frictionless experience for anyone involved. Just as Milton Berle recalled fighting for the presence of acts like the Four Step Brothers on *Texaco Star Theatre* in the early 1950s, so too did Eddie Cantor have to fight to keep the Will Mastin Trio on the *Colgate Comedy Hour*.[41] During their first appearance on the show on February 17, 1952, Cantor both blotted young Sammy's brow with his own handkerchief and put his arm around Davis near the end of their performance, remarking on his incredible talent. Aware of his transgression but doubling down on it, Cantor says, live on camera, "I'll probably get killed for this, but you're coming back here on my next show, four weeks from tonight." Hate mail was apparently sent to all parties involved: Davis, Cantor, NBC, and sponsor Colgate-Palmolive. Four years after Gene Kelly and the Nicholas Brothers had collapsed into a friendly pile on *The Pirate*, but four years before Elvis Presley's transgressive pelvis would more explicitly stoke white fears of miscegenation, Cantor's simple acts of *touching* Sammy Jr. inspired more disgust than the Trio's mere appearance and soon return on the program. A letter addressed to Cantor asked, "Where do you get off wiping that little coon's face with the same handkerchief you'd put on a good, clean, white, American face?" Similarly, a letter to Davis told him to "keep your filthy paws off Eddie Cantor he may be a jew but at least he is white and dont come from africa where you should go back to I hope I hope I hope."[42] A Morris Agency representative told Davis that another such upset could get Cantor's program pulled from the airways by a fearful Colgate-Palmolive.[43] But the Trio did return to the show the following month, and several times more over the next few years. On March 16, Cantor announced them as if there were no controversy at all: "Here they are again! They scored a great hit on our show last month, so by popular demand, and carrying on where they left off, is the Will Mastin trio starring Sammy Davis, Jr.!" The group literally starts in the middle of a song, but Sammy Jr. also offers a speedy tap solo, standing out from the others, clad in darker suits, by wearing a lighter one. Davis uses classical Africanist stylistics in his solo: he is bent and loose, swings his arms rhythmically but then tenses and straightens them in accented opposition; he also includes some exuberant starfish splays of explosive energy before Cantor interrupts to request impressions. His undeniable virtuosity here, and the extent to which his contrasting costuming draws the eye away from the elder members of the Trio, hint at the same tensions present in the Nicholas Brothers' dances a little over a decade prior; because Davis is clearly no longer a child, his virtuosity threatens to read as virility, and so must be shut down by Cantor's interruption before it gets out of hand.

Ultimately, despite the protestations of a vocal minority, Davis's television appearances were making him a recognizable star. At a café the day after his controversial initial appearance, Davis recalls being recognized by both the counterman and a fellow customer: "In over twenty years of playing nightclubs and theaters nobody had ever before recognized me, cold, like that. But the right presentation on just one television show had done it."[44] The television networks also recognized how quickly Davis was building star power, and perhaps also noticed the slippery slope of virtuosity as virility, so in 1953 ABC conceived a Black-cast sitcom entitled *We Three*, starring Davis and the Trio alongside the talented young Black dancer Frances Taylor, who was a member of the Katherine Dunham Company. Taylor was to play Davis's girlfriend in the program, providing a culturally safe (read: racially matched) romantic outlet for attractive young Sammy. Contracts were signed and a pilot was filmed in early 1954, but the program never found a sponsor.[45] Though America never got to see Davis starring in a sitcom and dancing his way through a youthful romance with a fellow Black dancer, this is where Davis's version of a romancing young Sinatra would have been established.

Sammy Goes Solo in Tight Pants

Having emerged in the public eye as a virtuosic young dancer, Davis was in his late twenties and developing a star text built on a charming, stylish masculinity. But just two years after Davis was first recognized "cold," a devastating car accident threatened that he might never dance again. On November 18, 1954, the Trio was performing at The Last Frontier in Las Vegas, and for the first time since first appearing in the nascent sin city, they were allowed to stay in the hotel itself rather than being banished to a rooming house on the segregated "West side" of town. Davis had also booked a Hollywood soundtrack recording for *Six Bridges to Cross* (1955); after he completed their performance late at night, Davis and his valet Charlie Head drove to Hollywood to record the next morning. They collided with a car that had backed up seeking an exit, causing major facial injuries for both men. Most critically, Davis's left eye had been pulled from its socket and was said to have been dangling by a thread next to his cheek. In his autobiography, Davis recalls waking up in the San Bernadino Community Hospital, confronting his new reality with grim acceptance: "'Well folks, I guess this wraps us up.' . . . They sure as hell aren't going to be laying down their money to see any one-eyed dancers."[46] In line with his fears, as he slowly recovered and prepared for a series of live shows at Ciro's (a swanky Los Angeles nightclub frequented by Hollywood royalty) in early 1955, a news article claimed that the announcement of his return "causes one to speculate as to whether the Sammy Davis, Jr. who'll open at Ciro's can possibly bear any resemblance to the dazzling figure of perpetual motion whose career only two months ago loomed as one of the brightest in show business."[47] Davis's initial attempts to return to dance with a glass eye and eye patch were indeed daunting, but he refused to give up on that aspect of his star persona:

> My balance and sense of depth had become pretty good for normal things but dancing was going to be something else . . . . It was as if I'd never danced before. My legs shook, I had almost no wind at all, every turn brought a knife-stab to my eye, the tempo seemed faster than it had ever been and I was fighting to keep up with it. I kicked myself in the leg and tripped . . . . I got up, picked out a slower record and stared dancing again. My eye burned and throbbed but I didn't dare stop.[48]

It was through this process of insistent self-retraining that Davis both solidified himself as a dancer at his core *and* most clearly updated his style toward the chameleonic mélange of suave stylistics that came to define his solo career.

Davis's solo style was built not only from his vaudeville training as a child and his performance experiences in the Army, but also from what he absorbed as a lover of Hollywood film. Indeed, he built a reputation for holding private film screenings in the Emerald Room of The Sands whenever he was performing there; "I had two features flown in from L.A. every night."[49] His careful attention to the ways musical stars, from his old friend Mickey Rooney to fresh talent like young Elvis Presley, were bringing dance to Hollywood is apparent in the hybrid style he develops for himself. On an April 3, 1955 episode of *Toast of the Town*, for example, Davis clearly fuses Gene Kelly's theatrical, spectacular jazz-tap with the mobile pelvis that Presley would make famous mere months later. Still wearing a black eye patch as a result of his accident, Davis first appears in a two-toned suit with the Trio and performs what might be termed "Trio material," including impressions. But as before, the more interesting portion comes later on with his solo work. One segment is an "audition" for an imaginary show called "That's Entertainment," for which young Sammy shows up as a "kid" (presumably meant to be playing the role of a naïf in his late teens or early twenties) dressed in jeans and a very tight tee-shirt, channeling Kelly channeling Brando. Davis the auditioner is very light on his feet, prancing about and adding a heel-click flourish alongside some large and active arms. Though the choreography is not complex, Davis here signals his familiarity with the movement vocabulary of a young Broadway aspirant; he also dances quite well in this idiom despite it being outside the training of his youth. However briefly, Davis here demonstrates his sponge-like ability to watch, absorb, and replicate a range of not only others' voices and mannerisms (which were more regularly featured in his stage and television acts) but also others' dance styles. When the cameras dissolve back to the "present," Sammy switches gears by singing and dancing a sensual version of "It Ain't Necessarily So," a song from the opera *Porgy and Bess*. It is particularly interesting to see Davis perform this number in 1955, mere months after its latest Broadway revival and U.S. tour (as this episode aired, the tour was continuing abroad), but still several years before Samuel Goldwyn secured the rights for a film adaptation featuring Davis as Sportin' Life—which I will discuss further below. In 1955, performing a segment on the widely viewed *Toast of The Town*, Davis has far more creative control to make the performance his own. In crafting his own Broadway-inflected version of the big city "dope peddler" Sportin' Life, he probes deeper into the fusion dance style he had begun developing prior to his accident.

This interpretation of "It Ain't Necessarily So" embodies the dangers of secular life by oozing sexuality, a departure from jazz singer Cab Calloway's interpretation of it in the recent stage revival. Davis begins with Presley-style pelvic isolations but soon sutures them into a Kelly-style Broadway jazz dance. Keeping his knees bent and arms supported throughout, Davis weaves together slow drag steps, big starfish poses, large sideways hops, barrel rolls, and athletic running back and forth, ending the number with a dramatic slide toward the camera on his knees. That Davis's dance here repeatedly centers his pelvis and highlights his athletic ability is dangerous for a Black man to do on television in the 1950s; even Presley, a white man, would soon be censored for his own active pelvis. But context and camera choices appear to rescue Davis from such a disaster; the song was well-known, by this point, as one associated with an evil fictional character, so there is a layer of distance between Davis himself and the sexuality on view. Additionally, the camera never frames Davis's body too tightly, so that his pelvic activities are not visually highlighted in the way that Presley's soon would be. Still, Davis's highly kinetic performance of the song demonstrates his understanding of precisely which combination of 1950s dance vocabularies would best capture the essence of the Sportin' Life character thirty years after his conception, and he takes full advantage of the opportunity to embody an explicitly sexy masculinity.[50]

On the heels of his 1955 television appearances, Davis actively attempts to "get bigger" by expanding the reach of his performer profile from mere nightclub performer who occasionally appears on television or records a song to a true multi- and trans-media star. Of course, some aspects of his burgeoning star text were not his idea. The crucial example here is his growing reputation as a Black man who wanted to be white, and as such was only interested in romancing white women. Fueled in particular by tabloid headlines about him with actresses Ava Gardner, Kim Novak, and Marilyn Monroe, this perception also made its way into the Black press. One such column, quoted in his autobiography, complains, "Clearly, Mr. Davis is doing nothing to discourage rumors that success has erased his memory for friends who knew him 'when.' His all-night, all-white, orgy-style parties are the talk of Las Vegas, where he is currently appearing. We are sorry to be the ones to remind Mr. Davis of his obligation to the Negro community, but even sorrier for the necessity to do so."[51] Though the historical record suggests that his only real big-name affair was with Kim Novak, Davis did, in fact, continue to cultivate a large circle of white friends. But the reaction to this choice in the Black press upset Davis; he saw it as a side-effect of his pursuit of greater fame. Because most of the highly successful people in show business were white, they were his natural social group as he set his sights on increased media exposure. The (white) mainstream press, on the other hand, mischaracterized Davis stylistically. During an interview with Jack Eigen for his late-night radio show "Chez Show" at the Chez Paree in Chicago, for example, Eigen rather sloppily links him to Bill Robinson. Rather than letting it slide, Davis highlights the subtle racism of this common mistake:

> Why do you compare me to Bill Robinson? . . . Jack, I want to make it clear that you are not the first person to do it. I hear it all the time and I see it in the papers and in magazines, and obviously nobody means it as anything but a compliment and I'm enormously flattered by the comparison—but it's a wrong one! . . . We are not the same kind of performers. Sure, I dance, but my style is totally different from his . . . . So if you're talking performance it would be much more logical to compare Fred Astaire to Bill Robinson, but I never heard that done.[52]

Davis is correct that his style bears little resemblance to the upright style of both Robinson and Astaire. And so, caught between what he saw as unfair characterizations by both the Black press and the white press, Davis redoubles his efforts to "get bigger" still.

Davis's true dance style by the late 1950s, as he breaks away from the retiring members of the Trio, is a blend of many others' styles which he delivers with modish panache. A chameleon in his dancing as much as in his impressions, what marks his dance as so interesting is the smoothness of integration, the near simultaneity of that multiplicity rather than bouncing from person to person with mannerism or vocal tone changes. Even when performing numbers not at all associated with Broadway, he fuses aspects of that style—especially those popularized on screen by Gene Kelly—with both the jazz of his youth and the popular dances of the present. This is most clearly exemplified by the segment that opened this chapter, from his May 5, 1957 appearance on *The Steve Allen Show*. The episode begins with a skit starring host Steve Allen, Sammy Davis, Jr., and famed writer/director/actor Orson Welles. Davis has by now shed his eye patch and has taken to wearing fashionably thick horn-rimmed glasses, which he wears here, though he is costumed in a turban as a "yogi"—with an also turbaned Allen as his "swami" counterpart—for this magic trick skit. The explicitly Orientalist context here functions to smooth over the multiracial collaboration that had spurred hate mail a few years prior, allowing for momentary racial indeterminacy for Davis not unlike the Nicholas Brothers' Latinesque exoticism in *Down Argentine Way* (1943).[53] Later in the episode, after the Trio has performed one of the final iterations of their usual act together—including impressions by Sammy Jr. and crouched, hopping, one-legged wings by an aging Will Mastin—Davis comes back out for his duet with Allen. His carefully crafted footwork is complemented by equally carefully crafted costuming, lighting, and camerawork that stands out from standard vaudeo fare, allowing his fashionable masculinity to shine through seamlessly alongside his virtuosic fusion dance.

Davis's joke about his "Cye Martin tight pants" being "all he needs" (before asking Allen for some rhythm) indexes his active attempts at this moment to reshape his image—beginning in 1955 or 1956, he approached the swanky New York City clothier Cye Martin and asked for quite slim slacks. Rather than the standard circumference of 22–24 inches at the knee, Davis requested 16 or fewer. He remembers telling Martin, "I want the pants so tight that I can barely sit down in them," and remembers Martin responding, "What you want is a flannel suit with leggings."[54] Implicit here is a more spectacular masculinity than he had indulged while still with the Trio, an everyday look more in line with the kind of tailoring that Gene Kelly reserved for dancing only. Then, melding together movement styles aligned with all of the previous case studies in this book (Kelly, but also the Nicholas Brothers and Elvis), Davis drives home his truly synthetic capabilities. This mélange of jazz tap, Broadway jazz, social dance, and some Davis signatures (the occasional ballet-style *developé* kick from a *plié* began here and continued through the sixties) represents several decades of Davis's observations of his peers, both Black and white, on stage, film, and television. And by doing it all in his signature tight pants, a sport jacket, popped collar, and ascot, he claims a fashionable and suave masculinity that balances the

170   WHITE SCREENS, BLACK DANCE

classic with the contemporary—much like the dance itself. However, his fleeting presence on variety shows was not "big enough" for Davis's vision of his potential stardom.

After several years of lobbying for more serious acting roles, Davis finally began to land some, but dancing remained the most remarked-upon aspect of his performances. On the one hand, his starring role in the 1958 "Auf Wiedersehen" episode of *General Electric Theater* was regarded with triumph by Morris agent Sy Marsh: "Well, sweetheart, you've made television history. When they write books about the tube they've got to write that Sammy Davis, Jr. was the first Negro actor to star in episodic television."[55] On the other hand, breaking down barriers to dramatic television got him less notice in the press than his first major film role, Danny in *Anna Lucasta* (1958). In the film, starring Eartha Kitt as Anna, Davis's Danny serves as the embodiment of wildness and debauchery. A sailor-turned-taxi driver, Danny prefers a good time over marriage and stability. Anna meets Danny in a gin joint out at the docks. The two appear to be of similar disposition, enjoying booze, cigarettes, gaudy jewelry, and lewd dancing together. Indeed, they don't even need music to dance so suggestively around the bar that the owner orders them to stop. But Anna is called home, a pawn in her family's game to con a young bachelor out of his money by marrying her off, though she eventually runs away again with Danny.

When Anna rejoins Danny in his lifestyle of revelry, the film breaks from its overall commitment to verisimilitude and instead offers a sort of drunken fever dream montage of Davis's Danny dancing, intercut with reaction shots of Kitt's Anna in her gin-fueled stupor. Suddenly, Danny is no longer in the crowded bar with Anna, but is instead alone in an empty space. The number both begins and ends with Davis's focused, intense, and seductive stare toward the camera-as-Anna, in medium close-up. With each cut, he pops back and forth between his current suit and his past sailor uniform, then dancing in a long shot to the hot jazz music with a mix of tap, mambo, and modern jazz (see Figure 4.5). Still in an empty, open space, he includes a few spins and emphatic, expansive arm gestures, providing a clear contrast between tight fists and open palms. He also includes the same Presleyesque isolated leg flaps that he'd begun to incorporate in the years prior. Despite this dancing style consistent with the rest of the late-fifties Sammy Davis star text, he is still acting, so the entire sequence is sloppier and his gaze more lolling and leering than his usual precision and sharpness when being himself. And yet, Davis peeks through Danny in cuts to him playing the drums and trumpet. Though the role of Danny is a relatively small one, Davis's performance is so electric it made its way into Bosley Crowther's negative review of the film: "Mr. Davis does sixteen wiggles for every one that the role requires."[56] Recalling the same kinds of complaints lodged against Presley's pelvis a couple

Figure 4.5 Alone in an empty space during the drunken fever dream sequence in *Anna Lucasta* (1958), Davis pops back and forth between his suit and a sailor uniform as he looks seductively into the camera (left) and dances in a mix of styles, including more Presley-style leg flaps (right).

years prior, the review unwittingly highlights that this was a rare opportunity for a Black man to be Presley-level sexy and virile on the silver screen.

This fever dream sequence is also the clearest indication of a fairly direct influence from Gene Kelly on Davis's late 1950s dance style. While this is not the first time Davis has used a Kellyesque movement vocabulary—as demonstrated above, he had been incorporating signature Kelly stances and the palm/fist dichotomy for several years by this point—this is the first time he dances in Kelly's signature sailor uniform. Kelly's dancing sailors of the decade prior were no doubt familiar to Davis, between his regularly hosted film screenings and the fact that his friend Frank Sinatra costarred as a sailor with Gene Kelly in both *Anchors Aweigh* (1945) and *On The Town* (1949). It is thus no stretch to surmise that he had studied Kelly's work and intentionally alluded to his style in this sailor performance; like many of his sung and spoken impressions on stage, this amounts to a danced impression onscreen. But unlike those sung and spoken impressions, which were often announced, the incorporealization is not remarked upon, and is instead integrated into a drunken character with Davis (and Presley!) twists on top. It is also an embodied example of what Gerald Early calls Davis's "interracialism."[57] Though Early conceptualizes Davis as interracial in general, through his personal trajectories as a celebrity, his performance of interracialism begins in his body itself. The result is a shapeshifting Sammy Davis introducing himself to Hollywood film audiences—through both Black dance and formerly blackbodied dance—as the embodiment of sexiness, temptation, and debauchery.

Davis had the opportunity to more fully explore Black sensuality and sexuality through film dances by winning the character of Sportin' Life in Samuel Goldwyn's big-budget film adaptation of *Porgy and Bess* (1959). The film originated as a 1925 novel by DuBose Heyward that was then adapted into a 1927

172   WHITE SCREENS, BLACK DANCE

play by Heyward and his wife Dorothy, and re-adapted into a 1935 Broadway opera by Heyward and composer-lyricist team George and Ira Gershwin. The story takes place in the so-called "Catfish Row" area of Charleston, where disabled beggar Porgy falls in love with drug-addicted Bess. She has only just escaped the clutches of an abusive relationship with Crown, a dockworker who kills his opponent in a game of craps at the film's start. Even as Porgy and Bess grow attached over the course of the narrative, her drug dealer, Sportin' Life, repeatedly tempts her with a more exciting and sinful life in New York City. Sportin' Life, who had been originated for the Broadway stage by John W. Bubbles (né Sublett), and subsequently embodied by Cab Calloway in the mid-1950s revival, is a complex figure—and a role that Davis campaigned relentlessly to play, at one point offering to take on the part for free.[58] Much has been written about the various versions of *Porgy and Bess*, which is at bottom a white man's fantasy of a poor Black community in the Jim Crow South, but which has been equally shaped by Black talent and (re)interpretive performance over time.[59] From its inception in the 1920s to its use as Cold War propaganda during the Eisenhower administration and beyond, *Porgy* has frequently been characterized as a somehow quintessentially American folk opera.[60] But by the late 1950s, when the Goldwyn film version was being produced, there was immense tension between the text and the values of both the NAACP and most of the actors Goldwyn was courting as potential stars—Goldwyn placated the NAACP by announcing that the film would "portray the people of Catfish Row as triumphant over racism" and pledging the film's profits to charity, but potential stars Harry Belafonte, Sidney Poitier, Dorothy Dandridge, Pearl Bailey, and Diahann Carroll all either refused the roles offered or remained extremely hesitant about the damaging messaging baked into the controversial story.[61] Against this backdrop, that Davis not only had no reservations but also actively pursued the role of Sportin' Life is once again indicative of his complex and unpredictable racial politics—this time, he appears not to act in solidarity with the Civil Rights vision shared by most of his contemporaries. And yet, he did claim to participate in the cast's active revision of the script to remove the more offensive bits of dialogue, particularly the heavy dialect.[62] Reviews were mixed, especially in the Black press, but the biggest names and outlets were disappointed; James Baldwin wrote for *Commentary* that *Porgy and Bess* "assuages [whites'] guilt about Negroes and it attacks none of their fantasies," and Era Bell Thompson wrote for *Ebony* (in an article titled "Why Negroes Don't Like *Porgy and Bess*") that the film was "the same old kettle of catfish."[63]

Despite its controversies, Goldwyn's *Porgy and Bess* gave Davis the opportunity to act alongside some of the most respected Black stars in Hollywood at the time (Sidney Poitier, Dorothy Dandridge, Pearl Bailey), and simultaneously helped to establish him onscreen as a Black Dandy—a persona that he worked to embody in a range of media appearances outside the evil figure of Sportin' Life. Davis recalled that Irene Sharaff, his costume designer for *Porgy*, ordered the pants for the role much as Davis ordered his own; when he commented that the test-pair "fit like skin," Sharaff told the tailor to "make them tighter. I want those pants so tight that you'll see him move all over his body .... Split the coat at the bottom. I want them to see everything he's got."[64] These pants formed the foundation of an equally tight three-piece suit (a major departure from the looser tailoring on Cab Calloway's suit for the role), with bow tie and matching pocket square, which were then accessorized with a cane, gloves, spats, and a bowler hat. So clothed, Davis interprets Sportin' Life by following largely in Bubbles' footsteps, drawing upon his vaudeville hoofing vocabulary but extending it with various light-footed flourishes—on Davis's petit frame, these flourishes read as decidedly more effeminate than did Bubbles'. In George Gershwin's original vision for Sportin' Life, he imagined "a humorous, dancing villain, who is likable and believable and at the same time evil;" correspondingly, director Rouben Mamoulian "had instructed Bubbles 'to make no movement except in the pattern of dance,' and it was principally by dancing that [Bubbles] took control of the stage."[65] It is unclear how much of this was passed on to Davis before Goldwyn replaced Mamoulian with Otto Preminger for the film version, but Davis, like Bubbles, is dancerly in his approach to every scene, even the ones where he is not explicitly dancing. He hops and glides about, such that the assessment "Bubbles's 'dancing' and his 'acting' were indistinguishable from one another" is equally applicable to Davis; from this perspective, it is little wonder that he campaigned so hard for the role.[66] Indeed, there was a certain equivalence between his personal identity and the character.[67] While he was certainly not intentionally predatory, by the late fifties Davis was settling into a life of nightly parties and debauchery in his hotel suites, so he was as much a figure of temptation and sin as Sportin' Life himself.[68] And of course, Davis was styling his wardrobe just as carefully and lavishly.

Davis's big number in *Porgy and Bess*, "It Ain't Necessarily So," which he had of course already performed on television, is as clear a reflection of Davis's own dandyism as it is of the sinful character he is playing (Figure 4.6). The number occurs during a church picnic on Kittiwah Island, where the song's lyrics have Sportin' Life casting doubt on stories in the Bible and further encouraging the denizens of Catfish Row to take its teachings "with a grain of salt." However, it is not his words but his vernacular jazz dance that is implied to be the most dangerous aspect of Sportin' Life's presentation to the believers; as he slithers out of frame at the end of the number, a pious church woman admonishes the now-dancing community: "Stop it! Shame on all you sinners! You call yourselves church members . . . and when the Christians turn their back, you start behaving like Sodom and Gomorrah! . . . Get on the boat, all you wicked children." While it

Figure 4.6 Davis's performance as Sportin' Life in *Porgy and Bess* (1959) embodies Davis's own style of dance and dandyism. Image courtesy of Gjon Mili/The LIFE Picture Collection/Shutterstock.

is unclear whether Sportin' Life's more philosophical arguments have taken hold, the one aspect of his "sermon" that has immediately resonated is his physicality, and it seems to read as much more dangerous to the pious woman than doubt in the Bible's teachings.[69] And this physicality is extremely anachronistic: he does not perform a Charleston, or even provide much focused tap dance, but rather the same mélange of soft-shoe footwork, syncopated hip thrusts, and occasional Broadway-style kicks, turns, and barrel rolls that Davis had been drawing together since first "going solo." Though he is more up-on-his toes in general than he had been on television, Davis here is so himself (including a slide through the dirt on his knees, which Sportin' Life surely would have avoided) that he exceeds the role and "conveys Davis's energy but not the character's aspirant urbanity."[70] Thus, we are ultimately faced not with Sportin' Life's dandy, but with Davis's dandy. Still, more than any other film role or television spot, Sportin' Life allowed Davis to present himself to the public *legibly* as a dandy—whose masculinity is seductive, dancerly, very well-dressed, slightly feminine, and a one-way ticket to sin city.

Mr. Perpetual Motion

Somewhat controversially, Gerald Early has argued, "I think a very plausible case can be made that in the 1960s Sammy Davis Jr. was a more influential and important person than either Malcolm X or Muhammad Ali, the two blacks, outside of Martin Luther King Jr., usually seen as the most seminal black personalities of the time."[71] Certainly, the sixties saw the peak of Davis's career, and were a period when he was almost omnipresent in American popular culture: in the first half of the decade, he was most often seen at The Sands Hotel in Las Vegas and in Hollywood films with a group known as the Rat Pack: Frank Sinatra, Dean Martin, Peter Lawford, and Joey Bishop; at the middle of the decade, he was starring in *Golden Boy* on Broadway and then helming *The Sammy Davis, Jr. Show* on NBC; by the end of the decade, he descended into parody on *Sweet Charity*.[72] The sixties are also the decade during which Davis's activism on behalf of the Civil Rights Movement is highly visible, from marches to benefit performances, and the decade during which his star text, now established via the historical figure of the Black dandy, pivots toward the contemporary figures of the playboy and then the hippie. The latter do not erase the former so much as offer new iterations of it for a swiftly changing cultural and political landscape. Thus, pushing away from Sportin' Life's 1959 Zip Coon of a bygone era, Davis the Rat Pack member establishes in the early sixties a type of Black "cool" whose glasses, goatee, and getup made a young Gerald Early think he was an intellectual; by the late sixties he morphs again to embrace the hippie counterculture look, leaving Sinatra, Martin, and the rest of his contemporaries to age in their bland suits and ties.[73] More than anything else, Davis understood his own reputation during the 1960s as "the figure of perpetual motion, the little guy with the dazzling energy. They love to say, 'Nobody works as hard as Sammy Davis!'"[74] As such, he danced his way through the decade with an attention to fashions both musical and sartorial, balancing Broadway with social dance with old school jazz tap, ultimately forging a protean masculinity of the "cool."

To kick off this decade of especially rapid chameleonic changes, Davis appeared in *Ocean's 11* (1960), the first Rat Pack film. That he was the only Black member of an otherwise white "clan" was made especially apparent in the film's casting;[75] while all eleven co-conspirators in the film's heist plot are World War II veterans of the same Army division, all but Davis's character are able to secure jobs at the Las Vegas casino they plan to rob. And though his earworming vocal performance of "Eee-O-11" is the film's sonic through-line, Davis's Josh Howard, a sanitation worker, has relatively less screen time than the rest of the Pack. He does not quite dance, either, even when he first sings "Eee-O-11" among other sanitation workers. Indeed, the most important aspect of Davis's appearance, here, is its irony. He holds precisely the role in this imagined Vegas that he was determined to be "too big" for in real life; the film's heist plot only works because Josh, the Black garbage truck driver, is functionally invisible to the seat of white power on The Strip. Davis in 1960 may have been a headliner at The Sands, on a first-name basis with manager Jack Entratter, and finally granted the freedom to roam about, gamble, and stay in a premium suite, but as Josh in the world of

176   WHITE SCREENS, BLACK DANCE

the film, he was pulled back to an earlier point in his career, when he "had to leave through the kitchen, with the garbage, like thieves in the night."[76] This uneasy sense of conditional membership in the Rat Pack, most publicly introduced through *Ocean's 11*, appears to define Davis's relationship to them throughout the 1960s. Davis's background as a poor Black Cuban American (though he claimed to be Puerto Rican instead) boy from Harlem who converted to Judaism seemed to parallel the all-American rags-to-riches class trajectory of the others (Sinatra and Martin hailing from working-class Italian American Catholic families, and Bishop from a working-class Polish American Jewish family), but in live shows at The Sands he remained the butt of many racial (and religious, when Bishop wasn't there) jokes amongst the group. One of the *less* damaging examples is a recurring bit in which Dean Martin picks Davis up and says, "I'd like to thank the NAACP for this wonderful trophy." Though they all constantly roasted each other, the other members were more often targeted for personal qualities, such as Martin's alcoholism and Sinatra's bad temper, rather than their ethnic or religious identities. Davis played along, but did occasionally highlight how rough they were on him, as in the album release of a 1963 show in which he says to the audience after a series of insults, "and these are the *best* friends I have."[77] So, although his film career during the 1960s is comprised almost entirely of Rat Pack movies, this group was not the only influence on Davis's sixties masculinity.

Despite his very public marriage to white Swedish actress May Britt in 1960, another major influence on Davis's performance of masculinity in the sixties was *Playboy* magazine founder Hugh Hefner. Davis appeared on Hefner's television shows at both the dawn (*Playboy's Penthouse*, 1961) and dusk (*Playboy After Dark*, 1969) of the decade, suggesting that his self-fashioning as a playboy was at least as important to his star text as his membership in the Rat Pack. *Playboy's Penthouse* (1959–1961) was a variety show disguised as a hip house party that filmed in Chicago; in late 1960, Davis was performing there and asked to be on the show. Filming for the second season had already wrapped, so Hefner had a new set built specifically to tape Davis's appearance, which aired during the show's final season in 1961.[78] When Davis "arrives" to the on-camera party, fashionably late, he is wearing a finely tailored, slim-fitting suit. While there, he is nearly always holding a cigarette and a cocktail (often in the same hand), and sometimes wears a fashionable pair of thick-rimmed eyeglasses. The company is notably entirely white, save for the mostly Black entourage Davis brings in with him. For the guests, Davis provides a mix of jazzy singing, suave soft shoe dancing, impressions, and equally performative drinking and smoking. In his primary soft shoe dance, which accompanies his vocal rendition of "The Lady Is a Tramp," Davis's driving kineticism finds its foundation in his contrasts between emphatically rooted downbeats with deeply bent knees and the buoyancy of his little pirouettes and jump off a balcony set piece back into

Figure 4.7 During his 1961 appearance on *Playboy's Penthouse*, Davis provides a contrast between movement qualities via deeply rooted downbeats (left) alongside the buoyancy of a jump off a balcony set piece (right).

the crowd (see Figure 4.7). His Africanist contrasts in movement quality accompany a set of steps primarily drawn from Black vernacular jazz dance, but he also includes flourishes drawn from European forms such as ballet. As a result, the overall dance style here is once again similar to that employed by Gene Kelly in the 1950s and once again a sort of embodied form of what Early terms Davis's "interracialism." Through such a dance in such a context, this can also be understood as Davis constructing his own image of the playboy. Hefner's imagined playboy figure, made famous via *Playboy* magazine, seemed to have been triangulated somewhere between himself, Frank Sinatra, and James Bond. As Elizabeth Fraterrigo has demonstrated in her book about *Playboy*, the magazine aimed itself at white, especially WASPy (white, Anglo-Saxon, Protestant), college-educated, liberal young men, and it encouraged not only a conspicuous consumption of expensive cars, high-tech apartments, and beautiful women, but also the cultivation of a taste culture rooted in jazz music, smart fashion, and fine liquor.[79] By 1960, Davis had established himself as a *performer* of jazz who also happened to love spending far too much money on expensive cars and smart fashion, so he and Hefner were a natural fit.

Davis's version of the playboy, however, is different from Hefner's: still triangulated in part alongside Frank Sinatra, but also drawing from Gene Kelly and a long line of "Black cool" figures he had watched or met since childhood. In the first case, that Davis was, at this time, emerging through regular "Summit" performances at the Sands Hotel and in *Oceans 11* as a central member of the Rat Pack—however conditionally—initially aligned him with Hefner's playboy image. In the words of Fraterrigo,

> As members of the Rat Pack, these entertainers achieved iconic status with their hip, cool style and reputation as all-around playboys. Like Hefner's, their

178 WHITE SCREENS, BLACK DANCE

> work often seemed like play, and they played with abandon ... they achieved their greatest acclaim at a time when they publicly reveled in a hedonistic bachelor life-style.[80]

This is all largely because Sinatra, as leader of the pack, had recently reemerged as a big star himself—not as the crooner beloved by bobbysoxers over a decade prior, but as the womanizing wolf he played in the film version of *Pal Joey* (1957), a persona solidified by his very public extramarital affairs. But the signifiers of Sinatra's lifestyle were equally in his self-presentation. As a 1958 *Playboy* article titled "The Word on Frank Sinatra" put it, "Hat set cockily on the back of his head, raincoat draped carelessly over a bony shoulder, this hip brand of love god ... casually ambles into the phantasies of females young and old, dances on the ceilings near their beds, bids them come fly with him down to Acapulco Bay."[81] As indicated earlier in this chapter, Davis had long modeled himself musically and sometimes stylistically after Sinatra, and this continues into the 1950s, when Sinatra is being recast as "combative, caustic, and sexually potent."[82] It is in this context that Davis borrowed "The Lady Is a Tramp" from its recent revival by Sinatra in *Pal Joey*. In his second autobiography, Davis explicitly says of his persona, "[t]he attitude, the cockiness was Sinatra. Black people weren't cocky in those days."[83] But while Sinatra may have danced in women's dreams, he couldn't really dance—at least, not without the extensive help of Gene Kelly. Davis, of course, *could* dance, and the fact that the dance he chose to perform on *Playboy's Penthouse* is rather in the style of Kelly (recall that he performed the same wolf character as Sinatra in the original Broadway version of *Pal Joey*) completes Davis's triangulation of white playboys. Thus, his image of the playboy certainly draws heavily from the one established by Sinatra and approved by *Playboy* itself, but its dance style also bears continuity with the Kelly-influenced mélange he developed on 1950s variety television. Jacobson finds this "highly pronounced masculinism," in Davis's usage, as part of "a wolfish, playboy culture where licentious sexuality could become a stand-in for freedom itself."[84] In short, Davis's Black dandy playboy used a blend of Black dance and re-appropriated, formerly blackbodied Black dance to exceed the limits of the white playboy playbook in seducing women—especially white women—and implicitly equated this sense of universal sex appeal with actual power. This is the crux of his sixties masculinity.

Beyond the influence of his personal and stylistic associations with white people such as Britt, Hefner, Sinatra, and Kelly, equally crucial to understanding Davis's performance of a distinctly "Black cool" masculinity was his very public involvement with the Civil Rights Movement. As Emilie Raymond has documented, Davis began appearing at civil rights-related benefit performances as early as 1956, when he performed at a Madison Square Garden rally to support the Montgomery bus boycott. By 1958, he was lending major help to the

NAACP's membership campaign, and he produced and promoted several benefit shows for organizations such as the Chicago Urban League, the Southern Christian Leadership Conference, and the Freedom Riders in the early 1960s.[85] In addition to hosting these events as well as many "house parties" to raise funds for the Student Nonviolent Coordinating Committee, Davis also personally donated large amounts of his own money to civil rights causes—more than many of the more outspoken Black celebrities of the time.[86] In 1963, he participated in the March on Washington, having been contacted by both Harry Belafonte and Robert "Bobby" Kennedy beforehand: the former asked him to appear and the latter asked him to be careful.[87] He recalled an early-sixties conversation wherein Kennedy said, "You're not popular with the Klan . . . or the White Citizens Council. You're on all of their lists. Whenever you plan to appear in public at anything controversial, anything to do with civil rights, be sure to call me a day or two in advance, and at least I can have a couple of men there looking out for you."[88] Raymond notes that Davis faced criticism for his unwillingness to go to the South for events—though few other Black celebrities were willing to risk their lives in the South, either—but in 1965, Belafonte convinced him to perform at the Stars for Freedom Rally in Montgomery, Alabama to support those on the (third) march from Selma to Montgomery.[89] Davis also recalled briefly joining the march itself:

> My stomach, my arms trembled. My legs were weakened and I walked heavily. But I was glad I was there. Those who watched us walking across their city recognized that our presence was causing cameras and printing presses to record what was happening, to bring our protest to tens of millions of other Americans. And they saw an era fading, a way of life coming to a close.[90]

Clearly marking this as one of the most significant moments of the movement for him, Davis also organized a benefit in New York City called "Broadway Answers Selma," which "brought a new interracial cohort of stars to the cause . . . and raised an impressive $150,000."[91] When Dr. King was assassinated in 1968, Davis remembered immediately making his way to all three major New York television studios, saying he "did the six o'clock news everywhere," apparently trying to convince Black America not to riot *en masse*; he later attended the funeral at Coretta Scott King's home.[92] In recognition of all such deeds, NAACP Executive Director Roy Wilkins awarded Davis with the 53rd Spingarn Medal on March 30, 1969, citing the "tireless sacrifices he has made" and "his generous and meaningful participation in the civil rights movement."[93]

The tension that both Early and Raymond find with regard to Sammy Davis in the sixties—"establishment rebel," "both daring and deferential"—begins to crystallize through the juxtaposition of not only his white-influenced playboy self

180   WHITE SCREENS, BLACK DANCE

and his civil rights-supporting self, but also the media spaces where he dances and the styles he uses to do so. Though he does continue to dance, he does so with increasing simplicity and brevity when performing amongst the Rat Pack. And in the films' diegetic contexts, these dances are often fraught. For example, Davis's singular dance scene for the western *Sergeants 3* (1962), in which he plays a freed slave named Jonah, is indicative of the ambivalence that remains for him in being the Black dancer entertaining a white cast and audience. In an 1870 saloon, Jonah wears a tattered hat, khakis, and cowboy boots to entertain customers by performing up on the bar, struggling to balance demands to dance against demands to play the trumpet. Jonah protests, "Gentlemen, now, I can either play, or I can dance, but I can't—" and a burly cowboy interrupts with "Oh yeah you can, you can play *and* dance." At this point, the cowboy cocks his gun threateningly and Davis's Jonah complies. As Matthew Frye Jacobson points out, this is framed as comedic hijinks in the film, but the trope of the "bullet dance" was a much grimmer lived reality for African Americans in the antebellum United States—and was among the tortures Davis endured from white soldiers while in the Army.[94] In Jacobson's reading, "the telescoping of historical time and the condensation of racialized meanings" is made particularly clear once the throughline is connected "[f]rom the historical reality of the bullet dance in antebellum North America, to its menacing replication in a racial skirmish on an Army base during World War II, to its putatively comic refrain in a lighthearted adventure film in the 1960s."[95] That Davis was comedically dancing his way through such condensations of Black trauma the year before joining the March on Washington indicates the tensions building in his star text. Stylistically, the dance itself is comprised of the fairly simple hoofing that Davis no doubt associated with the 1870s, offering little opportunity for Davis's talents to actually shine. It is also filmed unusually—from a perspective behind the bar rather than within the saloon's seating—which grants the spectator a mediocre view of Davis's dancing body but a full view of the uneasy context in which Jonah finds himself: at the whim of over a dozen armed, drunk, and white frontiersmen. The toned-down movement and tense air clearly separate Davis from the rest of the Rat Pack, who each emerge from rooms (and women) upstairs in the following shots. So, just as in *Ocean's 11*, Davis's character mirrors the kind of conditional membership across racial lines that was less obvious but just as relevant offscreen.

A similar dance on the bar in *Robin and the 7 Hoods* (1964), however, does seem to finally grant Davis some power, and despite the film not being a musical, offers a glimpse of how Davis might have danced as a musical star. Playing a gunslinger named Will, instructed by his mob boss to shoot up a rival's bar, Davis has full command of a large set and many opportunities to partake in *bricolage*. Shooting at some aspects of the set (cash registers, bottles, chandeliers)

Figure 4.8 As a gunslinger named Will in *Robin and the 7 Hoods* (1964), Davis performs a rather graceful, Astaire-style traveling tap sequence.

and dancing up and down others (the roulette table, the bar itself), Davis offers a surprisingly more graceful, Fred Astaire-style tap sequence with fewer Kelly or Presley elements (though these are not entirely absent). Davis combines almost propeller-like arms—a frequent strategy of Astaire's—with syncopated, travelling taps (see Figure 4.8). He does weave in comedy, a brief effeminate hip-swinging walk, a buoyant heel-click, and even a slide on his knees, allowing the Davis persona to shine through Will. Aspects of the dandy also remain: spats, very tight pants, skinny tie, and perfect slim tailoring on his shirt; like Sportin' Life, Will also relishes in his bad behavior. Overall, Davis manages to create the same balance of his own star persona with a seductive, dancing villain as he had in *Porgy and Bess*, which otherwise did not tend to happen when he was surrounded by the Rat Pack. And the dance itself, like the Nicholas Brothers' spectacular "Jumpin' Jive" number in *Stormy Weather*, reads as a hint of a road not taken in Hollywood: had Sammy Davis, Jr. had access to starring musical roles over the past several decades, what further range of compelling, multifaceted song-and-dance sequences might he have produced?

To balance out his seeming subservience to the white Rat Pack members in Hollywood (and Vegas), and perhaps also to implicitly highlight his Civil Rights work, Davis participated in at least one highly visible Black cultural project in the mid-sixties. As part of a CBS musical special entitled "The Strollin' 20s," which aired on February 21, 1966, Davis appears as a Bill Robinson-style tap dancer in Harlem. Among an all-star Black cast including Harry Belafonte, Sidney Poitier, George Kirby, Nipsey Russell, and Duke Ellington, Davis has a relatively minor role but provides a careful facsimile of the dance styles he was born into. Wearing a bowler hat and plaid suit in his primary scene, he taps upright rather than with a mobile upper body; he even adds a brief tap-up-steps sequence in the clearest nod to Robinson's famous stair dance. His characterization in the

182 WHITE SCREENS, BLACK DANCE

Belafonte-helmed special (set to Langston Hughes' poetic script) at first runs counter to his own star persona—serious, gentlemanly—but he reappears later in a light tan suit to accompany a group of chorus girls, transitioning into the comic mode which aligns more closely with Davis himself. He dances less in this portion, though he does briefly offer a slow, dragging tap introduction suggestive of a sand dance but lacking the sand itself. The program's star-studded nostalgia earned it a cover story for the February 4, 1966 edition of *LIFE* magazine—"Greatest Negro Stars Team Up"—with the cover image featuring the smiling visages of Belafonte and Poitier beside a tragicomically wincing Davis, hamming it up. It is almost as if years of being the butt of the Rat Pack's racial and often racist jokes led Davis to find relief in celebrating the Harlem Renaissance, reminding his audience (and perhaps himself) that his masculinity was playful, stylish, and *Black*.

Midlife Styleshifting

Also in the mid-1960s, Davis begins to transition away from the suit-and-tie swinger and showcases the chameleonic side of his masculinity. Across four episodes of the two-season NBC musical variety series *Hullabaloo* (1965–1966), three of which he hosted, Davis proves he is more than just a Vegas playboy.[96] Not only does he join in social dances with a multi-racial ensemble of dancers ten to twenty years his junior—he also begins to shed his tailored suit in order to blend in with the more casual fashions of the young Hullabaloo corps. When Davis appeared on this young-skewing, hip program, he was starring in *Golden Boy* on Broadway, also supported by an integrated cast of young performers. Thus, though Davis clings to his tailored suit and makes jokes about being in his thirties during his first two *Hullabaloo* appearances, he soon adapts to the context at hand. This transformation can be seen in his dances: he kicks off his first appearance, in February, with a dance largely in his own style. The Hullabaloo Dancers are clearly choreographed in a more Broadway style (rather than their usual social dance style) to match him; all partake in his deeply bent knees, and jazzy *pas de bourées* back and forth with accentuating leg extensions to the sides. Davis also adds a signature kick and a bit of soft-shoe to distinguish himself. However, the first clue of his stylistic shift for the program's sake is his performance of the mashed potato while he sings; the other dancers echo it later. Unlike Davis's usual dances, which require too much breath to be achieved while singing, the relatively simple mashed potato is a low-effort accompaniment that signals his willingness to blend in with the youth.

Later in this same episode, Davis changes into a deep-V sweater over an unbuttoned shirt collar to perform a medley from *West Side Story* with guest

Joey Heatherton and the Hullabaloo Dancers. Davis snaps and shoots out more syncopated leg extensions with an ironically diverse cast of "Jets," all returning to the Broadway idiom Davis began the episode with. Though the choreography is not particularly complex—mostly simple walks, turns, and poses with varying accents—Davis slides easily into Jerome Robbins's choreographic style, as it is simply a more balletic spin on the jazz he was already dancing in his own Broadway show. A dynamic multi-camera setup, with tracking, dolly, and high-angle shots, helps to render the kineticism of Davis and his group here and in their later "mambo" segment, where the hips on everyone are particularly mobile. The Jets' final phrase of choreography seems tailored to Davis again, with big starfish and a hitch-kick to top it off; when Davis runs back on stage to continue his hosting duties immediately afterwards, he is clearly winded. But the multiple stylistic shifts, from his own Broadway moves, to the youth's social dance, to Jerome Robbins' Broadway style as an edgy Jet clearly shows the chameleon at work. In fact, the constant shifts are even enough to distract from the irony of Davis taking on the guise of a white European immigrant (a "Jet"), who in *West Side Story* is staged in violent opposition to his own self-proclaimed (if false) Puerto Rican identity (the "Sharks")—and, in the original *East Side Story*, Jewish identity, also self-proclaimed by Davis.[97] Through all layers, here, Davis performs briefly as the enemy, more explicitly so than he had even as a child in blackface, and with a troubling crystallization of his embodied "interracialism;" the prejudice of the character he has taken on is very nearly the target he is fighting with Dr. King and other Civil Rights leaders offstage.

Thirteen years after the pilot for Davis's *We Three* sitcom vehicle failed to sell, he finally got his own show: *The Sammy Davis, Jr. Show* (NBC, 1966). In a period where Black-led shows were still rare, it served to solidify Davis as one of the biggest stars of the sixties, while also suturing together the "old" Rat Pack playboy with the "new" hip social dancer who kept up with the youth scene. As Davis tells it, he originally turned down the offer in an attempt to be more present with his family, but then he noticed how his star text was changing in the press:

> As I read the newspapers and watched the television news and talk show, I saw that my image was changing or fading. For "Sammy" to be in a town and not be in the middle of what's happening was a contradiction in style. Earl Wilson had said it, I was developing the domesticated animal image, which was great for Perry Como but not for "Sammy" the saloon singer, the legend of perpetual motion, the swinger, the boozer, and "Wowowowowowee-wow, it's a party!"[98]

Consciously placing his star-self in quotes throughout the passage to separate that persona from his real self, Davis demonstrates a hyper-awareness of how his married family life conflicted with the "perpetual motion" masculinism he had worked to develop for his public figure in the first half of the decade. He cites this disconnect as the reason he changed his mind and agreed to host the program. It did not do particularly well and was canceled early due to scheduling conflicts, format changes, and having started as a mid-season replacement program, but its existence nevertheless serves as a testament to Davis's ongoing and carefully-constructed star power, especially since many of the show's guests and guest hosts—such as Richard Taylor and Elizabeth Burton, Sean Connery, Milton Berle, the Nicholas Brothers, The Supremes, Judy Garland, Diahann Carroll, and Lola Falana—were lined up by Davis himself.[99] In addition to guest performances, each episode is generally interspersed with Davis solos or duets with the guests. Sometimes Davis replicates the social dance-heavy style with a group of dancers that he had grown accustomed to on *Hullabaloo*; other times he proves that he's "still got it" with a speedy and crisp tap number recalling his late forties or early fifties style.

The Sammy Davis, Jr. Show's series finale (only the fifteenth episode) captures the true breadth of Davis's talents; the entire hour is a one-man show. During it, Davis draws a parallel to his nightclub shows, suggesting "we always have a moment where we do something that reflects upon my early career as a hoofer." This leads to a long tap sequence, inaugurated by a slow, vaudeville-esque soft shoe number in a straw hat by the version of himself he calls "Mr. Tippy-Tap Toe." While certainly rhythmic, this portion is more about the carriage of Davis's full body, which looks rather like Davis doing Kelly doing Davis (see Figure 4.9), accompanied by George Rhodes on piano. To transition into the second half of the sequence, he grabs a comically large shoehorn and switches shoes, before launching into some of his best tap work of the decade. Davis achieves crystal clear machine-gun taps in a nearly upright Bill Robinson style. In a rare departure

Figure 4.9 During the series finale of *The Sammy Davis, Jr. Show* (April 22, 1966), Davis performs a tap number that first engages in a full-body dance style more reminiscent of Gene Kelly (left); after switching shoes, he taps in a more upright style with his hands in his pockets and his head bowed (right).

for Davis, he looks down and places both hands in his pockets, presenting the most unassuming and least showboating version of himself, encouraging all to merely listen in awe as he relaxes into his own speed—only occasionally accented by other sounds from George or his band. He brings his arms back out for a more intense portion, seeming to propel himself through to a slower, quieter ending. He completes the sequence without comment, not out of breath at all, merely grabbing the microphone and picking up where he left off in the middle of the song "Put on a Happy Face." Despite a decade full of playful, sexy social dance defining Davis's playboy era, he reminds us here of his roots and morphs once again into a more timeless, ageless, quiet masculinity, stripped of his bread-and-butter grandstanding for a brief moment.

Zooming out from this moment, however, perhaps *The Sammy Davis, Jr. Show*'s most important contribution to Davis's star text is its opening sequence, which through sheer repetition becomes a central reference point for Sammy in the sixties. Featuring Davis's silhouette performing against a plain white background, the sequence opens the first fourteen episodes with most everything *but* the tap portion of the Sammy Davis dance vocabulary: his classic side leg extension with the standing knee bent, his syncopated walks and a splayed starfish pose, leg flaps and a little hip-thrusting social dance, playful impish prancing, modified Mambo, and big heel-clicks stopped in freeze-frame. As a special treat, he performs the sequence again, "live," for the finale. Another clear signifier of his range and a reminder that he is a dancer first, the sequence cements a clear, black-and-white image of sixties Sammy's cool—and increasingly playful—masculinity. It is unfortunately balanced out by a closing scene parallel to the Nicholas Brothers' final film scene: just as their final image on film, performing "Be A Clown," was as a pair of undignified clowns trying to avoid a noose, Davis ends his television show and one-man finale by performing "Be A Clown" in an absurd clown/tramp costume (but no white face makeup). He does not dance much in his huge shoes, and while he is at first surrounded by fellow clowns (all in whiteface), he transitions in the final bars to a sad solo on a stool, singing "What Kind of Fool Am I?" as he removes components of the clown costume. Changing the lyrics to "What kind of *clown* am I?," Davis seems to let his "true" self through for a moment: fleetingly acknowledging that his entire career is built on the isolating imperative of being the only Black man clowning about amongst a sea of white network executives, colleagues, and audience members.

Soon afterward, Davis appears on the ABC variety show *Hollywood Palace* some ten times between 1967–1969, often as the host, joining other dancer-performers from Mickey Rooney to James Brown on the stage and ever more chameleonically adapting to their styles. It is in this venue that we can really see Davis's persona move far away from the playboy of the early sixties and into the hippie of the late sixties, while still preserving the dandy's attention to the weight and significance of his sartorial choices. Offscreen, Davis was spending the lion's share of his time in London, doing so much cocaine (and other drugs) with hippie icons like Jimi Hendrix that Sinatra wasn't really speaking to him and May Britt was initiating divorce proceedings. On *The Hollywood Palace*, he began to wear big patterns, bright colors, bell bottoms, and fringe, most of which he purchased in London:

> I was getting my gear at Mr. Fish on the King's Road, where Mick [Jagger] got his stuff. Everything was one of a kind. I had the long coats, beaded jackets, bell-bottoms, big puffed sleeves, military braid, beads from Carnaby Street, and the paisley shirts. My Nehrus came from France. Onstage I was wearing skintight solid-color jumpsuits with low-slung belts that hit below the waist. I had one made by Cartier and another by Hermès and they were a glittering offset.[100]

Davis's *Hollywood Palace* appearances also offer additional evidence of his again-transforming star text. While his first couple of 1967 episodes continue in the nostalgic tap dance vein started in the final episode of his own series (including a rare duet with tap elder Baby Laurence), by 1968 he is wearing his hair natural for the first time on screen (see Figure 4.10) and singing Ray Charles's "What'd I Say" with Aretha Franklin. Of course, the transformation did not take entirely, as nostalgia was expected from an aging hoofer in his forties, especially one whose bestselling autobiography was released two years prior.[101] The ready availability of Davis's life story also seems to encourage thoughtful commentary on the sheer span of his career. On the October 18, 1969 episode, for example, hostess Diana Ross is given the responsibility of introducing both Michael Jackson and the Jackson 5, and Sammy Davis, Jr. The writers, Jay Burton and

Figure 4.10 During his 1968 appearances on *The Hollywood Palace*, Davis begins to wear his natural hair onscreen (left) and, during a tribute sequence, lifts Diana Ross, Fred-and-Ginger style, in a relation of dependency (right).

Charles Isaacs, engineer a series of comedic mix-ups wherein Davis mistakes her description of young Michael Jackson as being about him—and later, vice versa: "I have the pleasure of introducing a great young star, who has been in the business all of his life. He has worked with his family, and when he sings and dances, he lights up the stage." Thus, viewers are implicitly encouraged to see Jackson as the "next" Sammy Davis, and reflect on the fact that Davis still (sort of) appears "young" and worth watching, forty years after his showbiz debut.

Though Davis then sings a hip Blood, Sweat, and Tears song, he is later pulled back into the realm of nostalgia as he and Diana Ross perform a medley tribute to Fred Astaire and Ginger Rogers. For Davis's part, this is an opportunity to both deepen his long history of imitating white performers and weave together several threads of his star image: the dandy once again meets the playboy. After each magically transforms into evening wear—including a lyrically reinforced top hat, white tie, and tails for Davis—they sing bits of the old musical numbers that made Fred and Ginger famous, and then launch into a dance duet. Surprisingly, Ross does far more solo dancing than Davis, leaving him to watch her in awe; this is the biggest departure from classical Fred and Ginger that they indulge. Otherwise, they manage to squeeze in all four arrangements of couple dancing that Richard Dyer has described in his analysis of heterosexual happiness in musical numbers: side by side, mirroring, mutually holding, and a relation of dependency.[102] In Dyer's reading of these old numbers, "the nearer you get to sex the less sameness and equality can be tolerated," so the "climax" of the number often requires the woman's full dependency on the man—he often lifts her into the air.[103] This is precisely what Davis and Ross accomplish, as the climax of their dance involves him lifting and spinning her in the air just as Astaire once did with Rogers (see Figure 4.10). And because it is 1969, he follows its completion with a bawdy playboy joke that may not have been airable in years prior. When he remarks that he is taking off the white tie, vest, and tails, and Ross replies "Oh, in case you're taking off anything else, I think we'd better have a staging break," Davis pulls her in close for a kiss and says, "You bet your *Oh! Calcutta!*, baby." *Oh! Calcutta!* was a theatrical revue that had recently debuted off-Broadway, composed of a series of sketches about sex in which the performers are often disrobing and nude. In a sense, then, Davis makes more explicit the danced innuendo they had just borrowed from 1930s musicals—he may be forty-three and Ross merely twenty-five, but this lascivious masculinity bears clear continuity with the playboy persona he has not entirely shed. Offscreen, he was participating in enough orgies that the public and private personae were starting to blur, and heavy onstage flirtation with a younger Black woman remained far more socially acceptable than with a white woman.

With *Sweet Charity* (1969), wherein Bob Fosse choreographs Davis's "Big Daddy" as a counterculture send-up, Davis performs a sort of logical

Figure 4.11 Outfitted in a hot pink chemise, gold necklace, and black leather boot-pants for *Sweet Charity* (1969), Davis as "Big Daddy" the cult leader does the swim as the camera frames him between the legs of one of his followers.

conclusion to the masculinity he had been building since his time in the Army. He is costumed in a hot pink stylized paisley chemise with round yellow glasses, thick gold necklaces, and skin-tight black leather boot-pants (see Figure 4.11). Davis absolutely loved the role and penned an enthusiastic article about the experience which appeared in the *Michigan Chronicle* about a month after the film's release. He writes,

> Around me are the weirdest, wildest, loveliest, loosest-jointed chorus of flower children, Carnaby mods, gurus and weirdos. And there I am, blessing my children, anointing them with my hands which show off eight big rings, rattling my love-in-necklaces in tempo, my black English glove leather pants with boots attached catching the light of a rhythmic flashing spotlight.[104]

We can once again see the proud dandy, though he is peacocking a very different style than he had at the beginning of the decade. Adding to his style shift is the extent to which Davis dives into the Fosse version of jazz dance for his "Rhythm of Life" number: in yet another departure from anything he had done previously, he adopts a birdlike stance with a pigeon-toed walk and a bobbing head. As an ironically petite cult leader, Davis's Big Daddy seems to both float and slither through the throngs of followers he beckons into his large garage full of "groovy" cars. In some respects, the Fosse signature is well-suited to Davis's preexisting style, since Fosse's style was built on the Africanisms of jazz artists like Davis (and, secondarily, blackbodiers like Gene Kelly) in the first place. With some of Davis's syncopated walking and prancing, for example, it is unclear whether the pelvis-forward, hip-thrusting nature of the steps is Davis's idea or Fosse's. There is also a smooth integration of both Davis's recently-learned popular dances—especially the swim—and his signature kick (made all the more identifiable thanks to the *Sammy Davis, Jr. Show* opening sequence) into the number (see Figure 4.11). Overall, Davis sings more than he dances, and the number's impact comes as much from interesting staging and camerawork as from his movement through the frame, but it serves as a meaningful capstone to the peak of his shapeshifting career for several reasons.

First, it was only his second but also his final appearance in a live-action film musical, a perhaps curious and surprising state of affairs for a song-and-dance man. But Davis reached Hollywood as the musical genre was dying and as other Black musical talent (like the Nicholas Brothers) were being forced abroad and/ or onto television. There is thus a hint of what could have been in the large gap—both temporal and tonal—between *Porgy and Bess* and *Sweet Charity*. Second, it highlights the breadth of Davis's protean movement range; the Fosse idiom is nearly as far as one can stray from early 1930s hoofing while still tracing the through-line of Black dance through midcentury America, and Davis proves himself capable of shapeshifting into it through the entire range of corporeality in between. Finally, it perfectly encapsulates the politics of Davis's dandy-chameleon masculinity. In the context of the film, Davis has become the Black leader to whom his range of largely white followers fly, swim, and—literally—crawl. What began in the Army as an attempt to demand recognition of his humanity, a forgetting of his Blackness, and a sort of awed respect, blossoms nearly twenty-five years later into (fictional) worship of him as nearly transcendent of humanity and into holiness, a paternalistic father figure whose Blackness is indexed briefly through scatting but otherwise, finally, irrelevant. In this figuration, his masculinity is *so* cool and modish that it is irresistible to all who encounter it, such that the only response is blind worship of little Big Daddy Davis.

So when Davis ends the decade rather where he started by appearing on Hefner's next program, *Playboy After Dark* (1969–1970), he looks entirely different. Hefner is still in a tuxedo, but Davis has switched to a loud print blouse and loose vest. During his March 1969 appearance (which was taped in December 1968), Davis explicitly states that he "gave up ties and shirts and tuxedoes like that about two years ago." He performs some groovy social dances with Sonny Charles of the Checkmates, Ltd.—no soft-shoe in sight. Though he continues to seek out majority-white spaces, and though his dances remain solidly rooted in Black vernacular movement vocabularies, the changes in dance steps and fashions have transformed Sammy Davis's star persona from a playboy marching for Civil Rights to a (stoned) hippie.

An Aging Dandy Dance Master

Though Sammy Davis never fully gave in to the nostalgia pressures that had been mounting against him since the late sixties, he did enter the seventies in a more reflective mode, emerging from the height of his drug use and partying to a scary picture of the health costs associated with so many years of so-called perpetual motion.[105] It was in this moment of transition—as Davis entered his later forties—that he encountered the song "Mr. Bojangles." Written by country music artist Jerry Jeff Walker between 1965–1967, the song has nothing to do with Bill "Bojangles" Robinson, but instead tells the story of an encounter Walker claims to have had with an unhoused white street performer in a New Orleans jail.[106] And yet, the song hits too close to home for Davis in 1969:

> I said, "I can't do that song. I hate it." I wanted nothing to do with it, with the character. It was the story of a dancer who became a drunk, a bum, and he died in jail . . . . The song spooked me, I had seen too many performers who'd slid from headlining to playing joints, then toilets, and finally beer halls and passing the hat, reduced to coming backstage to see the star, their pants pressed on a hot electric lightbulb, but with frayed collars and cuffs . . . . The song was my own nightmare. I was afraid that was how I was going to end.[107]

However, Welsh singer Ton Jones, who would soon host Davis on his television show, insisted that Davis perform the song, so he eventually agreed to a compromise in which Jones would sing the song and Davis would act it; this occurred on the April 2, 1970 season finale of *This is Tom Jones*. As Davis explains, "working with his choreographer, we found a way that I could do movements to show the young guy at the beginning, lithe, a dandy—then, by the end, old and doddering, drunk and pathetic."[108] That Davis uses the word "dandy" immediately after admitting he saw himself in the figure of "Mr. Bojangles" both confirms that this had been the persona he was embodying throughout the peak of his career, and illustrates the extent to which he felt this version of his star text slipping away in middle age.

At the opening of the number on Jones' program, Davis appears with white-gray hair, hunched over and unstable. His fraying and oversized clothes recall the clown/tramp costume he wore in a moment of seeming self-awareness at the end of *The Sammy Davis, Jr. Show*—and present the opposite of the slim tailoring that had defined Davis's image for decades. As the song continues, Davis de-ages a bit into a better-fitting suit and bowler hat, with less gray hair and better posture: he performs the song's lyrics in the set's jail cell with precision, dancing "a lick" before performing the jump and heel-click also described. As Jones repeatedly sings the titular Mr. Bojangles' name, followed by four empty beats,

Davis adds a signature series of four knee-pops. These are somewhere between a march and a wing, a more upright and compact version of Presley's early knee flaps. What is fascinating about this character is that he looks rather like an unexpected fusion of Bill Robinson and Gene Kelly (not quite Fred Astaire): he remains upright and proud, but his legs are turned out and even balletic. Among his first "lick" movements are *petits battements* bouncing his working leg around the ankle of his standing leg; as he returns to his cell's cot, he does a similar beat before a *rond de jambe attitude* bends his working leg around behind him to lay down. This stylistic mix remains as he transitions into the historical part of the song, dancing as a vaudevillian/minstrel man. Unlike Davis's own incorporations of Kelly's style, this caricature loses the smoothness and careful arm placement, leaving behind a pedestrian tap dancer of no particular note but with a desperate, plastered-on smile on his face. Davis's claim of having known many such performers rings true here, as the style is so distinct from his other channelings of both Kelly and Robinson that it instead seems to recall a different, specific amalgam of memories. But it has just enough of himself in it—the occasional kick outward before returning to central stability—that his feared future lies just beneath the surface of the past.

After his initial mime-only performance of "Mr. Bojangles" with Tom Jones, Davis got more comfortable with the song and it became one of his mainstays during the seventies and eighties, as exemplified in his March 2, 1972 appearance on *The Flip Wilson Show*. Significantly, Davis is here a guest on what is arguably the first successful Black-led variety show, made possible by his own failed variety show. After doing a comedy skit with Wilson, Davis returns in a skintight brown belted spandex jumpsuit—it is difficult not to see echoes of 1970s Presley in a white jumpsuit—that recalls his preferred costuming from his live shows in the 1960s. His "Mr. Bojangles" prop is a black bowler hat, and his dance moves once again involve turned-out legs (see Figure 4.12), but there is more Davis in Bojangles this time: the smoothness, rootedness, and active pelvis are back. He even accentuates the performance with a gooey slide, his arms raised (for "he danced a lick"). Here, Davis has once again transformed a borrowed style into his own. A fitting crossroads of the past and present—both the bowler hat plus bodysuit and the vaudeville heel click plus groovy slide—this performance seems to cap a lifetime in perpetual motion.

There are other summative moments for Davis in the seventies, including a second appearance on *The Flip Wilson Show* and a television special of his own entitled *Sammy!*, both in 1973. First, he explains the difference between "dancing" and "hoofing" for Flip Wilson's younger audience on January 25: essentially, he embodies the distinction between Europeanist and Africanist movement vocabularies, suggesting that "dancers" stand erect and stable, whereas a "hoofer" "gets in there and *deals with it*" (with bent knees and rootedness in his body). Interestingly, he then destabilizes his own distinction by first demonstrating hoofing the style of Pat Rooney, "who almost invented the waltz clog." Davis performs an upright, Irish jig style of tap dance to the song "The Daughter of Rosie O'Grady," almost directly cribbed from Rooney's performance of the same song from the 1935 Vitaphone short *All-Star Vaudeville*. He then demonstrates Bill Robinson's upright style with his fists on his hips, asking the audience to "listen to the taps" as he performs a segment of Robinson's "Doin' the New Low Down." He follows these with the "close to the ground" style that he described as popular in the 1940s, and which is quite close to his own style in the early fifties. He ends the segment with a tribute to his father and "uncle," demonstrating the basics of their flash act, where "you had the music going fast, and you did a lot of flashy steps." These include the trenches and "clock" trick that had been staples of the Trio's performances even through the fifties, until the older members retired. Though this might be understood as giving in to nostalgia, Davis also frames himself as the (still stylishly dressed) elder educator, providing an abridged history of his native art form—though hamming up his winded exhaustion and back pain just as Kelly had. On *Sammy!*, he offers a wide-ranging retrospective of his career with footage from *Rufus Jones for President*, a simplified performance of "Mr. Bojangles," a boxing sequence that nods to *Golden Boy*, a medley in which he duets with himself as both Sportin' Life *and* Porgy, interview snippets with his father, and an extremely *au courant* jazz-rock number with a supporting cast of backup dancers. The song is Chase's "Get It On" (1971), and Davis introduces it with a series of playful match-cuts featuring him sitting on a stool in a wide variety of outfits, offering a brief monologue:

> You know, through the years I've always believed in change because it's healthy; if you don't keep up with what's happenin', man, you could become old-fashioned, which is the worst thing that could possibly happen to any performer. But I also believe in being your own man. For instance, I never let any of these crazy new fashions influence me. I think you should wear whatever makes you comfortable; clothes have never been that important to me. A simple, basic wardrobe is all a guy really needs—it's what's inside that counts!

Clearly being played for laughs (and accompanied by what sounds like a laugh track), this brief segment offers a self-aware gesture towards Davis's dandyism, and helps transition to the almost anachronistic feel of Davis (and dancers) performing the "Get It On" number in Day-Glo yellow. Davis's plaid bell-bottoms, turtle-neck, and matching boots, worn alongside dancers who are likely less than half his age, finally bring with them the notion that he is trying *too* hard to stay relevant. And yet, his extremely pelvis-focused dance moves (appropriate to the song's topic) are still compelling to watch, whether thrusts, side sways, or

Figure 4.12 Davis performs "Mr. Bojangles" in a brown jumpsuit and bowler hat with turned-out legs on *The Flip Wilson Show* in 1972 (left), and "Get It On" in day-glo yellow with pelvic thrusts on his *Sammy!* special in 1973 (right).

circular grinds (see Figure 4.12). The camera sometimes denies a full view of all this activity in favor of his singing upper body, but as was true with Presley nearly twenty years prior, the evidence of movement is still there even so.

Thus, performing some of the final active dances of his career, Davis in 1973 insists on the same basic tenets of stardom that he had developed over fifty years on media screens: protean changeability and a flamboyantly current sense of style, undergirded finally by an explicitly sexual masculinity. While the sexual aspect of this impish dandy was more visually implicit in previous years, the interracial romance scandals of Davis's larger star text meant that his mobile-pelvis dances in increasingly tight pants were able to signify these dangers indirectly. Davis's chameleonic condensation of so many movement vocabularies in service of constructing this sensual dandy clarifies just *how* Davis embodied the contradictions of the sixties, as both Early and Jacobson have suggested he did. With a style of performance and a masculinity that were inherently mutable, Davis was perfectly equipped to dance his way through one of the most tumultuous decades in American history. That he attempted simultaneously to achieve widespread acclaim among both white and Black audiences *and* support efforts to secure civil rights for everyday Black folks made the shapeshifting necessary. As he himself repeatedly indicated, the result was a man in perpetual motion.

Epilogue
Masculinities Danced on Post-1970 Screens

I opened this book with the 1985 televised ceremony wherein Gene Kelly received a Life Achievement Award from the American Film Institute, and the Nicholas Brothers pointed out that some of his moves were stolen from them. That same year, Metro-Goldwyn-Mayer released a compilation film entitled *That's Dancing!*, a companion to its *That's Entertainment!* series celebrating the studio's history. Kelly served as executive producer and appeared as one of the hosts—alongside Sammy Davis, Jr., ballet dancer Mikhail Baryshnikov, vaudeville and Broadway performer Ray Bolger, and actress/singer Liza Minnelli (daughter of Kelly's former costar, Judy Garland, and director Vincente Minnelli). In a small corrective to the previous decades' frequent absenting of Black bodies from the history of dance on screen, this film attempted to give occasional credit where due. Bill Robinson, for example, is not merely featured as Shirley Temple's aged partner, but is also shown as the pathbreaking solo dancer he was with a clip from *King for a Day* (1934); Davis's voiceover narration explains the significance of Robinson's stylistic shifts in tap dance. Black dancer LeRoy Daniels, who was not originally given screen credit for his dance with Fred Astaire in *The Band Wagon* (1953), is restored his credit via narration when the "Shine on Your Shoes" clip appears. But inequities certainly remain; whereas the film includes numerous Fred Astaire segments, second clips featuring Davis and the Nicholas Brothers were removed in the editing process. So the Nicholases are only seen in *Down Argentine Way* (1940) and Davis is only seen in *Rufus Jones for President* (1933), though he stands out amongst the hosts as the only one who dances in the present tense as well; a carefully timed cut at the end of the *Rufus Jones* sequence brings us to a fifty-nine-year-old Davis completing the sequence he had danced as a child. Perhaps due to rights issues or time constraints, the film leaves out Elvis Presley, though it does include a brief clip of Ann-Margret from their "C'mon Everybody" number in *Viva Las Vegas* (1964).[1] The rest of this book's case studies, however, are present, as are the next generations of dancing men. Indeed, in its attempt to be relevant to the 1980s historical moment, *That's Dancing!* begins with young street dancers breakdancing in New York City and ends with Michael Jackson dancing in the music video for "Beat It" (1983). Just as Jackson's appearances on sixties television with Sammy Davis and seventies

White Screens, Black Dance. Pamela Krayenbuhl, Oxford University Press. © Pamela Krayenbuhl 2025.
DOI: 10.1093/9780197699119.003.0006

EPILOGUE   195

television with the Nicholas Brothers signaled a passing of the dancerly torch, so too does Kelly's narration over the final clip from "Beat It," which is used to represent music video dance in general: "The most innovative and certainly the most successful exponent of this new medium is a young and gifted composer, singer, dancer, and choreographer, who obviously will be leading the way for some time to come: Michael Jackson."

Kelly is certainly more generous to Jackson as the vanguard of MTV dance in the mid-1980s than he was toward Presley as the vanguard of rock 'n' roll dance in the late 1950s. Of course, Jackson's embodied ephebism is far less threatening to Kelly when he is receiving life achievement awards than was Presley's when he was trying to extend his career peak. While Kelly's white working-class brash athleticism could coexist alongside the Nicholas Brothers' embodiment of classiness and dignity (an Irish American hoofer was sufficiently distinct from Harlem's most elite African American terpsichorean talent), Presley's own white working-class masculinity was ultimately rather similar to Kelly's. Though he lacked the formal dance training, skipped the muscular feats, and represented a distinctly Southern bad boy, Presley and his hot new pelvic moves may well have helped push Kelly backward toward vaudeville and its minstrel connections in the late 1950s. Their coexistence on television invites a broader zoom-out at this juncture: how do we make sense of this entire range of masculinities, Black and white, upper and lower class, variously ambiguous, threatening, nonthreatening, and so on *all at once*?

Some would suggest that the distinct masculinity shifts in all case studies rather align with major historical events and their ripple effects over the course of the midcentury period. Masculinities prior to the U.S.'s entry into World War II were most directly related to turn of the century notions of social roles and stereotypes: Sammy Davis, Jr. began in Black vaudeville as a pickaninny, whereas the Nicholas Brothers represented W.E.B. Du Bois's "talented tenth" as children of members of the college-educated Black upper-class. As middle-class Gene Kelly gained his dancing and choreography chops during the Great Depression, he brought bits of Davis's vaudeville together with the American ballet and Broadway worlds that were developing alongside Black jazz, thanks to influences from interested outsiders like Soviet defector George Balanchine. Thus, the early 1940s masculinities of all four men reflected those histories: Davis was the hammy jack-of-all-trades with a big smile; the Nicholases embodied dignity and grace; Kelly found his mix of ballet and jazz could fill out his womanizing characters with muscle. But one could argue that all available conceptions of American masculinity were changed by World War II. Indeed, all of the case studies, except for Harold Nicholas (who was too short for the Draft Board), served in the U.S. military between 1943–1960; all appeared in films or television shows with narratives revolving around military service.[2] The war itself and a military-based typology of masculinity had a profound effect on all the case studies' careers: Davis's entire philosophy of performance before white audiences—his desire to dance away racist conceptions of him—was born during his Army service, but both he and the Nicholases found that most work available to them had dried up by the end of the war. Kelly's dancing sailor, whose suit was the closest "masculine" costume to ballet's tights, was also born of first imagined and then real experience in the Navy. While Presley did not serve until peacetime (he was ten years younger than Davis and twenty-three years younger than Kelly), his roles in *G.I. Blues* and *Blue Hawaii* helped morph his fifties greaser bad boy image into a cleaner cut but still alluring heartthrob. Finally, the hard push of the Civil Rights and Black Power Movements in the 1960s changed what was possible for the Nicholas Brothers and especially Davis on television. The de facto segregation of the media industries, alongside the deep fears of and laws against miscegenation that had so defined their careers in the forties and fifties, gave way to a newfound pelvic freedom and access to the defining medium of the 1960s: television. In fact, one could even argue that greater visibility for Black performers in the 1960s contributed to both Kelly's and Presley's fading into the background.

Another way to make sense of the masculinities simultaneously screendanced by the case studies of this book is to return to the minstrel-based stereotypes of Black men that I laid out in the introduction. Certainly the Nicholas Brothers and Sammy Davis were consciously attempting to upend and subvert racist notions of Black masculinity, overcoming them with stylistic strategies that refused comparison to the lazy coon or the dangerous and oversexed buck. Relatedly, it is worth noting that all three men—the three biggest Black dancing stars of the midcentury—were of a slight and petite build, so associations with the buck would be more difficult by default. The Davis case, of course, is complicated by his being ever-enamored of the dandy figure; to place such a premium on both style and strut as a Black man always risked association with Zip Coon. But the white men, too, constructed masculinities that depended on these stereotypes. Presley's constant centering of his pelvis-as-phallus calls forth conceptions of the same Black buck that the Nicholases and Davis actively avoided. And, as demonstrated by Kelly's duet with Sugar Ray Robinson, the muscularity of dance that he always emphasized also drew from the fetishized strength of Black men's bodies—a fetishization he actively invited with muscle tees and tight pants. It is thus the midcentury's cultural inheritance from blackface minstrelsy, even though the minstrel show itself was fading from view, that allows us to see the trajectories behind these masculinities as a group. This is why it is important to name Kelly's and Presley's masculinity constructions through Black dance as *blackbodying*—it captures an inheritance that might otherwise be far less obvious than a Black man directly engaging with (especially by actively rejecting) stereotypes of himself. But it is equally important to demonstrate that the lineage of inheritance from minstrelsy did not stop with this generation.

EPILOGUE   197

Nostalgic texts like *That's Dancing!*, which included silent film and music video but focused primarily on Classical Hollywood musicals, as well as years of those musicals being broadcast on television and distributed on home video and DVD, work to canonize such films as peak dance on screen. Similar circulations of the era's TV programs, whether homemade bootleg VHS tapes, formal DVD compilations, or digitized kinescopes now garnering views on YouTube, have a similar effect. And in canonizing these media texts and the performances themselves, the (re)circulation of them also serves to solidify the models of minstrelsy-informed masculinity immortalized in them. In *That's Dancing!* and other screendance texts from the 1970s to the present moment, we see the onward passage of both the processes through which midcentury stars constructed masculinities via Black dance *and* the resultant masculinities themselves. Young Michael Jackson was certainly paying attention when he shared television stages with the Nicholas Brothers and Sammy Davis, Jr., but co-presence was not necessary for later performers to be influenced by midcentury stars. Below, I provide a brief demonstration of these lineages in the star texts of not only Michael Jackson, but also John Travolta, Gregory Hines, and Channing Tatum. Afterward, I offer brief final thoughts on blackbodying and masculinity in the contemporary social media landscape, particularly on the popular mobile app TikTok.

Models of Masculinity Mutate Onward

A child of Motown and one of the definitive figures of the MTV era, Black singer-dancer Michael Jackson inherits from Sammy Davis a tendency to draw from many other dancers' styles at once.[3] In reading his dances, viewers have seen touches of Fred Astaire, Jackie Wilson, James Brown, and, indeed, Davis.[4] Jackson certainly names all of these men in his autobiography, plus Gene Kelly, as inspiring dancers—the book is dedicated to Astaire. Despite the dedication, Jackson notes that he "might have learned more from watching Jackie Wilson than from anyone or anything else."[5] In this and other ways, he bears a great deal in common with Elvis Presley. Both not only paid close attention to and modeled portions of their signature style after Jackie Wilson's performances, but also danced their way to global stardom primarily on television. In fact, Jackson's dance for his song "Billie Jean" on the 1983 *Motown 25: Yesterday, Today, Forever* NBC television special rather paralleled Presley's "Hound Dog" debut in 1956; while both men had certainly appeared and danced on television before, these landmark performances, which launched each man into superstardom, are remembered as much for their dances as anything else. And like Presley's, Jackson's global superstardom was built on both his "crossover" music and a public persona that challenged the neat divisions between Black and white, masculine and feminine, heterosexual and homosexual.[6] While Jackson's *Motown 25* performance of "Billie Jean" is most often remembered for its introduction of his signature moonwalk and tipped fedora, it also cemented his intensive pelvic thrust—and crotch-grab—as core aspects of his solo star text. From this point forward, peak Jackson, like peak Presley, fashioned a phallic masculinity with his dances. Both stars' crotch-centric performances often employed relatively stable upper bodies, allowing for dramatic pelvic motion that caused public uproar.

Jackson's phallic masculinity is built, primarily through Black dance, across his 1980s music videos. Like Presley's, Jackson's movement vocabulary is firmly rooted in Africanist wing dances and body part isolations—alongside Cab Calloway-style hair choreography. In his *Motown 25* solo, as well as his highly acclaimed videos for "Beat It" (1983, featured in *That's Dancing!*), "Thriller" (1983), "Bad" (1987), "The Way You Make Me Feel" (1987), and "Smooth Criminal" (1988), Jackson's style is both "liquid and percussive," providing contrasts between smooth glides and abrupt pelvic thrusts.[7] The thrusts are often emphasized by a hand placed at the belt line (often gloved in a contrasting color), which almost appears to mechanically pop the pelvis; other forms of visual emphasis include the explicit crotch grab, or more implicit costuming details such as a splayed open jacket or elaborate belt closure (as in "Beat It" and "The Way You Make Me Feel," respectively). Frequent cuts and close-ups on body parts (typical of what came to be known as "MTV-style" editing) also underscored the thrusts and other sharp isolations. Like Presley's, Jackson's tendency to freeze up on his toes provided an additional opportunity to accentuate the thrust of his pelvis. Unlike Presley, of course, Jackson was a Black man, so his construction of a phallic masculinity in the 1980s had to contend with the nineteenth-century negative stereotypes of Black men I laid out in the introduction to this book (the buck and coon in particular). So, with the addition of Astaire's grace and what many saw as the feminine glitz and glam of Diana Ross, cultural historian Kobena Mercer argues that "Jackson not only questions dominant stereotypes of black masculinity, but also gracefully steps outside the existing range of 'types' of black men."[8] For dance scholar Judith Hamera, "[h]is transitions from splaying knees to multiple spins emphasized mastery of vocabularies popularly regarded as both racially particular and universal . . . all the while performatively refuting racist charges of idleness and reduction to 'nature' (versus discipline and 'culture')."[9] Too feminine to be a dangerous buck and too electric to be a shuffling coon, Jackson in the 1980s used the steps and styles acquired from an array of dancing men (and at least one woman) to embody a destabilized phallic masculinity.

White actor-dancer John Travolta was also featured in *That's Dancing!*, with his disco moves from *Saturday Night Fever* (1977) sandwiched between clips from *West Side Story* (1961) and *Fame* (1980). Though arguably a watered-down (perhaps whitened) version of the dances developed by queer dancers of color in real-life discos, Travolta's use of vernacular movement in this film continued Elvis Presley's tradition of constructing a "cool," virile, and once again phallic white masculinity from Black dance.[10] Some of the film's most memorable sequences are built around everyday gestures as dances of virility, such as a scene wherein Travolta as Tony Manero gets ready to go out (edited as a montage of hair coiffing and getting dressed amongst overhead shots of a dance floor), and others where the camera captures him walking down the street—gender scholar David Buchbinder remarks that "even his ordinary walk is a sexual strut."[11] In these sequences, low camera angles and heights highlight Travolta's ever-mobile pelvis, helping to define Manero's masculinity and sexuality through the Black dances constantly coursing through his body. For the disco performances in particular, Travolta credited Black choreographer Lester Wilson for "infus[ing his] dancing with African-American rhythm"—Wilson had notably been a featured dancer in Sammy Davis, Jr.'s *Golden Boy* on Broadway.[12] Dance scholar Sima Belmar has additionally suggested that the corporeal performance of Travolta's Tony is undergirded not only by Wilson's coaching but also a complex mixing of dance forms and racial categories, shaped by the input of both Black and white dancers from both social and concert dance traditions.[13] While Travolta, his character Tony, and even *Saturday Night Fever*'s credits do carefully give Black dancers credit for originating disco, Travolta's adaptation of the moves as Tony Manero "repatriated" disco from its largely queer roots to a Presley-style working-class "tough guy" heteronormativity.[14] Ironically, Manero's tendency to focus his gaze and concentration as much on his own body as on those of women, together with the camera's fetishization of his body, read to critics like Pauline Kael as homoerotic.[15] In this way, Travolta-as-Manero performs a hypermasculinity through Black dance that is ultimately as ambiguous and potentially homoerotic as Gene Kelly's in *The Pirate* or Presley's in *Jailhouse Rock*.

Travolta's danced masculinity harkens even more directly back to Presley when he performs as the late-fifties greaser Danny Zuko in *Grease* (1978), but the dances themselves also borrow from Gene Kelly's playful athleticism and border on comedy, thus combining the two different approaches to blackbodying.[16] Travolta's dance to "Greased Lighting," for example, uses Presley-style vocals and a mobile pelvis, including an exaggerated wing dance (both legs and arms); he adds a signature Presley guitar hand placement (sans guitar) during the "Summer Nights" number. But where Presley remained dangerous in his sexually provocative postures and poses in the late fifties, Travolta's nostalgic interpretation of him leans into the innocuous, campy exaggeration of Broadway choreography and borrows Kelly's tendency to jump up onto the sets and strike a pose. The phallic references in "Greased Lighting" are similarly over the top and are entwined with *bricolage* that echoes Presley's pommel horse antics in *Viva Las Vegas*: Travolta descends from the ceiling while straddling a large car motor, and later rubs a roll of plastic wrap on his crotch. However silly his send-up of the fifties greaser image may be, Travolta's nostalgic performance of Danny nevertheless traffics in a spectacularized phallic masculinity that remains rooted in Black dance. When he leaves behind the Hollywood musical context, Travolta performs his most pelvic number: in *Perfect* (1985), he moves into the realm of aerobics. His character, a *Rolling Stone* journalist named Adam Lawrence, becomes an image of phallic spectacle in a fitness class. Surrounded by mostly women in high-cut leotards, Travolta joins them in erotic pelvic thrusts under the auspices of aerobic exercise. Released at the peak of the 1980s aerobics and Jazzercise fads, *Perfect* draws from both Travolta's existing star text and the actual erotic *Aerobicise* television program that aired on cable and was released on home video formats throughout the decade. Though the movements involved do not necessarily qualify as dance, the manner in which they are filmed draws in particular from the way Presley had been filmed dancing in prior decades. Thus, just as a pointed close-up of Presley's crotch in short shorts helped construct his phallic masculinity in *Blue Hawaii*'s "Slicin' Sand," a combination of cinematography and short shorts does similar work as Travolta works up a sweat in a series of reverse shots making eye contact with the instructor, Jessie Wilson (Jamie Lee Curtis). The reverse shots and eye contact reassure us that the pelvic thrusts are executed as an expression of heterosexual desire. Thus, Travolta continues to construct a phallic masculinity even as his movements stray further from the more identifiable Black dance idioms where he began.

Black dancer-actor Gregory Hines might be understood as the last tap dance star of the twentieth century. A major admirer of the Nicholas Brothers and Sammy Davis, Jr., Hines named these men as his idols in many interviews over the years; he also starred in *Tap* (1989) alongside Davis (with a cameo appearance by Harold Nicholas), which was Davis's final film appearance before his death. Of the contemporary case studies mentioned here, Hines embodied a masculinity closest to that of the Nicholas Brothers; while the roles available to him were often pointedly non-sexual, Hines worked to build a proud Black masculinity rooted in his tap virtuosity. With several of his earliest media appearances placing him among Muppets, Hines was coded as an asexual performer and friend to children. One of his first major roles after that was as Delbert "Sandman" Williams in *The Cotton Club* (1984). His brother, Maurice Hines, appeared with him in the film and they served as a focal point for the film's retelling of the nightclub's historic role in mob-infested Jazz Age Harlem. Though Gregory Hines is granted a love interest—Lila Rose Oliver (Lonette McKee), styled largely after Lena Horne—and a single love scene in the film, he is one of the few men in the main cast who is defined not by acts of violence

EPILOGUE   201

but by his dancing. Once again presented as a friend to nearby children while dancing to impress McKee's character, his only goals in the film are to marry her and to dance exceptionally enough to support his family.[17] Twice in the film, his dancing is framed as more powerful than the mob; once metaphorically, and once when he literally kicks a gun out of a boss's hands as it goes off. Thus, Hines was established early on as a family-friendly tapping miracle.

Hines constructs a more nonchalant masculinity when costarring with fellow dancer Mikhail Baryshnikov in *White Nights* (1985); the two play characters defecting to and from the USSR, respectively. In a sense, they serve as representatives of masculine Africanist versus Europeanist dance throughout the film. Even when they perform the same choreography in unison, they demonstrate contrasting comportments: Hines uses a lower center of gravity and incorporates greater opposition and counterbalance between legs and arms, whereas Baryshnikov uses a higher center of gravity and holds his arms in greater stasis. These qualities of movement (among others) help to build each man's version of masculinity in the film. Baryshnikov, as if rebelling against the rigid backbone of his form, is explosive and hubristic as Nikolai "Kolya" Rodchenko. In film scholar Dora Valkanova's reading, *White Nights*, as a Cold War film, works to "reestablish dominant ideology about the U.S. as a paragon of liberal multicultural democracy."[18] In pursuit of this project, Baryshnikov (as Rodchenko) embodies an egotistic individualism "that authorizes inclusion into Western hegemonic white masculinity."[19] Hines, as an African American Vietnam War veteran whose freer form matches his more easygoing attitude, is thoughtful, practical, and a bit sardonic as Raymond Greenwood. Having defected from U.S. to the Soviet Union, Greenwood is assigned by a KGB officer to keep tabs on Rodchenko after he attempts to defect from the Soviet Union to the U.S. Notably, Hines's Greenwood refuses any vestigial Uncle Tom typing in his relationship to Rodchenko. In a typical exchange between them, Hines as Greenwood makes it clear that "I'm not your servant and I'm not your babysitter;" when Rodchenko makes racist assumptions about his "natural rhythm," Greenwood responds by showing Rodchenko his middle finger. So constructed as a post-Civil Rights version of the dignified Black tap dancer, Hines is nevertheless also framed as postsexual and fatherly. Greenwood has a pregnant Russian wife, and the primary illustration of their relationship is his proposal that they leave the USSR for the sake of the child—which is initially received with a slap. Thus, against the driving force of Baryshnikov's hotheaded masculinity, Hines dances a smoother, quietly obstinate and family-oriented masculinity.

Hines remains largely in the realm of fatherly, nonthreatening masculinity for the remainder of his screendance career—in *Tap!* he develops camaraderie with his ex-girlfriend's son (played by Savion Glover); in *The Gregory Hines Show* (1997–1998), he plays a widower father of a twelve-year-old son (who rarely dances outside of the opening credit sequence). Though *Tap!* shows Hines at peak virtuosity as he defends a dying form, particularly in a scene that replicates the "challenge" environment of old-school hoofers (echoing his scene in a fictional Hoofer's Club in *The Cotton Club*), his masculinity remains frustrated and subdued. He plays a formerly incarcerated man whose desires are sublimated into his love for "true" (rather than theatricalized, watered down) tap dance, such that his rekindling romance is itself more about his future as a dancer. It is nearly always in his non-dance roles that Hines manages to expand his masculinity beyond these narrow confines; he even remarks in an interview about *Running Scared* (1986) that "usually the black guy has no sexuality at all," so he is "proud because this is the first film that stars a black guy and a white guy – and the black guy has all the sex scenes."[20] It is only much later in his career, in the made-for-television biopic *Bojangles* (2001) that Hines is able to expand his dancerly masculinity to include more overt sexuality. Serving as both executive producer and lead actor, Hines ensures that this version of Bill Robinson corrects for the version that 1930s Hollywood constructed: Hines's Robinson gets angry, stands his ground, flirts, and makes love. While he certainly preserves the dignified Black masculinity that he had learned from the Nicholases as a child, Hines extends the range of what that dignity can envelop. In one of his last dancing roles, he is finally able to imbue his own star text, and that of the first tap dancing film star, with a complex masculinity that pushes fully beyond the stereotypes and limitations Hollywood had always placed on Black dancing men.

White actor-dancer Channing Tatum is the twenty-first century star who most clearly demonstrates the ongoing power of blackbodying in both film and television. Like Gene Kelly, Tatum has used Black dance to construct a range of athletic and often comedic masculinities, but unlike Kelly, he did not receive formal dance training. He began his performance career as a stripper, model, and music video extra; his breakout year in Hollywood was 2006, when he was cast as the male lead in *Step Up*.[21] The film's narrative centers on a Baltimore class conflict romance between Tatum's character, Tyler Gage, a white male street dancer specializing in hip-hop and breakdance, and Nora Clark (Jenna Dewan), a white female student in the local dance conservatory who specializes in ballet and modern dance. Tatum's danced masculinity is established through a series of oppositions against Dewan's danced femininity: where she is petite, airy, and proficient in Europeanist dance, Tatum is muscular, rooted, and proficient in Africanist dance (a similar dichotomy to *White Nights*, though staging the distinction via gender rather than race). Through blackbodying, Tatum takes on hip-hop's "aesthetic of the cool," and his engagement with hip-hop is visually authenticated by scenes where Gage socializes with a predominantly Black community of peers. As performance scholar Raquel Monroe has indicated with regard to the similarly white main character in *Step Up 2*, a direct connection to

Black urban space is crucial to legitimizing white participation in hip-hop culture in the eyes of viewers, and both of the first two *Step Up* films use majority-Black or multiracial friend groups surrounding a white star to suggest that "race does not determine which . . . bodies can and should dance which styles; this is determined by specific class distinctions."[22] Thus, while such instances of twenty-first century blackbodying do implicitly acknowledge the Black community as the source of hip-hop dance vocabulary, they continue to replace Black bodies with white ones and, particularly in this case, use Black dance to construct a "cool" masculinity for a budding white star. Per Monroe, "Hip-hop dance forms render whiteness hyper-visible, but the white performance of black performativity becomes the selling point for films where black performers are cast as ancillary characters to authenticate the white protagonists."[23] The ultimate result thus remains greater access to stardom for the blackbodying white man than the Black dancers who originated these movements.

The "cool" masculinity developed by a street-dancing Tatum in 2006 continued to inform many of his future roles, including the 2012 film loosely based on his own early career, *Magic Mike*. In this film—and its two sequels, *Magic Mike XXL* (2015) and *Magic Mike's Last Dance* (2023)—Tatum stars as stripper Michael Lane, who performs in clubs and at private parties alongside a close-knit group of other male strippers. The plots of these films offer up various opportunities for Lane and co. to flex their muscles and practice their athletic craft; scholars have remarked on the extent to which, by spectacularizing hard male bodies thrusting and grinding to spark heterosexual desire (and thus embodying the ultimate phallic masculinity), these films enable women viewers to feel both seen and desired.[24] In this more sexually charged context, Tatum continues blackbodying in service of building a "cool" masculinity, though the tone becomes increasingly playful in the *Magic Mike* films—a similar trajectory to that of Travolta. Performance scholar Broderick Chow has helpfully demonstrated that the *Magic Mike* films are ultimately stories about precarious labor, and the precarity of white men's working-class labor in particular, wherein the concept of magic "draws a veil over an appropriation of black labor."[25] Comparing Tatum in *Magic Mike XXL* to both Gene Kelly and Elvis Presley, Chow explicitly frames Tatum's and other nonblack men's appropriation of Black dance in terms of "material questions of remuneration and credit for work performed."[26] While credit does seem to be clearly indicated in the film's finale, wherein Tatum's hip-hop-heavy performance is twinned by Black actor-dancer Stephen "tWitch" Boss as stripper Malik, Chow holds that the "embodied adoption of black aesthetics by the mainly white strippers unconsciously returns to the fact of which bodies are excluded from the primarily white fantasy of entrepreneurial self-making."[27] So, in a contemporary twist on the dissolves of Kelly and Presley into images of Chocolat and Claude Thompson, respectively,

Tatum's mirroring of Boss's Black dancing body serves as an extraction of virtuosity designed to build and authenticate Tatum's white masculinity.

Tatum's similarity to Gene Kelly in particular is made most explicit in *Hail, Caesar!* (2016), an irreverent parody of 1950s Hollywood. Here, Tatum's Burt Gurney character is the embodiment of the anxieties that surrounded Gene Kelly and his white song-and-dance man colleagues at that historical moment. In the film, we see Tatum's character, decked out in a sailor suit and obvious eyeliner, tap dancing (and performing *bricolage* with a broom) in a musical's barroom set. He and his buddies sing about shipping out and having "no dames" with whom to dance, so they practice dancing with each other, during which Tatum's character finds himself in a number of homoerotic positions. Near the end, we discover that he is a Communist sympathizer and he dramatically—one might even say flamboyantly—boards a submarine to the USSR. Tatum's send-up song-and-dance man in *Hail, Caesar!* works to further "queer" Kelly's already ambiguous star text, and makes no attempts to reassure the audience of his masculinity. But Tatum's performance of an effeminized song-and-dance man does not threaten the masculinity of his own star text, primarily because said "cool" masculinity was already so firmly established through the use of Black dance in his previous films. Of course, this queered version of Kelly also uses Black dance, but by 2016 any of the remaining Jazz Age "cool" associated with tap dance was quite overshadowed by the contemporary edge of hip-hop. Just as Travolta created a parodic Presley in *Grease* after already authenticating his masculinity through contemporary Black vernacular dance in *Saturday Night Fever*, so too is Tatum able to create a parodic Kelly in *Hail, Caesar!* after already authenticating his masculinity through contemporary Black vernacular dance in the *Step Up* and *Magic Mike* series. Thus, the comedic distance implicit in Tatum's playful queering of Kelly, as well as his other gender transgressions (such as his *Lip Sync Battle* performance of Beyoncé's "Run the World (Girls)" in drag just before the release of *Hail, Caesar!*), though achieved through blackbodying, offer a reaffirmation of his preestablished masculinity.

These brief glimpses into the star texts and masculinities of dancing men on film and television between the 1970s and 2010s have, I hope, sketched a picture of the ongoing lineages of the models constructed in the mid-twentieth century. As sociopolitical contexts in the U.S. continue to evolve, of course, so too will the typologies of masculinity that are shaped in mainstream media. One of the biggest recent industrial shifts that now affects these danced constructions has been the arrival and now dominance of the Internet. The digital mediascape has expanded the range of screenic venues where we encounter stars and dances, and indeed has reshaped the conditions of stardom itself. I would be remiss if I did not address this new kind of stardom in some way, especially because the 2020s have so far been dominated by dance on a particular kind of new media

EPILOGUE   205

screen. While I acknowledge that this move skips past a great deal of interesting danced masculinity in music video and on YouTube (the dance career of R&B artist Usher Raymond IV is particularly ripe for analysis), this book would not be complete if it did not wrangle with the COVID-19 pandemic era on TikTok.

TikTok and Blackbodying in New Media

Since the birth of so-called Web 2.0 in the early to mid 2000s, the very concept of stardom has been fractured—or perhaps refracted—by social media. "DIY celebrities" and "microcelebrities" developed seemingly organically, first on blogs and then on social networking websites and YouTube, rather than being carefully fashioned by media industry gatekeepers, as stars had been since the 1910s.[28] Today, most "internet celebrities" are developed on mobile applications (hereafter "apps") like Instagram and TikTok, often serving more as product marketing than entertainment sources, as in the case of the "Influencer."[29] Many of these "ordinary people" are not actively leveraging a particular talent, such as acting, singing, or dancing (as traditional stars do), but instead focus on producing "content," such as commentary on particular topics or lifestyle advice. And yet, even amidst this landscape of social media microcelebrities who are "ordinary," aspects of traditional stardom do survive. TikTok in particular was initially built on the basis of musical and dancerly talent: a Chinese app released to the international market in September 2017, it merged with similar lip-sync video app Musical.ly to become widely available in the U.S. in August 2018. Young people in particular flocked to the app by the millions in its first few years, and many of my students found it to be fundamental to their experience of the lockdown phases of the COVID-19 pandemic. At first limited to only fifteen seconds, but now up to one minute in length, TikTok's brief videos generally consist of a preselected "sound" alongside a video filmed to match that sound, or a sound and video recorded simultaneously.

Here, I would like to briefly discuss the genre of video that was dominant on TikTok between 2019 and 2021, and which still persists today even as the app has diversified into many niches and subcultures: the dance videos of "Straight TikTok."[30] These performance videos use excerpts from popular songs as their "sound" and viral dance choreographies as their visual accompaniment. Though TikTok dance has arguably evolved into its own unique style, its foundations—like Tatum's version of strip dances in the *Magic Mike* series—are in hip-hop. I offer the TikTok dance video here as a demonstration of the enduring nature of the concepts I have developed in this book; it is my hope that future work by other scholars will explore, in particular, occurrences of blackbodying across additional media and historical moments. Blackbodying occurs almost constantly on mainstream TikTok, though scholars have used other terms for the phenomenon.[31] Most publicized in mainstream news outlets are cases of direct stealing from individual choreographers and content creators. The most commonly cited example of uncredited choreographic poaching is the viral "Renegade" dance, set to an excerpt of K-Camp's song "Lottery." The dance, choreographed by Black Georgia teen Jalaiah Harmon (@jalaiahharmon) but uncredited when white Connecticut teen Charli D'Amelio (@charlidamelio) performed it with viral TikTok success, even serves as the titular exemplar for performance scholar Trevor Boffone's 2021 book *Renegades: Digital Dance Cultures from Dubsmash to TikTok*. As Boffone demonstrates, Black American youth today (those considered Generation Z, or "Zoomers") use music and dance apps like TikTok (and especially Dubsmash) not only to engage in the practice of creating cultural "content" like dances, but also to develop identities and digital community, and challenge the status quo whiteness of dominant culture.[32] Meanwhile, white creators have copied the hip-hop-based dances of these Black creators and used them to successfully attain or grow their (micro)celebrity status. While the "Renegade" dance was eventually credited to Harmon, largely thanks to a *New York Times* profile of her that "broke" the news of the viral dance's true authorship five months after its creation, dozens of other viral dances never were credited to their original creators.[33] In response, Black creators on TikTok went on a #BlackTikTokStrike in summer of 2021, demanding that they receive credit for their viral dances. Direct textual credit in the descriptions accompanying dance videos, usually shortened to "dc" for "dance credit," has since become a more standard practice on the app. Of course, this does not prevent blackbodying.

Recall that blackbodying is most often not a direct borrowing of specific steps from a singular individual, but rather a synthetic appropriation of Black vernacular movements and corporeality in general. This practice is quite common on TikTok, with white and other nonblack creators using a hip-hop vocabulary to both establish their own identities and build large numbers of "followers" to achieve microcelebrity status and potentially leverage that stardom into a stable performance career. Interestingly, as indicated in the Harmon–D'Amelio example above, the most common practitioners of TikTok dance are teen girls and young women, rather than the men I have focused on throughout this book. Communication and performance scholar Cienna Davis highlights this shift in gender with regard to minstrelsy-descended histories of Black dance appropriation, but she nevertheless reads the performance of TikTok dances as a means of gender identity building: invoking dance scholar Jasmine Johnson's concept of Black women's "flesh dance," Davis suggests that "a popular category of mimicry is that of scantily clad femmes using the [dance] challenge to assert their sexuality."[34] She argues that nonblack young women's self-fashioning of a sexually mature femininity both relies on stereotypes of hypersexual Black women (as seen in the Jezebel figure, similar to the Buck) and "reinscribes proprietary relations of domination that enforce Black women's precarity in American society."[35] Davis thus sees white femmes performing Black dance on TikTok as functioning quite similarly to how I've argued white men have performed Black dance on screen since the mid-twentieth century. Unsurprisingly, young men's TikTok dances operate in much the same way.

While men TikTok dancers are, on the whole, less visible than women TikTok dancers, they have also participated in and started the viral dance "trends" and "challenges" of Straight TikTok. Some of the most famous African American dancing men on TikTok, Jean-Victor Mackie (@jeanvictorm, ca. 9 million followers as of this writing) and Jeff Tingz (@jeffxtingz, ca. 3.2 million followers)—who have often collaborated in their videos—have been producing dance content on TikTok for over four years. They perform simple dances to popular song clips, choreographed by themselves or other creators, both solo and in unison with each other or alongside other friends. In their own choreography, they also incorporate athletic feats, such as backflips, echoing the flash elements of the Nicholas Brothers' dances from nearly a century prior. These two young men are known not only for their dances, but also for their fit bodies. Both have danced shirtless on the app since they were teens, and Tingz will sometimes simply flex a single muscle as a "dance." They both choose to make and participate in dances that "embrace the conflict" between fast and slow, allowing them to show off both their embodiment of a "cool" aesthetic and their chiseled physiques, which have become more pronounced as they have grown up. This hard-bodied masculinity, which has been a recurring image in popular culture since at least the 1980s, is certainly a popular model of contemporary masculinity across racial lines—it was a central feature of the *Magic Mike* series and almost seems to be an expectation of actors playing male superheroes, in particular. But for Black men, to perform a masculinity and construct a star text based primarily on the contracting flesh of the half-naked body risks a return to what scholars like Mercer and Fanon see as Black masculinity reduced to the penis itself. While TikTok's short-form videos reduce almost all users to pure spectacle, hard-bodied Black men dancing in an always-spectacularized format is fraught with the same tensions that have haunted Black performance for non-black audiences since at least the nineteenth century.

Nonblack dancing men on TikTok have used Black dance (once again comprised of hip-hop-based TikTok dance vocabularies) to construct "cool" masculinities not rooted in rippling muscle. A frequent collaborator of Mackie, white dancer Zack Lugo (@zacklugo, ca. 10.7 million followers), describes himself in his TikTok profile as a "small town boy chasing his dreams." Drawing on the same "humble beginnings" narrative that helped construct Presley's star text, Lugo emphasizes his semi-rural Idaho whiteness as contrast for his later big-city

208   WHITE SCREENS, BLACK DANCE

lifestyle after moving to Los Angeles. Historically fully clothed in his dance videos, Lugo's version of athletic masculinity is influenced by his simultaneous creation of both skateboarding *and* dance videos (though rarely in combination). Less skilled at the dances themselves, and with a limited dance vocabulary (similar to Presley), Lugo instead used the dance trends of Straight Tok to design his own clothing line and build a fashion/modeling career. For his star text, then, the clothes are part of the draw, shifting the focus away from the slim body wearing them. Michael Le (@justmaiko, ca. 51.8 million followers), the most-followed dancing man on TikTok, began his social media career on other platforms (primarily Instagram) but became the sixth-highest paid TikToker in the world by 2020—largely through brand deals.[36] Acutely aware of being the only Asian in the top tier of mostly-white TikTokers, Le stated in an interview that he wants to provide "good" representation for Asian artist-creators.[37] Le leans heavily into the hip-hop aesthetic through not only his dances but also his streetwear-based fashion (and merchandise promotion) on the app. Unlike the previous examples, he constructs his masculinity not as a solo star who does occasional collaborations with others, but through family. Le founded a content creation house called Shluv House, where his two brothers, sister, and mother now also reside and perform on social media with him. That said, he does also dance with other TikTok stars, especially dancers of color—this includes Mackie and Tingz, as well as his now ex-girlfriend Analisse Rodriguez and her sisters. Like Lugo (and Channing Tatum's character in *Step Up*), Le is careful to authenticate his performance of Black dance by visibly associating with Black friends; also like Lugo, he builds his masculinity away from his body by focusing on clothing and especially videographic tricks, making his screendances as much about their cinematographic effects as about his own moves. In fact, some of his more cleverly filmed and edited TikToks, featuring carefully timed dolly shots, graphic matches, and multiplications of the dancing body, are among his most watched—boasting up to 25 million views—and indicate that this is a crucial aspect of his cachet as a creator. Thus, though all of these young men construct a "cool" masculinity through their TikTok dances, the white and Asian men (while blackbodying) define it more through clothing and other aspects that *distract* from the body itself, whereas the two Black men construct it through a hyper-*focus* on their bodies and physicality.

There is certainly more work to be done on contemporary dance in relation to identity construction, both on screens and off, and I hope that the tools of this book—simultaneous focus on the dancing body and the role of the camera (and the media industries themselves), as well as blackbodying as a conceptual framework for understanding the use of Black dance in these processes of identity construction by nonblack people—will help future scholars in these endeavors. As nonbinary conceptions of gender gain traction in mainstream discourses, how are danced constructions of gender shifting? As the so-called middle class in the U.S. continues to shrink and income inequality exacerbates the gap between the very wealthy and the barely surviving, how are performances of gender shifting alongside the struggles of everyday people? And as U.S. society's other Others, including Latinx folks, Asian Americans, and Indigenous peoples finally achieve greater access to and representation in mainstream media—at the same time as later generations are born of increasingly mixed backgrounds—how will the blurring of ethnic and racial markers operate? I have no doubt that mainstream media industries will remain under largely white control, and that Black dance will remain a dominant aspect of U.S. popular culture, so blackbodying will likely continue as well. I therefore hope future work will continue to ask: How is Black dance being used?

Notes

Introduction

1. Sally Banes, "Balanchine and Black Dance," *Writing Dancing in the Age of Postmodernism* (Hanover, CT: Wesleyan University Press, 1994); Brenda Dixon Gottschild, *Digging the Africanist Presence in American Performance: Dance and Other Contexts* (Westport, CT: Greenwood Press, 1996); Ramsay Burt, *Alien Bodies: Representations of Modernity, Race and Nation in Early Modern Dance* (London: Routledge, 1998); Susan Manning, *Modern Dance, Negro Dance: Race in Motion* (Minneapolis: University of Minnesota Press, 2004).
2. Nadine George-Graves, "'Just Like Being at the Zoo': Primitivity and Ragtime Dance," in *Ballroom, Boogie, Shimmy Sham, Shake: A Social and Popular Dance Reader*, ed. Julie Malnig (Chicago: University of Illinois Press, 2009); Thomas F. DeFrantz, "Popular Dances of the 1920s and early 30s: From Animal Dance Crazes to the Lindy Hop" and "Popular African American Dance of the 1950s and 60s," in *Ain't Nothing Like the Real Thing*, ed. R. Carlin and K. Conwill (Washington, D.C.: Smithsonian Press, 2010); Meghan Pugh, *America Dancing: From the Cakewalk to the Moonwalk* (New Haven, CT: Yale University Press, 2015); Danielle Robinson, *Modern Moves: Dancing Race During the Ragtime and Jazz Eras* (New York: Oxford University Press, 2015); Julie Malnig, *Dancing Black, Dancing White: Rock 'n' Roll, Race, and Youth Culture of the 1950s and Early 1960s* (Oxford: Oxford University Press, 2023).
3. Thomas F. DeFrantz, "African American Dance: A Complex History," *Dancing Many Drums: Excavations in African American Dance* (Madison: University of Wisconsin Press, 2002), 5. Quoted in Takiyah Nur Amin, "A Terminology of Difference: Making the Case for Black Dance in the 21st Century and Beyond," *The Journal of Pan African Studies* 4, no. 6 (September 2011), 10.
4. Carole Y. Johnson, "Black Dance," *THE FEET*, July 1971, 1.
5. DeFrantz, "African American Dance," 15.
6. Richard A. Long, *The Black Tradition in American Dance* (New York: Smithmark Publishers, 1989), 8. The debates have continued since then; for a more thorough overview and a compelling contemporary argument for an expansive definition of Black Dance, see Amin, "A Terminology of Difference."
7. DeFrantz, "Popular Dances of the 1920s and early 30s," 67.
8. DeFrantz, "Popular Dances of the 1920s and early 30s," 68.
9. DeFrantz, "Popular African American Dance of the 1950s and 60s," 184.
10. See, in particular, the first two chapters of *Digging the Africanist Presence in American Performance*. Gottschild's schema builds on several prior works by Robert F. Thompson.
11. Gottschild, *Digging the Africanist Presence*, 12–17.
12. Ibid., 9. For more from Gottschild on the Black dancing body, see *The Black Dancing Body: A Geography from Coon to Cool* (New York: Palgrave Macmillan, 2008).
13. The exceptions to this rule were the eight Black-cast musicals that were produced between 1929 and 1959.
14. While white male bodies were frequently praised for borrowing and embodying Africanist dance during the twentieth century, Black male bodies were frequently discouraged or prevented from doing the same with Europeanist dance. This is due, in part, to the racist assumptions about Black dancing bodies that Gottschild described in my references above. For a brief overview of the racialized roles—governed by hyper-masculinity and "primitiveness"—available to the Black male body in ballet and modern dance, see Thomas DeFrantz, "Simmering Passivity: The Black Male Body in Concert Dance," in *Moving Words: Re-writing Dance*, ed. Gay Morris (London: Routledge, 1996).
15. See Donna Haraway, *Primate Visions: Gender, Race, and Nature in the World of Modern Science* (New York: Routledge, 1989) and Gail Bederman, *Manliness & Civilization: A Cultural*

212 NOTES

History of Gender and Race in the United States, 1880–1917 (Chicago: University of Chicago Press, 1995).

16. See Judith Butler, *Gender Trouble: Feminism and the Subversion of Identity* (New York: Routledge, 1990).
17. Marlon B. Ross's summary of this history in his review of several 1990s books about Black masculinity characterizes this paradox with clarity and nuance. See Marlon B. Ross, "In Search of Black Men's Masculinities," *Feminist Studies* 24, no. 3 (Autumn 1998): 599–626.
18. Ralph Ellison, *Invisible Man* (New York: Random House, 1952); James Baldwin, *Nobody Knows My Name: More Notes of a Native Son* (New York: Dial Press, 1961).
19. Daniel Patrick Moynihan, "The Negro Family: The Case for National Action (1965)," reprinted in *African American Male Research* (1997): 1–35.
20. While it had been building since the 1940s, this "crisis" of masculinity came to a head in 1958, when multiple books and articles were published addressing the matter. See, for example, Arthur M. Schlesinger, Jr., "The Crisis of American Masculinity," *Esquire*, November 1958 and *Look Magazine*'s series, *The Decline of the American Male*, 1958. A similar crisis of masculinity had struck during the Great Depression.
21. See E. Anthony Rotundo, *American Manhood: Transformations in Masculinity from the Revolution to the Modern Era* (New York: BasicBooks, 1993) and Michael Kimmel, *Manhood in America: A Cultural History* (New York: Oxford University Press, 2018).
22. Kimmel, *Manhood in America*, 81–104.
23. Ibid., 155–165.
24. Steven Cohan, *Masked Men: Masculinity and the Movies in the Fifties* (Bloomington: Indiana University Press, 1997), xiv. According to gender studies scholar Michael Kimmel, the sissy concept began to refer to weakness, dependency, helplessness, feebleness, and femininity around 1900. See Kimmel, *Manhood in America*, 104–105.
25. Bederman, *Manliness & Civilization*, 1–20.
26. See Gaylyn Studlar, "'Optic Intoxication': Rudolph Valentino and Dance Madness," in *This Mad Masquerade: Stardom and Masculinity in the Jazz Age* (New York: Columbia University Press, 1996).
27. Miriam Hansen, "Pleasure, Ambivalence, Identification: Valentino and Female Spectatorship," *Cinema Journal* 25, no. 4 (1986), 7.
28. The question of the relationship between masculinity and dance is not new. For some of these discussions, see: Marcia Siegel, "Men Dancing," in *The Shapes of Change: Images of American Dance* (Berkeley and Los Angeles: University of California Press, 1985) and Jennifer Fisher and Anthony Shay, eds., *When Men Dance: Choreographing Masculinities Across Borders* (Oxford: Oxford University Press, 2009).
29. This stereotypical perception arguably emerged with Sergei Diaghilev's Ballets Russes, which in 1909 reintroduced men into ballet after a long absence. Ramsay Burt describes how a constellation of factors coalesced at once to entrench an association between the male dancer and homosexuality and/or femininity, including the Oscar Wilde trial and widespread anxieties about the weakening of manliness in the modern city. For more, see in particular chapters 1–3 of Burt, *The Male Dancer: Bodies, Spectacle, Sexualities*, 2nd ed. (London: Routledge, 2007).
30. Burt, *The Male Dancer*, 64, 66. In an alternative reading, Peter Stoneley has focused on Diaghilev's earlier roles for Nijinsky to argue that he was in fact feminized—first as an exotic, "Oriental" Golden Slave in *Schéhérazade* (1910), and then as a rose in *Le Spectre de la rose* (1911). See Stoneley, *A Queer History of the Ballet* (New York: Routledge, 2007), 69–77. From my perspective, the two are not necessarily mutually exclusive; Stoneley's descriptions of the Diaghilev roles could be reasonably understood as the impetus for or mere stylistic differentiation from Nijinsky's later effort at reassurance/masculinization described by Burt.
31. Lincoln Kirstein, *Nijinsky Dancing* (New York: Knopf, 1975), 137.
32. Maura Keefe, "Is Dance a Man's Sport Too?: The Performance of Athletic-Coded Masculinity on the Concert Dance Stage," in *When Men Dance: Choreographing Masculinities Across Borders* (Oxford: Oxford University Press, 2009).
33. Donald Bogle, *Toms, Coons, Mulattoes, Mammies and Bucks: An Interpretive History of Blacks in American Films*, 5th ed. (New York: Bloomsbury, 2016), 4.
34. Marshall Stearns and Jean Stearns, *Jazz Dance: The Story of American Vernacular Dance* (New York: Macmillan, 1968), 83.
35. For more on buck and wing dancing and their place in the history of American tap dance, see Constance Valis Hill, *Tap Dancing America: A Cultural History* (New York: Oxford University

Press, 2009). See also this informative video for Duke University by Thomas F. DeFrantz: https://www.youtube.com/watch?v=A34OD4eA17o.

36. Stearns and Stearns, *Jazz Dance*, 122.

37. This is not to say that Black men have never been called sissies. For more on the figure of the sissy in relation to Black masculinity, see Marlon B. Ross, *Sissy Insurgencies: A Racial Anatomy of Unfit Manliness* (Durham, NC: Duke University Press, 2021).

38. Johanna Boyce, Ann Daly, Bill T. Jones, and Carol Martin, "Movement and Gender: A Roundtable Discussion," *TDR* 32, no. 4 (1988), 89–90. Quoted in Burt, *The Male Dancer*, 52.

39. Ronald L. Jackson II has helpfully enumerated and explained the set of "scripts" made available to Black masculine bodies in the twentieth century: 1) exotic and strange, 2) violent, 3) incompetent and uneducated, 4) sexual, 5) exploitable, and 6) innately incapacitated. For more, see Jackson, *Scripting the Black Masculine Body: Identity, Discourse, and Racial Politics in Popular Media* (Ithaca, NY: SUNY Press, 2006). See also Ronald L. Jackson II and Celnisha L. Dangerfield, "Defining Black Masculinity as Cultural Property: An Identity Negotiation Paradigm," in *African American Communication & Identities: Essential Readings*, ed. Ronald L. Jackson II (Thousand Oaks, CA: Sage, 2004).

40. Many film historians consider Hollywood's silent era, from 1915–1927, to be part of its Golden Age. While both the studio system and many of its cinematic conventions were solidified during this period, I consider its Golden Age to begin with the talkies. Relatedly, some see the Golden Age as lasting all the way to 1969. I am agnostic with regard to the end date, so I use 1962 here because it seems to be the majority opinion.

41. Of course, Broadway musicals themselves, especially the revue format, were heavily influenced by vaudeville. Film scholars Gerald Mast and Sean Griffin have further demonstrated the extent to which both 1930s Hollywood musicals in general and Fox musicals in particular (even into the 1940s) were just as much or more shaped by vaudeville than Broadway. See Gerald Mast, *Can't Help Singin': The American Musical on Stage and Screen* (New York: Overlook Press, 1987), 228 and Sean Griffin, "The Gang's All Here: Generic versus Racial Integration in the 1940s Musical," *Cinema Journal* 42, no. 1 (Fall 2002), 28–32.

42. See Rick Altman, *The American Film Musical* (Bloomington: Indiana University Press, 1987); Jane Feuer, *The Hollywood Musical*, 2nd ed. (Bloomington: Indiana University Press, 1993); Richard Dyer, "Entertainment and Utopia," in *Only Entertainment* (London: Routledge, 1992); and Dyer, *In the Space of a Song: The Uses of Song in Film* (London: Routledge, 2012).

43. Scholars have discussed the first wave of the rock 'n' roll musical in terms of its relationship to class, labor, authenticity, the popular music industry, and even race, since it has been widely established that rock 'n' roll is a Black musical genre colonized by whites throughout the midcentury period. See Keir Keightley, "Manufacturing Authenticity: Imagining the Music Industry in Anglo-American Cinema, 1956–62," in *Movie Music, the Film Reader*, ed. Kay Dickinson (London: Routledge, 2003); Kay Dickinson, "'The Motion Picture You're About to See is a Story of Music': The Migration of Cinema into Rock 'n' Roll," in *Off Key: When Film and Music Won't Work Together* (New York: Oxford University Press, 2008); Thomas Doherty, *Teenagers and Teenpics: Juvenilization of American Movies* (Philadelphia, PA: Temple University Press, 2010); and David E. James, *Rock 'n' Film: Cinema's Dance with Popular Music* (New York: Oxford University Press, 2016).

44. See "Plastic Years" in Eric Barnouw, *Tube of Plenty: The Evolution of American Television* (New York: Oxford University Press, 1990).

45. See Susan Murray, *Hitch Your Antenna to the Stars!: Early Television and Broadcast Stardom* (New York: Routledge, 2005).

46. Denise Mann, "The Spectacularization of Everyday Life: Recycling Hollywood Stars and Fans in Early Television Variety Shows," in *Private Screenings: Television and the Female Consumer*, ed. Lynn Spigel and Denise Mann (Minneapolis: University of Minnesota Press, 1992), 43.

47. See both Richard Dyer, *Stars* (London: British Film Institute, 1979) and Dyer, *Heavenly Bodies: Film Stars and Society* (New York: St. Martin's Press, 1986).

48. For a discussion of a wider range of midcentury Hollywood masculinities (predominantly white ones), see Susan Bordo, "Fifties Hollywood: The Rebel Male Crashes the Wedding" in *The Male Body* (New York: Farrar, Straus, and Giroux, 1999).

49. Steven Cohan, "'Feminizing' the Song-and-Dance Man: Fred Astaire and the spectacle of masculinity in the Hollywood musical," in *Screening the Male: Exploring Masculinities in the Hollywood Cinema*, ed. Steven Cohan and Ina R. Hark (London: Routledge, 1993. See

214 NOTES

also Laura Mulvey, "Visual Pleasure and Narrative Cinema" in *Feminism and Film Theory* (London: Routledge, 2013), 57–68.

50. Cohan, "'Feminizing' the Song-and-Dance Man," 61–62.
51. Ibid., 66.
52. Ibid., 47.
53. To my knowledge, the only work that offers sustained engagement with *dance's* role in constructing musical masculinity is choreographer Darcey Callison's dissertation, which analyzes fourteen Hollywood white male choreographies, ranging from Golden Age musicals to recent films. He concluded that in dancing the white masculinity of the "American Dream," these men in fact borrow heavily from the Black dancers that Hollywood contained and excluded. See Darcey Callison, "Dancing Masculinity for Hollywood: The American Dream, Whiteness and the Movement Vocabulary Within Hollywood's Choreography for Men" (PhD diss., York University, 2008).
54. See Murray, *Hitch Your Antenna to the Stars!*. Other scholars have examined the ways that non-white performers were framed in variety television. See Murray Forman, *One Night on TV Is Worth Weeks at the Paramount: Popular Music on Early Television* (Durham, NC: Duke University Press, 2012); and Meenasarani Linde Murugan, "Exotic Television: Technology, Empire, and Entertaining Globalism" (PhD diss., Northwestern University, 2015). Only Murugan addresses dance, examining the ways in which both white performers and performers of color danced notions of "the Orient" and uncovering opportunities for performers of color in particular to perform both cosmopolitanism and diaspora through the seeming "gimmick" of exoticism.
55. See, for example, Mary R. Desjardins, *Recycled Stars: Female Film Stardom in the Age of Television and Video* (Durham, NC: Duke University Press, 2015).
56. It has been argued that these policies were largely based on faulty data. See in particular Thomas Cripps, "The Myth of the Southern Box Office," in *The Black Experience in America: Selected Essays*, ed. James C. Curtis and Lewis L. Gould (Austin: University of Texas Press, 1970).
57. See Arthur Knight, *Disintegrating the Musical: Black Performance and American Musical Film* (Durham, NC: Duke University Press, 2002).
58. Mary R. Desjardins, *Recycled Stars: Female Film Stardom in the Age of Television and Video* (Durham, NC: Duke University Press, 2015), 39.
59. See Will Friedwald, "Years of Stardust, Night Lights, and Fear of the Dark: 1957–1959," in *Straighten Up and Fly Right: The Life and Music of Nat King Cole* (New York: Oxford University Press, 2020).
60. See Arthur Knight, "Star Dances: African American Constructions of Stardom, 1925–1960," in *Classic Hollywood, Classic Whiteness*, ed. Daniel Bernardi (Minneapolis: University of Minnesota Press, 2001); Mia Mask, *Divas on Screen: Black Women in American Film* (Urbana: University of Illinois Press, 2009); Charlene Regester, *African American Actresses: The Struggle for Visibility, 1900–1960* (Bloomington: Indiana University Press, 2010), and Miriam Petty, *Stealing the Show: African American Performers and Audiences in 1930s Hollywood* (Oakland: University of California Press, 2016).
61. J. Fred MacDonald, *Blacks in White TV: African Americans in Television Since 1948* (Chicago: Prentice-Hall, 1992); Herman Gray, *Watching Race: Television and The Struggle for Blackness* (Minneapolis: University of Minnesota Press, 1995); Melvin Patrick Ely, *The Adventures of Amos 'n' Andy: A Social History of an American Phenomenon* (Charlottesville: University Press of Virginia, 2001).
62. See, for example, Henry Louis Gates, Jr., *The Signifying Monkey: A Theory of Afro-American Literary Criticism* (London: Oxford University Press, 1988) and Mel Watkins, *On the Real Side: Laughing, Lying, and Signifying* (New York: Simon and Schuster, 1994).
63. For examples of such practices in Hollywood film and their reception by Black audiences, see Miriam Petty, *Stealing the Show*; for early television examples, see Christine Acham, "Reading the Roots of Resistance: Television of the Black Revolution," in *Revolution Televised: Prime Time and the Struggle for Black Power* (Minneapolis: University of Minnesota Press, 2004) and Mack Scott, "From Blackface to Beulah: Subtle Subversion in Early Black Sitcoms," *Journal of Contemporary History* 49, no. 4 (October 2014): 743–769.
64. Sean Griffin, "The Gang's All Here: Generic versus Racial Integration in the 1940s Musical," *Cinema Journal* 42, no. 1 (Autumn 2002): 21–45 and Karen McNally, "Featuring the Nicholas Brothers: Spectacle, Structure, and Racial Interventions in the Hollywood Musical," *Star Turns in Hollywood Musicals* (Dijon, France: Les Presses du réel, 2016).

NOTES 215

65. See, for example, *Tin Pan Alley* (1940), *Orchestra Wives* (1942), *Greenwich Village* (1944), and *You're My Everything* (1949), all produced by Twentieth Century Fox and featuring "dance specialty" numbers by the Nicholas Brothers, the Four Step Brothers, and the Berry Brothers, respectively.

66. I give hearty and grateful thanks to my colleague Mario LaMothe for coining and then gifting me the term *blackbodying* after I presented this work in its very early stages at the 2015 Mellon Dance Studies Seminar.

67. Brynn Shiovitz, *Behind the Screen: Tap Dance, Race, and Invisibility During Hollywood's Golden Age* (New York: Oxford University Press, 2023), 11.

68. Manning, *Modern Dance, Negro Dance*, 10.

69. Krin Gabbard, "Marlon Brando's Jazz Acting and the Obsolescence of Blackface," in *Black Magic: White Hollywood and African American Culture* (New Brunswick: Rutgers University Press, 2004), 19–20.

70. Gabbard, *Black Magic*, 33, 39. See also Joanna Dee Das, *Katherine Dunham: Dance and the African Diaspora* (New York: Oxford University Press, 2017), 106.

71. W.T. Lhamon, Jr., *Raising Cain: Blackface Performance from Jim Crow to Hip Hop* (Cambridge, MA: Harvard University Press, 1998), 41–43.

72. Eric Lott, *Love and Theft: Blackface Minstrelsy and the American Working Class* (New York: Oxford University Press, 1993), 6–7.

73. Lott, *Love and Theft*, 54–56.

74. Lott, *Love and Theft*, 105. One of the ways mainstream American culture was rather immediately "blackened" by blackface minstrelsy was in ragtime music and dance. For an in-depth analysis of this, see Danielle Robinson, "Performing American: Ragtime Dancing as Participatory Minstrelsy," *Dance Chronicle* 32 (2009): 89–126.

75. See Gottschild, *Digging the Africanist Presence*, 81–125 and Watkins, *On the Real Side*, 104–133.

76. Michael Rogin, *Blackface, White Noise: Jewish Immigrants in the Hollywood Melting Pot* (Berkeley and Los Angeles: University of California Press, 1996).

77. There is a fair amount of scholarship examining the 1930s blackface of these 1920s holdovers, particularly in relationship to their ethnic reckonings as Jews. See in particular Rogin, *Blackface, White Noise*; Knight, *Disintegrating the Musical*; and Shiovitz, *Behind the Screen*.

78. The standard structure of a blackface minstrel show in the 1850s included a first act wherein an "interlocutor" stood at center and engaged two "endmen" before a semicircle of the rest of the minstrel troupe. This structure is roughly replicated in *Dimples'* "Dixie-Anna." For more on Lincoln Perry as Stepin Fetchit, see Charlene Regester, "Stepin Fetchit: The Man, the Image, and the African American Press," *Film History* 6, no. 4 (1994): 502–521 and Miriam Petty, "Lincoln Perry's 'Problematic Stardom': Stepin Fetchit Steals the Shoat," in *Stealing the Show*.

79. In Harriet Beecher Stowe's narration of Uncle Tom's first encounter with Evangeline in *Uncle Tom's Cabin* (1852), he sees her as an angel. Patricia Turner has argued that the relationship between Temple and Robinson was consciously modeled after that between Eva and Uncle Tom. Completing the sequence of connections to minstrelsy, Lott reminds us that the stereotypes Stowe created, like the enduring "Uncle Tom," were not so different from similar types on the minstrel stage; he hammers this home by noting that T.D. Rice, famed "father" of minstrelsy and "Jump Jim Crow," ended his career playing Uncle Tom on the stage. See Patricia Turner, *Ceramic Uncles & Celluloid Mammies: Black Images and Their Influence on Culture* (New York: Anchor Books, 1994), 83 and Eric Lott, *Love and Theft*, 34.

80. See Shiovitz, 149–153 and Ara Osterweil, "Reconstructing Shirley: Pedophilia and Interracial Romance in Hollywood's Age of Innocence," *Camera Obscura* 24, no. 3 (72) (December 2009): 1–39.

81. Rooney and Garland teamed up for another blackface minstrel show (seemingly in the same costumes they wore for *Babes in Arms*'s minstrel show) in *Babes on Broadway* (1941), which also held several references to the New Deal. This included Rooney performing in drag (sans brownface) as Carmen Miranda, a famous Hollywood symbol of FDR's Good Neighbor Policy, singing her famous "Mamãe eu quero." Garland's main number during the minstrel show had her singing "Franklin D. Roosevelt Jones." The song's original lyrics were clearly meant to mock African Americans who name their children after presidents but this version also offers commentary on FDR himself, with "Maybe you'll balance the budget by and by" and "When this rascal goes to school, ABCs won't matter / Teach him plain old 'rithmetic / And of course some fireside chatter."

216   NOTES

82. For example, she dresses up as a male tramp when performing the reprise of "Be A Clown" with Gene Kelly in *The Pirate* (1948).
83. Rogin, *Blackface, White Noise*, 125–126.
84. Gottschild, *Digging the Africanist Presence*, 2–3.
85. Carol Clover, "Dancin' in the Rain," *Critical Inquiry* 21, no. 4 (1995), 740.
86. See Arlene Croce, *The Fred Astaire and Ginger Rogers Book* (New York: Outerbridge & Larzard, 1972), 107.
87. See Elizabeth Abel, "Shadows," *Representations* 84, no. 1 (November 2003): 166–199; Pugh, 63; Shiovitz, 183–189. See also Susan Gubar's reading of the number, which highlights evidence of the white man's sexual anxiety in comparison to Black men, harkening back to minstrelsy's original fascination with Black masculinity. Susan Gubar, *Racechanges: White Skin, Black Face in American Culture* (New York: Oxford University Press, 1997), 88–90.
88. Bubbles' style ultimately had a stronger influence on the majority of tap dancers in the 1930s and beyond. See Hill, *Tap Dancing America*, 88.
89. See Shiovitz, 193. For more on Powell's competence in relation to gender in Hollywood, see Adrienne L. McLean, "Putting 'Em Down Like a Man: Eleanor Powell and the Spectacle of Competence," in *Hetero: Queering Representations of Straightness*, ed. Sean Griffin (Albany, NY: SUNY Press, 2009).
90. In my reading, the focus on arms is where Powell's ballet training overshadows her tap training. But more importantly, as Shiovitz astutely suggests, the gestures she adds that Robinson never seems to have used himself, such as hands in pockets, reinforce some of minstrelsy's (and Hollywood's) stereotypes, such as the obedient servant. See Shiovitz, 198–199; 204–205.
91. Shiovitz, 176.
92. Rogin, *Blackface, White Noise*, 167–168.
93. Carol Clover, "Dancin' in the Rain."
94. Clover, "Dancin' in the Rain," 738–742.
95. She refers to the legacy of chattel slavery in the United States. Gottschild, *Digging the Africanist Presence*, 2–5, 9.
96. For a discussion of female stars' gestures, dances, and overall corporeality in musical films, see Erin Brannigan, "The Musical: Moving into the Dance," in *Dancefilm: Choreography and the Moving Image* (New York: Oxford University Press, 2011).

Chapter 1

1. See Rusty E. Frank, *Tap!: The Greatest Tap Dance Stars and Their Stories 1900–1955*, rev. ed. (New York: De Capo Press, 1994), wherein tap dancer LaVaughn Robinson explains that he was one of many tap dancers who developed his art on the streets of Philadelphia. He goes on to note that "The Nicholas Brothers, see they came outta Philadelphia, too. But they didn't hang on them corners. Yeah—well see—they were fortunate" (130).
2. For more on the contradictory positioning of Black stars in Hollywood, see Arthur Knight, "Star Dances: African-American Constructions of Stardom, 1925–1960," in *Classic Hollywood: Classic Whiteness*, ed. Daniel Bernardi (Minneapolis: University of Minnesota Press, 2001).
3. Maurice Hines, interview, in *The Nicholas Brothers: We Sing and We Dance* (New York: A&E, November 29, 1992).
4. Leonard Reed, interview by Bruce Goldstein, 1991. Quoted in Hill, *Brotherhood in Rhythm: The Jazz Tap Dancing of the Nicholas Brothers* (New York: Oxford University Press, 2000), 185.
5. Hill, *Brotherhood in Rhythm*, 200–201.
6. Constance Valis Hill, *Tap Dancing America: A Cultural History* (New York: Oxford University Press, 2010), 90.
7. Krin Gabbard, *Black Magic: White Hollywood and African American Culture* (New Brunswick: Rutgers University Press, 2004); Arthur Knight, "Star Dances," in *Disintegrating the Musical: Black Performance and American Musical Film* (Durham, NC: Duke University Press, 2002); Miriam Petty, *Stealing the Show: African American Performers and Audiences in 1930s Hollywood* (Oakland: University of California Press, 2016).
8. Hill quotes Fayard as having explained, "We were kids, but we danced like men." See *Brotherhood in Rhythm*, 52 and 95.
9. Hill is particularly dismissive of the Nicholases' television performances. See *Brotherhood in Rhythm*, 234–236.

NOTES 217

10. Fayard Nicholas, interview by Constance Valis Hill, 1995. Quoted in *Brotherhood in Rhythm*, 37.
11. Hill, *Brotherhood in Rhythm*, 42.
12. Constance Valis Hill, *Brotherhood in Rhythm,* 37–49.
13. Ibid., 41; Rusty Frank, *Tap!*, 67.
14. The time step is one of the basic sequences in tap dance, whose sounds are often used to set a rhythm. While there are many variations, it is most often described as "stomp, hop, step, flap, step" or "shuffle, hop, step, flap, step."
15. Fayard Nicholas, interview, 1999. Quoted in David Fantle and Tom Johnson, *Reel to Real: 25 Years of Celebrity Interviews from Vaudeville to Movies to TV* (Oregon, WI: Badger Books Inc., 2004), 83.
16. *The Nicholas Brothers: We Sing and We Dance*; Frank, *Tap!*, 67.
17. Marshall Stearns and Jean Stearns, *Jazz Dance: The Story of American Vernacular Dance* (New York: Macmillan, 1968), 279; Fantle and Johnson, *Reel to Real*, 83–84.
18. While Constance Valis Hill's biography of the Nicholas Brothers describes the advertising for their opening act at the Lafayette Theatre as still featuring the "Nicholas *Kids*" (for her, it seems the change to the "Nicholas *Brothers*" did not occur until their debut at the Cotton Club [*Brotherhood in Rhythm*, 64–68]), Fayard Nicholas himself recalls the name of their duo changing immediately upon their arrival in New York (See Frank, *Tap!*, 68).
19. Hill, *Brotherhood in Rhythm*, 61. See also Jervis Anderson, *This Was Harlem: A Cultural Portrait, 1900–1950* (New York: Farrar Straus Giroux, 1981), 339–341.
20. Interview with Fayard Nicholas by Constance Valis Hill, 1995. Quoted in Hill, *Brotherhood in Rhythm*, 65.
21. Ibid., 68.
22. Constance Valis Hill, *Tap Dancing America: A Cultural History* (Oxford: Oxford University Press, 2010), 87.
23. Ibid.
24. Hill, *Brotherhood in Rhythm*, 147–148.
25. Marshall and Jean Stearns, *Jazz Dance*, 279. The Stearnses cite "numerous interviews, conversations, and lecture-demonstrations," 1959–1966, for this information. It is also important to note, here, that the Nicholases were already famous for this style of dress three years before the introduction of Fred Astaire's signature "Top Hat, White Tie, and Tails" costume and song about the same in *Top Hat* (1935).
26. *The Nicholas Brothers: We Sing and We Dance*; Fayard echoes this recollection in Frank, *Tap!*, 68.
27. Hill, *Brotherhood in Rhythm*, 58.
28. Ibid., 61.
29. Donald Crafton, *The Talkies: American Cinema's Transition to Sound, 1926–1931* (Berkeley and Los Angeles: University of California Press, 1999), 106.
30. Thomas Cripps, *Slow Fade to Black* (New York: Oxford University Press, 1977), 291.
31. Hill, *Brotherhood in Rhythm*, 74 and *The Nicholas Brothers: We Sing and We Dance*.
32. Harold also performed alone with scantily clad women in a similar context in *The Emperor Jones* (1933).
33. Cohan was Irish-American, so his dance style reflected that influence. Like the Nicholases, Cohan began his performance career as a child; he sang and danced as part of his family's touring vaudeville troupe "The Four Cohans" for over a decade before becoming a prolific Tin Pan Alley songwriter.
34. Of course, as mentioned in the introductory chapter, Black blackface minstrels did exist historically. See Gottschild, *Digging the Africanist Presence in American Performance*, 81–125 and Mel Watkins, *On the Real Side: Laughing, Lying, and Signifying* (New York: Simon and Schuster, 1994), 104–133.
35. Kristen Hatch, *Shirley Temple and the Performance of Girlhood* (New Brunswick: Rutgers University Press, 2015), 21. Gaylyn Studlar has discussed the performance of girlhood from a different angle, namely via the lens of "juvenation" as a process linked to feminization and eroticization. This reading is also closed off to the Nicholases, whose eroticization and feminization seem to function independently rather than dependently due to their racial difference. For more on the "juvenation" approach, see Studlar, *Precocious Charms: Stars Performing Girlhood in Classical Hollywood Cinema* (Berkeley and Los Angeles: University of California Press, 2013).

36. Importantly, this is a very different conflation of childhood innocence and mature sexuality than Pamela Robertson Wojcik identifies in Shirley Temple films. Whereas Wojcik argues that Temple's characters "imitate the conventions" of the fallen woman, carrying a sexual knowingness about her, young Harold Nicholas bears no such quality. Instead, it is the Goldwyn Girls who perform the sexual knowingness; when Harold sings about his "sugar candy," he appears excited about literal candy, as most children might. But when the Goldwyn Girls repeat the chorus, they all wink when they sing about his sugar candy, as if it is a euphemism for something more sexual in nature. See Wojcik, "Shirley Temple as Streetwalker: Girls, Streets, and Encounters with Men," *Fantasies of Neglect: Imagining the Urban Child in American Film and Fiction* (New Brunswick: Rutgers University Press, 2016).
37. "Nicholas Boys Return to Cotton Club In N.Y.," *Chicago Defender*, March 16, 1935, 10.
38. Hill, *Brotherhood in Rhythm*, 95.
39. Ibid., 95–96. Hill refers here to Thomas Cripps, *Slow Fade to Black: The Negro in American Film, 1900–1942* (New York: Oxford University Press, 1977).
40. Fayard Nicholas, interview, in *The Nicholas Brothers: We Sing and We Dance*.
41. "Colored Theaters," *Atlanta Constitution*, March 9, 1941, 9.
42. Scholars of the film musical have performed extensive analyses of the non-integrated versus integrated musical format. In particular, see John Mueller, "Fred Astaire and the Integrated Musical," *Cinema Journal* 24, no. 1 (Autumn 1984): 28–40. See also Rick Altman, *The American Film Musical*, (Bloomington: Indiana University Press, 1987) and Jane Feuer, *The Hollywood Musical* (Bloomington: Indiana University Press, 1982).
43. Knight, *Disintegrating the Musical*, 13–25.
44. Feuer, *The Hollywood Musical*, 24.
45. For discussion of this *Summer Stock* number, see, for example, Feuer, *The Hollywood Musical*, 6, 20.
46. The 1940s and 50s were sprinkled with fleeting, one-off performances by other Black dancers. A prime example is the "Shine on Your Shoes" number from *The Band Wagon* (1953). In the number, Leroy Daniels shines Fred Astaire's shoes and performs a syncopated dance with his brushes and rag. According to Mark Knowles, Daniels had already become rather famous in Los Angeles as the "Bebop Bootblack" and was "discovered" by the film's assistant dance director, Alex Romero. Though Astaire happily welcomed Daniels into the film, he was uncredited for the performance. For more on this instance, see Mark Knowles, *The Man Who Made the Jailhouse Rock: Alex Romero, Hollywood Choreographer* (Jefferson, NC: McFarland, 2013), 82–83, 182–183.
47. Feuer, *The Hollywood Musical*, 3–7.
48. A. Philip Randolph, "The Pullman Company and the Pullman Porter," *Messenger* 7, no. 9 (September 1925): 312. For more, see Beth Tompkins Bates, *Pullman Porters and the Rise of Protest Politics in Black America, 1925–1945* (Chapel Hill: University of North Carolina Press, 2001).
49. For more on A. Philip Randolph and his role in the fight for Civil Rights, see Cornelius L. Bynum, *A. Philip Randolph and the Struggle for Civil Rights* (Urbana: University of Illinois Press, 2010) and Andrew Edmund Kersten and Clarence Lang, eds., *Reframing Randolph: Labor, Black Freedom, and the Legacies of A. Philip Randolph* (New York: New York University Press, 2015).
50. In fact, a later performance of the song by Dan Dailey, Jr. with the Berry Brothers in *You're My Everything* (1949) casts Nyas (Ananias) and Warren Berry as precisely these shoeshine boys/ Pullman Porters; Dailey sings "Boys, you can give me a shine" and the Berrys' corresponding choreography includes shining motions. While their flash tap dancing is more complex and visually appealing than Dailey's, the Berrys are not the primary focus of the number, much as actual Pullman Porters were expected to blend into the background. For more on the culture and rules surrounding Pullman Porters, see, for example, this 1952 "Instructions to Porters, Attendants and Bus Boys" booklet, provided by the Southern California Scenic Railway Association's online library: http://www.scsra.org/library/rulebook.html.
51. Leonard Reed, interview by Bruce Goldstein, 1991. Quoted in Hill, *Brotherhood in Rhythm*, 169.
52. Mary Harris, "Sun Valley Serenade, Palace, Reveals New Henie Abilities," *Washington Post*, October 3, 1941, 12.
53. Amiri Baraka [as LeRoi Jones], *Blues People: Negro Music in White America* (New York: Quill, 1963), 181.
54. Hill, *Brotherhood in Rhythm*, 177–178.

NOTES 219

55. Fayard Nicholas, telephone interview by S. Torriano Berry, February 7, 1999. Quoted in S. Torriano Berry with Venise T. Berry, *The 50 Most Influential Black Films: A Celebration of African-American Talent, Determination, and Creativity* (New York: Kensington Publishing, 2001), 67.
56. The Nicholas Brothers also executed these side splits in a promotional still for *Sun Valley Serenade* the year before, but they were not actually part of the choreography for their "Chattanooga Choo Choo" number.
57. Steven Cohan, "'Feminizing' the Song-and-Dance Man: Fred Astaire and the spectacle of masculinity in the Hollywood musical," in *Screening the Male: Exploring Masculinities in the Hollywood Cinema*, ed. Steven Cohan and Ina R. Hark (London: Routledge, 1993), 62.
58. Cohan, 63–64.
59. For more on Rick Altman's theory of the Hollywood musical's dual-focus narrative and dance numbers' role in resolving (sexual) difference, see Altman, *The American Film Musical*.
60. See, for example, VéVé Clark, "Performing the Memory of Difference in Afro-Caribbean Dance: Katherine Dunham's Choreography, 1938–1987" in *Kaiso!: Writings by and About Katherine Dunham*, ed. VéVé Clark and Sarah E. Johnson (Madison: University of Wisconsin Press, 2005); Susie Trenka, "Appreciation, Appropriation, Assimilation: *Stormy Weather* and the Hollywood History of Black Dance," in *The Oxford Handbook of Dance and the Popular Screen*, ed. Melissa Blanco Borelli (New York: Oxford University Press, 2014); and Shane Vogel, "Performing 'Stormy Weather': Ethel Waters, Lena Horne, and Katherine Dunham," *South Central Review* 25, no. 1 (2008): 93–113.
61. Knight, *Disintegrating the Musical*, 125.
62. Hill, *Brotherhood in Rhythm*, 214.
63. John L. Scott, "'Stormy Weather' Joyous Gathering of Sepia Stars," *Los Angeles Times*, July 30, 1943, 11.
64. Hill, *Brotherhood in Rhythm*, 212–213.
65. Ibid., 211.
66. Kobena Mercer, "Black Hair/Style Politics," *Welcome to the Jungle: New Positions in Black Cultural Studies* (New York: Routledge, 1994), 118.
67. Malcolm X with Alex Haley, *The Autobiography of Malcolm X*, 1964 (New York: Ballantine Books, 1992), 62–63.
68. Ibid., 119.
69. Hill, *Brotherhood in Rhythm*, 211.
70. Ibid., 214.
71. Fayard Nicholas, interview by Constance Valis Hill, 1995. Quoted in Hill, *Brotherhood in Rhythm*, 229.
72. This is not to say that musical films disappeared or ceased to be profitable in the post-studio era, but the "classical" Hollywood musical gave way to what might be termed the "roadshow" musical and other variations (such as the rock 'n' roll musical, to be discussed in Chapter 3.) For more on the post-studio musical, see Kelly Kessler, *Destabilizing the Hollywood Musical: Music, Masculinity and Mayhem* (New York: Palgrave Macmillan, 2011).
73. Milton Berle with Haskel Frankel, *Milton Berle: An Autobiography* (New York: Delacorte Press, 1974), 285.
74. Christine Acham, *Revolution Televised*, 19.
75. According to *The World Book Encyclopedia*'s entry on television, there were about 6 million television sets in the United States in 1950; by 1960, there were almost 60 million.
76. As stated at the outset of this chapter, Hill is one of these critics. See: *Brotherhood in Rhythm*, 234–236.
77. Hill, *Brotherhood in Rhythm*, 237. See also: *The Nicholas Brothers: We Sing and We Dance*.
78. For more on hard bop, see David H. Rosenthal, *Hard Bop: Jazz and Black Music, 1955–1965* (New York: Oxford University Press, 1994).
79. Hill, *Brotherhood in Rhythm*, 246.
80. Hill characterizes these performances as launching the "nostalgia" phase of the Nicholases' career, though not necessarily in a bad way—she suggests that their frequent repetition and recombination of old steps and stylistics served to "codify their own dance technique . . . in essence interpreting and reinterpreting their own jazz dance, as jazz musicians do when playing" (*Brotherhood in Rhythm*, 248–249). This is a compelling comparison. What Hill does not give sufficient attention to, however, is just how much the steps, moves, and rhythms have *changed*.

220 NOTES

81. One might argue that James Brown epitomized "soul dance" in 1970s funk; DeFrantz notes that funk "echoed the solo popular dance forms of the 1920s," sharing their "rhythmic response that deployed body parts as percussive instruments in space." See Thomas F. DeFrantz, "Unchecked Popularity: Neoliberal Circulations of Black Social Dance," in *Neoliberalism and Global Theatres: Performance Permutations*, ed. Lara D. Nielsen and Patricia A. Ybarra (Hampshire: Palgrave Macmillan, 2012), 137–138.
82. Harriet Jackson, "American Dancer, Negro," *Dance Magazine*, September 1966, 42. Quoted in Hill, *Brotherhood in Rhythm*, 246.
83. James Brown and Bruce Tucker, *James Brown: The Godfather of Soul* (New York: Macmillan, 1986), 153.
84. See R. J. Smith, *The One: The Life and Music of James Brown* (New York: Gotham Books, 2012), 149–152.
85. Portia K. Maultsby, "Soul Music: Its Sociological and Political Significance in American Popular Culture," *Journal of Popular Culture* 17, no. 2 (Fall 1983): 54.
86. Though the Nicholas Brothers themselves stayed out of politics, both of their first wives, Dorothy Dandridge and Geraldine Pate, were fairly active in World War II-era progressive organizations such as the Hollywood Democratic Committee.
87. For more on the history of the circle formation, see Katrina Hazzard-Donald, "The Circle and the Line: Speculations of the Development of African American Vernacular Dancing," *Western Journal of Black Studies* 20, no. 1 (Spring 1996): 28–38.
88. Matthew Delmont, "Michael Jackson & Television Before Thriller," *The Journal of Pan African Studies* 3, no. 7 (March 2010), 76. Notably, there is also an ambivalence here: *The Jacksons* was an artifact of the brothers' (minus Jermaine) move from the Black-owned Motown label (as "The Jackson 5") to white-owned CBS/Epic Records. The white CBS producers just as often booked popular white guests such as Sonny Bono, Betty White, and David Letterman for the show, leaving fewer opportunities for showcasing Black talent and instead once again courting whiter audiences.
89. See, in particular, *The Nicholas Brothers: We Sing and We Dance*.

Chapter 2

1. Brenda Dixon Gottschild, *Digging the Africanist Presence in American Performance: Dance and Other Contexts* (Westport, CT: Greenwood Press, 1996).
2. Rick Altman, *The American Film Musical* (Bloomington: Indiana University Press, 1987); Jane Feuer, *The Hollywood Musical*, 2nd ed. (Bloomington: Indiana University Press, 1993). For *bricolage* specifically, see Feuer, 3–7.
3. See chapters 4 and 5 in Richard Dyer, *In the Space of a Song: The Uses of Song in Film* (New York: Routledge, 2012). See also much of Beth Genné's work.
4. Carol Clover, "Dancin' in the Rain," *Critical Inquiry* 21, no. 4 (Summer 1995): 722–747.
5. See "Dancing with Balls: Sissies, Sailors, and the Camp Masculinity of Gene Kelly," in Steven Cohan, *Incongruous Entertainment: Camp, Cultural Value, and the MGM Musical* (Durham, NC: Duke University Press, 2005).
6. I will return to the concept of the Black dandy in Chapter 4, as it is also an important figure for understanding Sammy Davis, Jr.'s masculinity and stardom. For more on dandyism and Victorian masculinity more generally, see James Eli Adams, *Dandies and Desert Saints: Styles of Victorian Masculinity* (Ithaca, NY: Cornell University Press, 1995). For more on Black dandyism specifically, see Monica L. Miller, *Slaves to Fashion: Black Dandyism and the Styling of Black Diasporic Identity* (Durham, NC: Duke University Press, 2009). Particularly helpful for thinking about the Black dandyism of dancer-performers like Padilla is Barbara L. Webb, "The Black Dandyism of George Walker: A Case Study in Genealogical Method," *TDR: The Drama Review* 45, no. 4 (Winter 2001): 7–24.
7. Recall that Gottschild lists the "aesthetic of the cool" as a key Africanist aesthetic. See Gottschild, *Digging the Africanist Presence*, 16–17.
8. It is important to note that these tense hands were not unique to Kelly, as they became common in "masculine" tap-style show dancing during the second half of Kelly's career; for example, Tommy Rall and Bob Fosse used the flat palm/tight fist dichotomy often in their dancing, especially in their duet for *My Sister Eileen* (1955), choreographed by Fosse. It does seem that Kelly was "first" and most iconic among white male dancers to use them, and he used them most prolifically across dance styles.

NOTES 221

9. Michael Kimmel, *Manhood in America: A Cultural History* (New York: Oxford University Press, 2018), 103.

10. Clive Hirschhorn, *Gene Kelly: A Biography* (New York: St. Martin's, 1984), 25–26.

11. See Camille Hardy, "Bringing Bourrées to Broadway: George Balanchine's Career in the Commercial Theater," *World Literature Today* 80, no. 2 (2006): 16–18. See also Constance Valis Hill's analysis of Balanchine's work with (and inspiration by) the Nicholas Brothers on Broadway: Constance Valis Hill, "Babes on Broadway: 1936–1938," in *Brotherhood in Rhythm: The Jazz Tap Dancing of the Nicholas Brothers* (New York: Oxford University Press, 2000), 107–129.

12. Following *Darktown Follies*, another landmark show in bringing Black dance to Broadway was the Black-produced Black-cast musical *Shuffle Along* (1921), which Hill credits with establishing jazz on Broadway. See chapters 3 and 4 in Constance Valis Hill, *Tap Dancing America: A Cultural History* (New York: Oxford University Press, 2010).

13. Hill, *Tap Dancing America*, 6.

14. In chapters 2–5 of *Tap Dancing America*, Hill describes the development of popular tap styles from simpler buck and wing to include over-the-tops and trenches, and then the influence of jazz in the 1920s and 30s. For more on the individual elements of buck, wing, and jig, see this Duke University video of Thomas DeFrantz: https://www.youtube.com/watch?v=A34OD4eA17o.

15. This proverb opens the first chapter of Jacqui Malone, *Steppin' on the Blues: The Visible Rhythms of African American Dance* (Urbana: University of Illinois Press, 1996). See also Gottschild, *Digging the Africanist Presence*, 9.

16. See Hirschhorn, *Gene Kelly*, 25, and Tony Thomas, *The Films of Gene Kelly: Song and Dance Man* (New York: Carol Publishing, 1991), 10.

17. See Ramsay Burt, *The Male Dancer: Bodies, Spectacle, Sexualities*, 2nd ed. (London: Routledge, 2007) and Peter Stoneley, *A Queer History of the Ballet* (New York: Routledge, 2007).

18. Hirschhorn, *Gene Kelly*, 74.

19. See Maura Keefe, "Is Dance a Man's Sport Too?: The Performance of Athletic-Coded Masculinity on the Concert Dance Stage," in *When Men Dance: Choreographing Masculinities Across Borders*, ed. Anthony Shay and Jennifer Fisher (New York: Oxford University Press, 2009).

20. See, for example, Kay Proctor, "Hey, Irish!," *Photoplay* (May 1943), 36–37.

21. A great deal has been written about working class masculinity. Especially salient for my examination of Kelly are the questions of how working-class masculinity relates to physicality/tools and Irish American identity. See, for example, Roger Horowitz, *Boys and Their Toys?: Masculinity, Technology, and Class in America* (New York: Routledge, 2001) and chapters 5, 6, and 7 of David R. Roediger, *The Wages of Whiteness: Race and the Making of the American Working Class* (London: Verso, 2007).

22. *Reflections on the Silver Screen*, "Gene Kelly," AMC (aired February 2, 1994), quoted in Cohan, *Incongruous Entertainment*, 151.

23. Kyle Crichton, "Dancing Master," *Colliers*, May 19, 1945, 20.

24. Dance recital program, The Gene Kelly Studio of the Dance, Embassy Theatre, Johnstown, PA June 20, 1939, box 6, Gene Kelly Collection, Howard Gotlieb Archival Research Center, Boston University.

25. Robert Van Gelder, "Mr. Kelly, or Pal Joey: Portrait of a Dancer, From Pennsylvania to the Barrymore Theatre," *New York Times*, March 2, 1941, X3.

26. "Candid Close-Ups of Pictures and Personalities by Beverly Hills," *Liberty*, October 17, 1942.

27. If this latter term sounds familiar, it is because the "class act" was precisely how the Nicholas Brothers had presented themselves prior to joining Gene Kelly in *The Pirate*. Of course, "class act" does specific work for the Nicholases, providing them with a means of access to white audiences by sanitizing what might have otherwise been perceived as the "primitive rhythms" of Black dancers. Fred Astaire did not require these optics for the purposes of access, but instead used them to legitimize the role of "the hoofer" as a "respectable" dancer rather than, say, an interchangeable vaudeville act.

28. Gene Kelly, interview. Quoted in David Lewins, "Gene Kelly Explains: The Difference Between Astaire and Me," *Daily Express* (London), March 26, 1952.

29. Despite the seeming richness of the two styles interacting, Kelly and Astaire did not appear on film together again until the 1976 compilation film *That's Entertainment Part II* (Astaire, then seventy-six, never danced again on film).

222 NOTES

30. Kelly's training in ballet began with local Pittsburgh teachers when he was a child, but he did not train seriously in it until 1933, when he spent several summers taking master classes from the Chicago Association of Dancing Masters. His instructors, such as Berenice Holmes and Alexander Kotchetovsky, had associations with Diaghilev's Ballets Russes. For more on Kelly's dance training, see Yudkoff, *Gene Kelly: A Life of Dance and Dreams* (New York: Back Stage Books, 1999), 32–34.

31. "Kelly Not vs. Astaire," *Christian Science Monitor*, 1946, box 7, Gene Kelly Collection, Howard Gotlieb Archival Research Center, Boston University.

32. Whereas the author of this review appears to be presuming the whiteness of both modernism and its expressive qualities, the influence of Black dance on modern dance is well documented (by Gottschild, Burt, and Manning in particular). Moreover, Hill writes frequently of tap dance as an expressive form of a distinctly African American modernism, especially between the 1920s and 1950s. See, in particular, chapters 4 and 7 in *Tap Dancing America*.

33. Cohan, *Incongruous Entertainment*, 165. Cohan cites Phil Silvers, Oscar Levant, Donald O'Connor, and Van Johnson as other examples of Kelly's more diminutive buddies.

34. Betsy Blair, *The Memory of All That: Love and Politics in New York, Hollywood, and Paris* (New York: Alfred A. Knopf, 2003), 192; Norma McClain Stoop, "Gene Kelly: An American Dance Innovator Tells It Like It Was—and Is," *Dance Magazine*, July 1976, 71.

35. Hirschhorn, *Gene Kelly*, 116.

36. Gabbard, *Black Magic: White Hollywood and African American Culture* (New Brunswick: Rutgers University Press, 2004), 41. Though Gabbard offers no concrete evidence for this claim, there are numerous accounts and a photographic proof demonstrating that Brando took dance classes with famed African American dancer and choreographer Katherine Dunham (who had performed in *Stormy Weather* with the Nicholas brothers) during the 1940s.

37. Gabbard, *Black Magic*, 19.

38. Patricia Ward Kelly, "Spotlight on Gene Kelly: The Chicago Years" (lecture, The Newberry Library, Ruggles Hall, Chicago, IL, June 6, 2019). See also Hirschhorn, *Gene Kelly*, 44 and Alvin Yudkoff, *Gene Kelly: A Life of Dance and Dreams* (New York: Back Stage Books, 1999), 33.

39. "Slaughter on Tenth Avenue" was originally choreographed by George Balanchine for the Rodgers and Hart Broadway musical *On Your Toes* (1936), with a Hollywood film adaptation released in 1939. Balanchine's original included ballet with jazz infusions and then a tap segment, already reflecting heavy Africanist influence. For its inclusion in the Rodgers and Hart tribute *Words and Music* (1948), Kelly rechoreographed the number, removing the tap segment and deepening the jazz influence on the ballet.

40. Cohan, *Incongruous Entertainment*, 158.

41. Richard Dyer, "Don't Look Now," *Screen* 23, nos. 3–4 (1982): 61–73.

42. Kelly did receive lessons in Spanish flamenco dance in 1933 from Angel Cansino (Rita Hayworth's uncle) in Chicago. See Yudkoff, *Gene Kelly*, 33 and Hirschhorn, *Gene Kelly*, 44.

43. Cohan, *Incongruous Entertainment*, 173.

44. For example, one newspaper clipping from September 1945, "No Anchors on His Feet," describes the number thusly: "After a series of seven-foot leaps over tower parapets, Gene swings forty-five feet from rooftop to rooftop. An admittedly risky routine, the dance is performed forty feet in the air." Box 7, Gene Kelly Collection, Howard Gotlieb Archival Research Center, Boston University.

45. Bob Thomas, "Gene Kelly Lectures at U.C.L.A," Associated Press, 1946. Kelly is clearly making rhetorical reference here to the 1946 Broadway musical *Annie Get Your Gun*, specifically the "Anything You Can Do" number, which enacts a competition between a man and a woman who each argue that they are better at various tasks and achievements.

46. Ibid.

47. "Who Rules These Hollywood Roosts?," *Photoplay Magazine*, October 1944, 44–45, 90.

48. Cohan, *Incongruous Entertainment*, 176–177.

49. Cole Porter's lyrics for the song "Mack the Black," which Garland sings in the film, describe Macoco the pirate as having a "flaming trail of masculinity."

50. Ibid., 179. In the quoted text, Cohan refers to passages in Feuer's *The Hollywood Musical* (143) and Dyer's *Heavenly Bodies* (185).

51. Hill, *Brotherhood in Rhythm*, 230–231.

52. Alton Cook, "'The Pirate' Colorful, Lavish," *New York World Telegram*, 1948, box 8, Gene Kelly Collection, Howard Gotlieb Archival Research Center, Boston University.

NOTES 223

53. See Michael S. Kimmel, "Baseball and the Reconstruction of American Masculinity," *The History of Men: Essays on the History of American and British Masculinities* (Albany: State University of New York Press, 2005).

54. It is possible there were concerns about Kelly appearing to be "too" Irish in the early forties. According to Hirschhorn's biography of Kelly, when producer Arthur Schwartz suggested Kelly for the role of Rita Hayworth's costar in *Cover Girl*, Columbia Pictures studio head Harry Cohn exploded, "That tough Irishman with his tough Irish mug?! You couldn't put him in the same *frame* as Rita!!" See Hirschhorn, *Gene Kelly*, 107. The irony here is that Cohn originally deemed Hayworth (née Margarita Carmen Cansino) "too Mediterranean" so, to secure better roles, she played up her Irish American ancestry by changing her name, raising her hairline, and dying her hair red.

55. Robert Nowatzki, "Paddy Jumps Jim Crow: Irish-Americans and Blackface Minstrelsy," *Éire-Ireland* 41, nos. 3–4 (Fall/Winter 2006): 162–184.

56. Ibid. See also Eric Lott, *Love and Theft: Blackface Minstrelsy and the American Working Class* (New York: Oxford University Press, 1993), 70–78 and Margaret Greaves, "Slave Ships and Coffin Ships: Transatlantic Exchanges in Irish-American Blackface Minstrelsy," *Comparative American Studies* 10, no. 1 (2012): 78–94.

57. Roger Ebert, "An American in Paris," *RogerEbert.com*, October 2, 1992.

58. Patricia Ward Kelly, Panel Discussion at screening of *An American in Paris*, The Egyptian Theatre, Hollywood, CA, May 31, 2015.

59. For more on "Chocolat and Footit," situated among similar spectacles of the time, see James Smalls, "'Race' As Spectacle in Late-Nineteenth-Century French Art and Popular Culture," *French Historical Studies* 26, no. 2 (Spring 2003): 351–382.

60. As I mentioned at the opening of the chapter, Padilla himself often dressed in the form-fitting clothes of a dandy, especially when performing with Footit, which again complicates the performance of gender here.

61. For more detail about these types, see Donald Bogle, *Toms, Coons, Mulattoes, Mammies and Bucks: An Interpretive History of Blacks in American Films*, 5th ed. (New York: Bloomsbury, 2016).

62. Dick Williams, *Singin' in the Rain* film review, *LA Mirror*, April 10, 1952.

63. Clover, "Dancin' in the Rain," 728–729, 737. In the quoted text, Clover cites page 79 of Jerome Delamater's "Dance in the Hollywood Musical" (PhD diss., Northwestern University, 1981).

64. Clover, "Dancin' in the Rain," 729.

65. Ibid., 738. Though Clover does not attribute the quote within this sentence, it is Peter Wollen's claim in his *Singin' in the Rain*, 2nd ed. (London: BFI, 2012), 15.

66. The famed Bill Robinson is a notable example. See Hill, *Tap Dancing America*, 20.

67. Steven Cohan, *Incongruous Entertainment*, 50.

68. See, for example Altman, *The American Film Musical*, 198–200 and John Mueller, *Astaire Dancing: The Musical Films* (New York: Alfred A. Knopf, 1985), 12–13.

69. [Author and title unknown], *Toledo Blade*, January 26, 1957.

70. For more on gender, ethnicity, and performance on early variety shows, see Susan Murray, *Hitch Your Antenna to the Stars!: Early Television and Broadcast Stardom* (New York: Routledge, 2005). For more on (female) Hollywood stars moving to television, see Mary Desjardins, *Recycled Stars: Female Film Stardom in the Age of Television and Video* (Durham, NC: Duke University Press, 2015).

71. Anna McCarthy, *The Citizen Machine: Governing by Television in 1950s America* (New York: The New Press, 2010), 122.

72. Elizabeth L. Sullivan, "Kelly Makes Dancers of Cousy, Sugar Ray," *Daily Boston Globe*, December 22, 1958, 13.

73. Harry Harris, "Gene Kelly Proves Dancing IS a Man's Game in TV Debut," *Philadelphia Inquirer*, December 22, 1958, 22.

74. Gene Kelly, "Dancing, A Man's Game," *Omnibus*, NBC, December 21, 1958.

75. Hill, *Tap Dancing America*, 21.

76. Gene Kelly, interview, *Ottawa Citizen*, April 22, 1959.

77. Gene Kelly, interview with Edward R. Murrow, *Person to Person*, December 19, 1958.

78. Gene joined his siblings in performing as amateur vaudevillians in Pittsburgh during the 1920s; his mother Harriet named the family troupe The Five Kellys, perhaps modeled after the earlier Irish American vaudeville troupe "The Four Cohans," which birthed the famous minstrel man George M. Cohan. The Five Kellys sometimes stood in for their contemporary

224 NOTES

similarly named troupe "The Seven Little Foys" when they couldn't make it to their scheduled show in Pittsburgh. See Cynthia Brideson and Sara Brideson, *He's Got Rhythm: The Life and Career of Gene Kelly* (Lexington: University Press of Kentucky, 2017), 17–18 and Yudkoff, *Gene Kelly*, 9–14.

79. The ensemble dance movements here are only very vaguely related to the actual Cuban "Cha-cha-cha" dance whose name the number appropriates in an act of exoticization.

80. Kimmel, *Manhood in America*, 232.

81. It is worth noting at this juncture that both the "Cha Cha" group dance and Kelly's *pas de deux* with the "killer" exhibit a greater pelvic fluidity than many earlier Kelly dances. This does not necessarily correlate to more extensive blackbodying, however; it is during this era that Bob Fosse's choreography was becoming a standard fixture of both Broadway and late Hollywood musicals such as *Damn Yankees* (1955 Broadway, 1958 Warner Brothers). Itself influenced by Black dance and Kelly's early style, Fosse's work brought an extremely fluid pelvis into show dancing vogue. Kelly's choreography here and in the following special exhibit affinities with Fosse's style.

82. Ray Bolger, who was in the original Broadway cast of *Three to Make Ready*, also resurrected the song in a 1957 episode of *Washington Square*, another variety show.

83. The "Madame La Zonga" line is probably meant to reference the Jimmy Dorsey & Helen O'Connell song "Six Lessons from Madam La Zonga" (1940) that inspired a 1941 film by the same name.

84. In the 1910s, Irish Canadian minstrel man George Primrose was hailed as "the greatest soft-shoe dancer in the world." See Hill, *Tap Dancing America*, 61–62.

85. Clover, "Dancin' in the Rain," 729.

86. Photo caption, *TV Radio Mirror*, November 1959.

87. Meenasarani Linde Murugan, "Exotic Television: Technology, Empire, and Entertaining Globalism" (PhD diss., Northwestern University, 2015).

88. Andrew N. McLellan, "The Challenge of Television," *Dance Magazine* (January 1947), 19. Quoted in Murugan, "Exotic Television: Technology, Empire, and Entertaining Globalism," 39–40.

89. Altman, *The American Film Musical*, 55.

90. See Thomas DeFrantz, "Popular African American Dance of the 1950s and 60s," in *Ain't Nothing Like the Real Thing*, ed. R. Carlin and K. Conwill (Washington, D.C.: Smithsonian Press, 2010), 184 and Katrina Hazzard-Gordon, *Jookin': The Rise of Social Dance Formations in African-American Culture* (Philadelphia: Temple University Press, 1990), 87.

91. Danny Kaye sang all of these lyrics, with the exception of "and the girls were, too," which was an interjection by Kelly.

92. [Author and title unknown], *Radio Times* (London), October 1972.

93. Interview with Gene Kelly, *American Film* (Washington, D.C.), February 1979.

Chapter 3

1. Jack Gould, "TV: New Phenomenon: Elvis Presley Rises to Fame as Vocalist Who Is Virtuoso of Hootchy-Kootchy," *New York Times*, June 6, 1956, 67.

2. Ben Gross, *New York Daily News*, June 8, 1956. Quoted in Peter Guralnick and Ernst Jorgensen, *Elvis Day by Day: The Definitive Record of His Life and Music* (New York: Ballantine Books, 1999), 73.

3. John Crosby, "Could Elvis Mean End of Rock 'n' Roll Craze?," *The Washington Post and Times Herald*, June 18, 1956, 33.

4. See, for example, Michael Bane, *White Boy Singin' the Blues: The Black Roots of White Rock* (New York: Penguin Books, 1982); Simon Jones, "Crossover Culture: Popular Music and the Politics of 'Race,'" *Stanford Humanities Review* 3 (1993): 103–117; Michael Coyle, "Hijacked Hits and Antic Authenticity: Cover Songs, Race, and Postwar Marketing," in *Rock Over the Edge: Transformations in Popular Music Culture*, ed. Roger Beebe, Denise Fulbrook, and Ben Saunders (Durham, NC: Duke University Press, 2002); and David P. Szatmary, *Rockin' in Time: A Social History of Rock-and-Roll*, 5th ed. (Upper Saddle River, NJ: Prentice Hall, 2004).

5. Presley's records scored high positions on both country and R&B charts during the 1950s, indicating his mixture of "white" and "Black" sounds.

6. A number of scholars of dance, film, and music have made brief reference to the ways in which Presley's corporeality borrows from Black culture. Some have even linked this to his

masculinity and/or sexuality. See: Thomas F. DeFrantz, "Popular African American Dance of the 1950s and 60s," in *Ain't Nothing Like the Real Thing,* ed. Richard Carlin and Kinshasha Holman Conwill (Washington, D.C.: Smithsonian Press, 2010), 183; Brenda Dixon Gottschild, *Digging the Africanist Presence in American Performance: Dance and Other Contexts* (Westport, CT: Greenwood Press, 1996), 25–26 and 29; Linda Williams, *Playing the Race Card: Melodramas of Black and White from Uncle Tom to O.J. Simpson* (Princeton, NJ: Princeton University Press, 2001), 69; Michael T. Bertrand, *Race, Rock, and Elvis* (Urbana: University of Illinois Press, 2005), 99; and David R. Shumway, "Watching Elvis" in *Rock Star: The Making of Musical Icons from Elvis to Springsteen* (Baltimore, MD: Johns Hopkins University Press, 2014).

7. Jon Michael Spencer, "A Revolutionary Sexual Persona: Elvis Presley and the White Acquiescence of Black Rhythms," in *In Search of Elvis: Music, Race, Art, Religion,* ed. Vernon Chadwick (Boulder: Westview Press, 1997), 110–113.

8. Norma Coates, "Elvis from the Waist Up and Other Myths: 1950s Music Television and the Gendering of Rock Discourse," in *Medium Cool: Music Videos from Soundies to Cellphones,* ed. Roger Beebe and Jason Middleton (Durham, NC: Duke University Press, 2007), 235.

9. Jake Austen has pointed out that The Treniers, a Black jump blues/rock 'n' roll band, were doing equally wild, sexy, virile dance performances on 1954 and 1955 television variety programs that rivaled Presley's—wing dances, vibrations, and all—but suggests that they were not received with the same anxiety "because of the prevailing perception that these performances were simply a continuation of a long tradition of blacks entertaining whites." While this is plausible, I would argue that a more important factor in their case is the sheer number of group members: usually around seven. Thus, the wild dance moves are presented as band members playing around with one another, rather than individual enticements to young women. See Jake Austen, *TV a-Go-Go: Rock on TV from American Bandstand to American Idol* (Chicago: Chicago Review Press, 2005), 7–9.

10. Thomas F. DeFrantz, "Popular Dances of the 1920s and early 30s: From Animal Dance Crazes to the Lindy Hop," in *Ain't Nothing Like the Real Thing,* ed. Richard Carlin and Kinshasha Holman Conwill (Washington, D.C.: Smithsonian Press, 2010), 67–68. See also this demonstration of wing dances (among others) by DeFrantz: https://www.youtube.com/watch?v=A34O D4eA17o.

11. Gottschild, *Digging the Africanist Presence,* 12–17.

12. Peter Guralnick, *Last Train to Memphis: The Rise of Elvis Presley* (New York: Little, Brown, and Company, 1994), 50–53.

13. Guralnick, *Last Train to Memphis,* 99.

14. Albin Zak, *I Don't Sound Like Nobody: Remaking Music in 1950s America* (Ann Arbor: University of Michigan Press, 2010), 106.

15. Guralnick, *Last Train to Memphis,* 53.

16. Ibid., 110–111.

17. Ibid., 183.

18. See, for example, David E. James, *Rock 'n' Film: Cinema's Dance with Popular Music* (New York: Oxford University Press, 2016), 76.

19. Michael T. Bertrand, *Race, Rock, and Elvis* (Urbana: University of Illinois Press, 2005), 99 and 192–193.

20. Marshall and Jean Stearns, *Jazz Dance: The Story of American Vernacular Dance* (New York: Macmillan, 1968), 237. Quoted in Gottschild, *Digging the Africanist Presence,* 16.

21. Guralnick, *Last Train to Memphis,* 119, 128.

22. Marjorie Garber, *Vested Interests: Cross-Dressing and Cultural Anxiety* (New York: Routledge, 1992), 367.

23. Aldore Collier, "Little Richard Tells Us How He Got What He Wanted but Lost What He Had," *Jet,* November 26, 1984.

24. Ronald L. Jackson has described American popular culture's parallel representation of Black male bodies as inherently dangerous and hyper-(hetero-)sexual, and provides a helpful guide to additional literature on these subjects, in *Scripting the Black Masculine Body: Identity, Discourse, and Racial Politics in Popular Media* (Ithaca, NY: SUNY Press, 2006). As a Black man, Penniman's presence on stage is always already inscribed with these societal assumptions, so flamboyant stylings for him offset these stereotypes with homosexual connotations. As a white man, privileged to lack these societal assumptions, Presley is able to selectively apply signifiers of Blackness *alongside* this same flamboyance to "add on" presumptions about heterosexuality that deflect these homosexual connotations.

226 NOTES

25. Guralnick, *Last Train to Memphis*, 243.
26. DeFrantz, "Popular Dances of the 1920s and Early 30s," 68.
27. Jack Mabley, "Radio and Video," *Down Beat*, December 14, 1955, 46. Quoted in Murray Forman, *One Night on TV Is Worth Weeks at the Paramount: Popular Music on Early Television* (Durham, NC: Duke University Press, 2012), 203.
28. Media and performance scholar madison moore defines "hair choreography" as the use of "'haircrobatics' to punctuate a moment, a feeling, raising the stakes, the sex appeal, and even the energy in the audience," which occurs "in those moments of a live performance where the hair is flipped, whipped, dipped, spun and amplified during the most exciting, emotion-filled sounds and dance moves." See madison moore, "Beyoncé's New Weave Swing, or How to Snatch Wigs with Hair Choreography," *Sounding Out!*, September 29, 2014, https://soundstudiesblog.com/author/madisonianmoore/.
29. Calloway's soundies and Snader Telescriptions are still commercially available under compilation titles such as *The Swingtime Collection: Half Past Jump Time!* and *Cab Calloway: HI-DE-HO and other Movies*. His hair choreography is particularly evident in "I Can't Give You Anything but Love" and "Cab's Club: Calloway Boogie." For more on Calloway's hair choreography, see Nate Sloan, "Constructing Cab Calloway: Publicity, Race, and Performance in 1930s Harlem Jazz," *The Journal of Musicology* 36, no. 3 (2019): 394–395. Notably, similar "wild" hair shaking would soon become a primary characteristic of fellow rockabilly performer Jerry Lee Lewis's performance as well.
30. RCA-Victor's promotional materials for Presley in 1956 labeled him as the "nation's only atomic powered singer."
31. Jane Feuer, *The Hollywood Musical* (Bloomington: Indiana University Press, 1982), 3–7.
32. Kobena Mercer, *Welcome to the Jungle: New Positions in Black Cultural Studies* (New York: Routledge, 1994), 174.
33. Frantz Fanon, *Black Skin, White Masks*, 1952 (London: Paladin, 1970), 120. Quoted in Mercer, *Welcome to the Jungle*, 185.
34. Mercer, *Welcome to the Jungle*, 185.
35. "The Rat Race for Ratings," *Variety*, July 18, 1956.
36. Mary Cremmen, "TV NOTEBOOK: A New 'Chained' Presley, but Rest of Show 'Old Hat,'" *Daily Boston Globe*, July 2, 1956, 5.
37. "Allen Gives No. 2 Spot to Sullivan Via 'New' Presley," *Variety*, July 4, 1956.
38. "Sullivan Signs Elvis Presley for 3 TV Shows," *Chicago Daily Tribune*, July 14, 1956, 14.
39. Richard F. Shepard, "Presley Signed by Ed Sullivan: Singer to Appear on 3 C.B.S. Shows, Beginning Sept. 9, Reportedly for $50,000." *New York Times*, July 14, 1956, 33.
40. Walter Ames, "Sullivan Topped by Steve Allen; Teen-agers Are Mad," *Los Angeles Times*, July 3, 1956, B6.
41. Mary Cremmen, "TV NOTEBOOK: Charles Laughton and the 'Hound Dog,'" *Daily Boston Globe,* September 10, 1956, 28.
42. Guralnick, *Last Train to Memphis*, 378–379.
43. This jam session is referenced in numerous biographies of Elvis Presley; for my own analysis I used the following copy on YouTube: https://www.youtube.com/watch?v=Q8Ao-TN05V4.
44. Gottschild, *Digging the Africanist Presence*, 25.
45. Altman, *The American Film Musical*, 55.
46. Gottschild, *Digging the Africanist Presence*, 26.
47. Mae Tinee, "Elvis Rocks but Movie Stands Still," *Chicago Daily Tribune*, November 15, 1957, A3; Paul Jones, "Elvis Needs Jaircut in 'Jailhouse Rock,'" *Atlanta Constitution,* November 1, 1957, 47.
48. "Elvis Going Like Helvis!," *Variety*, November 6, 1957.
49. Mark Knowles, *The Man Who Made the Jailhouse Rock: Alex Romero, Hollywood Choreographer* (Jefferson, NC: McFarland & Company, 2013), 97–99.
50. James, *Rock 'n' Film*, 84.
51. Brett Farmer, *Spectacular Passions: Cinema, Fantasy, Gay Male Spectatorships* (Durham, NC: Duke University Press, 2000), 86.
52. James, *Rock 'n' Film*, 90–91.
53. DeFrantz, "Popular Dances of the 1920s and Early 30s," 68.
54. Peter Guralnick, *Careless Love: The Unmaking of Elvis Presley* (New York: Little, Brown, and Company, 1999), 11–12.

NOTES 227

55. For a detailed account of Elvis's reception in midcentury Germany, see Uta G. Poiger, *Jazz, Rock, and Rebels: Cold War Politics and American Culture in a Divided Germany* (Berkeley and Los Angeles: University of California Press, 2000), particularly chapters 2 and 5.
56. Brian McAllister Linn, *Elvis's Army: Cold War GIs and the Atomic Battlefield* (Cambridge, MA: Harvard University Press, 2016), 5.
57. Bosley Crowther, "G.I. Blues: Elvis – A Reformed Wriggler," *New York Times*, November 5, 1960.
58. Linn, *Elvis's Army*, 230.
59. Ibid., 268.
60. Many of the secondary characters and bit roles in *Blue Hawaii* were in fact filled by native Hawaiian singers and actors; however, Gates' half-Hawaiian girlfriend Maile was played by Joan Blackman, who has no known Hawaiian ancestry.
61. For more on the twist as a Black-originated social dance craze, see DeFrantz, "Popular African American Dance of the 1950s and 60s," 184.
62. Jig dances have a complicated African-Irish history, similar to tap-dancing. But unlike in tap dancing, the Africanist and Europeanist (to use Gottschild's phrasing) threads in jigging are more difficult to disentangle. Though Thomas F. DeFrantz classifies jigs, alongside buck dances and wing dances, among the nineteenth-century African American social dances that have since filtered into several generations of later American social dance trends, I am loath to claim that Presley et al.'s jigging is necessarily blackbodying here. Still, the lineage is important to consider. For more on jigs, see DeFrantz, https://www.youtube.com/watch?v=A34OD4eA17o and Constance Valis Hill, *Tap Dancing America: A Cultural History* (New York: Oxford University Press, 2009), 1, 6.
63. Steven Cohan, *Incongruous Entertainment: Camp, Cultural Value, and the MGM Musical* (Durham, NC: Duke University Press, 2005), 176–177.
64. Adam Victor, *The Elvis Encyclopedia* (New York: Overlook Duckworth, 2008), 44–45.
65. The exception is *Kissin' Cousins*, in which Presley simultaneously plays an Air Force lieutenant and his hillbilly cousin.
66. James, *Rock 'n' Film,* 102.
67. DeFrantz, "Popular Dances of the 1920s and Early 30s"; Gottschild, *Digging the Africanist Presence*.
68. Ironically, "Viva Las Vegas" was released as the B-side to Presley's version of Ray Charles' "What'd I Say," but charted separately. The primary song, which *was* explicitly connected to contemporary African American blues music, has long since been forgotten in the Presley repertoire, whereas "Viva Las Vegas" is now iconic.
69. See, for example, James, *Rock 'n' Film*, 93–113.
70. James, *Rock 'n' Film*, 115.
71. For more on the continuities between Elvis, Little Richard, and Liberace, see Garber, *Vested Interests*, 364–367.

Chapter 4

1. Emilie Raymond, "Sammy Davis Jr: Public Image and Politics," *Cultural History* 4, no. 1 (2015): 42–63; Gerald Early, "Sammy Davis, Jr., Establishment Rebel," in *This Is Where I Came In: Black America in the 1960s* (Lincoln: University of Nebraska Press, 2003).
2. In his biography of Davis, Wil Haygood exposes Davis's claims of being Puerto Rican as a lie; in fact, his mother was Cuban. See Wil Haygood, *In Black and White: The Life of Sammy Davis, Jr.* (New York: Alfred A. Knopf, 2003), 34–53.
3. Gerald Early, *The Sammy Davis, Jr. Reader: The Life and Times of the Last Great American Hipster—from Vaudeville to Vegas—As Seen Through the Eyes of His Public* (New York: Farrar, Straus, and Giroux, 2001), 19.
4. Marshall Stearns and Jean Stearns, *Jazz Dance: The Story of American Vernacular Dance* (New York: Macmillan, 1968; New York, De Capo Press, 1994), 219.
5. For a thorough analysis of both figures alongside Jim Crow, see Benjamin Miller, "Twisting the Dandy: The Transformation of the Blackface Dandy in Early American Theatre," *The Journal of American Drama and Theatre* 27, no. 3 (Fall 2015): 1898–1965.
6. Barbara Lewis, "Daddy Blue: The Evolution of the Dark Dandy," in *Inside the Minstrel Mask: Readings in Nineteenth-Century Blackface Minstrelsy*, ed. Annemarie Bean, James V. Hatch, and Brooks McNamara (Middletown, CT: Wesleyan University Press, 1996), 258.

228 NOTES

7. Ibid., 259, 269.
8. On George Walker, see Barbara L. Webb, "The Black Dandyism of George Walker: A Case Study in Geneological Method," *TDR* 45, no. 4 (Winter 2001): 7–24. On W. E. B. Du Bois, see Monica L. Miller, "W. E. B. Du Bois's 'Different' Diasporic Race Man," in *Slaves to Fashion: Black Dandyism and the Styling of Black Diasporic Identity* (Duke University Press, 2009), 137–175.
9. Monica L. Miller, *Slaves to Fashion: Black Dandyism and the Styling of Black Diasporic Identity* (Duke University Press, 2009), 19–20.
10. Ibid., 5, 10, 11–12.
11. Ibid., 11.
12. Ibid., 192–201.
13. Ibid., 16.
14. Raymond, "Sammy Davis Jr.," 42–63; Early, "Sammy Davis, Jr."
15. Early, *This Is Where I Came In*, 39.
16. Ibid., 38.
17. Matthew Frye Jacobson, *Dancing Down the Barricades: Sammy Davis Jr. and the Long Civil Rights Era* (Oakland: University of California Press, 2023), xxvi; xxi.
18. Sammy Davis, Jr., Jane Boyar, and Burt Boyar, *Yes I Can: The Story of Sammy Davis, Jr.* (New York: Farrar, Straus, and Giroux, 1965), 42.
19. Ibid., 23.
20. Ibid., 13.
21. Ibid., 106–107.
22. Ryan Jay Friedman, *Hollywood's African American Films: The Transition to Sound* (New Brunswick: Rutgers University Press, 2011), 76.
23. See, for example, Charlene Regester, *African American Actresses: The Struggle for Visibility, 1900–1960* (Bloomington: Indiana University Press, 2010), 267–270 and Jabari Asim, *What Obama Means . . . For Our Culture, Our Politics, Our Future* (New York: William Morrow, 2009), 79–80.
24. Jacobson notes that, "While the seven-year-old Davis was a talented dancer who had fully mastered the mugging cuteness that had won him a spot with Will Mastin's troupe, it is also true that child performers of this genre and skill were fairly common on the black vaudeville circuit." See Jacobson, *Dancing Down the Barricades*, 9. This is important to keep in mind, and a strong reminder that though this book builds its argument about masculinity through some of the most famous dancing men of the midcentury, each case study stands in for countless young men who either were, wanted to be, or could have been in the exact same positions as these stars. So, if the seed of Davis's suave and chameleonic adult masculinity is already present in his own childhood dancing persona, we might consider the extent to which the same ingredients were present in any other youth who did not quite "make it" as he did.
25. *Portrait of a Legend: Sammy Davis, Jr.* Produced by Essence Television Productions, Inc. Directed by Linda Howard, produced by Angela Thame, hosted by Susan Taylor. WNBC-TV New York, February 15, 1987. Though Davis claims he was between six and eight years old during the Robinson encounter, he mentions during the interview that Robinson was doing a show called *The Hot Mikado* at the time. This show was on Broadway in 1939, which would have made Davis thirteen years old for the encounter.
26. Rusty E. Frank, *Tap!: The Greatest Tap Dance Stars and Their Stories 1900–1955*, rev. ed. (New York: De Capo Press, 1994), 72. As film scholar Miriam Petty has demonstrated, Robinson's own star persona included a reputation for serving as mentor, teacher, and even industry advocate for young Black dancers. See Miriam J. Petty, *Stealing the Show: African American Performers and Audiences in 1930s Hollywood* (Oakland: University of California Press, 2016), 93–96.
27. Davis, Boyar, and Boyar, *Yes I Can*, 25.
28. Ibid., 42.
29. Katie Beisel Hollenbach, "Frank Sinatra and Constructions of Female Power and Fantasy in RKO's *Higher and Higher* (1943)," *Music and the Moving Image* 15, no. 1 (2022): 3–21.
30. Davis biographer Gary Fishgall has found no evidence that Davis was actually in an integrated unit, calling into question some of his recollections while enlisted. See Gary Fishgall, *Gonna Do Great Things: The Life of Sammy Davis, Jr.* (New York: Scribner, 2003), 30–34.
31. See Jacobson, *Dancing Down the Barricades*, 52–59.
32. Davis, Boyar, and Boyar, *Yes I Can*, 74.
33. Ibid., 74–75.

NOTES 229

34. Ibid., 101.
35. Ibid.
36. Ibid., 107.
37. Ibid., 110.
38. My thanks to Brynn Shiovitz for generously pointing this out to me. Robinson introduced this routine (which also included one of his famous stair dances) in the Black-cast Broadway musical revue *Blackbirds of 1928*. See Brynn Shiovitz, *Behind the Screen: Tap Dance, Race, and Invisibility During Hollywood's Golden Age* (New York: Oxford University Press, 2023), 38.
39. My thanks to Brynn Shiovitz and Lynn Dally for identifying the "Russian kick-outs" here.
40. Davis's song choice and rendition of it are notably racially fraught; while Davis changes the opening lyrics from "some darkies" to "some people," he is nevertheless one of the very few Black performers ever willing to touch the song's problematic retelling (both lyrically and soni-cally) of the blues. For more, see Jacobson, *Dancing Down the Barricades*, 32–34.
41. Milton Berle with Haskel Frankel, *Milton Berle: An Autobiography* (New York: Delacorte Press, 1974), 285; Arthur Silber, Jr., *Sammy Davis Jr.: Me and My Shadow* (Los Angeles: Samart Enterprises, 2003), 82.
42. Davis, Boyar, and Boyar, *Yes I Can*, 156–158.
43. Ibid., 158.
44. Ibid., 155.
45. Murray Forman, *One Night on TV is Worth Weeks at the Paramount: Popular Music on Early Television* (Durham: Duke UP, 2012), 263–264; Arthur Silber, Jr., *Sammy Davis Jr.: Me and My Shadow: A Biographical Memoir* (North Hollywood: Samart Enterprises, 2002), 90–93.
46. Davis, Boyar, and Boyar, *Yes I Can*, 205.
47. Ibid., 227.
48. Ibid., 228.
49. Sammy Davis, Jr., Jane Boyar, and Burt Boyar, *Why Me?: The Sammy Davis Jr. Story* (New York: Farrar, Straus, and Giroux, 1989), 65.
50. Davis also demonstrates clear knowledge of the number's performance history. Providing a clear stylistic contrast to Cab Calloway's 'hep' bandleader take on it, Davis instead chooses a movement approach that bears continuity with John Bubbles' original version, as described in Brian Harker, *Sportin' Life: John W. Bubbles, An American Classic* (New York: Oxford University Press, 2022), 155.
51. Davis, Boyar, and Boyar, *Yes I Can*, 249.
52. Ibid., 258–259.
53. For more on performances of exoticism and Orientalism by Black dancers in midcentury va-riety television, see Meenasarani Linde Murugan, "Electronic Salome: Exotic Dance, Early Television, and Black Modernism," *Écranosphère* 1 (2018), https://ecranosphere.ca/article.php?id=77.
54. Davis, Boyar, and Boyar, *Yes I Can*, 329–330.
55. Davis, Boyar, and Boyar, *Why Me?*, 78. Like other efforts to cross television's color line, getting the episode aired was no easy achievement, as the General Electric executives who reviewed the episode wanted to "kill" it before it could upset their white customers in the South. As Davis tells the story, Sy Marsh threatened to out GE's bigotry to the press if they did not agree to air it. See Davis, Boyar, and Boyar, *Why Me?*, 89–92.
56. Bosley Crowther, "'Anna Lucasta' at the Victoria; Old Play Is Revived With Eartha Kitt," *New York Times*, January 15, 1959.
57. Early argues that "Davis's interracialism, his sense of himself as an assimilated person, his insist-ence that he was as white as he was black, was equally threatening to the rigidity and conformity of 1950s America and to the polarized political vision of 1960s America." In Early, *The Sammy Davis, Jr. Reader*, 19.
58. Emilie Raymond, "Cleaning Up Catfish Row: Black Celebrity and the Making of *Porgy and Bess*," in *Stars for Freedom: Hollywood, Black Celebrities, and the Civil Rights Movement* (Seattle: University of Washington Press, 2015), 17, 20–21.
59. For book-length studies of *Porgy and Bess*, see: Hollis, Alpert, *The Life and Times of Porgy and Bess: The Story of an American Classic* (New York: Knopf, 1990) and Ellen Noonan, *The Strange Career of Porgy and Bess: Race, Culture, and America's Most Famous Opera* (Chapel Hill: University of North Carolina Press, 2012). The most exciting recent work includes Kai West, "Buckra: Whiteness and *Porgy and Bess*," *Journal of the American Musicological Society* 75,

no. 2 (August 2022): 319–377 and Daphne A. Brooks, "'A Woman Is a Sometime Thing': (Re) Covering Black Womanhood in *Porgy and Bess*," *Daedalus* 150, no. 1 (Winter 2021): 98–117.

60. For discussions of *Porgy* as a Cold War text, see David Monod, "'He is a cripple an' needs my love': Porgy and Bess as Cold War Propaganda," *Intelligence and National Security* 18, no. 2 (2003): 300–312; Michael Sy Uy, "Performing Catfish Row in the Soviet Union: The Everyman Opera Company and Porgy and Bess, 1955–56," *Journal of the Society for American Music* 11, no. 4 (2017): 470–501; and Lena Leson, "'I'm on My Way to a Heav'nly Lan'": *Porgy and Bess* as American Religious Export to the USSR," *Journal of the Society for American Music* 15, no. 2 (2021): 143–170.

61. Raymond, "Cleaning Up Catfish Row," 18–24.

62. Ibid., 28–29.

63. James Baldwin, "On Catfish Row: 'Porgy and Bess' in the Movies," *Commentary*, January 1, 1959; Era Bell Thompson, "Why Negroes Don't Like *Porgy and Bess*," *Ebony*, October 1959.

64. Davis, Boyar, and Boyar, *Yes I Can*, 476.

65. Robert Wyatt and John Andrew Johnson, *The George Gershwin Reader* (New York: Oxford University Press, 2004), 218; Harker, *Sportin' Life*, 155.

66. Harker, *Sportin' Life*, 156.

67. Critics (and Sublett himself) had claimed a similar equivalence between Sportin' Life and Bubbles, with Sublett at one point claiming, "I *am* Sportin' Life." See Harker, 158.

68. Davis, Boyar, and Boyar, *Yes I Can*, 249; Silber, *Sammy Davis Jr.*, 149–158.

69. This plot point is in line with a long history of white Christians (and some Black Christians) framing Black vernacular dances as dangerous, primitive, or too sexual, so it fits logically within this white-penned story. Though Heyward wrote the original novel *Porgy* as he was turning forty in 1925, during the Jazz Age, whites' associations of Africanist dances with primitivity had already been solidified via the "animal dances" of the ragtime era that he would have encountered as a younger man. See Nadine George-Graves, "'Just Like Being at the Zoo': Primitivity and Ragtime Dance," in *Ballroom, Boogie, Shimmy Sham, Shake: A Social and Popular Dance Reader*, ed. Julie Malnig (Urbana: University of Illinois Press, 2009), 55–71.

70. Arthur Knight, "It Ain't Necessarily So That It Ain't Necessarily So: Jazz Recordings of *Porgy and Bess* as Film and Cultural Criticism," in *Critical Voicings of Black Liberation: Resistance and Representations in the Americas*, ed. Kimberley L. Phillips (Münster: Lit Verlag, 2003), 90.

71. Early, *This Is Where I Came In*, 44.

72. The name originally referred to an earlier group of Hollywood friends during the 1940s–50s including Humphrey Bogart, Judy Garland, and others; Frank Sinatra was the common thread between all iterations of the group.

73. Early, *The Sammy Davis, Jr. Reader*, 38–39.

74. Davis, Boyar, and Boyar, *Why Me?*, 138.

75. In Davis's discussion of the "Rat Pack" years, he frequently mentions that they were also called "The Clan." News writers did refer to the group as "Frank Sinatra's Clan" or simply "The Clan" beginning as early as 1959, but that moniker seems to have been dropped by 1968; "Rat Pack" remains the dominant term today.

76. Davis, Boyar, and Boyar, *Yes I Can*, 123.

77. Frank Sinatra, Dean Martin, and Sammy Davis Jr., *The Rat Pack Live at The Sands*, Capitol Records, 2001, CD.

78. Hugh Hefner interview with Bill Zehme for the DVD release of *Playboy After Dark*, 2006.

79. Elizabeth Fraterrigo, *Playboy and the Making of the Good Life in Modern America* (New York: Oxford University Press, 2009).

80. Fraterrigo, *Playboy and the Making of the Good Life in Modern America*, 151.

81. Robert George Reisner, "The Word on Frank Sinatra," *Playboy* (November 1958), 63. Quoted in Karen McNally, *When Frankie Went to Hollywood: Frank Sinatra and American Male Identity* (University of Illinois Press, 2008), 145.

82. McNally, *When Frankie Went to Hollywood*, 1.

83. Davis, Boyar, and Boyar, *Why Me?*, 284.

84. Jacobson, *Dancing Down the Barricades*, xxiv.

85. Raymond, "Sammy Davis Jr.," 47 and 50–51.

86. Ibid., 51–52 and Early, "Sammy Davis, Jr., Establishment Rebel," 49.

87. Davis, Boyar, and Boyar, *Why Me?*, 145–146.

88. Ibid., 144.

89. Raymond, "Sammy Davis Jr.," 52–53.

NOTES   231

90. Davis, Boyar, and Boyar, *Why Me?*, 163.
91. Raymond, "Sammy Davis Jr.," 53.
92. Davis, Boyar, and Boyar, *Why Me?*, 211.
93. "Sammy Davis, Spingarn Medalist, Says Separatism 'Won't Work,'" *New York Amsterdam News*, April 12, 1969, p. 33.
94. Jacobson, *Dancing Down the Barricades*, xix–xx; Davis, Boyar, and Boyar, *Yes I Can*, 67–68.
95. Jacobson, *Dancing Down the Barricades*, xx.
96. Perhaps best understood as a variety show for the next generation (likely modeled on ABC's *Shindig!*), *Hullabaloo* aired in prime time and wove together Motown acts with British Invasion bands, alongside various other musical and dance artists and entertainers. Its production team had links to both Broadway and the music industry: it was directed by Steve Binder, who also directed the 1964 *T.A.M.I Show* (in which James Brown and the Famous Flames notoriously outperformed the Rolling Stones), and who would later go on to direct *Elvis: The Comeback Special* (1968), and its house dancers were choreographed by David Winters, who also choreographed for the *T.A.M.I Show*, *Viva Las Vegas* (1964), and later *Movin' With Nancy* [Sinatra] (1967). Winters had notably also performed the role of A-Rab in both the Broadway and film versions of *West Side Story* (1957; 1961).
97. For thorough readings of how Puerto Rican-ness was staged in *West Side Story*, especially in relation to the original Jewishness of *East Side Story*, see: Alberto Sandoval Sanchez, "*West Side Story*: A Puerto Rican reading of 'America,'" *Jump Cut* no. 39 (June 1994): 59–66 and Frances Negron-Muntaner, "Feeling Pretty: *West Side Story* and Puerto Rican Identity Discourses," *Social Text* 63 (Summer 2000): 83–106.
98. Davis, Boyar, and Boyar, *Why Me?*, 174.
99. One of the tragedies of the very incomplete U.S. television archive is that I have been unable to find footage of the Nicholas Brothers' February 18, 1966 appearance on *The Sammy Davis, Jr. Show*. Did the three of them dance together? In whose style? Perhaps someday a kinescope will surface to answer these questions.
100. Davis, Boyar, and Boyar, *Why Me?*, 202.
101. Gerald Early claims *Yes I Can* sold as well as or better than the biographies of both Malcolm X and Claude Brown in the 1960s, and that it kept publisher Farrar, Straus, and Giroux in business. See Early, *This Is Where I Came In*, 44.
102. Richard Dyer, "'I seem to find the happiness I seek': Heterosexuality and Dance in the Musical," in *In the Space of a Song: The Uses of Song in Film* (London: Routledge, 2012), 89–100.
103. Ibid., 99.
104. Sammy Davis Jr., "Sammy Sings a Song of Praise," *Michigan Chronicle*, May 10, 1969: A7.
105. Davis, Boyar, and Boyar, *Why Me?*, 222–225, 228–230.
106. Jerry Jeff Walker, *Gypsy Songman* (Emeryville: Woodford Press, 1999), 59–61, 67.
107. Davis, Boyar, and Boyar, *Why Me?*, 204.
108. Ibid.

Epilogue

1. Interestingly, as of this writing, the Internet Movie Database entry for *That's Dancing!* includes a still from *Jailhouse Rock* (1957) amongst its collection of related images, suggesting that a Presley clip may have been intended for inclusion in the film at some point. See https://www.imdb.com/title/tt0090152.
2. Regarding Harold's ineligibility to serve, see Constance Valis Hill, *Brotherhood in Rhythm: The Jazz Tap Dancing of the Nicholas Brothers* (New York: Oxford University Press, 2000), 215.
3. Dance scholar Judith Hamera describes Jackson as a "synecdochal" dancer representing a diverse corpus of dance histories and performance styles. See Judith Hamera, "The Labors of Michael Jackson: Virtuosity, Deindustrialization, and Dancing Work," *PMLA* 127, no. 4 (October 2012): 762.
4. For example, Barry Gordy, founder of the Motown record label, made many of these comparisons when recalling Jackson's famous debut of the moonwalk on the *Motown 25* television special. See Barry Gordy, *To Be Loved: The Music, the Magic, the Memories of Motown* (New York: Warner Books, 1994), 378.
5. Michael Jackson, *Moonwalk* (New York: Crown Publishing Group, 2009), 48.

232 NOTES

6. See, for example, David Brackett, "Black or White? Michael Jackson and the Idea of Crossover," *Popular Music and Society* 35, no. 2 (May 2012): 169–185 and Jaap Kooijman, "Michael Jackson: *Motown 25*, Pasadena Civic Auditorium, March 25, 1983," in *Performance and Popular Music: History, Place and Time*, ed. Ian Inglis (Brookfield: Taylor & Francis Group, 2006).

7. Margo Jefferson, *On Michael Jackson* (New York: Vintage, 2006), 87. Quoted in Hamera, "The Labors of Michael Jackson," 755.

8. Kobena Mercer, *Welcome to the Jungle: New Positions in Black Cultural Studies* (New York: Routledge, 1994), 34–35, 50.

9. Hamera, "The Labors of Michael Jackson," 762.

10. For a discussion of the differences between Travolta's disco and the vernacular dances that inspired it, see Alice Echols, *Hot Stuff: Disco and the Remaking of American Culture* (New York: W. W. Norton, 2010), 177–185.

11. Buchbinder also notes, in continuity with my discussion of the midcentury anxieties around white masculinity which undergirded this book, that figures like Travolta's Tony Manero also represent a certain angst around "traditional notions of masculinity . . . under pressure. That anxiety frequently expresses itself in these films through an accentuated or even exaggerated emphasis on the sexuality and/or pure physicality of the male character/performer." See David Buchbinder, "Color and Movement: The Male Dancer, Masculinity, and Race in Movies," in *Communicating Marginalized Masculinities: Identity Politics in TV, Film, and New Media*, ed. Ronald L. Jackson II and Jamie E. Moshin (London: Taylor & Francis Group, 2012), 67.

12. Sam Kashner, "Fever Pitch: How Travolta and the Bee Gees Shook the Night," *Vanity Fair*, August 15, 2013.

13. Travolta also claims to have drawn inspiration from dancers on the television dance program *Soul Train*, as well as disco dancers at the real 2001 Odyssey club. But his most direct disco dance teacher was uncredited white disco dancer Deney Terrio. See Sima Belmar, "Behind the Screens: Race, Space, and Place in *Saturday Night Fever*," in *The Oxford Handbook of Screendance Studies*, ed. Douglas Rosenberg (New York: Oxford University Press, 2016).

14. Echols, *Hot Stuff*, 185.

15. See Adrian Garvey, "Travolta Fever," in *"Grease is the word": Exploring a Cultural Phenomenon*, ed. Oliver Gruner and Peter Krämer (New York: Anthem Press, 2020), 88. See also Jeff Yanc, "'More than a woman': Music, Masculinity and Male Spectacle in *Saturday Night Fever* and *Staying Alive*," *Velvet Light Trap* 38 (Fall 1996): 39–51.

16. Film scholar James Morrison likens Travolta's Danny more to Ray Bolger or Donald O'Connor, determining that Danny represents a "a stylization of the body that amplifies 'masculine' postures and parodies them at the same time." See James Morrison, "In the Wings," in *Hollywood Reborn: Movie Stars of the 1970s*, ed. James Morrison (New Brunswick: Rutgers University Press, 2010), 229.

17. The song that has Hines surrounded by children while wooing McKee, "Tall, Tan, and Terrific," was cut from the original 1984 version of the film, alongside other material meant to flesh out the film's Black characters. Director Francis Ford Coppola re-released the film as *The Cotton Club: Encore* in 2019, restoring these cut portions. See Odie Henderson, "The Cotton Club Encore," *RogerEbert.com*, October 7, 2019. https://www.rogerebert.com/reviews/the-cotton-club-encore-movie-review-2019.

18. Dora Valkanova, "White masculinity in the 'New Cold War': Reading *Rocky IV* and *White Nights* as multidirectional memories," *Critical Studies in Media Communication* 39, no. 4 (2022), 327.

19. Ibid.

20. Philip Wuntch, "Gregory Hines: a dancer hits the screen and gets the girls," *Ottawa Citizen*, June 30, 1986.

21. *Step Up* spawned a franchise of four dance film sequels and a television series, though Tatum only reappeared in *Step Up 2: The Streets*.

22. Raquel L. Monroe, "The White Girl in the Middle: The Performativity of Race, Class, and Gender in *Step Up 2: The Streets*," in *The Oxford Handbook of Dance and the Popular Screen*, ed. Melissa Blanco Borelli (New York: Oxford University Press, 2014), 187, 192. Buchbinder also sees in Tatum's *Step Up* performances (as well as Travolta's in *Saturday Night Fever*) echoes of Gene Kelly's characters' "working-class origins and . . . intensity of physical performance." Buchbinder, "Color and Movement," 70.

23. Monroe, "The White Girl in the Middle," 195.

24. See, for example, Kristen J. Warner, "The Pleasure Principle of *Magic Mike XXL*: Sonic Visibility Toward Female Audiences," *Communication, Culture and Critique* 12, no. 2 (June

NOTES   233

2019): 230–246 and Amanda Ann Klein, "Grown Woman Shit: A Case for *Magic Mike XXL* as Cult Text," in *The Routledge Companion to Cult Cinema*, ed. Ernest Mathijs and Jamie Sexton (New York: Routledge, 2020).

25. Broderick Chow, "Every Little Thing He Does: Entrepreneurship and Appropriation in the *Magic Mike* Series," *Lateral* 6, no. 1 (2017).
26. Ibid., 14.
27. Ibid., 15. The absence of Black men in the main cast of *Magic Mike* was so palpable that a nearly identical Black-cast film, *Chocolate City*, was released in 2015 (starring Robert Ri'chard and Vivica A. Fox), which also spawned a 2017 sequel, *Chocolate City: Vegas Strip*.
28. For a theorization of "DIY celebrities," see Graeme Turner, *Understanding Celebrity* (Los Angeles: Sage, 2014), 70–77. For a theorization of "microcelebrities," see Theresa Senft, *Camgirls: Celebrity & Community in the Age of Social Networks* (New York: Peter Lang, 2008), 25–28. See also Alice E. Marwick and danah boyd, "I tweet honestly, I tweet passionately: Twitter users, context collapse, and the imagined audience," *New Media & Society* 13, no. 1 (2011): 114–133 and James Bennett, *Television Personalities: Stardom and the Small Screen* (London: Routledge, 2011).
29. See Crystal Abidin, *Internet Celebrity: Understanding Fame Online* (Bingley: Emerald Publishing Limited, 2018).
30. "Straight TikTok" is the vernacular term developed by users of the app to describe its mainstream dance video content and has nothing to do with sexual orientation.
31. Communication and performance scholar Cienna Davis sees it as an evolution of "digital blackface," a term coined by Joshua Lumpkin Green in 2006 which has since been marshalled by journalists and scholars to describe a wide range of appropriations of Blackness and Black culture by nonblack users online. Because the aspect of caricature is absent from most viral TikTok dance videos, I argue that blackbodying is a more accurate descriptor for this particular phenomenon. See Cienna Davis, "Digital Blackface and the Troubling Intimacies of TikTok Dance Challenges," in *TikTok Cultures in the United States*, ed. Trevor Boffone (New York: Routledge, 2022). See also Joshua Lumpkin Green, "Digital Blackface: The Repackaging of the Black Masculine Image" (Master's thesis, Miami University, 2006) and Lando Tosaya and Ralina L. Joseph, "A Look into Digital Blackface, Culture Vultures, & How to Read Racism Like Black Critical Audiences," *Flow*, April 27, 2021.
32. Trevor Boffone, *Renegades: Digital Dance Cultures from Dubsmash to TikTok* (New York: Oxford University Press, 2021).
33. Taylor Lorenz, "The Original Renegade," *New York Times*, February 13, 2020, https://www.nyti mes.com/2020/02/13/style/the-original-renegade.html. Boffone notes that Rebecca Jennings published an article for *Vox* on February 4, 2020 that included Harmon's story but considers that the Lorenz piece was more responsible for Harmon's "meteoric rise to fame." See Boffone, *Renegades*, 135.
34. Davis, "Digital Blackface," 31, 34. See Jasmine E. Johnson, "Flesh Dance: Black Women from Behind" in *Futures of Dance Studies* (Madison: University of Wisconsin Press, 2020).
35. Davis, "Digital Blackface," 33. For more on the Jezebel figure, see Patricia Hill Collins, *Black Feminist Thought: Knowledge, Consciousness, and the Politics of Empowerment* (London: Routledge, 2002), 81–85, 129–132.
36. Tom Ward, "Michael Le Is Building an Empire," *Forbes*, October 7, 2020, https://www.forbes.com/sites/tomward/2020/10/07/michael-le-is-building-an-empire.
37. Jamilah King, "TikTok's Michael Le Talks of Love of Dance and Asian Representation," *Teen Vogue*, February 17, 2021, https://www.teenvogue.com/story/michael-le-young-hollywood-2021.

Selected Bibliography

Abel, Elizabeth. "Shadows." *Representations* 84, no. 1 (November 2003): 166–199.

Acham, Christine. *Revolution Televised: Prime Time and the Struggle for Black Power.* Minneapolis: University of Minnesota Press, 2004.

Adams, James Eli. *Dandies and Desert Saints: Styles of Victorian Masculinity.* Ithaca, NY: Cornell University Press, 1995.

Altman, Rick. *The American Film Musical.* Bloomington: Indiana University Press, 1987.

Amin, Takiyah Nur. "A Terminology of Difference: Making the Case for Black Dance in the 21st Century and Beyond." *The Journal of Pan African Studies* 4, no. 6 (September 2011): 7–15.

Anderson, Jervis. *This Was Harlem: A Cultural Portrait, 1900–1950.* New York: Farrar, Straus, and Giroux, 1981.

Bane, Michael. *White Boy Singin' the Blues: The Black Roots of White Rock.* New York: Penguin Books, 1982.

Banes, Sally. "Balanchine and Black Dance." *Writing Dancing in the Age of Postmodernism.* Hanover, NH: Wesleyan University Press, 1994.

Bederman, Gail. *Manliness & Civilization: A Cultural History of Gender and Race in the United States, 1880–1917.* Chicago: University of Chicago Press, 1995.

Belmar, Sima. "Behind the Screens: Race, Space, and Place in *Saturday Night Fever*." In *The Oxford Handbook of Screendance Studies*, edited by Douglas Rosenberg. New York: Oxford University Press, 2016.

Bertrand, Michael T. *Race, Rock, and Elvis.* Urbana: University of Illinois Press, 2005.

Bogle, Donald. *Toms, Coons, Mulattoes, Mammies and Bucks: An Interpretive History of Blacks in American Films*, 5th ed. New York: Bloomsbury, 2016.

Bordo, Susan. *The Male Body: A New Look at Men in Public and in Private.* New York: Farrar, Straus, and Giroux, 1999.

Bould, Chris and Bruce Goldstein. *The Nicholas Brothers: We Sing and We Dance.* New York: A&E, November 29, 1992.

Brackett, Davis. "Black or White? Michael Jackson and the Idea of Crossover." *Popular Music and Society* 35, no. 2 (May 2012): 169–185.

Brannigan, Erin. "The Musical: Moving into the Dance." In *Dancefilm: Choreography and the Moving Image.* New York: Oxford University Press, 2011.

Brode, Douglas. *Elvis Cinema and Popular Culture.* Jefferson: McFarland & Co., 2006.

Brooks, Daphne A. "'A Woman Is a Sometime Thing': (Re)Covering Black Womanhood in *Porgy and Bess*." *Daedalus* 150, no. 1 (Winter 2021): 98–117.

Buchbinder, David. "Color and Movement: The Male Dancer, Masculinity, and Race in Movies." In *Communicating Marginalized Masculinities: Identity Politics in TV, Film, and New Media*, edited by Ronald L. Jackson II and Jamie E. Moshin. London: Taylor & Francis Group, 2012.

Burt, Ramsay. *Alien Bodies: Representations of Modernity, Race and Nation in Early Modern Dance.* London: Routledge, 1998.

Burt, Ramsay. *The Male Dancer: Bodies, Spectacle, Sexualities*, 2nd ed. London: Routledge, 2007.

Butler, Judith. *Gender Trouble: Feminism and the Subversion of Identity.* New York: Routledge, 1990.

Callison, Darcey. "Dancing Masculinity for Hollywood: The American Dream, Whiteness and the Movement Vocabulary Within Hollywood's Choreography for Men." PhD diss., York University, 2008.

236   SELECTED BIBLIOGRAPHY

Chow, Broderick. "Every Little Thing He Does: Entrepreneurship and Appropriation in the *Magic Mike* Series." *Lateral* 6, no. 1 (2017). https://doi.org/10.25158/L6.1.3.

Clover, Carol. "Dancin' in the Rain." *Critical Inquiry* 21, no. 4 (Summer 1995): 722–747.

Coates, Norma. "Elvis from the Waist Up and Other Myths: 1950s Music Television and the Gendering of Rock Discourse." In *Medium Cool: Music Videos from Soundies to Cellphones*, edited by Roger Beebe and Jason Middleton. Durham, NC: Duke University Press, 2007.

Cohan, Steven. "'Feminizing' the Song-and-Dance Man." In *Screening the Male: Exploring Masculinities in Hollywood Cinema*, edited by Steven Cohan and Ina R. Hark. London: Routledge, 1993.

Cohan, Steven. "Dancing with Balls: Sissies, Sailors, and the Camp Masculinity of Gene Kelly." In *Incongruous Entertainment: Camp, Cultural Value, and the MGM Musical*. Durham, NC: Duke University Press, 2005.

Cohan, Steven. *Masked Men: Masculinity and the Movies in the Fifties*. Bloomington: Indiana University Press, 1997.

Cripps, Thomas. *Slow Fade to Black*. New York: Oxford University Press, 1977.

Davis, Cienna. "Digital Blackface and the Troubling Intimacies of TikTok Dance Challenges." In *TikTok Cultures in the United States*, edited by Trevor Boffone. New York: Routledge, 2022.

DeFrantz, Thomas F. "African American Dance: A Complex History." In *Dancing Many Drums: Excavations in African American Dance*. Madison: University of Wisconsin Press, 2002.

DeFrantz, Thomas F. "Popular African American Dance of the 1950s and 60s." In *Ain't Nothing Like the Real Thing*, edited by Richard Carlin and Kinshasha Holman Conwill. Washington, D.C.: Smithsonian Press, 2010.

DeFrantz, Thomas F. "Popular Dances of the 1920s and early 30s: From Animal Dance Crazes to the Lindy Hop." In *Ain't Nothing Like the Real Thing*, edited by Richard Carlin and Kinshasha Holman Conwill. Washington, D.C.: Smithsonian Press, 2010.

DeFrantz, Thomas F. "Simmering Passivity: The Black Male Body in Concert Dance." In *Moving Words: Re-writing Dance*, edited by Gay Morris. London: Routledge, 1996.

DeFrantz, Thomas F. "Unchecked Popularity: Neoliberal Circulations of Black Social Dance." In *Neoliberalism and Global Theatres: Performance Permutations*, edited by Lara D. Nielsen and Patricia A. Ybarra. Hampshire: Palgrave Macmillan, 2012.

Delamater, Jerome. "A Critical and Historical Analysis of Dance as a Code of the Hollywood Musical." PhD diss. Northwestern University, 1981.

Delmont, Matthew. "Michael Jackson and Television Before Thriller." *The Journal of Pan African Studies* 3, no. 7 (March 2010): 64–78.

Desjardins, Mary. *Recycled Stars: Female Film Stardom in the Age of Television and Video*. Durham, NC: Duke University Press, 2015.

Doherty, Thomas. *Teenagers and Teenpics: Juvenilization of American Movies*. Philadelphia: Temple University Press, 2010.

Dyer, Richard. "Don't Look Now." *Screen* 23, nos. 3–4 (1982): 61–73.

Dyer, Richard. "Entertainment and Utopia." In *Only Entertainment*. New York: Routledge, 1992.

Dyer, Richard. *Heavenly Bodies: Film Stars and Society*. New York: St. Martin's Press, 1986.

Dyer, Richard. *In the Space of a Song: The Uses of Song in Film*. New York: Routledge, 2012.

Dyer, Richard. *Stars*. London: British Film Institute, 1979.

Early, Gerald. "Sammy Davis, Jr., Establishment Rebel." *This Is Where I Came In: Black America in the 1960s*. Lincoln: University of Nebraska Press, 2003.

Early, Gerald. *The Sammy Davis, Jr. Reader: The Life and Times of the Last Great American Hipster—From Vaudeville to Vegas—As Seen Through the Eyes of His Public*. New York: Farrar, Straus, and Giroux, 2001.

Fanon, Frantz. *Black Skin, White Masks*. 1952. London: Paladin, 1970.

Feuer, Jane. *The Hollywood Musical*. Bloomington: Indiana University Press, 1982.

Fisher, Jennifer and Anthony Shay, eds. *When Men Dance: Choreographing Masculinities Across Borders*. Oxford: Oxford University Press, 2009.

SELECTED BIBLIOGRAPHY   237

Forman, Murray. *One Night on TV Is Worth Weeks at the Paramount: Popular Music on Early Television.* Durham, NC: Duke University Press, 2012.

Fraterrigo, Elizabeth. *Playboy and the Making of the Good Life in Modern America.* New York: Oxford University Press, 2009.

Gabbard, Krin. "Marlon Brando's Jazz Acting and the Obsolescence of Blackface." In *Black Magic: White Hollywood and African American Culture.* New Brunswick: Rutgers University Press, 2004.

Gabbard, Krin. *Jammin' at the Margins: Jazz and the American Cinema.* Chicago: University of Chicago Press, 1996.

Garber, Marjorie. *Vested Interests: Cross-Dressing and Cultural Anxiety.* New York: Routledge, 1992.

Gates, Henry Louis and Gene A. Jarrett. *The New Negro: Readings on Race, Representation, and African American Culture, 1892–1938.* Princeton, NJ: Princeton University Press, 2007.

George-Graves, Nadine. "'Just Like Being at the Zoo': Primitivity and Ragtime Dance." In *Ballroom, Boogie, Shimmy Sham, Shake: A Social and Popular Dance Reader,* edited by Julie Malnig. Chicago: University of Illinois Press, 2009.

Gottschild, Brenda Dixon. *Digging the Africanist Presence in American Performance: Dance and Other Contexts.* Westport, CT: Greenwood Press, 1996.

Gottschild, Brenda Dixon. *The Black Dancing Body: A Geography from Coon to Cool.* New York: Palgrave Macmillan, 2008.

Gray, Herman. *Watching Race: Television and The Struggle for Blackness.* Minneapolis: University of Minnesota Press, 1995.

Griffin, Sean. "The Gang's All Here: Generic versus Racial Integration in the 1940s Musical." *Cinema Journal* 42, no. 1 (Autumn 2002): 21–45.

Hamera, Judith. "The Labors of Michael Jackson: Virtuosity, Deindustrialization, and Dancing Work." *PMLA* 127, no. 4 (October 2012): 751–765.

Hansen, Miriam. "Pleasure, Ambivalence, Identification: Valentino and Female Spectatorship." *Cinema Journal* 25, no. 4 (1986): 6–32.

Hatch, Kristen. *Shirley Temple and the Performance of Girlhood.* New Brunswick: Rutgers University Press, 2015.

Hazzard-Donald, Katrina. "The Circle and the Line: Speculations of the Development of African American Vernacular Dancing." *Western Journal of Black Studies* 20, no. 1 (Spring 1996): 28–38.

Hill, Constance Valis. *Brotherhood in Rhythm: The Jazz Tap Dancing of the Nicholas Brothers.* New York: Oxford University Press, 2000.

Hill, Constance Valis. *Tap Dancing America: A Cultural History.* New York: Oxford University Press, 2010.

Jacobson, Matthew Frye. *Dancing Down the Barricades: Sammy Davis Jr. and the Long Civil Rights Era.* Oakland: University of California Press, 2023.

Jackson, Ronald L. *Scripting the Black Masculine Body: Identity, Discourse, and Racial Politics in Popular Media.* Ithaca, NY: SUNY Press, 2006.

Jackson, Ronald L., and Celnisha L. Dangerfield. "Defining Black Masculinity as Cultural Property: An Identity Negotiation Paradigm." In *African American Communication & Identities: Essential Readings,* edited by Ronald L. Jackson. Thousand Oaks, CA: Sage, 2004.

James, David E. *Rock 'n' Film: Cinema's Dance with Popular Music.* New York: Oxford University Press, 2016.

Jones, LeRoi [Amiri Baraka]. *Blues People: Negro Music in White America.* New York: Quill, 1963.

Kimmel, Michael S. *Manhood in America: A Cultural History.* New York: The Free Press, 1996.

Knight, Arthur. *Disintegrating the Musical: Black Performance and American Musical Film.* Durham, NC: Duke University Press, 2002.

Knight, Arthur. "It Ain't Necessarily So That It Ain't Necessarily So: Jazz Recordings of *Porgy and Bess* as Film and Cultural Criticism." In *Critical Voicings of Black Liberation: Resistance*

238 SELECTED BIBLIOGRAPHY

and Representations in the Americas, edited by Kimberley L. Phillips. Münster: Lit Verlag, 2003.

Knight, Arthur. "Star Dances: African American Constructions of Stardom, 1925–1960." In *Classic Hollywood, Classic Whiteness*, edited by Daniel Bemardi. Minneapolis: University of Minnesota Press, 2001.

Knowles, Mark. *The Man Who Made the Jailhouse Rock: Alex Romero, Hollywood Choreographer*. Jefferson: McFarland & Co., 2013.

Kraut, Anthea. *Choreographing Copyright: Race, Gender, and Intellectual Property Rights in American Dance*. New York: Oxford University Press, 2015.

Kraut, Anthea. *Choreographing the Folk: The Dance Stagings of Zora Neale Hurston*. Minneapolis: University of Minnesota Press, 2008.

Lewis, Barbara. "Daddy Blue: The Evolution of the Dark Dandy." In *Inside the Minstrel Mask: Readings in Nineteenth-Century Blackface Minstrelsy*, edited by Annemarie Bean, James V. Hatch, and Brooks McNamara. Middletown, CT: Wesleyan University Press, 1996.

Lhamon, W T. *Raising Cain: Blackface Performance from Jim Crow to Hip Hop*. Cambridge, MA: Harvard University Press, 1998.

Linn, Brian McAllister. *Elvis's Army: Cold War GIs and the Atomic Battlefield*. Cambridge, MA: Harvard University Press, 2016.

Long, Richard A. *The Black Tradition in American Dance*. New York: Smithmark Publishers, 1989).

Lott, Eric. *Love and Theft: Blackface Minstrelsy and the American Working Class*. New York: Oxford University Press, 1993.

Malone, Jacqui. *Steppin' on the Blues: The Visible Rhythms of African American Dance*. Urbana: University of Illinois Press, 1996.

Mann, Denise. "The Spectacularization of Everyday Life: Recycling Hollywood Stars and Fans in Early Television Variety Shows." In *Private Screenings: Television and the Female Consumer*, edited by Lynn Spigel and Denise Mann. Minneapolis: University of Minnesota Press, 1992.

Manning, Susan. *Modern Dance, Negro Dance: Race in Motion*. Minneapolis: University of Minnesota Press, 2004.

McCarthy, Anna. *The Citizen Machine: Governing by Television in 1950s America*. New York: The New Press, 2010.

McNally, Karen. "Featuring the Nicholas Brothers: Spectacle, Structure, and Racial Interventions in the Hollywood Musical." *Star Turns in Hollywood Musicals*. Dijon: Les Presses du réel, 2016.

McNally, Karen. *When Frankie Went to Hollywood: Frank Sinatra and American Male Identity*. University of Illinois Press, 2008.

Mercer, Kobena. *Welcome to the Jungle: New Positions in Black Cultural Studies*. New York: Routledge, 1994.

Miller, Benjamin. "Twisting the Dandy: The Transformation of the Blackface Dandy in Early American Theatre." *The Journal of American Drama and Theatre* 27, no. 3 (Fall 2015): 1898–1965.

Miller, Monica L. *Slaves to Fashion: Black Dandyism and the Styling of Black Diasporic Identity*. Durham: Duke University Press, 2009.

Murray, Susan. *Hitch Your Antenna to the Stars!: Early Television and Broadcast Stardom*. New York: Routledge, 2005.

Murugan, Meenasarani Linde. "Electronic Salome: Exotic Dance, Early Television, and Black Modernism." *Écranosphère* 1 (2018), https://ecranosphere.ca/article.php?id=77.

Murugan, Meenasarani Linde. "Exotic Television: Technology, Empire, and Entertaining Globalism." PhD diss., Northwestern University, 2015.

Noonan, Ellen. *The Strange Career of Porgy and Bess: Race, Culture, and America's Most Famous Opera*. Chapel Hill: University of North Carolina Press, 2012.

SELECTED BIBLIOGRAPHY   239

Petty, Miriam. *Stealing the Show: African American Performers and Audiences in 1930s Hollywood*. Oakland: University of California Press, 2016.

Pugh, Megan. *America Dancing: From the Cakewalk to the Moonwalk*. New Haven, CT: Yale University Press, 2015.

Raymond, Emilie. "Sammy Davis Jr: Public Image and Politics." *Cultural History* 4.1 (2015): 42–63.

Raymond, Emilie. "Cleaning Up Catfish Row: Black Celebrity and the Making of *Porgy and Bess*." *Stars for Freedom: Hollywood, Black Celebrities, and the Civil Rights Movement*. Seattle: University of Washington Press, 2015.

Regester, Charlene. *African American Actresses: The Struggle for Visibility, 1900–1960*. Bloomington: Indiana University Press, 2010.

Robinson, Danielle. *Modern Moves: Dancing Race During the Ragtime and Jazz Eras*. New York: Oxford University Press, 2015.

Rogin, Michael. *Blackface, White Noise: Jewish Immigrants in the Hollywood Melting Pot*. Berkeley and Los Angeles: University of California Press, 1998.

Rotundo, E. Anthony. *American Manhood: Transformations in Masculinity from the Revolution to the Modern Era*. New York: Basic Books, 1993.

Shiovitz, Brynn W. *Behind the Screen: Tap Dance, Race, and Invisibility During Hollywood's Golden Age*. New York: Oxford University Press, 2023.

Spencer, Jon Michael. "A Revolutionary Sexual Persona: Elvis Presley and the White Acquiescence of Black Rhythms." In *In Search of Elvis: Music, Race, Art, Religion*, edited by Vernon Chadwick. Boulder, CO: Westview Press, 1997.

Stearns, Marshall and Jean Stearns. *Jazz Dance: The Story of American Vernacular Dance*. New York: Macmillan, 1968.

Studlar, Gaylin. "'Optic Intoxication': Rudolph Valentino and Dance Madness." In *This Mad Masquerade: Stardom and Masculinity in the Jazz Age*. New York: Columbia University Press, 1996.

Studlar, Gaylin. *Precocious Charms: Stars Performing Girlhood in Classical Hollywood Cinema*. Berkeley and Los Angeles: University of California Press, 2013.

Trenka, Susie. "Appreciation, Appropriation, Assimilation: *Stormy Weather* and the Hollywood History of Black Dance." In *The Oxford Handbook of Dance and the Popular Screen*, edited by Melissa Blanco Borelli. New York: Oxford University Press, 2014.

Vogel, Shane. "Performing 'Stormy Weather': Ethel Waters, Lena Horne, and Katherine Dunham." *South Central Review* 25, no. 1 (2008): 93–113.

Webb, Barbara L. "The Black Dandyism of George Walker: A Case Study in Genealogical Method." *TDR: The Drama Review* 45, no. 4 (Winter 2001): 7–24.

West, Kai. "Buckra: Whiteness and *Porgy and Bess*." *Journal of the American Musicological Society* 75, no. 2 (August 2022): 319–377.

Williams, Linda. *Playing the Race Card: Melodramas of Black and White from Uncle Tom to O.J. Simpson*. Princeton, NJ: Princeton University Press, 2001.

Wojcik, Pamela Robertson. "Shirley Temple as Streetwalker: Girls, Streets, and Encounters with Men." *Fantasies of Neglect: Imagining the Urban Child in American Film and Fiction*. New Brunswick: Rutgers University Press, 2016.

Index

For the benefit of digital users, indexed terms that span two pages (e.g., 52–53) may, on occasion, appear on only one of those pages.

Figures are indicated by an italic *f* following the page number.

Acham, Christine, 156
aesthetic of the cool
  as Africanist aesthetic element, 4
  Channing Tatum use of, 203–4
  Elvis Presley use of, 123–24, 127–28
  Gene Kelly use of, 107*f*, 107–8
  James Brown use of, 66–67
  Sammy Davis, Jr. use of, 150, 174–75, 177, 185, 189
African American dance. *See* Africanist aesthetics; Black Dance
Africanist aesthetics. *See also* Black dance; blackbodying; ephebism
  characteristics of, 4–5, 95, 96*f*, 128–29, 133–34, 135, 164–65
  definition of, 2–3
  Elvis Presley use of, 28, 114–15, 116–17, 119–20, 121*f*, 122, 139–40, 142–43
  Europeanist perspective of, 4–5
  Gene Kelly use of, 27–28, 72–73, 81–83, 85, 96*f*, 107–8
  Nicholas Brothers use of, 32, 63
  Sammy Davis, Jr. use of, 149–50, 155, 159–60, 163*f*, 163–64
All Star Revue: The Ed Wynn Show. See under Nicholas Brothers
An All-Colored Vaudeville Show. See under Nicholas Brothers
Allen, Steve, 14, 124, 125–26, 149, 168–69
Altman, Rick, 51–52, 70–72, 106–7, 129–30
ambiguous masculinity. *See also* Kelly, Gene; masculinity; Presley, Elvis
  Elvis Presley use of, 28, 114, 117–18, 130–31, 134–35, 145–47
  Gene Kelly use of, 70–72, 73–74, 82, 83, 84–85, 86, 105–6
  John Travolta use of, 198–99
  Michael Jackson use of, 198
"American Dancer, Negro" (Jackson), 64–65
American Film Institute, 1, 194–95
The American Film Musical (Altman), 70–72

An American in Paris. See under blackbodying; Kelly, Gene
"An American in Paris" (Gershwin), 90
Amin, Takiyah Nur, 3
Anchors Aweigh. See under Kelly, Gene
Anna Lucasta. See under Davis, Sammy, Jr.
Ann-Margret, 143–47, 145*f*, 194–95
appropriation, cultural. *See* blackbodying; blackface minstrelsy; invisibilization
Army, U.S. *See* U.S. Army
Astaire, Fred
  "The Babbitt and the Bromide," 76–77, 77*f*
  "Bojangles of Harlem," 20–21, 79–81, 86
  bricolage use, 45–46, 70–72
  collaboration with Gene Kelly, 76–78
  contrast with Gene Kelly, 76, 79–81
  dance style, 34, 50–51, 78
  films of, 45–46, 76–77, 101–2, 194–95
  influence on Michael Jackson, 197–98
  masculinity style, 51–52, 77–78
  portrayal in *That's Dancing!* 194–95
  relationship with the Nicholas Brothers, 56–57
athletic masculinity. *See also* Kelly, Gene: "Dancing, A Man's Game"
  as counter for gender ambiguity, 8, 82–83, 95
  dancing as physical exercise, 75
  Gene Kelly association with, 27–28
  Gene Kelly use of, 81–82, 87, 105–6, 107–9
  Nicholas Brothers use of, 50
The Autobiography of an Ex-Colored Man (Johnson), 151–52

"The Babbitt and the Bromide" (performance). *See under* Astaire, Fred; Kelly, Gene
Babes in Arms, 19–20
Bailey, Pearl, 171–73
Balanchine, George, 1–2, 72–73, 195–96
Baldwin, James, 6, 171–72
ballet, 1–2, 8, 50–51, 91. *See also* Kelly, Gene
ballin' the jack (dance), 27–28, 106–7, 139–40

242 INDEX

"Ballin' the Jack" (performance). *See under*
Kelly, Gene
Baraka, Amiri, 48
Baryshnikov, Mikhail, 194–95, 201
"Be a Clown" (performance). *See under* Davis,
Sammy, Jr.; Kelly, Gene; Nicholas Brothers
Bederman, Gail, 7
Belafonte, Harry, 171–72, 178–79, 181–82
Belmar, Sima, 198–99
Berle, Milton, 14, 57–59, 111, 120–21, 122–23
Berry, Chuck, 14, 66–67, 122, 128–29
Berry Brothers, 14, 26, 159
"Billie Jean" (performance). *See* Jackson,
Michael
Billy Ward and his Dominoes, 128–29
Bishop, Joey, 174–76
Black, Bill, 115–16, 119
Black dance. *See also* Africanist aesthetics;
blackbodying; blackface minstrelsy; Davis,
Sammy, Jr.; invisibilization; Kelly, Gene;
stereotypes
Afro-Cuban dancers, 70
assumptions about, 100
characteristics, 27–28, 120
danced masculinities from, 22–23
dances, 3–4, 9, 19–20, 33–34, 67–69, 90
definition, 2–3
Elvis Presley use of, 118–21
"flesh dance" of Black women, 206–7
Nicholas Brothers use of, 32–33
reception of, 4–5
social dance, 128–29, 139–40, 143
Black dandy, 70–72, 151–52. *See also* Davis,
Sammy, Jr.; stereotypes
Black masculinity. *See* masculinity, Black
The Black Network. See under Nicholas
Brothers
Black Power Movement, 6, 67, 195–96
Black short films, 36–37, 43, 55, 154–55
The Black Tradition in American Dance
(Long), 3
blackbodying. *See also* Africanist aesthetics;
blackbodying-as-masculinity; blackface
minstrelsy; invisibilization; Kelly, Gene;
Presley, Elvis; Tatum, Channing
in *An American in Paris*, 70–72, 90,
92*f*, 92–93
appropriation of steps, 1
definition, 14–16, 206–7
Elvis Presley use of, 96–97, 128–29,
143, 196
gender shift on social media, 206–7
in *The Gene Kelly Show*, 102–4, 106–7

Gene Kelly use of, 27–28, 72, 74, 84–85, 88–
89, 100–1
influence on white masculinity, 15–16
inheritance from black minstrelsy, 196
in *Les Girls*, 95, 96*f*
modern, 202–4, 208–9
purpose of, 112–13, 114
in *Singin' in the Rain*, 22, 94
on TikTok (app), 205–8
transition from covert minstrelsy to, 22
blackbodying-as-masculinity. *See also*
blackbodying; masculinity
Channing Tatum, 202–4
definition, 26, 196
Elvis Presley use of, 113, 114, 118–
19, 122–24
Gene Kelly use of, 72–74, 79–83, 89–96, 98–
99, 103–4, 106–7, 109–10
John Travolta use of, 198–200
blackface minstrelsy, 2, 14–23, 37–38, 157–58.
See also blackbodying; covert minstrelsy;
dialect, Black; racism; stereotypes
Blue Hawaii. See under Presley, Elvis
Boffone, Trevor, 205–6
Bogle, Donald, 8–9, 13–14
Bojangles (film), 201–2
"Bojangles of Harlem" (performance). *See
under* Astaire, Fred
Boss, Stephen "tWitch," 203–4
"Bossa Nova, Baby" (performance). *See* Presley,
Elvis: in *Fun in Acapulco*
Boyar, Burt, 152
Boyar, Jane, 152
Brando, Marlon, 12–13, 15–16, 79–81,
81*f*, 94–95
brash masculinity. *See* wolfish
masculinity
bricolage, 45–46, 50, 52–53, 70–72, 122, 180–
81, 199–200, 204
Britt, May, 149–50, 176–77, 185–86
"Broadway Melody" performance. *See* Kelly,
Gene: in *Singin' in the Rain*
Broadway theater, 1–2, 10–11, 72–73
*Brotherhood in Rhythm: The Jazz Tap Dancing
of the Nicholas Brothers* (Hill), 32
Brotherhood of Sleeping Car Porters (BSCP),
46
Brown, James, 65–67, 185–86
Bryant, Willie, 33–34, 90
Bubbles, John. *See* Sublett, John W. "Bubbles"
Buchbinder, David, 198–99
buck and wing dancing, 9, 28, 98–99, 114–15,
120, 143

Burt, Ramsay, 8

Calloway, Cab, 34–35, 52–53, 54, 120, 167–68, 171–72
camera
  censorship of Elvis Presley, 126–27, 128
  film vs. television, 11–12, 24, 101
  framing in films, 18–19, 130–31, 133–34, 188f, 188–89, 198–99
  Nicholas Brothers
    use of, 42–43, 50, 62–63
    role in displaying masculinity, 97–98, 140–41, 144, 145f, 208–9
  Sammy Davis, Jr. use of, 163–64, 167–68
Cantor, Eddie, 17, 21–22, 37–38, 39–40, 161–63, 164–65
caricature. See blackface minstrelsy; stereotypes
Caron, Leslie, 70, 91, 101–2
Carroll, Diahann, 171–72, 183–84
Castle, Nick, 34, 44, 50
challenge dance. See Hoofers Club (New York); Nicholas Brothers
chameleonic masculinity. See Davis, Sammy, Jr.; modish and chameleonic masculinity
Charisse, Cyd, 94, 101–2
Charleston (dance), 3–4, 19–20, 32, 70, 90, 94
"Chattanooga Choo Choo" (performance). See Nicholas Brothers: in Sun Valley Serenade
Chitlin' Circuit, 82–83
Chocolat (dancer). See Padilla, Raphaël
Chocolat dansant dans un bar (Lautrec), 70–72, 71f, 92–93
Chow, Broderick, 203–4
Chrichton, Kyle, 74–75
civil rights, 1–2, 6, 32–33, 46, 63–64, 153, 171–72, 195–96
Civil Rights Act of 1964, 64–65
class act. See Will Mastin Trio
classy and dignified masculinity, 26, 27, 39–40, 43, 51–52, 69, 201–2. See also masculinity; Nicholas Brothers
Clover, Carol, 19–20, 22, 70–72, 93–94
"C'mon Everybody" (performance). See Presley, Elvis: in Viva Las Vegas
Coates, Norma, 113
Cohan, George M., 21–22, 37–38, 73
Cohan, George M., Jr., 157–58
Cohan, Steven, 6–7, 12–13, 51, 70–72, 82–86, 94–95, 134–35, 141
Cole, Nat King, 13
The Colgate Comedy Hour. See under Davis, Sammy, Jr.; Nicholas Brothers
Como, Perry, 118–19

concert dance, 8, 9, 73–74, 97, 143
conked hair. See hair, Black
Cooke, Alistair, 97–98
cool aesthetic. See aesthetic of the cool
costuming. See also Davis, Sammy, Jr.; Kelly, Gene; Nicholas Brothers; Presley, Elvis
  aesthetic of the cool, 4–5
  blackbodying through, 72, 79–81, 92–93, 94–95
  Elvis Presley, 117–18, 122–23, 127–28, 141
  ethnic blurring in, 82–83, 85f, 86, 168–69
  Gene Kelly, 70, 78–79, 81f
  Nicholas Brothers, 37, 47, 48–49, 55, 58–60
  popular fashion as, 67–69, 182, 185–86, 186f, 189, 192–93
  problematic, 86–87, 156
  rock 'n' roll aesthetic, 95, 117–18, 120, 147–48
  Sammy Davis, Jr., 153, 166–67, 169–70, 172–73, 180–81, 190–91
  ties to sport, 8
  Will Mastin Trio, 154, 159–60, 161–65
  of working-class masculinity, 90
The Cotton Club (film), 200–1
Cotton Club (New York), 30–31, 34–35, 37–38, 61–62
covert minstrelsy, 14–15, 17, 20–22. See also blackbodying; blackface minstrelsy; Hollywood musical
credit to Black performers, 17–18, 19–20, 22, 147–48, 194–95, 198–99, 203–4, 205–6
Cremmen, Mary, 125, 126–27
Cripps, Thomas, 36–37, 41
crisis of masculinity, 1–2, 6–7, 83–84, 195–96
Crowther, Bosley, 136–37, 170–71

D'Amelio, Charli, 205–6
dance, social. See social dance
dance crazes, 3–4, 7, 139–40. See also social dance
"Dancin' in the Rain" (Clover), 22, 70–72
"Dancing, A Man's Game" (television special). See under Kelly, Gene
Dancing Down the Barricades: Sammy Davis Jr. and the Long Civil Rights Era (Jacobson), 152
Dandridge, Dorothy, 43, 46–47, 47f, 58–59, 171–73
dandy, 37–38, 70–72, 151–52. See also Black dandy; Davis, Sammy, Jr.
Daniels, LeRoy, 194–95
The Danny Kaye Show. See under Kelly, Gene
Darktown Follies, 72–73
Davis, Cienna, 206–7

244 INDEX

Davis, Sammy, Jr. *See also* aesthetic of the cool;
    Africanist aesthetics; costuming; modish
    and chameleonic masculinity; Rat Pack
  in *Anna Lucasta*, 170–71, 171*f*
  "Auf Wiedersehen," 170
  autobiographies, 152
  "Be a Clown," 185
  "Birth of the Blues," 161–63, 163*f*
  as Black dandy, 153, 172–74, 174*f*, 188–89,
    190, 193, 196
  Black stardom, 13–14
  bricolage use, 180–81
  car accident, 165–66
  chameleonic qualities, 166–67, 174–75
  civil rights activism, 149–50, 157–58, 174–75,
    178–79, 182–83
  on *The Colgate Comedy Hour*, 161–
    63, 164–65
  comedy use, 149–50, 159–60, 192–93
  comparison to Michael Jackson, 186–87
  dance style, 28–29, 155, 159–60, 161–64,
    166–67, 179–80
  "The Daughter of Rosie O'Grady," 191–92
  early career, 153–55, 156
  evolving masculinity, 26, 28–29, 150, 164–65,
    169–70, 181–82, 184–85
  explanation of hoofing vs. dancing, 191–92
  eye, loss of, 165–66
  on *The Flip Wilson Show*, 191–92, 193*f*
  "Get It On," 191–93
  in *Golden Boy*, 174–75, 182, 198–99
  hippie image, 174–75, 187–88, 189
  on *Hollywood House*, 159–61, 162*f*
  on *Hollywood Palace*, 185–87
  on *Hullabaloo*, 28–29, 153, 182–83
  influence of other dancers, 156–57, 168–69,
    171, 176–77, 178, 184*f*, 184–85
  influence on other dancers, 174–75
  integrated dancing, 182
  interracialism of, 149–50, 168, 171, 176–
    77, 182–83
  Jewish identity, 182–83
  "The Lady Is a Tramp," 178
  military service, 157–58, 179–80
  "The Most Outstanding New Personality of
    the Year" (*Metronome*), 158–59
  "Mr. Bojangles," 153, 190–91, 193*f*
  nicknames, 149–50, 184–85
  in *Ocean's 11*, 175–76, 177
  personal life, 149–50, 172–73, 185–86, 190
  playboy image, 176–77, 178, 187
  on *Playboy* television shows, 176–77,
    177*f*, 189

  popular dance, 182, 188–89
  in *Porgy and Bess*, 151, 152–53, 166–68,
    171–74, 174*f*
  preservation of performances, 24–25
  public reputation, 165, 168
  racism experienced by, 157–58, 164–66
  re-appropriation of Black dance, 178
  in *Robin and the 7 Hoods*, 180–81, 181*f*
  role models, 158–59
  in *Rufus Jones for President*, 154–55,
    156*f*, 194–95
  on *Sammy!* 191–92, 193*f*
  on *The Sammy Davis, Jr. Show*, 174–75,
    183–85, 184*f*
  in *Seasoned Greetings*, 156
  in *Sergeants 3*, 179–80
  sexuality in performance, 161–63, 167–68,
    170–72, 173–74, 193
  short films, 154–55, 159–60
  Spingarn Medal award, 179
  on *The Steve Allen Show*, 149, 168–69
  "The Strollin' 20s," 181–82
  in *Sweet and Low*, 159–60, 160*f*
  in *Sweet Charity*, 28–29, 153, 174–75, 187–
    89, 188*f*
  in *Tap*, 200–1
  tap style, 159–60, 180–81, 184–85
  television appearances, 28–29, 149–50, 159–
    60, 161–63, 164–65
  in *That's Dancing!* 194–95
  on *Toast of the Town*, 161–63, 166–67
  vaudeville career, 101–2, 155, 158–
    59, 161–63
  in *We Three*, 165, 183
Davis, Sammy, Sr., 153–54, 156
Dean, James, 12–13, 15–16, 117–18, 135–36
DeFrantz, Thomas F., 3, 4–5, 118
Dewan, Jenna, 202–3
dialect, Black, 14–15, 16, 19–20, 154–55, 171–
    72. *See also* blackface minstrelsy
Diddley, Bo, 116–17, 128–29
disco, 198–99
Donen, Stanley, 73–74, 81–83, 94
Dorsey, Tommy, 118, 156–57
"Down Argentina Way" (performance). *See*
    Nicholas Brothers: in *Down Argentine Way*
Down Argentine Way (film). *See under* Nicholas
    Brothers
Du Bois, W.E.B., 34–35, 151–52, 195–96
Dunham, Katherine, 15–16, 165
Dyer, Richard, 187

eagle rock (dance), 106–7

INDEX 245

Early, Gerald, 150, 152, 171, 174–75, 179–80, 193
The Ed Sullivan Show. See under Presley, Elvis
Edison films, 9
Eigen, Jack, 168
Ellington, Duke, 34–35, 165
"Elvis - A Reformed Wriggler" (Crowther), 136–37
"Elvis from the Waist Up and Other Myths: 1950s Music Television and Gendering of Rock Discourse" (Coates), 113
"Elvis Rocks but Movie Stands Still" (Tinee), 132–33
Elvis's Army: Cold War GIs and the Atomic Battlefield (Linn), 136
Entratter, Jack, 175–76
ephebism, 4, 27, 106–7, 195. *See also* Africanist aesthetics
ethnic blurring, 5, 41–42, 43, 86, 141–42, 168–69
Europeanist aesthetics, 4–5, 73
Everybody Sing (film), 18–19

Fanon, Frantz, 123–24, 207
Farmer, Brett, 134–35, 141
femininity, 6–7, 72–73, 145–47, 202–3, 206–7
Fetchit, Stepin, 17–18, 43–44, 100
Feuer, Jane, 44, 45–46, 50, 70–72
film noir, 12–13, 101–2
film to television transition, 11–12, 57–58, 96–97
flamenco, 82–83, 104–5
flash dance, 31–32, 82–83, 154, 207
The Flip Wilson Show. See under Davis, Sammy, Jr.
Fosse, Bob, 101–2, 187–89
Four Step Brothers, 14, 26, 57–58, 60–61
Franklin, Aretha, 186–87
Fraterrigo, Elizabeth, 176–77
Friedman, Ryan Jay, 154–55
Fun in Acapulco. See under Presley, Elvis

Gabbard, Krin, 15–16, 32–33, 79–81
Garber, Marjorie, 117
Garland, Judy, 18–20, 85
gender. *See* femininity; masculinity
The Gene Kelly Show. See under blackbodying; Kelly, Gene
Gene Kelly Studio of the Dance, 75
Gershwin, George, 171–73
"Get It On" (performance). *See under* Davis, Sammy, Jr.
G.I. Blues. See under Presley, Elvis
Girls! Girls! Girls! See under Presley, Elvis
Glenn Miller Orchestra, 46–47, 47*f*, 48–49

Glover, Savion, 201–2
Golden Age musical. *See* Hollywood musical
Golden Age of Hollywood. *See* Hollywood
Golden Boy. See under Davis, Sammy, Jr.
Goldwyn, Samuel, 37–38, 166–67, 171–72
Gottschild, Brenda Dixon, 2–3, 4–5, 19–20, 22–23, 106–7, 114–15, 116–17. *See also* invisibilization
Gould, Jack, 111, 112, 124
Grease. See Travolta, John
The Great American Broadcast. See under Nicholas Brothers
"Greatest Negro Stars Team Up" (*LIFE Magazine*), 181–82
Greco, José, 82–83, 104–5
Gross, Ben, 112, 126
Guralnick, Peter, 128–29, 136–37

Hail, Caesar! 204
hair, Black, 43, 54, 67–69, 186*f*, 186–87
hair choreography, 28, 113, 120, 122, 128, 130–31, 141*f*, 198. *See also* hair, Black; Presley, Elvis
Hamera, Judith, 198
Harlem (New York), 34–35, 151–52, 153–54
Harlem Renaissance, 6, 34–35, 40, 151–52, 181–82
Harmon, Jalaiah, 205–6
Hefner, Hugh, 176–77, 189
Heyward, DuBose, 171–72
Hill, Constance Valis, 32, 36, 40–41, 54–55, 72–73
Hines, Gregory, 1, 29, 31–32, 197, 200–2
Hines, Maurice, 31–32, 200–1
hip-hop, 4, 202–4, 205, 207–8
Hirschhorn, Clive, 72–73
Hollywood, 1–2, 4–5, 10, 12–13, 24, 57, 96–97
Hollywood House. See under Davis, Sammy, Jr.
Hollywood musical, 10, 11–12, 24, 28, 57, 73, 96–97, 197. *See also* covert minstrelsy; Hollywood
The Hollywood Musical (Feuer), 70–72
The Hollywood Palace. See under Davis, Sammy, Jr.; Nicholas Brothers
Hoofers Club (New York), 35, 52
hoofing. *See* tap dance
Horne, Lena, 43–44, 52, 200–1
"Hound Dog" (performance). *See under* Presley, Elvis
Hullabaloo. See under Davis, Sammy, Jr.

"I Want to Be a Minstrel Man" (performance). *See under* Nicholas, Harold

246 INDEX

In Dahomey, 9
Incongruous Entertainment (Cohan), 70–72
The Ink Spots, 45–46
integration, racial, 13, 86–87. *See also*
    segregation
Internet influence, 205
interracial relationships. *See* miscegenation
invisibilization, 19–20, 22–23, 70, 81–82, 90,
    92–94, 98–100, 134. *See also* Black dance;
    blackbodying; Gottschild, Brenda Dixon;
    jazz dance; Kelly, Gene
Invitation to the Dance. See under Kelly, Gene
Irish American history, 88–89
Irish dance, 4, 37–38, 38*f*, 73, 87–88, 100. *See*
    also Europeanist aesthetics; tap dance
"It Ain't Necessarily So" (performance). *See*
    Davis, Sammy, Jr.: in *Porgy and Bess*
"(I've Got a Gal In) Kalamazoo" (performance).
    See Nicholas Brothers: in *Orchestra Wives*

Jackson, Harriet, 64–65
Jackson, Janet, 67–69, 186–87
Jackson, Michael, 67–69, 68*f*, 186–87, 194–
    95, 197–98
The Jacksons. See under Nicholas Brothers
Jacobson, Matthew Frye, 152, 179–80, 193
Jailhouse Rock. See under Presley, Elvis
"Jailhouse Rock" (performance). *See* Presley,
    Elvis: in *Jailhouse Rock*
James, David, 134, 135, 142, 147–48
jazz acting, 15–16
jazz dance, 2–3, 4, 8–9, 32, 36, 48, 73. *See*
    also Davis, Sammy, Jr.; invisibilization;
    Nicholas Brothers
jazz music, 48–49, 73
The Jazz Singer, 14–15, 86, 154
Jeffries, James J., 7
Jeux (ballet), 8, 73–74
Jewish people, 7, 12–13, 17, 19–20, 57–
    58, 182–83
Johnson, Carole Y., 3
Johnson, Jasmine, 206–7
Jolson, Al, 14–15, 17, 21–22, 79–81, 86, 154
Jones, Bill T., 9–10
Jones, Tom, 190–91
Jongintaba, Yahya, 113, 124
The Julie Andrews Show. See under Kelly, Gene
"Jumpin' Jive" (performance). *See* Nicholas
    Brothers: in *Stormy Weather*

Kael, Pauline, 198–99
Kaye, Danny, 13, 26, 107–8
Keefe, Maura, 8

Kelly, Betsy, 83–84
Kelly, Gene. *See also* Africanist aesthetics;
    ambiguous masculinity; athletic
    masculinity; blackbodying;
    blackbodying-as-masculinity; costuming;
    invisibilization; palm/fist dichotomy;
    virile masculinity; wolfish masculinity;
    working-class masculinity
adaptation of dance style for television, 101
ambivalence towards television, 101
in *An American in Paris*, 70, 71*f*, 89–91, 92*f*
in *Anchors Aweigh*, 78–81, 80*f*, 81*f*, 82–
    83, 84–85
asymmetrical male friendships on screen, 78
"The Babbitt and the Bromide," 76–77, 77*f*
ballet use, 73, 81–83, 84–85, 89–91, 101–
    2, 107–8
"Ballin' the Jack," 106–8, 107*f*
"Be a Clown," 55–61, 86–87
bricolage use, 70–72
"Cha Cha Coffee House," 101–2
collaborations with other male dancers,
    76–78, 86–87
contrast with Fred Astaire, 76, 79–81
dance style, 72–73, 78, 82–83, 87–88, 92–
    93, 99–100
dance training, 74–75, 79–81
"Dancing, A Man's Game," 27–28, 97–101,
    98*f*, 99*f*, 103–4
on *The Danny Kaye Show*, 107*f*, 107–8
defense of dance as masculine, 72–73, 74–75,
    83–84, 89, 97–98, 135–36
early life, 74–75
erotic spectacle in choreography, 84–85
ethnic blurring use, 82–83, 86, 105
evolving masculinity, 27–28, 70, 78, 95–97,
    100–1, 102–3
film career, 70–72, 74
flash dance elements, 72–73, 81–83
gender indeterminacy of, 82–86, 94–95
on *The Gene Kelly Show*, 100–4
at Gene Kelly Studio of the Dance, 75
integrated dancing, 98–99
in *Invitation to the Dance*, 78–79, 113
Irish heritage emphasis, 27–28, 72, 73, 87–89,
    103–4, 107–9
on *The Julie Andrews Show*, 78–79,
    108*f*, 108–9
lectures at Los Angeles universities, 83–84
in *Les Girls*, 94–95, 96*f*
Life Achievement Award, 1, 194–95
as "likeable heel," 76, 78
military service, 82–83

nostalgia in later career, 63–64, 74, 100–4, 107–9
"The Old Soft Shoe," 102–4
in *On the Town*, 78–79, 89–90
opinion on rock 'n' roll, 95, 102–4
in *Pal Joey*, 76, 178
personal life, 83–84
in *The Pirate*, 55–56, 56*f*, 82–87, 84*f*, 85*f*, 92–93, 198–99
in *Pontiac Star Parade*, 104–7, 106*f*
preservation of performances, 24–25
racial ambiguity performed by, 86, 88–89, 104–5
relationships with other dancers, 102–3, 195
similarities to Nicholas Brothers, 84*f*, 84–85
in *Singin' in the Rain*, 45*f*, 70–72, 89–94, 101–2
in *Summer Stock*, 44
in *Take Me Out to the Ballgame*, 78, 87–89, 88*f*
television career, 27–28, 74, 96–97, 100–2, 109–10
in *That's Dancing!* 194–95
in *Words and Music*, 79–81, 81*f*
"The Worry Song," 79–83, 80*f*
"You're Just in Love," 105–6
in *Ziegfeld Follies*, 76–77
Kelly, Kerry, 83–84
Kennedy, Robert "Bobby," 178–79
Kid Millions. See under Nicholas Brothers
King, Jean, 147–48
King, Martin Luther, Jr., 149–50, 174–75, 179
King Creole. See under Presley, Elvis
Kinsey report on gender, 6–7
Knight, Arthur, 32–33, 44, 52

"La Cumparsita" (performance). *See* Kelly, Gene: in *Anchors Aweigh*
"The Lady Is a Tramp" (performance). *See under* Davis, Sammy, Jr.
Latinesque dance, 41–42, 43, 82–83
Lautrec, Henri Toulouse, 70, 71*f*, 92–93
Lawrence, Carol, 104–5
Le, Michael, 207–8
Les Girls. See under blackbodying; Kelly, Gene
Lewis, Jerry Lee, 26, 120, 128–29
Lhamon, Jr., W.T., 16
Linn, Brian McAllister, 136–37
Little Richard, 111, 117–18, 120, 128–29
London Palladium, 59–60
Long, Richard, 3
"Long Tail Blue" (song), 151
Lott, Eric, 16–17, 39–40

"Lottery" (K-Camp), 205–6
Loving You. See under Presley, Elvis
Lugo, Zack, 207–8
Luman, Bob, 116–17
lynching, 56–57, 86–87

Mackie, Jean-Victor, 207
Magic Mike. See Tatum, Channing
Malcolm X, 54, 174–75
Mamoulian, Rouben, 172–73
"Mandy" (performance). *See* Nicholas Brothers: in *Kid Millions*
Manning, Susan, 15–16
Marsh, Sy, 170
Martin, Cye, 149, 169–70
Martin, Dean, 150, 174–76
masculinity. *See also* aesthetic of the cool; ambiguous masculinity; athletic masculinity; blackbodying-as-masculinity; classy and dignified masculinity; crisis of masculinity; modish and chameleonic masculinity; Nicholas Brothers: masculinity, childhood; phallic masculinity; virile masculinity; wolfish masculinity; working-class masculinity
capitalism influence on, 6–7
codes of, 6
concept of, 72–73, 109, 195–96
conflation with race and class, 23
contemporary, 207–8
dancers as models of, 2, 204–5
ethnic, 12–13
midcentury, 6–7, 8
military influence on, 195–96
physical fitness as, 6–7
proof of, 6–7, 72–73
threats to. *see* crisis of masculinity
workplace importance to, 6–7
masculinity, Black. *See also* Davis, Sammy, Jr.; Nicholas Brothers
contemporary, 207
James Brown as model of, 67
Little Richard as model of, 117–18
stereotypes as model of, 8–10
Sugar Ray Robinson as model of, 98–99
Mastin, Will, 153–54, 156, 168–69
Maultsby, Portia K., 67
McCarthy, Anna, 97
Mercer, Kobena, 54, 123–24, 198, 207
Merman, Ethel, 105–6
Metro Goldwyn-Mayer (MGM), 70–72, 94–95, 194–95
midcentury, definition of, 1–2, 23

248 INDEX

Miller, Monica L., 151–52
The Milton Berle Show. See under Presley, Elvis
minstrelsy. *See* blackface minstrelsy; whiteface
  minstrelsy
minstrelsy, metaphorical. *See* Manning, Susan;
  modern dance
miscegenation, 38–39, 113–14, 124, 134, 149–
  50, 195–96
modern dance, 1–3, 15–16, 144, 147*f*, 147–48
modish and chameleonic masculinity, 28–29,
  150, 153, 168–70, 182, 185–86, 189, 193.
  See also Davis, Sammy, Jr.; masculinity
Monroe, Raquel, 202–3
Montgomery Bus Boycott, 124
Moore, Scotty, 115–16, 119, 120
Morris Agency, 164–65, 170
Motown 25: Yesterday, Today, Forever, 197–98
Moynihan report, 6
"Mr. Bojangles" (performance). *See under*
  Davis, Sammy, Jr.
"Mr. Bojangles" (song), 190
Mulvey, Laura, 12–13
Murugan, Meenasarani Linde, 104–5
musicals. *See* Hollywood musical

National Association for the Advancement
  of Colored People (NAACP), 13–14,
  54, 171–72
New Deal, 18–20
New Negro. *See* Harlem Renaissance
Nicholas, Dorothy, 33–34
Nicholas, Fayard. *See also* Nicholas Brothers
  comments on time step, 34
  early life, 27, 33–34, 37
  handwork, 34, 60*f*, 60–61, 79
  military service, 55
  personal life, 58–59
  split without hands, 33–34
Nicholas, Harold. *See also* Nicholas Brothers
  early life, 33–34, 37, 153–54
  "I Want to Be a Minstrel Man," 37–40, 38*f*
  personal life, 46–47, 58–59
  return to United States, 63–64
  singing career, 63, 64, 65
  solo performances, 55, 200–1
Nicholas, Harolyn Suzanne, 58–59
Nicholas, Tony, 58–59
Nicholas, Ulysses, 33–35
Nicholas, Viola, 33–35
Nicholas Brothers. *See also* costuming; jazz
  dance; masculinity, Black; Nicholas,
  Fayard; Nicholas, Harold; stereotypes,
  precocious innocent

adaptation to television, 58–59
on *All Star Revue: The Ed Wynn Show,*
  30, 59–60
in *An All-Colored Vaudeville Show,* 36–37
armwork, 50–51, 60–61, 62
ballet elements, 50–51
"Be a Clown," 55–57, 86–87
in *The Black Network,* 36–37
bricolage use, 50
career limitations, 27, 30–31, 54–55,
  57, 63, 69
challenge dance, 36, 41–42
choreography, 60–63, 64
as class act, 35–36, 37, 51–52, 69
on *The Colgate Comedy Hour,* 60*f*, 60–61
contract with Twentieth Century Fox, 43–44,
  53–55, 69
Cotton Club performances, 27, 34–36
dance style, 32–33, 36, 44, 52–53, 63–
  64, 65, 69
in *Down Argentine Way,* 30, 41–44, 42*f*, 58–
  59, 69, 194–95
early career, 34, 36
ethnic blurring use, 82–83
in Europe, 63
evolving masculinity, 27, 55–57, 58–
  59, 63–65
film career, 36–37, 55–56, 57
flash dance elements, 31–32, 47–48, 50–51,
  62, 65–66
at Gene Kelly Life Achievement Award
  ceremony, 1, 84–85, 194–95
in *The Great American Broadcast,* 45*f*, 45–46
on *The Hollywood Palace,* 63–64, 65*f*, 65, 66*f*
influence, 30–31, 159, 201–2
innovation, 31, 67, 69
integrated dancing, 27, 44, 45–46, 56–57
on *The Jacksons,* 67–69, 68*f*
in *Kid Millions,* 37–40, 38*f*, 39*f*, 43,
  57, 157–58
masculinity, childhood, 32–33, 37–40, 43, 54
micro-resistances of, 31, 32–33, 41, 45–
  46, 48, 69
as model of Black masculinity, 32–33,
  41, 54, 69
"My Kind of Town" performance, 64
as novelty act, 4–5, 14, 30–31
in *Orchestra Wives,* 48–49, 49*f*
parallels to Fred Astaire, 51–52
partnering style, 63–64
in *Pie, Pie Blackbird,* 36
in *The Pirate,* 27, 55–56, 56*f*
popularity, 43–44, 67

preservation of performances, 24–25
racial ambiguity of, 43, 52, 55–56
reception by audience, 37, 40, 47–48
rhythm, use of, 48
as role models, 69
sexuality of, 27, 43, 47, 49, 51–52, 53–54, 58–59
short films, 55
as spectacle, 51–52, 55–56
in *Stormy Weather*, 27, 51–53, 53*f*, 57, 67–69, 180–81
in *Sun Valley Serenade*, 46–48, 47*f*
television career, 27, 32–33, 58
on *Texaco Star Theater*, 30, 58–59
in *That's Dancing!* 194–95
on *Toast of the Town*, 61–63
Nicholas Collegians, 33–34
Nicholas Kids, 33–34
Nijinsky, Vaslav, 8, 73–74
"Niña" (performance). *See* Kelly, Gene: in *The Pirate*
Novak, Kim, 168
novelty acts, 14

Ocean's 11. See under Davis, Sammy, Jr.
O'Connor, Donald, 13, 26, 93, 94, 104–6
O'Hara, John, 76
"The Old Soft Shoe" (performance). *See under* Kelly, Gene
Olsson, Ann-Margret. *See* Ann-Margret
Olympiad (stage performance), 8
On the Town. See under Kelly, Gene
Orchestra Wives. See under Nicholas Brothers
Osterweil, Ara, 17–18

Padilla, Raphaël, 70–72, 71*f*, 92–93, 203–4
Paget, Debra, 95–96, 123–24
Pal Joey (film), 178
Pal Joey (novel), 76
Pal Joey (stage show). *See under* Kelly, Gene
palm/fist dichotomy. *See also* Kelly, Gene
  defining characteristic of Gene Kelly, 70, 79, 83, 110
  definition of, 27–28
  Gene Kelly use of, 80*f*, 81–83, 84*f*, 84–85, 91, 106–7
  as masculinity, 74, 95, 113
Paramount, 14, 113, 159–60
Paramount Decree (1948), 57
Parker, "Colonel" Tom, 118, 135–36, 143–44, 147–48
Pate, Geraldine, 58–59
Penniman, Richard Wayne. *See* Little Richard

Perfect (film). *See* Travolta, John
Perkins, Carl, 26, 119–20, 122–23
Perry, Lincoln. *See* Fetchit, Stepin
Petty, Miriam, 32–33
phallic masculinity. *See also* masculinity; Presley, Elvis; virile masculinity
  Channing Tatum use of, 203–4
  definition of, 123–24
  Elvis Presley as model of, 28, 143, 148
  in Elvis Presley films, 132–34, 133*f*, 140–41, 144–45
  John Travolta use of, 198–200
  Michael Jackson performance of, 197–98
  pelvic thrusts as characteristic of, 96–97, 113, 123–24
Phillips, Dewey, 115–16
Phillips, Sam, 115, 118
Pie, Pie Blackbird. See under Nicholas Brothers
The Pirate. See under Kelly, Gene; Nicholas Brothers
"The Pirate Ballet" (performance). *See* Kelly, Gene: in *The Pirate*
Playboy After Dark, 176–77, 189
Playboy's Penthouse, 176–77, 178
Poitier, Sidney, 171–73, 181–82
Pontiac Star Parade. See under Kelly, Gene
popular dance. *See* social dance
Porgy and Bess (film). *See under* Davis, Sammy, Jr.
Porgy and Bess (novel), 171–72
Porgy and Bess (stage show), 166–67, 171–72
Powell, Eleanor, 20–21
Presley, Elvis. *See also* aesthetic of the cool; Africanist aesthetics; ambiguous masculinity; Black dance; blackbodying; blackbodying-as-masculinity; costuming; hair choreography; invisibilization; phallic masculinity; virile masculinity; working-class masculinity
  as Army propaganda, 136–37
  bad boy image, 129–30, 135–36, 147–48
  as bejeweled spectacle, 114–15, 147–48
  Black music influence on, 112–13
  blackbodying, transition from, 147–48
  in *Blue Hawaii*, 138–42, 140*f*, 141*f*, 144–45, 195–96, 199–200
  "Blue Suede Shoes," 119–20
  bricolage use, 122
  censorship of, 125, 126–27, 127*f*
  code switching, 127–28
  "Comeback Special," 28, 114–15, 147*f*, 147–48
  commercial desirability of, 125–26

250 INDEX

Presley, Elvis (*cont.*)
  commercial desireability of, 126
  comparisons to other performers, 113, 118–
    19, 134–35, 141, 197–98
  dance role in stardom, 112, 118
  dance style, 113, 116–17, 118, 121, 129–30,
    139–40, 142, 148
  early life, 115
  on *The Ed Sullivan Show*, 125–27, 127*f*,
    128*f*, 128–29
  facial choreography, 126–27, 138
  female fan reaction to, 114, 130–32
  film career, 114–15, 129–30
  fistfights as masculinity, 95–96, 135–36
  in *Fun in Acapulco*, 142–43
  gender ambiguity of, 114–15, 117–18, 121,
    122–23, 127–28, 141, 144–48
  in *G.I. Blues*, 136–37, 138*f*, 195–96
  in *Girls! Girls! Girls!* 142*f*, 142–43
  "Hound Dog," 111, 112*f*, 114–15, 120,
    122, 124
  as ideological symbol, 136–37
  in *Jailhouse Rock*, 131–35, 133*f*
  in *King Creole*, 135
  as "the king" of rock 'n' roll, 112–13
  in *Les Girls*, 94–95
  in *Loving You*, 130–32, 132*f*
  military service, 28, 136–37
  on *The Milton Berle Show*, 111, 112*f*, 118–19,
    120–21, 122
  music career, 115–16
  as "the Pelvis," 28, 96–97, 118, 122–
    29, 133–34
  post-Army film career, 114–15, 136–37, 138,
    142, 143
  preservation of performances, 24–25
  public reception of, 112, 114, 124
  "reform" of, 136–37, 138
  signature pose, 111, 122
  spectacular sexuality of, 113, 134–35, 144–45
  Stage Show appearances, 111, 118, 119–
    20, 121*f*
  on *The Steve Allen Show*, 124–26
  television career, 28, 111, 113, 124, 147–48
  touring career, 116–17, 119, 127
  transgressions of performance, 130–
    31, 134–35
  "the twist" influence, 139–40, 142–43
  in *Viva Las Vegas*, 28, 114–15, 143–47, 145*f*,
    146*f*, 194–95
Presley, Gladys, 115
Presley, Jesse Garon, 115
Presley, Vernon, 115

prop dances. *See* bricolage
Pullman Porters, 45–46

race riots, 7, 54
racial blurring. *See* ethnic blurring
racial integration. *See* integration, racial
racial miscegenation. *See* miscegenation
racism, 30, 43–44, 54–55, 100, 168, 181–82,
    201. *See also* blackface minstrelsy;
    stereotypes
Radio Corporation of America (RCA), 10–
    11, 118
Randolph, A. Philip, 46
Rat Pack, 28–29, 153, 174–78, 179–82
Raymond, Emilie, 178–80
RCA. *See* Radio Corporation of America (RCA)
Reed, Leonard, 31–32, 33–34, 47–48, 90
"Renegade" (dance), 205–6
*Renegades: Digital Dance Cultures from
    Dubsmash to TikTok* (Boffone), 205–6
Robbins, Jerome, 182–83
Robeson, Paul, 6
Robin and the 7 Hoods. See under Davis,
    Sammy, Jr.; Sinatra, Frank
Robinson, Bill "Bojangles"
  dance contest win over Harry Swinton, 100
  dance style, 9, 20–21, 81–82, 159–60, 191–92
  early life, 40
  mentorship of young Black performers, 156
  New York nightclub career, 35
  portrayal in *That's Dancing!* 194–95
  Shirley Temple partnership, 17–18
  as source material for other dancers, 14–15
  "stair dance," 21
  in *Stormy Weather*, 52, 54–55
  as subject of *Bojangles*, 201–2
  on *Texaco Star Theater*, 57–58
  "tributes" to, 20–21
Robinson, Sugar Ray, 98–99, 196
rock 'n' roll music, 48, 112–13, 115–16, 147*f*,
    147–48. *See also* costuming: rock 'n' roll
    aesthetic; Presley, Elvis
Rodriguez, Analisse, 207–8
Rogin, Michael, 17, 19–20
Romero, Alex, 133–34, 135–36
Rooney, Mickey, 13, 18–20, 158–59, 166–
    67, 185–86
Ross, Diana, 186–87, 198
Rufus Jones for President. See under Davis,
    Sammy, Jr.

Sammy! See under Davis, Sammy, Jr.
The Sammy Davis, Jr. Reader (Early), 150

The Sammy Davis, Jr. Show. See under Davis, Sammy, Jr.

Sanchez, Elvera, 153–54

The Sands Hotel, 166–67, 174–76, 177

Saturday Night Fever. See Travolta, John

segregation, 43, 44, 46, 165–66, 195–96. *See also* integration, racial

Sergeants 3. See under Davis, Sammy, Jr.

Sharaff, Irene, 172–73

Shawn, Ted, 8, 73–74

Shiovitz, Brynn, 14–15, 17–18, 21

short subject film. *See* Black short films

Sinatra, Frank. *See also* Rat Pack
  dancing ability, 178
  Gene Kelly collaborations, 78–79, 87, 171
  as model for Sammy Davis, Jr., 153
  movement in performance, 118–19
  in *Pal Joey*, 178
  playboy image, 176–77, 178
  relationship with Sammy Davis, Jr., 156–57, 159, 171, 185–86
  in *Robin and the 7 Hoods*, 64

Singin' in the Rain. See under blackbodying; Kelly, Gene

"Slaughter on Tenth Avenue" (performance). *See* Kelly, Gene: in *Words and Music*

Slaves to Fashion: Black Dandyism and the Styling of Black Diasporic Identity (Miller), 151–52

"Slicin' Sand" (performance). *See* Presley, Elvis: in *Blue Hawaii*

social dance, 1–3, 4, 73–74, 113. *See also* dance crazes; twist, the (dance)

social media. *See* TikTok (app)

Stage Show. See Presley, Elvis: *Stage Show* appearances

Stearns, Jean, 8–9, 35–36, 150

Stearns, Marshall, 8–9, 35–36, 150

Step Up. See Tatum, Channing

stereotypes. *See also* Black dance; Black dandy; racism; *Uncle Tom's Cabin* (Stowe)
  Black dance, 4–5, 8–9, 92–93
  Black gender, 196, 206–7
  Black sexuality, 123–24
  blackface minstrelsy, 8–9, 14–23
  buck, 8–9, 196
  coon, 8–9, 14, 196
  ethnic, 5, 7, 88–89, 105
  influence on Black dance, 9
  Jim Crow, 6, 151, 171–72
  Long Tail Blue, 151
  pickaninny, 8–9, 18–19, 195–96
  precocious innocent, 40–41

Zip Coon, 151, 174–75, 196

The Steve Allen Show. See under Davis, Sammy, Jr.; Presley, Elvis

Stormy Weather. See under Nicholas Brothers; Robinson, Bill "Bojangles"

A Streetcar Named Desire, 79–81, 81*f*, 89–90

Studlar, Gaylyn, 7

Sublett, John W. "Bubbles," 20–21, 35, 150, 159–60, 171–73

Sullivan, Ed, 14, 61–62, 125–26, 127–28

Sun Records, 115, 118, 119–20

Sun Valley Serenade. See under Nicholas Brothers

Sweet and Low. See under Davis, Sammy, Jr.

Sweet Charity. See under Davis, Sammy, Jr.

swing music, 48

Swing Time. See Astaire, Fred: "Bojangles of Harlem"

Take Me Out to the Ball Game. See under Kelly, Gene

T.A.M.I. Show, 66–67

"Tango Twist" (Wiggins), 33–34

Tap, 200–1

tap dance, 2–3, 4, 9, 73, 88*f*, 100. *See also* Davis, Sammy, Jr.; Hoofers Club (New York); Kelly, Gene; Nicholas Brothers; Robinson, Bill "Bojangles"

Tap Dancing America (Hill), 32

Tatum, Channing, 29, 197, 202–4. *See also* blackbodying-as-masculinity

Taylor, Frances, 165

Teenage Awards Music International Show (*T.A.M.I. Show*), 66–67

television, rise of, 10–12, 96–97. *See also* vaudeo

Temple, Shirley, 17–18, 194–95

Texaco Star Theater. See under Nicholas Brothers; Robinson, Bill "Bojangles"

That's Dancing! 194–95, 197

Theater Owners Booking Association (T.O.B.A.), 90, 153–54

This is Tom Jones, 190

Thompson, Claude, 147*f*, 147–48

TikTok (app), 29, 197, 205–8

Tinee, Mae, 132–33

Tingz, Jeff, 207

Tip, Tap, and Toe (musical act), 156–57

Toast of the Town. See under Davis, Sammy, Jr.; Nicholas Brothers

T.O.B.A. (Theater Owners Booking Association), 90

Travolta, John, 29, 197, 204

Tucker, Earl "Snakehips," 3–4, 116–17, 119–20

252 INDEX

Twentieth Century Fox, 14, 27, 31–32, 41–42, 43–44, 48–49
"The Twist" (song), 139–40
twist, the (dance), 4, 28, 114–15, 139–40, 143

Uncle Tom's Cabin (Stowe), 8–9, 17–19
U.S. Army, 136–37, 157–58. *See also* Presley, Elvis

Valentino, Rudolph, 7, 82–83
Valkanova, Dora, 201
variety television. *See* vaudeo
vaudeo. *See also* television, rise of; vaudeville
  Elvis Presley participation in, 118
  filming methods, 24
  Gene Kelly participation in, 96–97, 100–1, 103–4, 107–8, 109
  Nicholas Brothers participation in, 14, 57–58, 63–64
  Sammy Davis, Jr. participation in, 64–65, 159–60, 169–70, 178, 185
vaudeville, 8–9, 10–11, 90, 151–52, 153–54. *See also* vaudeo
Vested Interests: Cross-Dressing and Cultural Anxiety (Garber), 117
virile masculinity. *See also* Kelly, Gene; masculinity; phallic masculinity; Presley, Elvis
  Elvis Presley as model of, 28, 113, 123–24, 148
  in Elvis Presley films, 130–31
  Gene Kelly examples of, 83–84, 85, 94, 95, 96–97, 102–3, 110
  John Travolta performance of, 198–200
  Sammy Davis Jr. use of, 170–71
Vitaphone, 27, 36, 55, 154–55, 191–92
Viva Las Vegas (film). *See under* Presley, Elvis

"Viva Las Vegas" (performance). *See* Presley, Elvis: in *Viva Las Vegas*

Walker, George, 9, 81–82, 151–52
Warner Brothers, 36–37, 154–55
Waters, Ethel, 154–55
We Three. See under Davis, Sammy, Jr.
White Nights, 201
whiteface minstrelsy, 15–16, 79–81, 154–55
"Who Rules These Hollywood Roosts?" (fanzine article), 83–84
"Why Am I So Gone About That Gal?" (performance). *See* Kelly, Gene: in *Les Girls*
"Why Negroes Don't Like *Porgy and Bess*" (Thompson), 171–72
Wiggins, "Ginger" Jack, 31–32, 33–34
Will Mastin Trio, 153–54, 156–57, 158–63, 160*f*, 164–65, 168–69, 191–92
Wilson, Flip, 191–92
Wilson, Jackie, 28, 128–29, 197–98
Wilson, Lester, 198–99
wing dancing. *See* buck and wing dancing
wolfish masculinity, 78–79, 107–8, 178
"The Word on Frank Sinatra" (*Playboy*), 178
Words and Music. See under Kelly, Gene
working-class masculinity. *See also* Kelly, Gene; Presley, Elvis
  Elvis Presley as embodiment of, 28, 95–96, 125, 131, 134–35
  Gene Kelly demonstration of, 72, 74–75, 78, 79–81, 83, 88–89, 108–9
"The Worry Song" (performance). *See under* Kelly, Gene

Yes I Can (Davis, Jr.), 158–59

Zak, Albin, 115–16
Ziegfeld Follies. See under Astaire, Fred; Kelly, Gene

The manufacturer's authorised representative in the EU for product safety is Oxford
University Press España S.A. of El Parque Empresarial San Fernando de Henares,
Avenida de Castilla, 2 – 28830 Madrid (www.oup.es/en or product.safety@oup.com).
OUP España S.A. also acts as importer into Spain of products made by the manufacturer.

Printed in the USA/Agawam, MA
July 30, 2025

891003.005